Articulating Life's Memory

Articulating Life's Memory

U.S. Medical Rhetoric about Abortion in the Nineteenth Century

Nathan Stormer

LEXINGTON BOOKS
Lanham • Boulder • New York • Oxford

LEXINGTON BOOKS

Published in the United States of America
by Lexington Books
A Member of the Rowman & Littlefield Publishing Group
4720 Boston Way, Lanham, Maryland 20706

12 Hid's Copse Road
Cumnor Hill, Oxford OX2 9JJ, England

British Library Cataloguing in Publication Information Available

Library of Congress Cataloging-in-Publication Data

Stormer, Nathan, 1966-
    Articulating life's memory : U.S. medical rhetoric about abortion in the nineteenth
century / Nathan Stormer.
        p. cm.
    Includes bibliographical references and index.
    ISBN 0-7391-0429-2 (cloth : alk. paper) — ISBN 0-7391-0430-6 (pbk. : alk. paper)
    1. Abortion—United States—History—19th century. 2. Abortion—Moral and
ethical aspects—United States. 3. Abortion—United States—Religious aspects. I.
Title.

    HQ767.5.U5 S767 2002
    363.46—dc21   2002009862

Printed in the United States of America

⊖™ The paper used in this publication meets the minimum requirements of American
National Standard for Information Sciences—Permanence of Paper for Printed Library
Materials, ANSI/NISO Z39.48–1992.

For Mom and Dad, who, ever since I wrote a story at age nine about Abe Lincoln and his talking cat, were convinced I would one day write a book. This, however, is not what I think they had in mind.

Contents

List of Figures

Preface

It is common to feel that rhetoric about abortion is at an impasse, that the issues at stake are fairly well decided for most people such that attempts at persuasion are an exercise in futility or self-justification. And yet, we continue to argue vociferously, usually employing the same sets of arguments over and over. The *persistence* of such an impasse is itself interesting, raising questions about the value of taking a position. What kind of cultural work is done by preserving opposed standpoints on the issue? Further, what are the grounds of the debate such that its intractability becomes its hallmark? For a very long time now, long before *Roe v. Wade*, one frame for the abortion debate in the United States has been the concept of the individual, politically and religiously defined, argued largely on the terms of biomedicine. Yet, there is more at stake than the individual, or even individualism, in the debate. Abortion rhetoric has a history, initially a strongly antiabortion history, in the United States, and individualism has not always been the dominant frame for discourse. Yet biomedical knowledge of the human body has continually served to set the terms. I do not claim to know a way to break the impasse, but I do claim to have an idea about how to understand better why we have an impasse: learn the history of the rhetoric. Exactly what I mean by the history of that rhetoric, however, is likely not what you think. We need to look at rhetoric about abortion *other* than through individualism, *other* than through arguments about individualism. If we want to understand how it is we have become locked into a loud public debate about the first moments of the individual *we need to ask what other rhetorical work is being done that we are failing to notice.* Like a flame, the light of a central point of contention can black out a multitude of other rhetorical effects, especially from other forms of rhetoric.

This book is a step toward understanding abortion rhetoric against the grain of individualism, and that means I have to approach rhetoric against the grain of individualism. Specifically, I look to the predominant antiabortion rhetoric in the early period. To analyze abortion rhetoric from within more conventional horizons of rhetorical studies would circumscribe the very possibility of working against individualist assumptions. Neoclassical and modernist rhetorical studies, indebted as they are to understanding civil reproduction through public discourse, share the ideological proclivities of abortion rhetoric. To presume an intentional, rights-bearing subject operating in a civil discursive environment is to share the same ideological ground as those who argue for the sovereignty of the fetus or the pregnant woman. As Karen Newman argues in *Fetal Positions*, supporters and opponents of abortion both rely on humanist realism wherein the naturalness of the individual originates the very possibility of rights. Similarly, neoclassical and modernist theories of rhetoric rely on humanist realism wherein the naturalness of speech originates the very possibility of the individual. These two strands of individualism are inextricably entwined. To look to what is persuasive or not about early opponents of abortion would proceed directly to evaluating the strategic qualities of discourses that attempt to speak within individualism and would suspend questions of how medical practices have helped articulate the very parameters of such discourses. In fact, one might argue that rhetoric as persuasion in its more normative forms operates in conjunction *with* the prenatal space articulated by biomedical practices.

I am not arguing we should dispense with analyses of persuasion. It would be of great worth to analyze how H. R. Storer, the chief antiabortionist of the nineteenth century, convinced colleagues and legislators of his agenda. However, if we do not analyze how knowledge of abortion was produced, the space of its debate was formed, and the materiality of the bodies involved was naturalized, we would miss the ways in which Storer's persuasion was a function of forces greater than his artful use of language. We would also deflect attention from the rhetorical impact the medicalization of abortion *opposition* has had on culture, not just on agents of change. Looking to persuasion rather than to the performative rhetorical work of medical practices would lead me away from exactly that which I argue is overlooked.

What follows is a not-so-humanist rhetorical analysis, then. I have chosen to account for the "lateral, unintended" rhetoric of medical practice by asking how such practices articulate cultural memory, or rather the performative order manifested by medical practice. I will attempt to provide nominal definitions for the key terms performativity, articulation, and memory as I proceed. In particular, articulation refers to the production of bodies, language, and the space of their interaction through the ligature of diverse material and semiotic elements.[1] In this case, articulation describes the reproductive interconnection of woman, privileged whiteness, nation, and various institutions through the rituals of exposure in medical investigation. The practices of direct examination articulated cultural memory through the criminalization of abortion. It also provided a mode of cultural regeneration *independent* of abortion rates (certainly unintended and lateral to the direct goal of eliminating abortion). My analysis is not-so-humanist because I am looking at the rhetoric of practices, not people; the performative order choreographed in the sometimes silent actions of doctors probing bodies; the memory work accomplished when no public audience was immediately present.

Studies of rhetoric typically remark on the context that conditions the rhetorical practices in question, and on the effects of these practices. I will do so as well, working in two parts. Part I, "Memory in Early Medical Abortion Opposition," provides a layered context for understanding medical practices within the rhetoric of memory formation. Chapter 1, "Medical Practice, Memory, and Antiabortion Rhetoric," sets forth the basic dynamic of early antiabortion rhetoric: abortion is a kind of cultural amnesia, a lost knowledge of the truth about life in the womb that can be recalled through examination of women's bodies. Medical practices are understood as rituals of exposure that participate in the rhetoric of "body criticism" established during the Enlightenment, understood here as a kind of archival process, or *hypomnesis*. Further, within early antiabortion opposition, this rhetoric operates through the epistemological motif of knowing as remembrance, or Neoplatonic *anamnesis*. Faced with a rise in abortion rates, the rhetoric of medical examination practices was to uncover the forgotten "truth" about life from within women's bodies in an effort to reeducate women's minds about maternal duty. Chapter 2, "The Politics of Life and Memory," sets early antiabortion efforts into the larger picture of nineteenth-century biopolitics and racism. At a time of great unease about the vigor of the bourgeois body, physicians were preoccupied with the consequences of abortion on native-born, white, privileged Americans, more so than its consequences on the population generally. Further, as a way of separating themselves from competition, American Medical Association physicians used abortion as a litmus test of quackery, thus using biopolitics in the realm of professional competition. Finally, chapter 3, "Somatic Confessions," places the memory work of early medical practices into the rhetorical genre of confession and explains the basic parameters of such rhetoric. The rituals of exposure identified in chapter 1 are described as forensic exegesis, the reconstitution of the past in the present through inspection of material traces. This, in turn, has a genealogical effect by creating lines of descent and emergence of current values, acts, and things. The effect is that the body confesses its knowledge under the pressures of forensic exegesis, thereby producing the memory of hidden truths in the very exposition of said truths. It is a performative rhetoric, wherein the memory reconstituted does not preexist its exposition, but is formed during exegesis.

In part II, "Articulating a Memory of Life," I discuss the rhetorical effects of the practices contextualized in part I by examining the substance of the memory constituted by early medical practices. Working with the concept of articulation, I analyze how the female body was made to "speak" the "true" discourse about reproduction, how the practices of medical examination embodied the patient-physician relationship, and how space was produced by those practices. Chapter 4, "Organic Discourse," sets forth what the female body confessed about life, abortion, and reproduction. The female body was treated by physicians as the source of memory about life's real meaning and the proper order of reproductivity within culture. I talk about how the uterus, ovaries, menstruation, and the fetus were read as texts that spelled out maternal duty in the face of increasing numbers of abortions. Also, I look at the inherent threat to life the maternal body posed to early physicians. Politically, life became its own enemy, thereby offering a permanent justification for medical stewardship of reproduction and a means by which cultural norms could be regenerated *independent* of abortion rates. Chapter 5, "Embodying a Matrix," addresses the interconnections forged by medical practices and the embodiment of a new physician-patient relationship regarding reproduction. Another aspect of the rhetoric of medical practices was to connect women to medical institutions and to the state, thus embodying women as a matrix of culture. This was not a rhetoric of representation, it was a rhetoric of enactment that accompanied the work of producing discursive representations. Chapter 6, "Prenatal Space," delineates the space produced by the enactment of these medical practices and the discourse they generated. The womb, as the space for constituting prenatal life, is a crossroads for institutional practices and discourses that are directed toward managing that life. Prenatal space is a material and semiotic space through which divergent interests in "life" arrange themselves, with biomedical nomenclature, imagery, and practices in a privileged position as the common vernacular for negotiating that space. A new space was articulated by early medical practices through which life could serve as a terminal for cultural as well as biological reproduction.

The conclusion, "In Living Memory," argues that articulation of cultural memory through reproductive control in early antiabortion rhetoric set the parameters by which abortion could be understood intelligibly, providing not only the language and bodies necessary to think of abortion as nationally, racially threatening, but also the space in which and through which to make sense of the relationship of individual women and the collective. I close by speculating about the relation of memory work as a constraint on cultural invention. Invention, or the tension between the novel and the familiar in cultural acts, depends on the maintenance of memory. As such, memory both limits and compels cultural invention.

A word on the genre of this volume, and this is directed mostly to readers who may feel resistant to my introductory remarks for a number of reasons. This is a feminist critical history of medical practice as rhetoric. I use such a convoluted description because of the waywardness of my approach. It has no "true" home in the sense that it is not a social history, not a history of medicine, not a history of the body, not a history of a system of thought, and not even a history of rhetoric as that might typically mean. I draw on each of these genres substantially and stylistically at various points, but none of them govern the overall argument of the book. There is no persistent narrative that unfolds chapter by chapter; no biographies or canonized texts predetermine the endpoint of the analysis. Many different narratives, bodies, and texts are woven together to analyze a complex form of rhetoric. The project is critically interpretive, it is historical, and it relies on a feminist rhetorical perspective, but it is not located wholly within the generic conventions of those forms listed. One could say it is a materialist history of the reformulation, within a specific context, of a rhetorical commonplace: to reproduce is to remember ourselves.[2] Because I chose to work against the habits of individualism and to understand the rhetorical ramifications of medicalized abortion opposition on a cultural, rather than a strictly persuasive, level, I have had to formulate an approach where none quite existed. Many concepts and methods spoke *to* my interest, but none *fulfilled* them. Thus, the continual presence of theory and theorizing is an effort to inform the reader of how I have formulated my analysis. This is not a strictly "theoretical work" although theory necessarily developed out of it. In that light, the theoretical contribution of the volume is the conceptual convergence of memory, articulation, and performativity in order to describe a memory formation. Rhetorical studies has seen these concepts pursued independently, whereas I am attempting to fold them together to provide a different lens for analysis. Further, I hope to impress on readers the value of theorizing the enactment of memory within systems of rhetoric. Despite the deductive introduction of theory, these concepts were adapted and formed from the ground up as I struggled with, even deciding what counted as, evidence.

This leads me to method. I have surveyed hundreds of texts from the nineteenth century, although I concentrate on those from the latter half, including case reports, professional and popular education tracts, committee reports, editorials, as well as legislative records, court reports, and letters in some cases. I have reviewed the majority of what was written from a medical perspective about abortion from that era and supplemented that with some nonmedical texts. Handling these works, I am less interested in exploring exactly what an author may or may not have meant in the sense of recreating a state of mind. Instead, I am interested in how these texts functioned. Also, because I am concerned with medical practices that can only be represented in retrospect, I use texts as records of action, recognizing that such construction of referent is never perfect and is, in fact, performative on my part. As a result, the works analyzed not only are reconstructed records of events, but also performances. The methodological contribution of this work is the configuration of a critical approach to rhetorical history that enables one to analyze how a form of rhetoric creates its own conditions of possibility, meaning its sources of memory and their relation to invention. To this point, the manner by which kinds of rhetoric make room for themselves in culture, how rhetorics establish their capacity to act and the space in which to act, has remained opaque to us. My hope is that this book marks a step toward clarity.

Gayatri Chakravorty Spivak has called for "scrupulous and plausible misreadings" to break up too-familiar stories, stories that have come to protect as much as they divulge. Such "misreading" is reading against the conventions that may dictate prematurely and without question what is the correct version of history and what is incorrect. Given the confines of the current debate on abortion, I contend we have prematurely and without question constrained our attention in ways that must be challenged by scrupulous and plausible misreadings of the record. I am acutely aware that abortion and the writing of history are both over-politicized and that "getting it right" according to one perspective or another may sometimes be more important to people than a fresh look. My hope is that readers, even those predisposed to want only a certain kind of story about abortion either for disciplinary or ideological reasons, may come away with a sense that this work, although appearing as a purposeful "misreading" to begin with, is in fact a worthy and helpful recharacterization of a vexed and often stagnant issue.

This project owes its completion to many people who have kindly given their time and support to me as I have researched and written it. It was a privilege to have access to the wealth of information that is contained in the Owen H. Wangensteen Historical Library of Biology and Medicine at the University of Minnesota, the U.S. National Library of Medicine in Bethesda, and the Special Collection on Women and Medicine housed at Allegheny University. Boasting some of the finest holdings of medical literature in the world, they were remarkable resources. Many special thanks are owed to the staff at Wangensteen, where I did the bulk of my work: Michele Schicker, Maria Falconer, and Colleen Allen, library assistants, and Elaine Challacombe, curator. They copied endlessly for me and made my excursions profitable and pleasant.

I also must thank my friends and mentors who have discussed and argued with me as I worked through my many drafts. Britt Abel, Gail Lippincott, Jane Miller, Sharon Preves, Jennifer Stromer-Galley, David Noon, Angela G. Ray, Naomi Rockler, and Corey Schlösser-Hall all have had a hand in improving this manuscript. In particular, I want to thank Rob Brookey and Kerry Brooks for the many debates that sharpened my understanding of what it is I am saying. Also, special thanks to Amy Kaminsky, Randy Lake, Richard Leppert, Ed Schiappa, and Robert Scott for their wise advice, good example, and persistent support as I jumped feet first and hoped for a soft landing. Each has helped me greatly.

I owe a liturgy of thanks to my advisers, Karlyn Kohrs Campbell and Jacquelyn N. Zita. I began this project years ago when I took a class from each during the same term. Dr. Zita has challenged me to consider why I think the way I do more times than I can recall. With her ability to grasp my intent far better than I can and her insistence on doing justice to my argument, she has kept me excited about my own work—a rare gift. Dr. Campbell deserves much more space than I have. My mentor for what seems an age now, she has taught me the value of rigor, perspicuity, and that rhetoric is vital and its limits are only those that we accept. She has always been my greatest advocate and my life in academics would have been pale without her support and guidance.

Finally, my greatest thanks goes to Naomi Jacobs. Her warm, generous support has made the difficult years of moving this manuscript along more than bearable. She has made the burdens light. As an academic companion, her rigorous editing and "tough love" have consistently made this project better, made me better. As a life companion, I cannot say in real fairness all that she has given me, but peace in the world comes close. All my love.

Part I
Memory in Early Medical Abortion Opposition

Chapter One
Medical Practice, Memory, and Antiabortion Rhetoric

Within antiabortion rhetoric, abortion is a metaphor for cultural amnesia. Calling one of the most charged issues of the nineteenth or twentieth century metaphorical, I do not intend to dematerialize the intensity or depth of the physical and emotional experiences of the millions who have attempted abortion, provided abortions, supported others making a difficult choice, or who have worked relentlessly to suppress or to protect the right to abort. Rather, I mean that to speak of abortion is to bring together a great many things and discourses under one heading. Abortion is cessation, but cessation of what? Some would say it is the cessation of a human being—others of a human becoming. I am of the latter view in that I think the final outcome of a pregnancy belongs in the hands of potential mothers as embryos go about becoming. Holding this perspective, I have grown increasingly preoccupied with the question, what *else* quickens *with* the fetus? Life, as it has been embodied in the fetus, has a vast array of institutions, groups, and economic and political markets congealing about it. Families are typically defined by their progeny. Industries of medicine are built on maximizing life. Industries of science define themselves by the search for the essence of life. Churches take as a reason for being the protection of what they see as part of the body divine. Industries of natal products and equipment grow as does the population. Political entities tie their existence to life as an issue. Culture, alongside and through the fetus, quickens itself. From the perspective of cultural amnesia, what does it mean to abort? To argue for the right to abort? What does it mean to prevent abortion?

The rhetoric that condemns abortion grimly elevates it as well. Abortion has become a metaphor for the benighted disconnection of sexual reproduction from cultural reproduction, a figure of inconceivable personal and collective loss materialized in the act of terminating a pregnancy. As such, abortion implies that someone has forgotten about a life in the womb, forgotten the great dependence of culture on children, forgotten women's duty to reproduce and nurture civilization. And there are consequences for forgetting, such as losing custody of what one has been charged to remember. After years of frustrated attempts to understand the grounds of the conflict, I have come to believe that, for its opponents, abortion refers to a loss of fundamental knowledge about humanity. Rather than treating abortion as an organized effort to consciously perpetrate a form of genocide, antiabortionists have more frequently construed abortion as mass murder caused by a willful estrangement from the "truth" of life. Treating abortion as a loss of knowledge about life places abortion practices in a dialectic of life-death wherein death is a function of ignorance and the proper regeneration of life is a function of knowledge. The slogan "They're Forgetting Someone" that has been used on placards and billboards in the last two decades is at least cursory evidence to that fact.[1] Operating from the narrative that we have fallen as a culture into a dangerous kind of amnesia about the meaning of life, antiabortion rhetoric attempts to remember a "true" knowledge of life. Or, if the number of abortions indicates a kind of forgetfulness about the truth, efforts to embody prenatal life are acts of remembrance. To say that antiabortion rhetoric articulates life's memory is to describe a normative rhetoric founded in the basic trope of a lost truth recovered. However, to assume that this professed true knowledge of life is solely that a "fetus is a person" overlooks the extraordinarily complex cultural investments of embodying, naming, and valuing human life in a prenatal form.

In contemporary public discourse, abortion is frequently debated through the commonplace of the life of the fetus versus the sovereignty of the woman's body. This privileged filter for discussion obscures as much as it clarifies what is at stake in such a divisive and emotional issue. If antiabortion rhetoric is one of re-collecting lost truths, then for prochoice advocates the almost exclusive emphasis on the fetus as a person is forgetting the woman in pregnancy. Likewise, the narratives of women who have aborted are acts of memory formation. Foregrounding the fetus over the pregnant woman or vice-versa creates competing claims of erasure and parallel acts of memory formation to combat the perceived erasures. When the clash between a fetus and its potential mother dominates our field of vision, however, it is difficult to see *how* it is that we as a culture are focusing so intently on abortion, to see the practices that structure these opposed rhetorics. I believe we would benefit from redirecting our attention for a moment from a contest between the unborn fetus and the individual woman to the ways in which culture separates itself unevenly, provides itself with historical divisions and cross purposes, through the body of the pregnant female, and how power is exercised to do so.

Over the last two decades, a formidable collection of feminist scholars has critiqued the rhetoric around abortion and the structure of the contest between fetus and woman. In particular, recent investigations of fetal imagery have raised powerful questions about the complicated palimpsest that is the fetal icon. Subtexts about individual rights, a gendered social contract, Western assumptions of seeing as self-evident knowledge, and the politics of biomedical perception are all present in the seemingly innocent vision of a floating, placid fetus. Scholars in science and technology, political theory, rhetorical criticism, art history, and cultural studies have questioned the presumed difference between rights talk and biological discourse. A general theme of this work has been to discuss how the visualization of the fetal individual occurs at the expense of the pregnant woman, arguing that a division and opposition is thereby established between a potential mother and her unborn.[2] One exceptionally skilled study, Karen Newman's *Fetal Positions,* is indicative of this scholarship. Studying the history of fetal imaging from the earliest illustrations in the second century to the highly stylized photos and videos of today, she demonstrates that the fetus has been interpreted through humanist individualism for centuries, albeit in different ways in different contexts. A constant in the process of fetal visualization has been the disembodiment of women as full human subjects and the embodiment of the fetus as the sign of the individual, a trade-off of one subject for another. Further, she argues that both the political right and left rely on the humanist vision of the individual to defend *or* attack abortion as a practice. Both seek a real vision of the individual grounded in material nature. Newman's insightful thesis is that the rhetoric of this visualization is grounded in the discourse of humanist realism.

The research that Newman exemplifies, however, addresses only a portion of the range of cultural work accomplished by the rhetoric of abortion, particularly beyond the semiotics of fetal imaging or the immediate politics of reproductive freedom. On one hand, this corpus of scholarship is clarifying and persuasive in contending that the visualization of reproduction and gestation has largely erased the female as individual from birthing. Women often are portrayed as environments for fetuses or as birthing machines, if they are portrayed at all, while the fetus is imbued with the rights of the individual (overwhelmingly represented as male). The ramifications of this rhetoric reach to the basic assumptions of individualism and of what counts as truth about humanity, as Mary Poovey has argued.[3] On the other hand, the theme of antagonism between woman and fetus clouds consideration of other rhetorical functions of abortion and the fetus, in that it frequently confines the debate to gender ideology operating through biologized individualism. The parameters of individualism that frequently set the limits of abortion discourse and its commentary resist understandings that are not intended to reflect directly on reproductive rights, thereby occluding many possible avenues of critical inquiry.

Not only have abortion practice and its opposition been used to constitute the individual, but also they have been used to constitute whole populations, institutions, and cultures. To the extent that abortion concerns the definition and management of life, it has been more than a stage for gendered individualism and bodily sovereignty. It has been a theater for *aggregate* life and the struggle of different races, ethnicities, sexualities, and classes to make themselves vital. Cross-cultural studies of abortion are typically more attuned to issues of collective biological politics and the relative power of the offspring of whole categories of people, but they typically focus on public policy issues rather than the rhetorical work accomplished through reproductive medicine. Some, such as Barbara Duden, Dion Farquhar, and especially Donna Haraway, have stepped outside the internal conflict of Western individualism within abortion rhetoric to ask, in effect, what creations other than individuals, fetal or adult female, arise through the attempt to manage life in the womb? Has reproductive control generally, and abortion specifically, been used as a source of cultural invention, and if so, how?[4]

In an effort to push aside the confines of individualism, if only briefly, this volume is dedicated to understanding some of the "what else" that has been articulated through the memory work implicit in antiabortion rhetoric. Many years ago, when I began to study abortion issues in today's context, I first felt the weight of flesh, of aggregate life, pressed upon the womb by antiabortionists or, rather, the investment of whole populations in the organs of reproduction by an act either of God or of nature. This led me to explore the history of the abortion controversy in the United States, not at the level of policies or rights, but at the level of the *bodies* most directly involved, in order to understand the ways in which the *actions* of pregnant women and their medical attendants were connected to the rest of culture. Two assumptions, both obvious and taken for granted, stood out to me from a survey of accounts of abortion before *Roe v. Wade*, from the literature of medical and religious antiabortionists, from talks with women who have aborted or refused to abort, and from conversations with men who felt entitled at least to a voice in the decision to abort and at most to full control over reproduction. One assumption is common to opposition to abortion practice: women have a duty to *others* (to God, to society, and to the fetus) to carry fetuses to term, and their decisions to abort either reject that duty by placing *women* first or are the result of ignorance regarding maternal duty. The other assumption is more general, crossing all segments of society, but is directly relevant to abortion rhetoric: the body is taken as a neutral, natural object that, left alone, is free of ideology. Correspondingly, medical language about the body is understood as naive description, language that awaits political use, but does not partake in politics per se. Looking to the history of abortion discourse and foregrounding its rhetorical configuration of a neglected reproductive burden and its assumption of a natural body uncontaminated by politics, one can imagine abortion as a metaphor for cultural amnesia that has linked and expressed a great many interests through the bodies of women. Or, at least, let me imagine it for you.

The rhetorical constitution of abortion in the United States as a kind of forgetfulness initially occurred in the mid-nineteenth century. The import of abortion to U.S. culture took a decided turn at this time with the physicians' antiabortion campaign. Given the presence of the natural body and its physiological laws in antiabortion discourse, both past and present, it is especially important to recognize that early opposition was predominantly medical and argued on grounds of the public body's well-being. "The years of 1850 to 1880 saw abortion emerge as a mass political issue in America for the first time," which, however, was not directly connected with the early woman's movement. Instead, as historian Carroll Smith-Rosenberg contends, the period from 1860 to 1880 saw the first successful lobbying effort by the newly formed American Medical Association, with the cooperation of the Roman Catholic Church and many of the Protestant clergy, to make abortion illegal for the first time in the United States. However, church support was tepid and, according to Carl Degler, "[n]o churches of any denomination were especially interested in the matter at the time the laws were passed." Before the passage of antiabortion statutes, terminating pregnancy before quickening, or during "the first four months," was legal.[5] Unlike today's debates in which medical issues are pervasive but submerged in a wrangle over woman's rights versus fetal rights, the health concerns of the collective body in relation to its overall fertility were at the forefront of the early struggle. Physicians demonized abortion by advocating society's dependence on reproduction and began to promulgate medically grounded rules for safe, effective, and sufficient procreation.

Change in terminology about abortion indicates the effect of the physicians' crusade. Before the AMA campaign, the term "abortion" was synonymous with miscarriage, whereas "criminal abortion" referred to abortion after quickening; and even then criminality typically referred to the risk to the pregnant woman in aborting. Pregnancy was not assumed until after the first trimester, and "most people believed that fetal life began at quickening."[6] After the AMA campaign, "criminal abortion" referred to any artificial abortion of fetal life. This shift in terms marked a turn in the basic character of "legitimate" discourse about reproduction and abortion. By the 1880s, discourse about women's reproduction had been professionalized, and abortion as an object of discourse about reproduction had changed as well.

Hence, prior to the nineteenth century, the fetus was partially disarticulated from notions of life, in that life was not taken by most people and most institutions to begin at conception. It was through the early practices of medical investigation, physicians' ways of knowing, that abortion was articulated with life such that to abort was deemed criminal. By "articulate," I do not mean simply giving voice to an as-yet unpopular or unknown idea. I mean articulate in its multiple senses: to produce intelligible speech, to interconnect, and to create order.[7] The expert knowledge that made abortion comprehensible as a kind of crime against nature, society, and God was embedded in a system of practices that constructed the female reproductive body as the anchor for society. Physicians did more than simply redefine abortion. They necessarily reconstituted the concept of life by producing a new discourse about life, new linkages between women's bodies and the state, and a new cultural order through prenatal space. The imperative to maximize life, a "prolife" mandate in the broadest sense, permeated these articulations. Abortion is death only if we can embody life in the womb; thus, the biomedical practices by which life is made a knowable, visible object are crucial. Such biomedical practices are necessarily intertwined in the believability and intelligibility of antiabortion rhetoric due to the dialectic of life and death that structures abortion discourse. One cannot constitute abortion as loss of life without recollecting what life is. The question then becomes, where is the source of this knowledge that is recollected and how is it remembered to prevent further loss of life? The rhetoric of the early medical practices used to criminalize abortion also, and of necessity, articulated life's memory.

Medical opposition to abortion became a mechanism through which culture was reproduced. Antiabortion politics of the nineteenth century carried an agenda to optimize cultural *life*, not only multiple biological *lives*. The idea that a way of life or a culture is passed on through children is an ancient commonplace around the world, and it has always been a commonplace for rhetorics of remembrance. In the United States, a version of that rhetoric was reiterated, this time through the *practices* of early scientific medicine. The rhetoric lies in the medical rituals of the era; physician's practices ordered a kind of dangerously unprocreative sexuality as well as its corrective: an inherent biological knowledge of reproductive normality. Through direct examination of patients—initially a controversial development in medical practice—and through autopsies, physicians inspected women's bodies to uncover the truth about abortion. Explicitly bypassing women's testimony in favor of what their bodies would confess, not only about specific instances of abortion but also about the essence of womanhood, physician's rituals of investigation were rhetorically inventive. The performative capacities of such rituals enabled physicians to embody women as the locus of racial, national health, and, in turn, enabled the production of vast amounts of authoritative discourse on reproductive "hygiene."

Rituals of Exposure

The memory work of physicians' epistemological practices, the practices of direct examination in particular, is the topic through which I explore some of the "what else" articulated by antiabortion rhetoric. However, the rhetoric of these practices was not unique to antiabortion efforts; it was and is common to general truth-seeking rituals that date from the Enlightenment and that physicians instantiated in the drive to modernize medicine in the nineteenth century. These epistemological practices developed into what Barbara Maria Stafford aptly termed a form of "body criticism" because the body became the dominant metaphor for the unseen and the mysterious. This criticism was enacted through *rituals of exposure* that became the province of experts. Stafford writes:

> There were proper and improper rituals for scanning, touching, cutting, deforming, abstracting, generating, conceiving, marking, staining, enlarging, reducing, imagining, and sensing. Constituting visual styles or manners of behavior, these procedures provided right or wrong sensory and intellectual strategies for "open-

ing" recalcitrant materials and otherwise impenetrable substances. Normal or abnormal processes and modes for proceeding could assure one, or not, of getting
a glimpse into secretive physiognomies. Body tropes thus provided critical clues
for how insight might be gained into the interior of any concealed territory. This
held equally for the realm of the fine arts or that of the natural sciences.[8]

What determined the truthfulness of a discourse, be it a textual description or an
image, was not the texts or images per se, but the method of perception involved
in making it, because the difference between the true and the false was considered
invisible to the senses. In other words, the criteria for truth inhered in the exposition of an object, not the object's appearance. The rhetoric of early medical rituals
of exposure was a particular instance of a general form.

To appreciate how medical rituals of nineteenth-century reproductive medicine were imbricated in the Enlightenment rhetoric of "body criticism," one must
delineate exactly which practices are in question and contextualize how they
emerged on the U.S. medical scene. As the sciences of the body, medicine and
biology were fundamental Enlightenment discourses that provided rich metaphors
and practices for the excision of truth from hidden recesses. As Michel Foucault
demonstrates in *The Birth of the Clinic*, rituals of exposure were definitive characteristics of an emerging clinical medicine in Europe. Moreover, the allopathic
(now AMA-based) medical community in the United States explicitly advocated
emulation of Europe, as witnessed by hospital reform and the adoption of European clinical methods in medical schools.[9] This process was full of internecine
conflicts, but U.S. medicine had begun to achieve its clinical aspirations by the
end of the century.

Initially, ritualized exposure in medicine centered on the corpse as the basic
text, because in the early modern period understanding life was predicated on understanding morbidity, thereby making "Death . . . the great analyst." Life was
presumed to be the antithesis of death. As a way of knowing, morbidity presumed
the doctor to be reading backward through death and across life as cadavers analogically taught doctors about the weaknesses of living bodies. Pioneered by
Marie-François Xavier Bichat, pathological anatomy, or the systematic embodiment of illness in tissue, came to define medical knowledge and institutions in the
nineteenth century. As Foucault put it, "the corpse became the brightest moment
in figures of truth. Knowledge spins where once larva was formed."[10]

In part, the early premise that death revealed life was shaped by technological
limitations of perception. Autopsies and anatomical dissection have to be done
after the death of the body, which prohibits one from seeing life at work. Ironically, Foucault notes that life "hides and envelops," whereas death "opens up to
the light of day the black coffer of the body." With the advent of technologies
such as the exploring needle or the speculum, the medical gaze opened the living
body as well. For example, James Younger Simpson, a Scottish obstetrician and
one of the foremost nineteenth-century specialists, remarked:

> As the knowledge of the structural lesions which the various organs may undergo
> from disease, has of later years extended in the hands of the pathological anato-
> mist, from his [sic] examination of the body after death, the practical physician
> has, for the purpose of his diagnosis and the guidance of his treatment, exerted
> himself in discovering means of detecting these same morbid alterations during
> the lifetime of his patient, and thus studying, if I may so speak, necroscopic anat-
> omy upon the living body.

In a typical enactment of this conception of medical knowledge, the English obstetrician Alfred Meadows wrote a paper titled "Remarks on Ovarian Physiology
and Pathology." In his essay, Meadows stresses that a better understanding of
physiology would reveal the real nature of the pathology of the ovaries.[11]

Long before clinical conditions fully saturated medical practice the preferred
mode of clinical perception had made its way into medicine. Within obstetrics and
gynecology, French clinical lectures were translated and published in U.S. journals, and Commonwealth physicians, such as Simpson and Edward Tilt, were
read and studied by many. Simpson typified the shift to a clinical mode of perception as he equated diagnostic method with truth and progress: "In fact, the medical science of the present day owes its superiority over that of an earlier date to no
circumstance more than to the increased degree of attention that has, for a considerable time past, been devoted to the study and improvement of Physical Diagnosis." Tilt, an English gynecologist and a key figure of his age, echoed this sentiment: "Continental obstetricians, having been the first to investigate scrupulously
the diseased organs of generation by the combined assistance of *the touch and the
eye*, have been able in many instances to detect hidden causes of those diseases."[12] Note that truthfulness is conferred by technique and that the body is an
ambiguous text requiring exegesis to be deciphered. AMA physicians clearly
adopted the mantle of Enlightened science, as defined by their European counter-
parts, complete with its antipathy for imposture and its search for invisible truths.
No clearer example can be found than in an 1853 address before the American
Association for the Advancement of Science that was published in *The Peninsular Journal of Medicine*. In that address, the president of the Association called
on the "New World" to surpass the standard set by Europe in the search for the
"philosopher's stone, the true *elixir vitae*, the fruit of the tree of knowledge, and
the footprint of Him of whom the earth is the footstool."[13]

Accordingly, in this period exposure to the senses became the primary method for diagnosing and treating women's reproductive ailments. Tilt marked the
beginning of gynecology at 1816, when Joseph Claude Anthelme Récamier "insisted on the necessity of studying the diseases of women as much as possible by
ocular demonstration, like all other diseases," which Tilt credited as "taking gynecology out of the shadowy regions of conjecture." In this period, the speculum,
widely believed to have been developed and first introduced in modern times by
Récamier, became the premiere tool for investigation (Fig. 1.1). T. Gaillard Thomas, one of the most respected obstetricians of his day, argued that Récamier

popularized an instrument that had been in use with little fanfare since the mid-1600s.[14] Regardless, the speculum became so popular that J. C. Nott, a New York physician, proclaimed in 1870, "that every new month brings forth a new vaginal speculum." Some, like Fleetwood Churchill, a professor of midwifery at the King and Queens College of Physicians in Ireland, felt the speculum to be overused and preferred digital examination (rectal and vaginal), the sound, the exploring needle, and the microscope as means to sensory knowledge of a woman's body; however, he did find the speculum of "great value" in diagnosis and largely responsible for many of the advances obstetricians were claiming in the latter

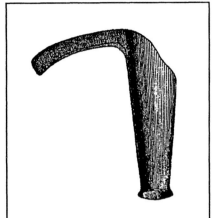

Figure 1.1. Récamier's speculum from William Jones, *Practical Observations on Diseases of Women.*

part of the century. Churchill was more modest than others in his accolades for the speculum. Throughout the late 1800s many U.S. physicians sang the praises of the speculum for its use in vaginal diagnostics. Augustus Gardner of New York, wrote that "in the same manner that the telescope analyzes the milky way, the speculum makes clear" the true nature of vaginal discharges as symptom rather than disease; in addition to "obstinate and continued" forms of discharge, for "repeated abortion, the importance and value of this instrument cannot well be exaggerated."[15] Gardner's telescopic metaphor indicates an assumption that better means of sensing women's reproductive organs, especially visually, would reveal the truth of "female maladies."

Occasionally, a critic would challenge the self-evident truth of specular examinations, such as Warren Stone. In 1855, Stone contended that the eminent physician Lisfranc, like many other obstetricians, "got a uterine twist in his mind which he never got over." In other words, technology did not remove the subjectivity of the medical observer in visualizing what was presupposed to be seen. Still others argued that the speculum was indecent and redundant with a refined sense of touch. The belief by many that touch was preferable to direct visual examination did not place tactile methods outside a system of visual documentation, however. The emphasis on visuality also encompassed the sense of touch as all direct examinations were moved into the visual register of textual literacy through pictorial description and images. Further, touch became a companion to sight in modern obstetric and gynecological practice, giving the eye a sense of texture and the hand a sense of color. Both senses were coordinated to maximize empirical observations as the feeling of the fingertips and the impressions of the eye both

were made into visual data. By the 1870s, few physicians questioned the truthfulness and propriety of the speculum and its use with other methods of direct
sensory examination.[16] Between 1800 and 1900, direct physical examination grew
in popularity until it became the premier method of the ob/gyn.

Direct contact significantly changed medical practices and reorganized the
space physicians and patients occupied. Physical diagnosis presumes a theory of
pathology that assumes diseases have a seat or originary site, rather than resulting
from an imbalance in bodily humors, as had been assumed for centuries. Direct
examination of a woman's reproductive organs became the best way to diagnose
her ailments. This was a radical shift from the earlier method of asking questions
and inferring illness largely from the verbal reports of patients. It was also quite
different from the methods practiced by midwives, who saw themselves more as
part of the process of birthing.[17] Accordingly, the methods used by physicians in
the daily course of medical care assume great significance. Physical diagnostic
practices were forms of body criticism, exegetical methods whereby the exposed
body could be transformed into knowledge. To study the performative rhetoric of
rituals such as these, one must account for the apparent truths culled from hidden
recesses, the dynamics of the rituals themselves, and the space through which
bodies act. It is crucial to understand how perceptual practices are normalized in
order to appreciate the simultaneity of creating knowledge and remembering culture. Maurice Halbwachs contended in *On Collective Memory*, that in order to
remember, "we must tread the same path that others would have followed had
they been in our position," and that "[t]here is no memory without perception."[18]
The normalization of body criticism within early medicine enabled a normalization of perception that sustained a memory of culture within a knowledge of life.
Thus, the performance of physicians in their daily rituals can be analyzed and
evaluated rhetorically as a mnemonic process. Similarly, women's participation in
and resistance to medical examination can be understood in relation, not only to
norms of reproductive healthcare, but also to norms of cultural regeneration.

Anamnesis and Hypomnesis

Epistemologically, the presumed outcome of rituals of exposure is knowledge. In this case, medical knowledge about life in the womb was to alter the
meaning of abortion and, in theory, stem the rising tide of ignorance regarding
pregnancy. How did ways of knowing like medical exams function as a kind of
memory work, however? The process of "discovery as recollection" was the
implicit, dominant epistemic motif of antiabortionists' discourse and practices.
For regular physicians, a central cause of abortion was women's ignorance of
abortion's "true nature." The rapid increase in abortions by middle- and upper-
class women, noticed in the decades after the 1840 census, was explained as a
loss of knowledge that women had formerly been in touch with. Physicians ar-

gued women were becoming dissociated from their inner, true selves, and offered the solution of reeducating women about their womanly essence and their place in the reproductive scheme of culture. The lost knowledge physicians elaborated was located in the body itself, in the natural laws that determined health and illness. Memory as used in this study is not about the recollection of one's individual experiences or even lessons one has been taught, but about a reconnection with essential knowledge by "unforgetting," or the Neoplatonic epistemology of *anamnesis*. The memory work of physicians' medical practices not only was addressed to certain individuals; it was addressed to a culture that had forgotten itself. "Memories in this view," Barbie Zelizer writes, "become not only the simple act of recall but social, cultural, and political action at its broadest level."[19] What can be referred to as an Enlightened "search for truth" through ritualized exposure may be described epistemologically as a kind of anamnesis, a remembering of what has been forgotten.

My use of memory as a critical concept is not a recitation of physicians' favorite term, a trope employed for persuasive ends during the nineteenth century; it is an analytical descriptor for the epistemological dynamics of lost and revivified knowledge. That is, the formation and use of memory is fundamental to all rhetoric to the extent that rhetors appeal to truths and experiences to make themselves known, whether or not they choose explicitly to use the trope of memory. Early physicians worked with the tropes of "ignorance," "civilization in decline," and "true knowledge." The epistemological dynamics of how ignorance and knowledge operated within their rhetoric, however, involve a form of anamnesis. I use memory as a way of analytically organizing the central epistemic motif of early antiabortion rhetoric, to name that which has heretofore remained nameless, not as a means of explaining physicians on their own terms.

Anamnesis is part of a long epistemological tradition of "knowing as remembrance." Dating to Plato's theory of the Forms, the notion of an immaterial, hidden truth has been a core value in Western intellectual cultures. What is not commonly stressed when considering the Platonic legacy (for science, philosophy, or otherwise) is that for Plato knowing was fundamentally remembering. According to Plato, anamnesis was the recollection of a divine, "essential reality" that humans implicitly knew but could not manage to recall. If truth is eternal and persistent, it exists as a pristine, metaphysical set of memories, as Jacques Derrida wrote of Plato: "Memory and truth cannot be separated."[20] Of course, Platonic remembrance is a function of the dialectic of two souls questioning each other to recall the truth within. In the case of physicians' investigative practices, the interlocutor is replaced by the body and the dialectic becomes a kind of somatic confessional induced by the physician. Medical antiabortionists employed a materialistic Neoplatonism.[21] Accordingly, antiabortion physicians' materialization of an instinctual, corporeal knowledge of maternal duty was a kind of memory formation that invested the reproductive order of culture within the body's organs and sympathies. They reiterated the pattern of eternal truths recalled to disabuse the world of its confusion, only here the eternal truths are etched into women's biology by God and nature, rather than being planted in the soul of another dialectician. I note the Neoplatonist overtones to indicate the manner in which instinctual knowledge of reproduction was offered as normative. Neoplatonist memory is a blueprint for "ought," not just a record of "was." It is an idealized genealogy of what is supposed to be.

In 1854, Gunning Bedford, a colorful lecturer on midwifery, captured the motif of forgetfulness well as he lamented the perils faced by young women. He decried the seductions of the city, the allure of a single life full of suitors, gaiety, and the "lascivious polka." He recalled the imperative of the ovaries and the great natural function for which they were destined. He described young women as somehow *unaware* of what their bodies knew, of what he knew: that women must follow their destiny because it was written in their biology. As J. B. W. Nowlin put it, "[t]he dread to assume the care and responsibilities of maternity may be assigned a most potent factor in the causation of this most reprehensible practice. The pleasures and calls of society are assumed to be paramount to all other considerations . . ." D. H. Storer, father of H. R. Storer, echoed this view in an essay that he wrote in the 1850s but that was published in 1872 in his son's journal: "The fashionable young bride . . . wishing still to enjoy the immunities of unmarried life—to be free, unshackled as ever—she will not endure the seclusion and deprivations necessary with the pregnant condition, but resorts to means, readily procurable, to destroy the life within her, *apparently unconscious* that she is not only committing a crime in the sight of the law, but also a sin in the sight of her Maker."[22] Over and over in the medical literature, women who aborted were portrayed as unconscious of or unable "to realize that the being within them is indeed animate," as Hugh Hodge, an important player in the early antiabortion movement, stated. Whether one looks to the early antiabortion figures such as D. H. Storer or Hugh Hodge, to certain homeopathists like Edwin Hale, to leading women physicians like Elizabeth Blackwell, to little noticed writers such as Andrew Nebinger or Nowlin, or to young physicians such as those studying at the Women's Medical College of Pennsylvania, the motif persists of an evil ignorance about woman's essential nature. There were other rationales routinely offered, like adultery, cowardice, prostitution, or poverty, but these were typically offered as excuses made plausible due to fundamental ignorance of the truth about abortion, "this dense ignorance" as Joseph Johnson called it.[23]

No treatise better illustrates the claim of ignorance as a kind of Neoplatonic forgetfulness than H. R. Storer's widely publicized and award-winning 1866 work, *Why Not? A Book for Every Woman.* He repeatedly invoked ignorance as "the only excuse that can be given with any show of plausibility" for increased abortions. His rationale was that reproduction was a natural, maternal instinct: "Nature does all her work, of whatever character it may be, in accordance with certain simple and general laws, any infringement of which must necessarily cause derangement, disaster, or ruin." Women are naturally bound to bring forth children; thus, abortion is "a thing so frightful and so repugnant to every instinct" that after an abortion, even if induced out of ignorance, the truth would affect the woman through "a touch of pity . . . a trace of regret . . . a trace of shame . . . a trace of remorse for what she knows to be wrong, no matter to what small extent."[24] For some, the psychic affect of "unwarrantably interfering with nature" could result in "moral shock" resulting in death:

> We have seen that, in some instances, the thought of the crime, coming to the mind at a time when the physical system is weak and prostrated, is sufficient to cause death. The same tremendous idea, so laden with the consciousness of guilt against God, humanity, and even mere natural instinct, is undoubtably able, where not affecting life, to produce insanity. This it may do either by its first and sudden occurrence to the mind, or subsequently, by those long and unavailing regrets, that remorse, if conscience exists, is sure to bring. Were we wrong in considering death the preferable alternative?

For Storer and many others in the antiabortion campaign, instinctual knowledge of the evils of abortion was always present in the woman if only she could be induced to remember it, either through prodding her conscience or through reminder. Indeed, knowledge of the wrong of abortion was so powerful that women would not only be driven insane by the realization after the fact, but also must be considered insane for attempting abortion with full knowledge of its character. He wrote that the act of abortion by one who was "cognisant of their [abortions'] true character, should almost be looked upon as proof of actual insanity."[25] His reasoning, typical of late nineteenth-century psychology, was that mental instability was visited upon women by "uterine excitation" of any kind so that pregnant women were prone to derangement.[26] Hence, women aborted because they were so ignorant of their own bodies that either they had lost touch with the maternal instinct or they were mad.

What could cause the loss of an instinctual knowledge so deeply felt that it might cause death or madness? Almost uniformly, antiabortionists cried, "Fashion!" That label referred to the corruption of contemporary society. In earlier times, it was argued, women knew their biological role, but modern "fashion often forbid[s] a woman from bearing children." H. R. Storer explained in reference to families of early settlers that:

> It was found, that the families comprising the first generation, had, on an average eight and ten children; the next three generations averaged between seven and eight to each family; the fifth generation about five, and the sixth less than three, to each family. What a change as to the size of the families since those olden times! Then, large families were common; now the exception. Then, it was rare to find married persons having only one, two, or three children: now, it is very common. Then, it was regarded a calamity for a married couple to have no children; now, such calamities are found on every side of us; in fact, they are fashionable.

According to authors of the time, polkas, boyfriends, shopping, gossiping, and keeping up with the Smythes were concerns that overpowered women's ability to discern their purpose in life and had led to ubiquitous "calamities." It had become customary to abort for frivolous reasons, so modern women, displaying weak mental faculties, followed the herd and ignored their biological imperative. A sense of astonishment often accompanied these remarks, an amazement at how women could be so ignorant of their own bodies' instincts. As Alice B. Stockham stated in her popular manual on healthy life practices, *Tokology*: "The maternal instinct is inherent in every woman's heart. It seems strange that any morbid idea of pleasure could antagonize the natural aspirations to such an extent that she could destroy the viability of her own offspring."[27]

Changing reproductive customs were attacked by many physicians as a source of corruption to maternal instinct and as a sign of "civilization" in decline, an attack that seemed to strengthen by the turn of the century. For more than one writer, abortion became the measure of whether or not the United States was civilized, arguing that the nation had descended either to or below the level of "savages." The narrative of ignorant, murderous decline framed the charge to remember the natural and divine truth about maternal duty. Calling abortion a "moral leprosy," G. Maxwell-Christine cast the antiabortion effort in strikingly clear Neoplatonic terms, as the work of enlightened leaders laboring to recall civilization to a pure state prior to original sin: "whilst there may be grave doubts of the possession by our race of the strength and vigor of former ages, much is being done toward a return to its former pristine condition. But this restorative project is a battle, fortunately presided over by the best of the race. Each one of us must join with watchful eye, willing heart, and ready hands in the crusade."[28] The comment vividly illustrates how Neoplatonic epistemology helped generate Christian arguments against abortion. The story of the fall blended effortlessly with the story of an invisible truth about women's duty being scripted into her anatomy. Christine-Maxwell's remark also hints at the racism that helped a decline in birth rates to appear as a threat to civilization, a topic I return to in the next chapter.

In virtually all cases, medical antiabortionists presumed that women's biology, when properly induced to reveal its secrets, would remind women of their destiny. The curative to a creeping ignorance was education, particularly among the apparently too-civilized bourgeoisie. At the height of the campaign, the outgoing president of the Philadelphia County Medical Society, Nebinger, wrote a thoroughly typical call to educate: "I am also convinced, that a wide-spread diffusion of the necessary information among women, by those in whom they have confidence as moral and religious instructors, will in a brief cycle very perceptibly diminish, and finally almost entirely prevent, the commission of the crime of abortion." By the turn of the century, physicians were still making the same call, as Jennie G. Oreman exemplifies: "Education of the young will alone rectify the evil."[29] Education centered on the principle that the fetus was alive at conception, a religious precept made biological, such as with the use of comparative anatomy of kangaroos, birds, tortoises, and fish. Further, it was argued that abortion resulted in demonstrable physical harm to the woman, to any future offspring, and to society, and that such biological harm proved abortion was contrary to natural and divine law. There were a host of messages women's bodies were interpreted as sending against abortion, the substance of which is detailed in chapter four. Because women somehow had forgotten their life's purpose, it was the physician's duty to remind them of what the female body always knew.

Documenting the forgotten messages of the body in order to educate the desires of modern women was a hypomnesic act, *hypomnesis* being the consignation of recollections to a place external to the memory (an archive in Derrida's terms). Hypomnesis is a documentary "apparatus" that includes the tools, practices, and rituals necessary to record memory with the anticipation of future use. As I read antiabortion rhetoric, new obstetric and gynecologic diagnostics are treated as hypomnesic practices, efforts to materialize a biological memory of cultural order in a public, medicalized archive. To treat what are typically considered predicates of therapy as mnemonic practices is to pursue scrupulously, if by some accounts implausibly, the idea that "[t]he archive takes place at the place of originary and structural breakdown of said memory." One marks down what is often forgotten at the point of loss, not elsewhere. To think of medical diagnostics as rhetorical memory aids requires that one understands that an archive is not a library, not a structure full of books, because it is a set of enactments both textual *and* corporeal. As a result, "[o]ne will never be able to objectivize it with no-remainder," Derrida writes. The bodies of women, the medical texts which ostensibly mirrored them, and the relationship between the two mediated by medical practice repeatedly reconstitute the archive as well as that which is presumptively contained within it, "and that is why [the archive] is never closed." In its performative character, what the act of hypomnesis "does" is to embody culture in the repetitive recuperation of truths. Building a cultural archive, a living memory, "can only illuminate, read, interpret, establish its object, namely a given inheritance, by inscribing itself into it . . . There is no meta-archive." Meticulously documenting the hidden truth that women's bodies, in their very physiology, bear the future of culture, physicians embodied culture not so much in the exact record they kept, for it kept changing, but in the very "scene of reading"—in women lies the truth of life and, as indicated by abortion rates, women no longer were capable of heeding that truth.[30]

The patronizing and infantilizing characterization of ignorant or mad women as threatening their health and that of the nation by aborting their unborn did not go unchallenged.[31] One piece, a direct response to Storer, ostensibly an anonymous letter by "the wife of a Christian physician," was published in 1866 in *The Boston Medical and Surgical Journal* with an editorial footnote recommending the letter for serious consideration. Titled, "'Why Not? A Book For Every Woman': A Woman's View," it was a powerful rebuttal to the presumption of women's ignorance:

> The true and *greatest* cause of abortion is one hidden from the world, viz.: un-
> happiness and want of consideration towards wives in the marriage relation, the
> more refined education of girls, and their subsequent revolting from the degrada-
> tion of being a mere thing—an appendage. . . . They are not independent, but
> subject; and all teaching tends to keep them so. Here is just where the trouble
> begins. This is why they rebel. Save themselves from the *cause* they cannot. The
> consequence is mainly within their power, and the temptation is strong to throw
> off the bond which confines them to the fireside. . . . Abortion is a crime, and
> women are guilty of it, but they sin not alone. . . . and the more intelligent they
> are, the more they recoil in disgust from the life they are led; for, mark it, it is not
> the ignorant class who are guilty of procuring abortion.

Note that the author adheres to a similar moral standard and is of a similar class
as the physicians she addresses. Her words resonate with the call for voluntary
motherhood, a predominantly middle-class position advanced in the latter part of
the century by suffragists, social reformers, and free lovers alike. On the principle
that women had the right to control their bodies and refuse sex, "they opposed
contraception and abortion but endorsed voluntary motherhood achieved through
periodic abstinence; they believed that women should always have the right to
decide when to bear a child," as Linda Gordon put it. Even many contraception
advocates came to oppose abortion, for that matter. Further, advocates of voluntary motherhood insisted on viewing procreation within a sociological rather than
a strictly biological framework. Accordingly, the author indicts male supremacy
with a critique that covers marriage, education and power, and calls abortion rebellion. Reversing the claims of antiabortionists, she argues that education and
knowledge lead to abortion. Any "forgetfulness" is moral and a result of subjuga-
tion: "What wonder if she for a time forget her moral obligations in her extremity,
and is indifferent to the life which is no longer a blessing."[32] It is a surprisingly
sharp condemnation to be published in a medical journal, let alone in a journal
known for its opposition to women's education. Set against the growing ortho-
doxy of medical opinion on abortion, the abrasion of the author's letter exposes
the surface of power in early antiabortion rhetoric. She highlights the motif of
"unforgetting" and offers a counter-memory that abortion is a knowing, reluctant
rebellion against marital despotism and *not* a kind of cultural amnesia.

The anonymous author's attitude is far more radical than that of women physicians toward the male-dominant antiabortion campaign. Almost always voluntary motherhood advocates, early women physicians such as the venerable Marie
Zakrweska, who established the New England Hospital in 1862, or Sarah Dolley,
the third woman to receive a chartered medical degree in the United States, supported the campaign and strongly opposed abortion. For example, Rachel Gleason
wrote in *Talks to My Patients* that "[t]here are conditions when it seems as if
pregnancy should be avoided. Remember, I say avoided, *not* interrupted." In fact,
Gleason refers her readers to Storer's "Why Not?" for further proof. Elizabeth

Blackwell, the first woman to enter regular medical school in the United States, cited opposition to abortion as an early motivation for her medical career: "The gross perversion and destruction of motherhood by the abortionist filled me with indignation, and awakened active antagonism. That the honourable term 'female physician' should be exclusively applied to those women who carried on this shocking trade seemed to me a horror. It was an utter degradation of what might and should become a noble position for women." According to Regina Morantz-Sanchez, "[m]ost female physicians expressed shock at the prevalence of abortion among middle-class women" and, quite frequently, "revered motherhood in senti-mental Victorian fashion" along with their male colleagues. Many pursued an ever greater normalization of motherly efficiency, or a kind of "scientific mother-hood," like Prudence Saur. Nonetheless, these doctors largely rejected their breth-ren's implication that women alone were to blame. They typically pointed to men's shared responsibility for abortion, as did the anonymous author, thus wid-ening the circle of condemnation, rather than rebutting the basic theme of the campaign. On the whole, women physicians' attitudes and practices toward abor-tion were consonant with those of the male principals behind the campaign.[33]

As acts of memory formation, early physicians' investigative practices were themselves a form of performative rhetoric. Not only did such practices produce medical language by which to talk of abortion, they embodied women as a source of cultural memory and physicians as privileged guardians of that memory. Fur-ther, in the effort to recover a "true" knowledge of abortion from the very organs of women, medical practices constituted a new *cultural* space of reproduction, prenatal space, in which the institutions of medicine, the family, the state, and religion were conjoined in cultural as well as biological reproduction. Discourses to legislators or various publics used the language of medicine, assumed the natu-ralness of medically constituted bodies to justify claims, and operated *in*, *with*, and *through* the emerging prenatal space. As a result, the discourse of antiabor-tion physicians reiterates forms produced by medical practices themselves.

In this book, my attention is focused on a specific memory formation estab-lished within early antiabortion medicine, not cultural memory formation in gen-eral. In that sense, I am paying heed more to "official" rather than "vernacular" memory.[34] I do not contend that remembrance is strictly an activity that favors prevailing power asymmetries. As the letter from the "wife of a Christian physi-cian" indicates, the rhetoric of memory *and* counter-memory are part and parcel of all political rhetoric, dominant and resistant.[35] The contention that early medi-cal practice established a normative cultural memory reformulates the intersection of medical practices and political rhetoric about abortion by intentionally relocat-ing the threshold of when and where such rhetoric begins. Rather than bracket the physician-patient relationship as generating disinterested knowledge that was then put to public political use, I stress the character of the physician-patient interac-tion itself to destabilize the medical "ground" of early rhetoric on abortion. In-stead of treating antiabortion arguments as a linear form of rhetoric from rhetor, through text, to audience, this book examines the lateral, unintended rhetorics accomplished as physicians acted upon preexisting discourses about reproduction and created new knowledge they then disposed in expert texts. I treat medical practices as of a piece with the discourse of physicians by examining their mutually constituting relationship. As such, I am interested more in the performative rhetoric of how medical text and practice interact in the patient-physician scene than with deliberative rhetoric of how text and audience interact in the advocate-legislator scene.

Antiabortion rhetoric invests fetal life with more than individuality; it invests fetal life with cultural constancy. Coming to the understanding that culture quickens itself alongside and through the fetus, I have focused on the confluence of reproduction and remembrance. In particular, I have looked to the moment when modern, biologically defined, life in the womb became an articulate site of recollection for cultural reproduction. At that moment, although not exclusively the province of physicians, life and its memory were largely articulated through medical body criticism; or, the rhetoric of examination and knowledge creation. What is striking about this rhetoric is that as a form of cultural "mnemonics," regardless of whether or not women stopped aborting, it enabled the *opposition* to abortion to normatively regenerate a raced, classed, and gendered order to national identity and entitlement in the form of medical knowledge. Further, the practices that blurred patients and criminals, medicine and law, reconfigured the power arrangements of women, physicians, and the state. This raises the question, "What was at stake in articulating a biological memory of culture?" To set the context for how medical practices could produce such a memory, I first must address the regenerative politics of the era.

Chapter Two
The Politics of Life and Memory

On the broader level of demographic patterns and social policy, abortion involves issues of national commitment to population control or expansion, the acceptability of woman's participation in the economy, and, more broadly, woman's appropriate role within the home and society. It exemplifies political control of the personal and the physiological. It thus bridges the intensely personal and the broadly political. On every level, to talk of abortion is to speak of power.

— Carroll Smith-Rosenberg, *Disorderly Conduct*

Rhetoric and politics go hand in glove. It has been written that rhetoric is always doubled, taking up in its forms whatever substance is at hand such as ethics or philosophy.[1] Since classical times, the unavoidable doubling of rhetoric with politics has at times made it unclear as to where one ends and the other begins. One hardly can imagine a politics that does not operate rhetorically nor a rhetoric that does not impact political culture on some level. Knowing that early physicians' efforts to criminalize abortion operated via a certain rhetoric, it is impossible to ignore the political character of their efforts by appeal to an ethos of disinterested science and self-evident truth. If there was a rhetoric to remembering a maternal imperative, there was a politics of life involved, and understanding the scenography and topography of that rhetoric's performance requires a map of the politics.

A Regenerative Campaign

Orchestrated by the AMA, the move to criminalize all induced abortions was clearly directed at bourgeois women and was precipitated by H. R. Storer. He was not alone, however, working with support from prestigious medical elders, such as Walter Channing (brother to William Ellery Channing) and Hugh L. Hodge. At the beginning of the campaign, Dr. Storer was a young, "professionally ambitious" obstetrician/gynecologist. During the 1840s, a few states had made abortion "before quickening a misdemeanor." In the early 1850s, opposition to abortion was beginning to grow among physicians, but it was diffused throughout the rank and file. Storer worked with antiabortion sentiment and focused it. He began by writing prominent physicians around the country who were already working for antiabortion legislation:

> After gaining support of key physicians . . . Storer opened his crusade publicly in May 1857 by introducing to the Suffolk County Medical Society a resolution that called for the formation of a committee to "consider whether any further legislation is necessary in this Commonwealth, on the subject of *criminal abortion*, and to report to the Society such other means as may seem necessary for the suppression of this abominable, unnatural, and yet common crime."[2]

The efforts of the AMA and its allies fostered antiabortion legislation in the 1870s such that "by the early 1880s, most states had enacted harsh antiabortion laws." However, notes Janet Farrell Brodie in her *Contraception and Abortion in 19th-Century America*, "many state laws regulating abortion provided a therapeutic exception that a physician could perform an abortion to save a woman's life."[3]

The AMA was hardly unified on this issue, however. The leading opponents were, like Storer, obstetric/gynecologic specialists; they were typically urban, frequently East-coast specialists. Among the many internal battles in the early days of professional medicine, Eastern urbanites and "country" doctors squared off over issues of ethics and education, and general practitioners attacked specialists as quacks. In these highly volatile days, "regular" physicians (as AMA allopaths called themselves) disagreed over most things, reflecting schisms as much over medical practice as competition for respect and clientele. Some physicians criticized Storer's proposal, but resistance quickly wilted in the heat of abortion opposition. An initially small group of specialists, in effect, popularized and successfully instantiated antiabortion principles within the Association.[4]

The emergence and execution of this antiabortion campaign spun a web of normative constraints around the practice and perception of reproductivity, and these entanglements surpassed the establishment of abortion as a crime. Prevailing histories of the period dwell on different motives for antiabortion efforts. James Mohr's *Abortion in America*, although acknowledging feminist issues regarding reproductive control, frames the campaign as professionally opportunistic, an outgrowth of the AMA's vision of itself as a custodian of national health. Smith-Rosenberg, although acknowledging the professional aspirations of the AMA, frames the campaign as institutionally sanctioned gender ideology at work, a reassertion of patriarchal reproductive control through scientific medicine. Brodie, although acknowledging Mohr's and Smith-Rosenberg's arguments, suggests briefly that the psychology of people such as Storer might account for the move to criminalize. These explanations have significant merit; however, they under-emphasize the decided presence of the biopolitics of abortion and the rhetoric of physicians' practices in the service of such politics.[5] Although not an exclusive consideration, the politics of managing "life" through individuals, as well as through racial, ethnic, and class reproductivity, permeates early opposition to abortion. Further, medical practices provided a rhetoric that not only lead to criminalization, but also formed a new space for reproduction and its management in the United States. Biopolitics and its rhetoric must be considered when evaluating the impact of early medical opposition to abortion. Despite the excellence of the aforementioned histories, there is as yet no adequate account of the rhetoric by which antiabortionists concatenated reproduction to the life of a (white) nation and the consequences of such a rhetoric.[6]

It is important, then, to frame abortion opposition as a restorative rhetoric that attempted to counteract white women's perceived estrangement from their maternal duty. The memory of that duty, or the recollection of lost knowledge, was articulated through medical practices. Rather than searching for a local motive, I place such a restorative project within the broad, purifying rhetoric of permanent social war against biological-cultural threats to society "born in its own body."[7] The criminalization of abortion took place at a time when the growing white bourgeoisie in the United States was experiencing significant anxiety about its overall health, fitness, and vitality. Facing radical cultural changes that were the very conditions of the creation of a modern, class-based society, many within the wealthier portions of white society reacted with fear to nonprocreative sexualities among their own ranks and their effects on the body politic. In a time marked by a sense of crisis regarding middle- and upper-class women's fertility, abortion manifested itself as an "enemy within" through declining numbers of births. But what does it mean to perceive a crisis in reproduction?

One *can* read the great ruptures in the United States of the 1800s as stoking bourgeois anxiety regarding fertility. Briefly, in the nineteenth century, the United States underwent major societal upheavals that serve now, and did then, as an index of disruption: industrialization, urbanization, slave emancipation, Western expansion, and immigration. The U.S. economy erupted in the early nineteenth century as industries proliferated, such as textile mills and shoe factories. Monopoly ownership of technologies and of resources to enable industries (buildings, transportation, raw materials, steam power, and electricity, for instance) radically influenced labor relations. Experts in law, medicine, business, and academics increased in number and kind as the bourgeoisie and the working classes took shape within a new systemic mix of wage laborers, capitalists, and budding professionals. Additionally, agrarian culture was disrupted as cities and towns burgeoned and many rural dwellers moved to urban centers. Hitherto unknown numbers of people came to dwell interdependently and in close proximity to one another. A profound sense of dislocation in the form of loss, decay, and anomie rippled through many authors' writings as new urban spaces emerged. Apartheid in the United States shifted from an outright slave institution to a set of segregated, post-slavery institutions. The Western territories were rapidly settled in conjunction with formal and informal wars on Native Americans. Finally, immigrant populations swelled several times, generally coming from Northern Europe in mid-century and Southern and Eastern Europe in the latter part of the century.[8] The cross-cultural friction of shifting ethnic populations, many bloody redefinitions of race relations, and the incorporation of millions of new residents in cities and towns further aggravated whatever sense of cultural unity and cohesion people felt and the emerging white affluent classes had.

Thus, one *could* situate the perceived crisis in middle- and upper-class reproduction within a larger theater of unease, presuming that such sweeping disruptions are aberrant irritations to social order, that stability more than conflict is the set point. From this perspective, the formulation of domestic ideals for womanhood might be read as a stabilizing project, an attempt to steady society through gender normalization. Nineteenth-century ideals of womanhood are now well documented and can be made to fit the story of a culture seeking order through reconfiguration of complementary gender inequality. The presumed responsibilities of women took on new connotations, entered new political webs, and created concomitant transformations in reproductive control. As has been documented by Sara Evans, Aileen Kraditor, Smith-Rosenberg, and Barbara Welter, among others, the ideal of womanhood shifted from that of a matron of the extended family within an agricultural and artisanal economy to one who was solely responsible for nourishing and maintaining the health and morality of the nuclear family in an increasingly urban, industrial economy. In particular, Welter and Smith-Rosenberg document the creation of the ideal bourgeois matron within moral, medical, and political discourses of the era. Little elaboration is necessary on the ideals of *republican motherhood* in the late eighteenth and early nineteenth centuries and the cult of *true womanhood* of the mid- to late nineteenth century. Republican motherhood was a sentimental vision of the domestic woman who used gentle persuasion to carry out her role in the social contract: to protect and nurture "children, the home, and morality" and, thus, create good citizens. True womanhood was a more rigid codification of these ideals into the feminine virtues of purity, piety, domesticity, and submissiveness.[9] These were profoundly white, privileged images of femininity, rife with contradictions, that did not reflect the many schisms in female identity in terms of class, race, sexuality, and region. Nonetheless, normative reproduction of culture was part and parcel of what was considered good about these ideals, and the complementary nature of womanhood to manhood was seen as a pillar of order within affluent, white society.

However, working from Ann Laura Stoler's brilliant rereading of Foucault, I believe it is more profitable to interpret the insistence on complementary gender normativity as part of an antagonistic project, not a stabilizing one. Foucault added a wrinkle to the narrative of normalizing procreation that is crucial for understanding the rhetoric of reproductive politics, however oblique his intention to speak to ideals of womanhood. In *The History of Sexuality*, he argued that in the era of the modern state, kinship systems of old, which had largely dictated mar-

riages and appropriate lineage according to stable family units associated with
land and birthright, were folded with an emerging system of dutiful heterosexuality within families that were increasingly unmoored geographically and socially.
Whereas lines of kinship had once regulated sexuality, a ubiquitous sense of sexual purity and natural obligation became the principles for normalizing sex. The
European aristocracy formerly had "asserted the special character of its body, but
this was in the form of *blood*, that is, in the form of the antiquity of its ancestry
and of the value of its alliances; the bourgeoisie on the contrary looked to its
progeny and the health of its organism when it laid claim to a specific body. The
bourgeoisie's 'blood' was its sex," meaning that identity was dependent on sexual
conduct. Instead of tracing a blue bloodline, one traced a line of sex practices to
guarantee the pedigree of the upper- and middle-class body. Stoler clarifies that
this reconfiguration of sexuality (where class and race are conflated) was not *precipitated* by the emergence of an industrial capitalist class-system, as many have
taken Foucault's thesis. Rather, sexuality, race, and class were intersecting vectors within the "permanency of war-like relations inside the social body."[10]

Feminists have long understood and argued that the body is, as Barbara Johnson stated, "the focal point over the shape of power." The shift Stoler describes
inverts the focus on the body within power relations, and thus inverts modes of
struggle over power, in the modern state. Foucault's argument was that power
within a "normalizing society" has come to operate along biological dimensions,
through the investment in life forces and their optimization individually and collectively. *Biopower*, as he described it, is "the power to *foster* life or *disallow* it to
the point of death," thus making regulation and discipline regarding sexual conduct a primary means of struggle between groups. "Healthy" sexuality and corresponding ways of life have become connected to cultural dominance through the
politics of what one does with one's body. Stoler notes that the nineteenth-century
expansion of biopower as a mode of conflict was marked by "increasing intervention in the ethics of conduct, geared to the management of 'how to live.'. . . It is
through the technologies of sexuality that the bourgeoisie will claim its hege-
mony, its privileged position, its certified knowledge and jurisdiction over the
manner of living, over the governing of children, over the civilities, conduct and
competencies that prescribe 'how to live.'"[11]

This process of normalizing how to live had medicine as its "common denominator," linking knowledge of class and race through knowledge of healthy living.
Foucault wrote, "[t]he works, published in great numbers at the end of the
eighteenth-century, on body hygiene, the art of longevity, ways of having healthy
children and of keeping them alive as long as possible, and methods for improving the human lineage, bear witness to the fact: they thus attest to the correlation
of this concern with the body and sex to a type of 'racism.'"[12] Expressed through
normative sexuality and the bodily arts of the "good life," race and class became
modes of separation and hostile juxtaposition of populations. This trend continued and intensified in the nineteenth century. Published in 1852, C. W. Gleason's

Seven Lectures on the Philosophy of Life and the Art of Preserving Health is indicative. In it he argues that women were declining in health and thereby decreasing the population, and that the health of "mankind" depends on the health of the individual who must in turn obey the "fixed laws" of physiological nature, like a machine. In terms of reproductive medicine and abortion, to maintain the body of the bourgeoisie, life had to be protected at that most vulnerable point, gestation. Many marriage and maternity guides in the United States reveal similar theses.[13]

Stoler argues convincingly that in his lectures that pertain to *The History of Sexuality*, Foucault presents biopower as a "set of strategies not only of self-affirmation, but self-defense of a bourgeois society against the internal dangers it had produced." Instead of operating on the principle that "we must defend ourselves against society," Foucault argued, the state and professional institutions affiliated with social regulation began to proceed on the principle that "we must defend society against all the biological dangers of that other race, of that sub-race, and that counter-race that despite ourselves we are constituting." Rather than seeing conflict between races as the means of bringing a nation into existence, keeping in mind the complicated integuments of class and race, survival required a permanent "internal war as a defense of society against itself."[14] To survive, the individual and collective body needed persistent, vigilant cleansing of any biological degeneration that was feared to weaken culture.

Instead of seeing racism as an act of scapegoating, where a darkened enemy is conjured to blame for other social stresses, Stoler contends that when viewed in terms of biopower, racism is a constitutive element of cultural norms about how to live: "racism is more than an ad hoc response to crisis; it is a manifestation of preserved possibilities, the expression of an underlying discourse of permanent social war, nurtured by the biopolitical technologies of 'incessant purification.' Racism does not simply arise in moments of crisis, in sporadic cleansings. It is internal to the biopolitical state, woven in the weft of the social body, threaded through its fabric."[15] Placing abortion into the complex weave of race, class, and sexuality that textures "biopower" requires us to consider abortion as a scene of *constitutive* conflict, not as a *problem* of differences that has yet to be solved. More than an anxious response to external disruptions to society's otherwise stable set point, abortion can be understood as an internal expression of permanent social war. What if the conflict over abortion is examined as part of a politics that *maintain* a culture of severe differences in power?

Reproductivity and Regeneration

In a context where disciplined procreative sexuality became central to white identity and to race survival, abortion became a significant element of the perceived reproductive crisis among certain classes. Levels of population and the relative fertility and mortality of different groups became primary sources of public consternation. From scientific racists like Francis Galton, who "coined the term 'eugenics,'" to popular figures like Jacob Riis, whose famous photographic surveillance of "the other half" posed the danger of a growing underclass living in urban tenements, the white bourgeoisie was concerned about the vigor of its body in relation to other populations. Furthermore, the debates inaugurated by Malthus (and later taken up by Darwin and Spencer) made populations and reproducing populations much more visible to the medical imagination. At the same time, abortion rates increased dramatically. Mohr cites a number of indicators that abortion rates rose from 1840 to 1880. A general indicator is the decline in Euro-American fertility rates from 7.04 children in 1800 to 3.56 children in 1900. According to Linda Gordon in *Woman's Body, Woman's Right*, the decline appears sharper still when available data for African American fertility are included. More direct evidence such as the rise of an industry around abortion drugs and services, the reportage of the popular press, court records, private correspondence, and physicians' statements in medical journals indicates that abortion became a common practice in these years among all strata of society. Like abortifacients, abortionists were widely available and ranged from respectable physicians to "infamous" figures such as the often pilloried Madame Restell of New York City, the most well-known abortionist of the century.[16]

However, the pervasiveness of abortion by itself was not the real issue for many physicians. The AMA was concerned predominantly about the bourgeois white woman because of the threat she posed. Smith-Rosenberg argues that "the good bourgeois wife was to limit her fertility, symbolize her husband's affluence, and do good within the world." Yet she was also to be "domestic, docile, and reproductive." In short, the "good wife had become a potentially dangerous social phenomenon" not only because her increased activity outside the home conflicted with the domestic limitations of true womanhood, but also because her restraint in reproduction to enable greater affluence heightened the bourgeois sense of risk from a racialized, working-class threat. As Smith-Rosenberg states, "The medico-scientific insistence that women's biology was women's destiny must be seen in this light." Compared to the more favorable view of bourgeois family limitation as moral in the earlier half of the century, Dennis Hodgson writes that, ideologically, "The 'prudence' and 'pride' of the upper classes became 'selfishness' and 'excessive materialism.'" Among those who objected to the new bourgeois way of life, early feminism was considered a source of reproductive immorality. Although antiabortionists often did not attribute family limitation to early feminists specifically, they did object to redefinitions in womanhood frequently advocated by feminists.[17] From a performative perspective, doing womanhood differently was seen as insecure artifice, a false enactment of what women are, that had dire consequences for the future of the white bourgeoisie. The restricted breeding habits of the new bourgeois woman were set against those of more fecund foremothers, thereby connecting earlier generations' reproductivity to truth and current generations' relative lack of reproductivity to corrupt lifestyle aesthetics.[18]

For example, working from census data of Hancock county in Georgia, E. M. Pendleton of Sparta argued "that the blacks are much better breeders than the whites, and, by consequence, the natural increase of the one race is as much larger than that of the other, as 2.42 is larger than 2.05." Similarly, H. R. Storer, in his most ambitious work, *Criminal Abortion*, spent over forty pages demonstrating the lower level of Protestant, native-born fertility to "foreign" fertility. His argument was that when still-births, sterility rates, and spontaneous abortions were accounted for, the remainder must have been the result of an upsurge in induced abortion that left "Americans" at risk. From the medical community's standpoint, abortion among bourgeois women was the apex of these procreatively based fears. An anonymous letter to Walter Channing captures the sentiment quite well:

> I will take this occasion to ask if any one can foresee the result of criminal abortion, and other means of interrupting procreation, so extensively practised at this time? In localities where I am acquainted, though the population is chiefly Anglo-American, full three fifths of the children born and reared are of German, Irish, or other foreign parents, principally in the lower walks of life, who either have less repugnance to rearing families, or have not been initiated into and adopted 'modern improvements' (?). [*sic*] Waiving all consideration of the moral tendency, what is to be the physical result of this widespread violation of a great natural law? Is it invalidism and premature decay of the female portion of the present generation, and final decay of the race?[19]

Notice the confluence of ethnicity and class as non-Anglos of "lower walks" were deemed more amenable to breeding, whereas "modern" Anglos of better walks somehow were detached from their biological burden.

The reasons for race suicide fears were convoluted but, nonetheless, predictable. Protestants aborted more than Catholics, such that Storer once claimed "that the average number of births to each Protestant family is less than it was half a century ago." Further, Anglo-Saxons were believed by many whites, physicians and otherwise, to be the most civilized and refined "race," superior to non-Anglo European, East Indian, Asian, or African peoples. On the hierarchical continuum from nature to culture that organized nineteenth-century scientific racism, Anglos were farther from natural sexual impulses and biological imperatives. Massachusetts physician, Clarkson Collins observed: "It needs but slight observation to see that the fairest and best of God's creation, in our country, are becoming sickly and puny; the very contrast of our New-England mothers. If the refinements of civilization bring upon us incurable diseases, we had better at once go back to primitive habits . . . For the sake of the species it is to be hoped that this same feeling will increase." T. Gaillard Thomas was more explicit in his comparison: "The Indian squaw or Southern freedwoman may go half naked while menstruating, carry heavy burdens from morning till night, or rise to labor or to travel in a day or two after parturition, and yet no evil will result; but to the civilized woman any one of these imprudences may prove a source of disease." This line of thinking is indicative of research on the presumed "sickening" of bourgeois women in Victorian culture. Refined women were thought to be weakened by their station on the pedestal of womanhood and thus constitutionally susceptible to disease and nervous insanity. Images of the swooning, pale lady, a "fragile and ethereal creature" from puberty, epitomized well-to-do femininity and circulated through medical literature, fiction, and the popular press.[20]

The production of white supremacist knowledge that became so popular in nineteenth-century science also pervaded discussions of reproduction and the fecundity of undesirable groups relative to the pathogenically abortive character of "white, married, Protestant, native born women of the middle and upper classes." J. S. Andrews couched abortion as perversion expressly in terms of white Anglo-Saxon decline relative to supposed ethnic, racial inferiors:

> We pity their ignorance; we are shocked at their degradation, and appalled at their cruelty, but in this humanized, civilized, christianized and enlightened land are found those who without the compulsion of the African mother, without the devotion of the Hindoo, but only from a false pride and cowardly fear, or inexcusable selfishness, wilfully destroy their own God given offspring, and knowingly or ignorantly forsake the law of nature, break the law of man and despise the law of God, and the doctors keep silent.

Annetta Kratz neatly captured the affront that abortion had became to racial supremacy: "It would not be astonishing to find it among savage tribes, but that christian communities should be found to tolerate and practice it seems almost incredible."[21]

Treating abortion as a sign of civilized decline was perfectly consonant with the dominant themes of early racial theory, as described by Robert J. C. Young, wherein "race became the fundamental determinant of human culture and history" and "the yardstick of racial difference consist[ed] of the 'excess of fertility' of the primitive over the civilized races." It was a very particular yet unstable set of racisms whose tangible markers were intertwined in a Gordian knot of sexual lineage, including skin color, ethnicity, nationality, religion, and wealth. Notice among antiabortionists' writings the array of "others" collected in a multiform threat to white Anglo civilization: Africans, African Americans, Native Americans, South Central Asians, Germans, Irish, the poor, and the catch-all category of "primitives." The complexity and nuance of the scientific debates over race that raged in the century never fully emerged in medical antiabortion texts. For example, discussions of monogenesis versus polygenesis were missing from the literature. Nonetheless, the "production of 'internal enemies'" through naturalized racism was powerfully evident.[22]

Such concerns are present in numerous physicians' writings. Even before the Civil War, a reactionary fear of "race suicide" was developing in response to increases in immigration and lowering birth rates among the white bourgeoisie. Gordon notes that "physicians in particular noticed demographic patterns" and that "medical journals carried many . . . articles of warning." Indeed, Hodgson notes that "fertility decline among city dwellers and the well-to-do, was noticed quite early."[23] In 1935, Joseph Spengler, a sociologist who extensively reviewed medical and sociological rationales for the decrease in fertility rates in the nineteenth century, summarized the literature as follows:

> While there is evidence that the American birth rate has been declining for a century and a quarter, and while the testimony of contemporaries indicates that contraceptive and abortionist practices have been known for nearly as long a period, the decline in the rate of natural increase was not discovered until after the census of 1840. A number of writers saw in the decline of family size evidence of racial decay, moral laxity, and unhealthy living conditions in parts of the United States. Their concern, however, was primarily with the fact that the so-called "native stock" was being out-bred by the foreign-born and not with any possible undesirable militaristic and economic effects.

The fear of race degeneracy and race suicide represents what Hodgson calls a kind of "biological Malthusianism" because of its focus on the health of racial "stock" and rejection of reduced fertility rates among the bourgeoisie. Amid the flowering of statistical methods, census data, and Malthusian theories of resource dispensation, the *population* became a new, foreboding unit of analysis.[24]

The scope of my argument might seem far removed from today's clashes over abortion rights. In the nineteenth century, however, the limits of antiabortion debate were no less than eugenic population warfare. Shortly after the Civil War, at the conclusion of his prize-winning exhortation *Why Not?*, H. R. Storer put it better than any of his colleagues:

> This subject, at all times so important for the consideration of the people at large, is invested with unusual interest at a period like the present, when, at the close of a long and closely contested war, greater fields for human development and success are opened than ever before. All the fruitfulness of present generation, tasked to its utmost, can hardly fill the gaps in our population that have of late been made by disease and the sword, while the great territories of the far West, just opening to civilization, and the fertile savannas of the South, now disinthralled and first made habitable by freemen, offer homes for countless millions yet unborn. Shall they be filled by our own children or by those of aliens? This is a question that our own women must answer; upon their loins depends the future destiny of the nation.[25]

Normalizing sexuality was a means of social defense against biopoliticized enemies; the manifest destiny of the nation and the biological destiny of a privileged group of women became one. Accordingly, within medical literature the consequences of abortion were depicted as manifold and dire, as concern over the population crisis reached a fever pitch. The editors of the *Boston Medical and Surgical Journal*, one of oldest and most prestigious journals of the time and later the *New England Journal of Medicine*, declared that "the moral and physical evils which it [abortion] entails can hardly be exaggerated; and nothing can be said in condemnation of it, or for the purpose of enlightening and warning those who, in ignorance of its serious consequences, may be tempted to practise it, can be supererogatory."[26] Physicians expressly linked the destiny of the nation with women's relative fecundity and reiterated hierarchies of race and privilege in the warrants of these claims.

Consequently, the presumed obligation to bear children shifted in value. Not only did a woman seem to carry the fate of her kin in her womb, she seemed to carry the fate of an entire class, ethnicity, race, and nation. Appropriate class, ethnicity, and race were the very parameters that defined "acceptable" bourgeois sex and that marked as a "national threat" improper or insufficient amounts of sex. Child-bearing was no longer the continuation of the family tree *per se* as the family began to blend with the overall population. As Foucault identified them, the Malthusian couple that curtailed its fertility and the hysterical woman who possessed a dangerous, unpredictable sexuality were central threats to the newly configured nuclear family, the focus of intense scrutiny regarding breeding habits. A medically grounded "pathogenic value" was attributed to birth control practices among couples, and women were "thoroughly saturated with [a dutiful] sexuality" that placed their bodies in "organic communication" with the body politic, the bodies of their children, and the home space that nurtured both. Two other figures, the masturbating child and the perverse adult, were also the subject of intense scrutiny and corrective treatment, in part because they also were deemed threats to appropriate procreative behavior. Thus, the nineteenth century witnessed the medical pathologization of onanism, homosexuality, birth control, and women's reproductive organs as the middle and upper classes became mired in moral-biological necessity. To be more precise, the bourgeoisie were to embody the rules of procreation that provided a means of defense for a time of perceived population crisis. Medical opposition to abortion, grounded in this moral-biological necessity, articulated a normative, collective memory of white bourgeois entitlement and the duty to preserve that entitlement.[27]

For example, H. R. Storer perfectly understood the relationship of sexual discipline and power, as illustrated by a passage that is remarkable in light of current understandings of biopower and its ubiquity:

> The sexual relations lie at the very foundation of society; their aberrations are not the result of chance, but of an efficient cause; when general and common, then, these are occasioned by habits and customs which rest directly upon the moral sense of the community. The abnormal customs referred to [abortion] are productive of much disease and of many kinds; and these, like all others, whatever their symptoms, can only rationally be treated by treating their cause. It is untrue that discussion but spreads evil. To cure a fetid and burrowing sore, it must be freely laid open and exposed.[28]

In a few lines, Storer spelled out in no uncertain terms the need to discipline the sexual customs of individuals and to choreograph the performance of heterosexuality so as to protect the body politic from fluctuations in fertility. The means to do so was to open abortive practices to intense scrutiny.

Yet, as a deployment of biopower, the medicalized criminality of abortion was a disciplinary failure in the strict sense. We well know that women did not become docile and disciplined regarding abortion, that they resisted mightily, and that the campaign succeeded only in driving abortion underground and making it far more deadly. In fact, it was the brutal legacy of botched and septic abortions that would lead physicians such as Frederick Taussig to call attention to the dangers of underground abortions in the 1936, or Planned Parenthood to organize an international conference to debate the merits of legal abortions in 1958. Leslie Reagan's *When Abortion Was a Crime*, Carol Joffe's *Doctors of Conscience*, or Rickie Solinger's *Wake Up Little Suzie* speak to the mortal resistance carried out by women and their medical attendants during the near-century of criminalized abortion. Where the antiabortion campaign did succeed was at the regulatory level in linking the bodies of women, the bodies of physicians, and the body politic through medical practices such that, whether or not women procured fewer abortions, white bourgeois culture had configured a way to remember itself. Put differently, it was the medically institutionalized power relations organized to *oppose* abortion, and not an actual decrease in abortions, that became culturally regenerative. If abortion came to exemplify the threat of the Other, then prenatal life became a commonplace for recalling cultural identity and supremacy.[29]

Stoler notes that racial difference plays a significant role in configurations of cultural memory: "Racisms provide truth claims about how the world once was, why social inequities do or should persist, and the social distinctions on which the future should rest." Thematically, racially regenerative rhetoric like that of early antiabortionists typifies the interrelation of women's reproductivity, race/ethnicity, class, and nationalism. Nira Yuval-Davis and Floya Anthias succinctly type ways in which woman, as person and as gender construct, has been enmeshed in nationalism and the state: as biological reproducer of ethnic groups; as ideological reproducer and transmitter of ethnic/national cultures; as spatial reproducer of ethnic/national boundaries; as symbolic reproducer of difference used in the signification of ethnic/national categories; and as constituent in struggles national, economic, political, and military. As they point out, "different historical contexts will construct these roles not only in different ways, but also the centrality of these roles will differ." In light of the biopolitics of early antiabortionists, I would add class as a central construct to these functions as well. Elaborating on Yuval-Davis and Anthias, Radhika Mohanram characterizes the interaction of these roles simply, stating that historically "woman 'is' the nation in that her function, literally, is to reproduce it and maintain its boundaries." Several important works have documented the importance of maternal and domestic discourses to nationalism, as well as to imperialism, and one easily can see the same dynamic at play in the medical opposition to abortion as described thus far.[30] As I will amplify throughout this volume, increased abortion rates among affluent whites indicated more than personal failures for early physicians; they were an affront to the basic nationalistic telos of maternal duty and, thus, warranted an articulation of woman as place and origin of privileged white culture.

Anxiety about bourgeois culture's insufficiency as a source of national order was not unique to nineteenth-century antiabortion rhetoric. In *Healing the Republic*, Joan Burbick analyzes fictional, medical, and scientific literatures to discern the political relation of different physiologies to nineteenth-century nationalism (specifically the brain, heart, nerves, and eyes). She describes generally how, in the wake of dissatisfaction with the unifying power of bourgeois norms, nationalistic desire motivated a turn to the new medical body:

> [T]he laws and assumptions of the middle class did not hold the nation together. The desire for a language of unity and order drove many to look for a more stable ground for nationhood. The emerging physiologies of the body offered supposedly a set of laws beyond dissent. Here at last was a way to guide the people toward proper action in a republic. But could the body, as a universal autonomous structure, provide a sense of certainty for the republic? Once encoded in the flesh, these laws obscured political debate, established cultural authority for particular groups, and, unlike the forms of republican government did not contain "checks and balances" to ward off abuses of power.

Burbick's work is a powerful example of the "two bodies" relationship that Mary Douglas noted: "The physical experience of the body, always modified by the social categories through which it is known, sustains a particular view of society. There is a continual exchange of meanings between the two kinds of bodily experience so that each reinforces the categories of the other."[31] Similarly, by embodying a properly fecund sexuality for the affluent classes in the laws of sex, rather than in gender fashion, antiabortion rhetoric of the era solidified the connection of cultural memory within women's bodies and the biopolitics of a society at war with itself. The laws of sex, in turn, could be used to educate the public to affirm white bourgeois dominance through reproductivity and to justify a warlike, biological relationship between different social strata.

Quackery and Regeneration

For female reproductivity to be articulated with cultural, racial regeneration, the medical profession needed to provide the means of articulation. Hence, the regenerative biopolitics that undergirded the antiabortion motif of knowledge versus ignorance should also be understood in terms of the larger professional debate on "quackery" versus science. Max Horkheimer and Theodor Adorno open the *Dialectic of Enlightenment* arguing that "the program of the Enlightenment was the disenchantment of the world; the dissolution of myths and the substitution of knowledge for fancy." In their now-classic volume, Horkheimer and Adorno demonstrate that Enlightenment thought is deeply connected to Greek philosophy and literature and that enlightening, rationalizing, and demystifying is an ancient pursuit.[32] The AMA's goal was nothing less than to disabuse the nation of any belief in alternate forms of medical care and especially to demystify the process of reproduction so that only obstetricians and gynecologists would be credible speakers on matters of abortion and contraception.

According to Mohr, after the establishment of the American Medical Association in 1847, "regular physicians, committed to the forward-looking tenets of what would eventually become scientific medicine, began a concerted, self-conscious, and eventually successful drive to improve, professionalize, and ultimately control the practice of medicine in the United States," a process "not fully realized until the twentieth century." Regular physicians framed the conflict between AMA and other practitioners "as science versus quackery; the irregulars framed it as free competition versus monopoly."[33] Journals published by and for regulars repeatedly condemned false medicine practiced by homeopaths, hydropaths, abortionists, eclectics, botanics, and midwives. Homeopaths, for example, were described as taking money from patients while watching them suffer, whereas midwives were said to have stolen medical practice from men only to put pregnant women and their unborn at risk. By virtue of sex alone and regardless of the medicine they practiced, women were considered quacks by so many that even women trained as regulars, like Elizabeth Blackwell, were excluded from local societies, like the prestigious Massachusetts Medical Society, prompting the formation of women's medical societies. Nationally, Sarah Hackett Stevenson was the first woman "seated in a state delegation to the American Medical Association."[34]

The extent and evil of irregulars was treated almost as a pestilence, as indicated by an address of George Coggeshall, President of the New York College of Pharmacy, in 1854:

> The monstrous growth of quackery in modern times has, at least, kept pace with the advancement of the age in arts and sciences designed to benefit, or when State policy requires, more expertly to destroy the human race. It protrudes itself with the most business-like assurance into all classes and circles of society; it is ever present at the corners of the streets and in our dwellings; mixes with our daily news, buying up the easily-purchasable public press, which in great measure subsists upon it . . . and promptly makes up all deficiency of fact with brazen falsehood.

Even malpractice suits, which were only beginning to take shape in legal forums, were treated as a kind of conspiracy against regulars by the forces of evil that sustained irregulars. In an 1851 letter, O. W. Randall described malpractice suits as an "inhuman cruelty and injustice pursued against the profession by a portion of [*sic*] community whose main object seems to be to break down the regular system of medicine."[35]

Abortion, as one of the issues used to promulgate an image of professional competence, raised especially loud cries of quackery from regulars because many allopaths provided abortions discreetly. In 1851, J. P. Leonard, a regular physician, captured the antipathy and contempt for abortionists that was blossoming within in the AMA:

> While the Association, through its committees, has made excellent suggestions, pointed out valuable improvements, and discountenanced quackery in most of its forms and devices, it has not yet struck any decided blow on that most diabolical kind of quackery, that high-handed villainy, which characterizes the *abortionist*. That this kind of charlatanism is rife, and is practised by regular members of the profession, that is men who have *diplomas*, there can be no doubt; and I believe that some who are promoted to *office in our medical societies* are of this order of quacks. That such men *are quacks*, no one will question—the *epithet* belongs to the *unprincipled* as well as to the *ignorant*.[36]

As threats to life of the public, quackery generally, and abortion quackery specifically, marked certain classes of doctors as especially dangerous internal enemies against whom society must protect itself.

When the AMA officially declared war on abortion in 1859, its manifesto spoke in the language of knowledge and truth. The AMA's "Report on Criminal Abortion" listed three causes for the rate of abortion: general ignorance, lack of proper training among regulars, and laws based on "mistaken and exploded medical dogmas." Abortion quackery was characterized as stemming from ignorance and falsehood among the public, the profession, and the legislature. Thus, the AMA took upon itself the responsibility to educate the public about abortion's "true nature" and to correct the "doctrinal errors of the profession of a former age" through strict adherence to antiabortion principles. This responsibility was mirrored by the expectation that the public would heed the AMA's advice, not only for abortion but for all matters medical. Indeed, in Chapter III, Article II, Section I of the National Code of Medical Ethics, "Obligations of the Public to Physicians," the AMA declared, "[t]he public ought likewise to entertain a just appreciation of medical qualifications; to make a proper discrimination between true science and the assumptions of ignorance and empiricism."[37]

Along the way, however, regular physicians had to constitute the knowledge, or rather the practices that would reify the knowledge, that would make them credible. For my purposes, it was not a difference between truth and falsehood that grounded opposition to abortion; it was a difference between what counted as knowing, as knowledge, and what counted as ignorance. Ways of knowing built into the very act of perception, rather than truth, demarcated regular physicians from abortionists. As such, I am interested in the relationship between the knower and the object of knowledge, the physician and the female body, and how the practices that established that relationship articulated life's memory.

Regulars routinely leveled the charge of mere empiricism against irregulars. In the context of early modern medicine, empiricism implied practice with sparse anatomical knowledge, education by lore or tradition, and experience by trial and error. Typically learned through an unsystematic patchwork of verbal instruction supplemented by hand-written and printed texts, empirics were a collection of medical practices in transition from the oral-tactile traditions that predated the Enlightenment to the textual-visual traditions that have dominated since. Many kinds of empirics were rooted in the European humoral pathology of Aristotle and Galen, wherein physicians of old would ask patients questions about their state of being, occasionally using touch to determine a patient's condition. The patient's temperament in conjunction with heat and cold, dryness and wetness were signs used to diagnose the balance between the four humors: blood, lymph, and black and yellow bile. Similarly, pregnancy was understood largely by how the pregnant woman said she felt, not through anatomical investigation of her physical condition. Lay healers in the United States also drew from or practiced the herbal medicine of Native Americans and slaves. Rigorous anatomical and physiological investigation was foreign to these arts as well. However, there was a significant but unsystematic appropriation of scientific medicine, the lore of anatomical texts and clinical observation, into irregular practice. The empiricism of irregulars rested uneasily between ancient and modern medicines. The methods of irregulars constitute a set of paradigms in transition that, on one hand, still emphasized the tactile basis of older methods while struggling with modern visual techniques; on the other hand, they relied on oral traditions more so than texts. In the 1900s, reproductive healthcare was learned and practiced in a robust *oral-visual* milieu that has been termed domestic medicine or medical counter-culture.[38]

The case of midwifery illustrates what the charge of "empiricism" meant in this context. After a review of English midwifery guides from the seventeenth century, Jane Donegan argued that midwives' education was demonstrably empirical. Laurel Thatcher Ulrich's work with the diary of Martha Ballard, a New England midwife from the late eighteenth to the early nineteenth century, confirms that most midwives learned through apprenticed observation: "most midwives began as observers, gradually assuming a more active role, until one day, when the old midwife was delayed or willing, they 'performed.'"[39] Midwives also learned from parturition themselves, other popular medical traditions, and self-education. In the United States, women began more formal training in the early nineteenth century, however, in classes offered by physicians such as William Shippen or at schools for irregulars such as Eclectic and Homeopathic institutions. In 1848, when the Boston Female Medical College was opened by Samuel Gregory as the first regular medical school for women, formal allopathic education became available to midwives. But these formal opportunities were hard to come by, especially from regulars, because of the antipathy toward women who worked outside the home and the exclusion of women from AMA institutions.[40] Midwives were seen largely as threats by regular physicians. On the whole, midwives learned their art from an incohesive array of sources, few of which were well-versed in the new anatomy or the visual style of a budding medical science.

Those who followed other medical traditions had similarly limited educational options. For example, the Botanical movement developed out of the Thomsonian health movement promulgated by Samuel Thomson. Thomson opposed the heroic allopathic methods of his time (bleeding and purgatives, primarily) and learned botanical healing from an "old-style empiric doctoress." Hydropathy, a doctrine of regulated water-intake and baths that traces its origins back to Europe, was very popular among well-to-do women, such as Catharine Beecher. It was primarily practiced according to empiricism and custom, although Russell Thatcher Trall, who founded the hydropathic Hygienic Institute in Manhattan, was educated at Albany Medical College. Other sects drew more explicitly on allopathy. Eclecticism, an off-shoot of Botanical medicine, took its methods from both botanics and allopathics. Homeopathy, a doctrine of minimal intervention and restrictive drug therapy that became popular among East-coast upper classes, was based on German traditions brought to the United States by Samuel Hahnemann. Over the years, homeopaths gradually incorporated methods from allopaths into their schools. Within the medical counter-culture generally, however, as with midwives, the study of anatomy and visual techniques was sparse and uneven.[41]

In addition to these more sectarian routes, women and their physicians could learn from popular discourse. Lay healers of many types wrote manuals on health and physiology and a lively circuit of itinerant lecturers discoursed on matters from "marriage and divorce, obstetrics and gynecology, sexuality and even reproductive control," occasionally with the aid of anatomical manikins. For instance, Sarah Coates, a Quaker from West Chester, was a physiological lecturer from 1849-1851. Lydia Folger Fowler, "the second woman to receive an official medical degree in the United States" according to Brodie, lectured on anatomy, physiology, and hygiene from the 1840s to the 1860s. After the death of her husband in 1845, woman's rights advocate Paulina Kellog Wright Davis lectured widely on anatomy and physiology.[42] Frederick Hollick, a former Owenite organizer who claimed to have a medical degree from Edinburgh, lectured and wrote for decades on reproductive control and greatly contributed to the "respectability" of lectures on such delicate matters. As for printed sources of information, among contraception manuals, Robert Dale Owen's *Moral Physiology* and Charles Knowlton's *Fruits of Philosophy* were among the most popular. Others specifically explained methods of birth control and abortion, such as A. M. Mauriceau's *The Married Woman's Private Medical Companion*, Eugene Beckland's *Physiological Mysteries*, or James Ashton's *The Book of Nature*.[43] A woman could acquire medical knowledge, in some cases the knowledge and the means to abort, from any number of sources, including mail-order pharmaceuticals, self-help manuals, midwives, homeopaths, hydropaths, Botanical doctors, and self-styled abortionists of any medical background.

However, the distinction between these alternative medical traditions and regular medicine, which allopaths characterized as mere empiricism versus science, depends on another distinction. In the medical parlance of the day, medical science was associated with systematic observation, a loose notion of experimentation, and educated rationality. By these criteria, the walls between early allopathy and other traditions were thin. Although many, like eclectics and homeopaths, were influenced by allopathy, allopaths were in turn influenced by eclecticism and homeopathy. Herbal drug therapies commonly were incorporated into regular practice, for instance. Also, allopaths generally were educated poorly and none too scientifically until the latter nineteenth century. For instance, the heavy use of leeches and cautery in obstetrics and gynecology until the early 1860s was based on "mere empiricism," as allopaths used the term. In 1859, Lind University of Chicago sported the first medical school in the United States to offer a graded, sequential curriculum. Lind was followed in the subsequent decades by a handful of other schools (Harvard, Johns Hopkins, Michigan, and Pennsylvania) that also introduced basic laboratory science. Even by 1890, only eight percent of regular physicians had college degrees. By their own standards, regulars were typically wretched "scientists," preferring rational observation over clinical research. Further, because some regulars performed abortions, the charge of ignorant empiricism is suspect. The allopaths' concept of medicine as systematized, educated science is not adequate to explain the antiabortion position of regulars and the relatively abortion-tolerant position of irregulars. In fact, opposition to abortion grew within the homeopathic and eclectic ranks after the AMA campaign began.[44]

If abortion tolerance is itself a sign of ignorance, as regulars argued, then the question of truth was no longer dependent on the rigor of one's method, no longer tied to the distinction between "good" and "bad" science. Any medical practitioner who supported abortion was, by definition, a quack. The issue was about who had the perceptive abilities to use women's physiology to confirm what was already believed about women's place. The tension of forgetting and remembering that permeates the medical literature serves to frame the rhetoric of knowledge versus ignorance, science versus empiricism. It attaches questions of rhetorical purpose to dominant modes of perception. The idea of unveiling life's secret within the hidden recesses of the womb was not the singular worry of the "new male midwives." It was part of a historical shift in the project of science, a shift toward a textual-visual basis for perception in which obstetricians and gynecologists participated. To remember the "true" purpose of women's bodies meant that one had shed light on a darkened subject and documented the act of illumination, something empirics and unprincipled regulars were less able or not willing to do. The status of memory in antiabortion rhetoric rests on Enlightenment principles with which the AMA simultaneously staked its claims to professionalism and reproductive stewardship. Obstetricians and gynecologists differentiated themselves from irregulars and abortionists, not so much by the rigor of their methodology as by a mode of perception. The empiricism of irregulars and abortionists, because it could not properly induce the body to speak, only perpetuated the ignorance that threatened the white affluent classes with an abortion epidemic.

Chapter Three
Somatic Confessions

I believe that matter came into existence by the creative will of God; and from the forgoing facts I am led to assume that when God created mass or matter, in the abstract, he endowed it with the properties of life and mind, the phenomena of said properties to be the more manifest, as matter became developed; that is to say, as organisms or concretes were evolved from abstract matter. The whole universe is matter, in one degree or another, all subject to natural laws, so that there is nothing of the natural order outside of nature; nature is one great whole, a whole of which man and all other organisms form an integral part.
— Henry Howard, "The Somatic Etiology of Crime"

The moment the body gains a cultural purpose, it becomes rhetorical. When it gains a destiny, it becomes a source of memory. Medical antiabortionists produced this investiture through the rituals of exposure mentioned earlier. Acts of knowledge production must also stipulate the origin of knowledge, thus constituting a source of memory in the act of exposition. Without memory, knowledge is an impossible concept, in that to persist from one moment to the next some remembrance must be assumed. In an effort to have the female body speak its natural purpose and destiny as redress to the forgetfulness induced by a degraded civilization, physicians' examination practices induced *somatic confessions* about what they took as the truth of life, and thus of abortion as the negation of life. If women were presumed ignorant of pregnancy's "true" nature, their bodies would confess its real purpose to them, and with it the unnaturalness of abortion. In those moments of confession, the source of knowledge, its memory, was constituted and archived.

Knowledge of life was located twice over: in female reproductive biology and in biomedical discourse, which ostensibly mirrored that biology symbolically. The discourse of female physiology and anatomy, one body, doubled the lived corporeality of the female, another body, in a presumably perfect concordance. In this configuration, a "transgenerational memory" of life's design was given substance and place through the interplay of two bodies, one organic and one textual. The practices of body criticism established such a duplexed record of life's memory by creating a *genealogical effect*, a path of origination and normalization, through *forensic exegesis*, an interpretive embodiment of the past in the present. Through the epistemological rituals adopted by physicians, specifically direct examination, antiabortion obstetricians and gynecologists produced a kind of biomedical archive of bourgeois racial, sexual identity such that a genealogy could be extracted for the cultural order of white middle and upper classes. In this chapter, I place these practices in the broad framework of their rhetorical dynamics because they are not unique to antiabortion efforts, but are a manifestation of a kind of epistemological rhetoric within expert, elite memory work. In short, the form of rhetoric analyzed in this study is placed into its context, just as the thematic and politics of the rhetoric have been contextualized. I situate the *anamnesic* and *hypomnesic* practices of early physicians as a particular reiteration of an ancient epistemological tradition, accounting for the gendered dynamics of this reiteration within mechanistic philosophy; then I discuss the tropes of revelation endemic to such an epistemological tradition in light of the importance of confession to Western truth-seeking.

Treating truth-seeking as rhetorical, I consider memory as the capacity for a certain kind of epistemological work that etches the present in the likeness of experiences, places, events, things, and people of a refigured knowledge. I do not take memory as an idiosyncratic storehouse of knowledge that one rediscovers or recapitulates through discourse, as in a traditional conception of memory. It is not a resource for *representation* existing outside of or before language, in other words. Memory is not prearticulated. Rather, remembrance is performative, an "*action* . . . a kind of doing," in the sense that cultural practices constitute what they articulate.[1] From a rhetorical perspective, memory does persist from moment to moment, but only in its articulation and rearticulation. In this light, anamnesis or "knowing as remembrance" is understood as an act of memory formation, not memory retrieval. Further, hypomnesis or "archiving" also is understood as an act of memory formation, not exclusively of memory representation, that is mutually constitutive with anamnesis. Formation and representation of memory are the shared effects of the same acts. Performatively, recollection embodies through practices in the present an archive for a knowledge that the rhetor offers as preceding articulation. That memory seems to exist outside manipulation and only to be articulated more or less faithfully is the result of its rhetorical embodiment.

Genealogical Effect: Anamnesis

Genealogy sits on the cusp of materiality, culture, and memory. Mnemonically, genealogy recalls the provenance of things, such as institutions, families, races, knowledges, values, and so on. To the extent that cultures attempt to adumbrate the future by reinscribing the present in the worn marks of the past, memory formation is the genealogical effect of cultural practice. Elements of the past are disposed in old or new arrangements, establishing lines of "descent" and moments of "emergence" for the events of the present. Materially, recollection is traced through the descent and emergence of the body of such things, be it the corporeal body or bodies composed of "monuments, artifacts, and even texts which themselves bear a definite relationship to space."[2] Like Donna Haraway, I understand "bodies" as material-semiotic entities, being at once earthly and meaningful, and yet wavering in their makeup *as* bodies as they materialize within different historical arrangements. Culturally, "objects like bodies do not pre-exist as such" for they must be animated by articulation within some kind of material-semiotic matrix. Hence, to embody is to "give force, real effect, power, life, authority to something by placing it within a viable framework or working system." *The flesh is not the body* in that even the human corpus must be "embodied" via some framework that makes it intelligible, such as moral physiology. As Haraway argues, "[b]odies . . . are not born, they are made. Bodies have been as denaturalized as sign, context, and time." In regard to cultural memory, then, corporeal and/or social bodies' significance exceeds the mere fact of their existence, for they secure the life history of an institution, family, race, knowledge, or value that they concretize. In that sense, the "accuracy and authenticity" of remembrance must "accommodate broader issues of identity formation, power and authority, and political affiliation."[3] The genealogical quality of remembrance is normative in that it is an effort to incorporate contemporary social order, identity, and being through a play on, reaction against or mimicry of the recreated past, thereby containing the present within a lineage of past events, institutions, people, and customs. Memory formation is necessarily caught up in the politics of embodying cultural, material reproduction.

The particular kind of memory formation in early antiabortion rhetoric was neoclassical anamnesis ("unforgetting") conjoined with a modern scriptural hypomnesis ("archiving"). To understand how physicians' practices reiterated an ancient epistemological tradition in modern circumstances, it is important to begin with anamnesis and sketch the similarities and differences of its classical forms with those common to early scientific medicine. "Knowing as remembrance" dates to the preclassical and classical era in the ligature of the feminine and truth seeking, as Page duBois elegantly states in *Torture and Truth*: "links with secrecy, female potentiality, the tempting, enclosed interiority of the body, links with both treasure and death, with the mysteries of the other" exist in Homer's *Odyssey*, the Delphic oracle myth, and notably in the Hippocratic texts. "Each of these sites of meaning in ancient culture—the epic, oracles, sacred buildings, the medicalized body—lay out pattern of obscure hidden truth that must be interpreted. . . . These images of interiority are associated in ancient culture with female space." These linkages persisted through secularization in classical Athens and were refurbished in the writings of Plato, particularly in his theory of the Forms. Other scholars have noticed these patterns, particularly in the metaphor of "unveiling nature," in the history of modern science and medicine, but their work does not foreground the mnemonics of recalling hidden truths.[4] I want to stress the ancient form of this pattern because it highlights the cultural memory work of unearthing truth from feminine recesses.

A quintessential example of Platonic anamnesis is the *Phaedrus*, a philosophical dialogue between Socrates and his ideal student, Phaedrus. Here, Plato writes that prior to embodiment, human souls glimpse truths as part of a divine communion, but that when born into corporeality, we are bereft of those truths. He presents his system of recollection mythologically through the story of a charioteer who represents the disembodied soul of the individual. This charioteer orbits the heavens, following Gods who are the epitomes of true Forms, such as justice, beauty, love, kingly nature, and so forth. When the charioteer falls from the heavens, as all humans do when they are incarnated, the truth beheld in the heavens is forgotten but not lost. Truth is thus within each of us, slumbering, and it is recoverable if properly sought after through Plato's method of dialectic, the dialogic exercise of definition, analysis, and synthesis. Sensing the inner truth that lies hidden within the other dialectician, two interlocutors attempt to see through the chaotic clutter of their embodied existences, questioning one another systematically until they awaken their internal knowledge of divine Forms. A key component of this search is the impassioned drive to recall the secrets within, a form of madness that is the love of truth visited by Eros on philosophers. This scenario is grounded in the assumption that all things are of the same divine structure, and, although temporarily estranged, already are known to one another. Coming to know the truth is a form of recommunion such that "the knower and that which is known . . . are essentially kindred."[5] The search for knowledge is a kind of eroticized, divine mnemonic that reunites the subject and the object of knowledge in the unity of a transcendental, incorporeal memory. The Platonic tradition of truth seeking as remembrance dapples truth with the shadows of mimesis and aesthetics. Platonic anamnesis was caught up in the politics of cultural order and rhetoric: the false appearances and manufactured seeming of rhetoricians would give only the facade of truth while in fact leading the public away from truth. The dialectical return to original, hidden truths would stand against such potential debasement. Remembering essential reality was a curative for dissembling aesthetics that might corrupt a culture.[6]

duBois observes, "We have for centuries idealized this description of truth seeking." European intellectuals from the Renaissance forward were deeply indebted to Plato's model. By the time of the Enlightenment, the ultimate immateriality of reality had become a given for many. Key architects of the Enlightenment in science, philosophy, and art (e.g., Francis Bacon, René Descartes, Gottfried Wilhelm Leibniz, John Locke, Isaac Newton, and Johann Winckelmann) were Neoplatonists who subscribed to the immateriality and invisibility of truth despite the many differences between them. Scholars granted validity and power to the Idea while designating all things physical as manifestations of some invisible, metaphysical prototype that superseded the physical. Both Descartes and Newton placed the ultimate realization of truth in the mind alone. For both, coming to know was a matter of communion with God's grand design, of seeing what was real through the "inner eye" of the mind. Charging themselves with the duty to expose nature's secrets, and thus to know truth, Enlightenment scholars became "specialists in the invisible . . . authorities about everything opposite to manufactured seeming," as Stafford put it.[7] As with Platonic anamnesis, knowledge of immaterial verities was apprehended by the mind's eye upon inner reflection, sight as a function of pure thought, and not upon passive observation of physical semblances of the real.

There were critical differences between Platonic anamnesis and that of many Enlightenment thinkers that are relevant to the memory work of physicians' antiabortion rhetoric. The first is traceable to seventeenth-century French mechanistic philosophy, whose premiere advocate was Descartes. Cartesian philosophy grounded an abstract reality and a physical immateriality in a *monistic* sense of rational divinity. In Descartes's *Meditations*, he contended that all that is real is derived from God's infinity because the finite nature of humanity must emanate from something greater. Moreover, he argued that all that is verifiably real is that which is clear and distinct to the mind, like the geometry of a triangle. For Descartes, it was possible to "understand nothing other than God himself or the ordered network of created things which was instituted by God." The corporeal was rationalized into abstract, mechanical principles that paralleled the certainty of geometric proofs. The body was understood in its eternal, divine reality as form and function, as an "object of pure mathematics" rather than as flesh. It was transformed into the much discussed "body-machine," as illustrated by Descartes's extended discussion of the heart as a kind of pump, a model he derived from William Harvey's demonstration of blood circulation. His anatomical work, *Treatise of Man*, is based on the presupposition that the human body is "an earthen machine" manufactured by God.[8]

Medicine has since walked in a Cartesian shadow, although mechanistic rationalism was not absolute in its power. David Hume, for example, leveled significant challenges to the immaterialism of Western rationalism, directly on the issue of perception and embodiment. Early medical science, however, paid little heed and largely developed its practices within mechanistic rationalism. Mechanistic theories of pathology and treatment developed to make sense of the body-machine, and obstetrics and gynecology were no exceptions. Respected teacher and practitioner, Bedford laid out the body-machine model in commonly used terms in a series of lectures reprinted in *Nelson's American Lancet* in 1854. He described a woman's reproductive organs in terms of "the important influence they exercise over the economy—in health ensuring harmony to the mechanism, whilst under the influence of morbid action they produce the most varied disturbances." A woman was a "mechanism" that functioned like an economy. Moreover, this mechanism "produced" health or disturbance. In her study of medical metaphors, Emily Martin argues that the body as machine is still the dominant metaphor in contemporary obstetrical medicine. After looking back on nineteenth-century implements used in parturition, Martin argues that doctors were effectively body mechanics not only in their "relatively low [social] status" at the time, but also in their treatment of patients.[9]

Unlike the highly poetic, polytheistic abstractions that were Plato's Forms, the ultimate vision of Cartesian truth was a divine Reason such that discovery of God's "network" was synonymous with *a rediscovery of a universal rationality*. The Forms were reduced to The Form, in effect. The human corpus, like any other thing to be known, dissolved through "abstraction, the tool of the Enlightenment," which "liquidates" the object of its eye, to use Horkheimer and Adorno's words. An axiom of disembodied remembrance undergirded attempts to Enlighten for Descartes and many after him: That which can be known is already known in the abstract and awaits liberation from the irrational chaos of human imperfection. Truth was a transcendent memory already known to the inquisitor, and by necessity invested *within* the inquisitor by God, by virtue of its generation from a singular, unifying logic. Thus, I read Neoplatonic anamnesis *through* Descartes rather than work directly from Descartes. Descartes's own explanations of memory do not acknowledge the more transcendent mnemonics I have described, emphasizing as he did "corporeal" brain traces of direct experience and "intellectual" memory of abstractions within individuals. Descartes was concerned with how the individual remembers corporeal and noncorporeal things from his or her experience. Descartes echoed classical techniques for personal recollection early in his career as they related to intellectual method, whereas I am concerned with how humans apparently recall higher truths embedded in the natural world. Given the emphasis on moral deception and the recovery of higher truth from women's flawed body-machines among early antiabortionists, analyzing their rhetoric as a Neoplatonic remembrance reconfigured for a Cartesian universe is a more descriptive and profitable line of inquiry.[10] Within the rhetoric of medical practices that essentialized women through biology, to recommune with the greater purpose of "woman" required disclosure of her body's secrets.

A second important difference from Platonic anamnesis was in the relationship between the divine and the natural world, a vital connection that natural philosophers such as Francis Bacon, Robert Boyle, and Isaac Newton would sever and transform. For Plato, all that was around us was simply an imperfect embodiment of greater, universal Forms. The natural world was a dynamic, spiritually animated yet inferior manifestation of a transcendent "reality." Similarly, in the Middle Ages, the world often was described as having a living soul. In contrast to a divinely infused and operated mechanism, many later thinkers argued that nature was separate from God, a machine set forth from a perfect mind but no longer personifying divinity. The analogy of the world as a great clock was a popular illustration of this viewpoint in the seventeenth and eighteenth centuries. As the Father of creation, God was a clock maker whose craft scientists struggled to comprehend through His handiwork. At this moment of separation from the infinity of God, the corporeal became conceptually finite and, therefore, knowable in a direct sense. As a machine, nature became measurable and lay within the grasp of scientific inquiry.[11] This crucial transformation gave structure to a working model of *complementary antagonism* between a masculinized mind and a feminized body in the scientific quest to reunite with God's Reason, a concept I come back to in a moment.

Further, when Nature became nature, the terminology for discussing God's "network" also changed. Mechanistic *life*, rather than God, became the hidden force driving a mechanical *nature* as the language of the natural sciences acquired a new key term. The age of *life* had begun. Echoing Carolyn Merchant's argument, Barbara Duden argues in *Disembodying Women* that life was conjured to replace the divine animation of nature. Duden writes, "Life as a substantive notion appears a good century after the final demotion of Aristotle as the great science teacher, or about two thousand years after his death. In 1801, Jean-Baptiste Lamarck introduced the term *biology* into the French language. The new science defined 'life' as its object." As science, biology's task has been to systematically articulate life's embodiment, "successively searching for [life's] organization in tissues, then cells, then protoplasm, then the genetic code, and by now . . . in morphogenetic fields." Even preceding Lamarck, biological studies have presumed a transcendent, unseen fabric that connects individuals to the world like visible links in a great chain of invisible ontology that supersedes us.[12] Life took its station as the primordial essence of all being from which each living thing descended as a momentary individuation of that essence. The vague, mysterious presence of life in all of existence functioned as the hidden memory that needed unearthing, the divinely rational plan that organized the material world. To know life was to reunite with that hidden ontology.

Concomitantly, a discourse emerged within medicine that construed life as a rational, mechanical force within the body. Bichat, the French physician who played a significant role in the development of clinical medicine, claimed that "life is organization in action." This definition was popular in Europe and the United States. One doctor who anonymously called himself "A Midland Surgeon" explicitly drew upon Bichat's definition and extended it by equating the development of the "Doctrine of Life" in biology to the discovery of the steam engine. As with an engine, "life is a method of force" that manifests itself in organized action. Therefore, "an arrest of co-ordination is death, and that imperfect co-ordination is disease."[13] Disease was physical irrationality, the disorder of imperfection. Pathology or the study of abnormality became, in effect, the study of poor reasoning on the part of the patient, the patient's body, or both. Within the community of antiabortion physicians, rational instinct was unquestionably to procreate prodigiously. It was the divine and natural law of life, a law that woman ignored

with the plan of life, the secrets of the womb needed to be laid bare in order to be remembered.

The feminization of life's corporeality contained a paradox that explains the acting principle of complementary antagonism between science and nature, Man and Woman. Nature was taken as a relic of Godly intervention, and as such it hid the secrets to, or rather stored the memory of, God's vision. The brute matter of female nature was a precious substance in that it was treated as the storehouse of eternal truths. Rational Man perceived God's "network" through the body of Woman, or female nature in its most general personification. The search for truth relied on a complementary relationship between the masculine observer and a feminized object, a relationship something like a mechanized muse revealing visions to genius. A sexed relation in truth-seeking was part of the general doctrine of sexual complementarity in politics, biology, and society at large that became common coin during and after the Enlightenment and that has shaped European societies so dramatically. Schiebinger argues that the ancient concept of sexual complementarity powerfully reemerged in Europe of the late seventeenth century and "taught that men and women are not physical and moral equals but complementary opposites." Carole Pateman, too, has documented carefully the reinvestment of complementarity in social contract theory of that age. Notions of political liberalism, work, education, and family structure were built around the productive polarity of the male and the female.[16] The objectification of nature as a feminine, divinely created artifact meant for masculine use is another aspect of this doctrine in the process of scientific inquiry.

However, the feminine also was denigrated in two ways as it was reified in nature: first, nature deceptively concealed its secrets, in effect burying knowledge intended for Man within itself and away from the eyes of God's sons; second, nature and Her organisms threatened humanity's continued existence because of dangerous imperfections. In regard to secrecy, as Nature was separated from God and transformed into a feminized machine an antagonism emerged; Evelyn Fox Keller writes, "the language of secrets acquired its most radically new implication: not respect for the status of things as they are and must be, but first, permission, then, a challenge, and finally, a moral imperative for change." Once God was believed to have left nature as a black box for Man, the need to open it, to remember what had been forgotten in the slumbers of the flesh so as to commune with God's wisdom, grew to greater and greater significance. Foucault observed, truth was "in the existence—mute, yet ready to speak, and secretly impregnated with a potential discourse—of that *not-known* from which [Man was] perpetually summoned towards self-knowledge."[17] Nature had the ambiguous status of being both the means and an obstacle to truth.

Nature was considered an imperfect, untrustworthy, even dangerous machine and yet essential as the medium by which to reconnect with a higher order of life's rationality. Long removed from God's act of creation, nature was deemed to be as open to malfunction and degeneration as to perfectibility. Living organisms were seen as highly mutable during the seventeenth and eighteenth century, as malfunction was theorized through biological instabilities.[18] The antagonism of nature hiding Her secrets was given a sense of immediacy and compounded by the perceived antagonism toward Man posed by nature's degenerative whims. Not only was Woman (as nature or womb) both an obstacle and a means, Her power was both a threat and a mode of salvation. The complementary antagonism of science and nature became directly implicated in issues of genealogy. Woman, either as womb or nature, was both deceptive and revelatory, life-taking and life-giving. What had been a moral imperative to know what God intended for Man through the bodily memory of Woman had become a means to manage biopolitical crises. In other words, the corporeal world always remembers what we need to know to maximize and perfect rationally the biological potential of desirable populations against the threats of undesirable ones.

Biomedical methods of diagnosis and treatment can be understood as disciplined cultural memory work, then, even though there is no experience to recall in the conventional sense, no past events to recollect. Under a biological paradigm, an invisible fabric joins the myriad life forms in the world as expressions of a greater plan. The organic body becomes a repository of life's secrets or the living memory of nature's knowledge of its own inner workings. In a nineteenth-century context, Henry Howard captured this idea perfectly in his "Somatic Etiology of Crime":

> I believe that matter came into existence by the creative will of God; and from the forgoing facts I am led to assume that when God created mass or matter, in the abstract, he endowed it with the properties of life and mind, the phenomena of said properties to be the more manifest, as matter became developed; that is to say, as organisms or concretes were evolved from abstract matter. The whole universe is matter, in one degree or another, all subject to natural laws, so that there is nothing in the natural order outside of nature; nature is one great whole, a whole of which man and all other organisms form an integral part.

Many physicians proclaimed themselves the privileged exegetes of this higher order, as Samantha S. Nivison argued in 1855: "The Physician in his [sic] true character, as Nature's minister & interpreter holds the sublimest vocation on earth. As a sage it is his province to explore the profounder secrets of the universe, & to develop the ultimate laws of things. He may follow the outline of the ways of God."[19] As life replicates itself, it remembers its secrets and preserves them in each and every life form. When those "secrets," as biological knowledge, are used to remind us of a "proper" order of culture by virtue of natural law, we are being asked to remember through our bodies our "true" selves and our "true" place in the world. We are called to return to a nostalgic past by way of the organism.

In the escalating antiabortion climate of the late nineteenth century, women were abjured repeatedly in newspapers, medical manifestos, and home reproductive guides not to forsake their biological duty to bear and rear children, in effect being asked by bourgeois society to remember the script of gender roles written in sexual anatomy. Unlike the memory of my first childhood pet or the complicated feelings that bubble up when looking at photos of my deceased father, these biological recollections presumably tapped into the eternal memory of nature, bringing to consciousness what the body always knows but conceals. Through a materialistic anamnesis, cultural boundaries and identity were articulated through the biologized essence of what women had been, what they had become, and what they should be in the future. Like all forms of memory work that lament a loss of origin, antiabortion rhetoric gave emerging social needs an ancestral body through the bodies of the living, making individuals' anatomy and physiology speak a collective destiny. With remembrance predicated on the assumption of discovering essential knowledge recently lost, physicians produced a genealogical effect in the very practices of patient examination as a precondition of being able to claim knowledge: the descent and emergence of *culture* was dependent on woman's forgotten *nature*.

Forensic Exegesis: Hypomnesis

Through the professionalization of reproductive medicine and abortion services, a formerly inarticulate, miraculous, and seemingly uncontrollable power was made normal and regular. As part of the body that was still unfamiliar to us, reproduction was both menacing and irresistible. Despite thousands of years of midwifery, life was still largely inexplicable by today's standards. The development of nineteenth-century biomedicine brought the almost magical power of life into the orderly confines of scientific knowledge. Life did not lose its fearful qualities or its wonder in the process. On the contrary, it became necessary to explain life exactly because it was now wonderful, frightening, *and* articulate. As life became more familiar, its power could be mobilized for rhetorical purposes, specifically to produce genealogical effects that provide normative identity for culture and its institutions. The mechanism by which life could be mobilized to create genealogical effects was *forensic exegesis*, the practice by which physicians could produce a record, a memory supplement with which to reeducate the public. Through analysis of patients' bodies, physicians articulated abortion, as an object of medical knowledge, as a measure of lost or degenerating culture. Medical diagnostic practices themselves were the means of articulation by which they performatively enacted a rhetoric of revelatory confession.

The body of the physician became a set of mnemonic devices by which simultaneously to perceive and to transcribe the truth of life in the form of secrets recalled from women's interiors. Thus, anamnesis was joined with *hypomnesis*, constituting a mnemonic supplement which Derrida describes as "an *external place* which assures the possibility of memorization, of repetition, or reproduction, or of reimpression." The anamnesic practice of unveiling essential truths from a feminized object had as its corollary the hypomnesic practice of documenting that truth in medical texts and images. Like the body of history, the corporeal body became a voiceless resource full of potential discourse that awaited expression in the form of a body of knowledge, as Michel de Certeau explained in his volume on historiography:

> An analogous change takes place when tradition, a lived body, is revealed to erudite curiosity through a corpus of texts. Modern medicine and historiography are born almost simultaneously from the rift between a subject that is supposedly literate, and an object that is supposedly written in an unknown language. The latter always remains to be decoded. These two "heterologies" (discourses on the other) are built upon a division between the body of knowledge that utters a discourse and the mute body that nourishes it.[20]

In a moment of perceived ignorance about life, the knowledge of abortion generated by a certain group of physicians and the bodies of their patients that nurtured that knowledge functioned as an archival memoir of the recovered truth about life. The process of coming to know, of making the mute body speak its knowledge in the language of medicine, was limited by certain rituals, accomplished through certain tools, and practiced according to a set of rules that condensed cultural essence into specific bodily organs and functions: the uterus, ovaries, menstruation, and the fetus. Perceptual practices of physicians performatively established not only the relationship but also the quality of the distinction between what was perceived and what was said. Literally, what physicians *did* with their hands and eyes articulated life's memory as a bifold archive of flesh and text.

duBois, in her study of the comingled origins of torture and truth in classical Greece, says that all truth-seeking is associated with interrogation of one sort or another. Because truth historically has been presumed to exist elsewhere, in a hidden location outside the observer, it has been deemed necessary to pry truth from its hiding place and recreate it in the more accessible form of discourse. Whether it is the testimony of a witness or the knowledge that nature secrets away from God's sons, sources of truth are interrogated in ways that range from polite to brutal and the knowledge divulged is catalogued in more or less systematic fashion. In particular, the confession has held a special place in regard to the truth of human sexuality, as Foucault wrote in *The History of Sexuality*:

> The confession was, and still remains, the general standard governing the production of the true discourse on sex. It has undergone considerable transformation, however. For a long time, it remained firmly entrenched in the practice of penance. But with the rise of Protestantism, the Counter Reformation, eighteenth-century pedagogy, and nineteenth-century medicine, it gradually lost its ritualistic and exclusive localization; it spread; it has been employed in a whole series of relationships: children and parents, students and educators, patients and psychiatrists, delinquents and experts.

Foucault refers here to verbal confessions. However, as duBois points out, the ancient compulsion to have feminized objects of truth divulge secret knowledge is also a form of confession. The memory work of antiabortion physicians is yet another aspect of this phenomenon, although the diagnostic practices of bodily examination produced a somatic rather than a psychic confession of inner truth. In that sense, physicians participated in the nineteenth-century "invention of sexuality as the repository of human truth."[21]

In confession, the physician becomes more than a translator of bodily truths. The physician sits atop an Archimedean hierarchy, employing methods of investigation, authorizing the discourse produced, evaluating its merit as true or false, and enforcing norms through judgment and treatment. Likewise, the patient's body becomes more than a storehouse of hidden truths. It becomes a place of potential transgression. Foucault outlines the interrogator-interrogated relationship:

> The confession is a ritual of discourse in which the speaking subject is also the subject of the statement; it is also a ritual that unfolds within a power relationship, for one does not confess without the presence (or virtual presence) of a partner who is not simply the interlocutor but the authority who requires the confession, prescribes and appreciates it, and intervenes in order to judge, punish, forgive, console, and reconcile; a ritual in which the truth is corroborated by the obstacles and resistances it has had to surmount in order to be formulated; and finally, a ritual in which the expression alone, independently of its external consequences, produces intrinsic modifications in the person who articulates it: it exonerates, redeems, and purifies him [sic]; it unburdens him of his wrongs, liberates him, and promises him salvation.[22]

Again, Foucault does not consider the possible differences in kinds of confessions. When dealing with the story told by a woman's body versus the story she tells a doctor about her reproductive state, we are faced with the possibility of the body confessing that woman to be a "criminal." This somatic confession need not unburden or purify her—it may condemn her through a sort of testimony. Her individual body holds the traces of personal and transgenerational memory, a record of her compliance with or resistance to moral-biological destiny.

Confession is a forensic practice. Traditionally, as the rhetoric of legal forums, forensic rhetoric is preoccupied with reconstructing the past in order to render judgment. What happened and what should be done about it? To the extent that medical practices reconstruct corporeal memory in order to evaluate health and pathology, physicians' epistemological work participates in that kind of rhetoric through forensic exegesis. As a record of pathological and possibly criminal behavior, the individual bodily history of a woman who aborts is judged against the larger biological/historical narrative of her "natural burden" as part of a collective matrix. The imbrication of natural and juridical law enables the ready incorporation of scientific medicine as a technology of law enforcement and prosecution and speaks to the interwoven rhetorical action of medicine and law. To gain a kind of "speech," to be able to confess the memory of some higher truth, women's bodies needed to be placed into a particular interpretive scheme. Halbwachs wrote, "[n]o memory is possible outside frameworks used by people to determine and retrieve their recollections."[23] One could posit that a significant aspect of the linkage of medical perception to forensic discourse has been at the level of memory formation, of appropriating scientific medicine as a hermeneutic device.

Examples of this relationship are common in the medical literature, as one might expect. For instance, a Dr. Jackson dissected and measured a woman's entire reproductive system in order to determine that "no appearances were found which tended to show that instruments had been used with a view to abortion." Her body announced her lack of guilt. A. G. Helmick wrote to *Nelson's American Lancet* in 1854 about such a confessional with a living patient. He attended a slave, already the mother of seven, who had abdominal pains, was feverish, and had vomited. Helmick recounted his examination:

> I made an examination, per vaginum, and found the os tincae undilated, and a lump, as the patient termed it, within the womb the size of a foetus of three months. The patient positively denies being pregnant, and has from the first, saying it can't possibly be so, from the fact of her having no husband. She pleaded with tears, to have no more medicine given her, to prevent uterine contractions. . . . I caused her to be confined strictly to a horizontal position, and ordered opium to be given in commanding doses, should anything like labour pains again make their appearance . . . I visited my patient until during which time, she had occasionally, symptoms of abortion, and was promptly met and relieved by opium. *The patient at last confessed* she was pregnant, and promised faithfully not to attempt again to bring on abortion.

The body, as inspected by the physician, was the woman's confession. Only later, after Helmick made it clear he would continue to drug her, did she confirm his diagnosis. Finally, Rachel Gleason left us an unnerving example of physician-as-confessor when she chastened her patients considering abortion: "I know your burdens are heavy, but sin is heavier. Be the true mother, whether you are among the weary ones of the earth, or those so worn that the dear Lord gives them release from mortal care." Jackson's and Helmick's cases, as well as Gleason's admonishment, illustrate how the nineteenth-century doctor had moved into the double position of a bodily healer/interrogator, authorized to take the truth from the body and then "judge, punish, forgive, console, and reconcile" as was deemed appropriate.[24]

Although unaware of the deeper significance of his comments, Storer made the power relationship plain when he described the physicians' office as "in reality a confessional." He continued: "the only positive evidence by which to judge the real frequency of the crime is *confession*, and it is from the confessions of many hundreds of women, in all classes of society." A review of medical cases indicates that a somatic confession was the basis of the "regular" medical episteme. Further, medical testimonies in court relied on the bodily confession as forensic evidence in abortion cases. Only when the bodies of women revealed what they knew about the practices of abortion would the truth come out.[25] In *Out of the Dead House*, Susan Wells demonstrates that women physicians, who were commonly described as easier to talk to, used less overt tactics to induce a patient to share her medical history, taking a "heart history" as Wells terms it. Offering "a more understanding ear to the transgressor" in cases of abortion, however, did not mean women physicians eschewed the disciplinary position of a confessor. In general, "women physicians also understood their medical practice as support for, and regulation of, motherhood. . . . the physician, male or female, African American or white, could take up the role of interrogator or refuse the patient's explanation."[26] For this reason, I frame the narrative of a manifest, procreative destiny tied to woman's organs as a series of confessions of the body. The reproductive organs remembered the dutiful place of the bourgeois matron in the segregated biological order of the late nineteenth century. They further contained the record of each woman's relative fidelity to that maternal destiny. Through confession, the diagnostics of medical science produced an archive of the hidden memory of reproductive truth in the face of the pestilence of abortion.

In practice, the difference between what we normally think of as confession and the kind of confession that comes from unveiling "nature" involves the relationship between the knower and the known, the difference between oral questioning and reading. This difference is fundamental for understanding the rhetoric of early antiabortionists because it deals with the basic rules for crafting discourse about expert perception, the literate practices that must be engaged for one to say anything authoritative about what crosses one's field of perception. Plato believed the interchange between two impassioned, living beings was necessary to produce a discourse on truth. The relationship between the ritualized opening of the body and hidden memories of biological truths therein is quite different. For one, how can biomedical science rely on this method of recollection if the physical traces of biological truths are at best deceptive, at worst illusions? How can it rely on a sense of vision that is not to be trusted? The answer lies in a kind of "double vision" reserved only for the sagacious observer.[27]

Simple apprehension, or *empirical vision*, is passive observation that takes its cues from the observable, hence learning from what nature has to show for itself in sensate "clutter" or "the chaotic accumulation of context" experienced by the senses. It is based wholly on the physical evidence available to the embodied senses and is not epistemically active or revelatory. It is suspect in its materiality because mere sensory data are not considered authoritative. Note that this includes all the senses, although I favor vision as the overarching metaphor for medical perception, given the privileged position of the eye in Western epistemologies. Stafford writes in *Body Criticism*: "the major epistemological trends of the eighteenth-century removed unruly sensory experiences—especially those originating in sight—from the sphere of intellectual and public importance. In addition, these individual modes of judging the flux of ordinary life were relocated to a false, inferior, and subjective domain."[28] Her claim that the Enlightenment was profoundly anti-ocular refers to the presumed insufficiency of empirical vision. Antiabortionists' distaste for "empiricism" is yet another instance of the demotion of untrained observation.

Because the hidden memories of life's rational biological order hover *between* their earthly mechanisms and their higher order of being, the keen observer must possess a deeper sense of perception, a *transcendental vision* of the soul. This is an active, searching observation of the invisible, metaphysical world for signs of God or nature's secret plan. Based on the musings of the "mind's eye," transcendent vision looks *through* the corporeal to the incorporeal by visualizing the unseen behind the visible. One must know how to read the body for what it conceals, to decipher the cryptic meanings buried in corporeal folds. The authoritative observer looks past colors and textures, past the movement of fluids, the degradation of flesh, in search of rational patterns. In turn, these patterns guide the reader in future attempts to decipher the body. These two kinds of seeing, although seemingly at odds, act together to expose the object of investigation and to liberate its concealed memories. The interdependence of the empirical and the transcendental is a key assumption of body criticism as Stafford discusses it. Keller and Foucault also have argued that a defining characteristic of modern intellectual paradigms is that the physical and the metaphysical traverse one another in an effort to know both.[29] Two seemingly disparate, oppositional sources of light, one in the visible realm and the other in the invisible, are shed on objects of study with the transcendental illumination in the superior position. In the materialistic Neoplatonism of early modern medicine, the observer read through the "concrete" manifestation of "abstract matter" toward the "creative will of God," as Howard put it; or, as duBois described Platonic remembrance, to look toward that "metaphysical zone beyond the reach of mortal experience."[30]

For this double vision to have any epistemic clout, one must know where to look to shed light on truth. The logical predicate to valid confession is that one has asked the right source the right questions. As a result, the trope of revelation in science is dependent on *metonymy*, the condensation and substitution of part to whole. The idea that one reads abstract truth from specific, transient empirical clutter does not make sense without the metonymic trafficking of essence in immanence. The reduction of woman's essence to her pelvic organs, and with that to the reproductive life of culture through biology, is a clear example of metonymy that I will detail in the following chapter. That scientific rhetoric would rely on metonymy would be the case in a less obviously ideological instance as well, but with the metonymic necessity of positing source location to justify revelation, there is always the strategic possibility of naturalizing cultural norms in biology.

I do not want to lose track of the tangible efforts that provided these physicians with messages to convert to text, however. In arguing that metaphysically guided reflections usurped the authority to see from the unaided eye, thereby enabling a strategic ambiguity incumbent to materially locating abstract truths, I have accounted for only part of the rhetorical action of revelation. The other part involves the act of exposition, which in the case of revelation involves *chiasmus* or rhetorical inversion. The hidden truth has to be turned out to view. The Enlightenment was overwhelmingly concerned with demystifying the world by shedding the light of reason; Henri Lefebvre has argued that the Enlightenment was intent on the social construction of luminous spaces, areas socially coded and arranged for optimal visibility.[31] In biomedical studies, the truth of the living body can only be discerned by opening the body to the light, by producing a radiant medical space. The rituals of exposure that became the metaphorical template for the embodiment of ways of thinking were also acts of illumination; they performed the physical labor of Enlightenment rationalism. As Stafford demonstrates, however, an illuminated space was not self-sufficient nor self-evident; it had to be textually mediated, commented upon, its brilliance deciphered so that what was seen was not mistaken by some trick of the eye or uneducated speculation. Casting radiance on formerly dark recesses, such as bodily cavities, did not mean the body was necessarily intelligible. In the modern era, the luminous spaces of knowledge were necessarily communicated spaces. The chiasmatic character of revelation involves not only inversion, but also transformation of perception to language. Thus, hypomnesis is the confirmation of correct perception: that the body has been rendered in authoritative language implies that it has been perceived as it wants to be perceived, as it really is.

In medical science, the double vision of empiricism and transcendentalism was melded into a single illuminating, communicative gaze that Foucault termed the "speaking eye." I am drawn to Foucault's metaphor because it emphasizes the connection between a knowledgeable gaze that unlocks hidden memories and the words of the observer who enunciates those memories. The speaking eye highlights the relationship between "reading the body" and "reading aloud," in which the patient's body comes to speak through a physician who translates cryptic anatomical signs into language. As a figure, the "speaking eye" encompasses the metonymic and chiasmatic qualities of textually mediated, optic revelation. Medical perception is both a seeing and saying practice that simultaneously configures the field of perception as it configures the field of discourse. In *The Writing of History*, Certeau explains the connection of perception to discourse in modern medicine:

> Here modern medicine is a decisive figure, from the moment when the body becomes a *legible* picture that can in turn be translated into that which can be *written* within the space of language. Thanks to the unfolding of the body before the doctor's eyes, what is seen and what is known can be superimposed or exchanged (be translated from one to the other). The body is a cipher that awaits deciphering. Between the seventeenth and the eighteenth century, what allowed the seen body to be converted into the known body, or what turns the spatial

organization of the body into a semantic organization of a vocabulary—and vice versa—is the transformation of the body into extension, into open interiority like a book, or like a silent corpse placed under our eyes.

Foucault observed that this exegetical practice postulates "a moment of balance between speech and spectacle. A precarious balance because it rests on a formidable postulate: that all that is *visible* is *expressible*, and that it is *wholly visible* because it is *wholly expressible*. . . . the reversibility, without residue, of the visible in the expressible." This postulate is "more the dream of a thought than a basic conceptual structure," however, because "total *description* is a present and ever withdrawing horizon."[32] As a form of rhetoric, it was necessarily a *metaleptic* practice, meaning a substitution whereby a transformation is wrought. Here, the metonymy of locating life's truth in female reproductive organs was substituted by a chiasmus that transformed the corporeal into a textual extension. Physicians constituted medical discourse and its object, the corporeal body, as mirror-like records of the same essential laws, each dependent on the other for coherence.

The body's finitude, the acting principle that the body's limits and all essential knowledge of life stored within the human corpus could be exhausted through description, rendered in words, justified exposure of the inside as a valid means for understanding the abstract order of biology. It folded empirical observation and metaphysical meditation into one action—translation of spectacle to speech without residue. In the discourse of early medical science, language focused a blurred empirical vision by having the body speak its secrets, as if medical speech was "given by the visible" itself and, in turn, "made it possible to see" the body clearly. Duden argues that the lay person has come to mistrust her or his own eyes, displacing "concreteness" onto the visualization commanded by the authoritative gaze.[33] That is, only when one sees as the knowledgeable authority tells one to see, does one see accurately. In an elision of the observer into the observed, the physician was assumed to enunciate clearly what was perceived, as if the means of perception, the technologies and the understandings of the body that enabled the physician to speak in a clinical manner, were outside the act of perception. The relation between the two bodies that archived life's memory in flesh and text was organized by a correspondent double vision: the perceptual clutter of the corporeal body revealed a higher order, that metaphysical zone, when converted to abstraction in the form of medical discourse. Symbolized observations were the convergence point of the empirical and the transcendental in a self-evident medical text, bringing the sensory powers of the body to bear for the purposes of the mind under the signs of language.

The style of the new scientific medical observer was an austere descriptive realism that mimicked the precision of measurable sense stimuli in "images mechanically reproduced and published warts and all; texts so laconic that they threaten to disappear entirely." For example, the first plate in Augustus Gardner's *The Causes and Curative Treatment of Sterility* is a lithograph of a specular exam from the vantage point of the physician (Fig. 3.1). The reader is positioned to see the afflicted cervix of a patient. No detail is spared in the image—folds and shadows in the sheets that cover the patient are depicted, as are the minute ripples in her flesh, individual pubic hairs, the colors of the ailing cervix, even the shadow thrown by the screw of the speculum on her body. The image attempts to capture the examination as if one were seeing through Gardner's eyes. Similarly, textual imagery attempted to render in words the experience of the senses. In a case report of an abortion typical of the discursive conventions of mid-nineteenth-century medicine, J. B. Treadwell described the body of Mrs. L. as he examined her: "Vagina hot and dry. Os uteri dilated to the extent of three fourths of an inch in diameter, with the edges very ragged, as if they had been lacerated and torn . . . Pulse 120. Hot skin, and considerable thirst." The transposition of spectacle to speech was accomplished by the sup-

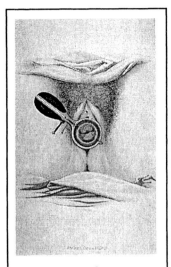

Figure 3.1. Lithograph from Augustus Gardner's *The Causes and Curative Treatment of Sterility.*

pression and objectification of the observer's perspective into direct sense data, a kind of "pictorial objectivism."[34]

Paradoxically, the transcendental vision that marked the perspicuity of the physician was obscured *and* foregrounded by the textualization of the senses. Medical perceptions were presented as self-evident, supposedly purified experiences that denied the presence and subjectivity of the interlocutor, the physician. The body seemingly spoke itself. At the same time, perceptions were not self-evident if they were not symbolized correctly. Those who did not have access to the requisite language of medicine, which was based in certain ritualized methods of perception, could not demonstrate their ability to perceive the hidden patterns of the body. It was the wisdom of trained inner reflection that enabled one to mirror the body in language. The laconic gaze of the Enlightened physician became "the separating agent of truths," establishing the difference between real and quack medicine, life and death.[35]

It was not the body that spoke truthfully, then, but the body transformed into text. As the descriptive discourse of medicine, anatomy and physiology became the screens through which one could see clearly or, rather, through which one could see the body as it presented itself to the eye. Equally a process of reading *and* writing, medical perception is necessarily a scriptural practice that induces the body to remember itself in language in a kind of somatic confession. The physician helps the body write itself for the medical gaze to read. A "more general operation" than treatment, perception "consists in *making the body tell the code*" of physiological norms, realizing "a social language" in the flesh. Perception is rhetorical action that embodies social codes such that "*the history of perception* [is] *the intermediary link between the content of thought and the structure of society.*"[36] As a result, rituals of exposure that were the preconditions of medical study functioned mnemonically to inscribe memories of truth into the body of woman as they recalled them from a mute flesh. As the body-machine was opened to view, the "speaking eye" of medicine separated out constituent parts, rationalized interactions between organs, liquidated matter into operative principles, and invested mechanical theories of pathology and health into the body. These acts, in effect, reflexively drafted the body's memory as they recorded it. As a book of anatomical and physiological truths, the female body could aid the public, especially young fashionable women, in recollecting what had been forgotten.

when criminally aborting or her body ignored when spontaneously aborting. To forget the reason behind life was to court insanity and disease, the physical traces of imbalance. This shift to life as a key term for nature's action within biology and medicine meant that to recover the plan of life's "network" was to gain some measure of control over biological dynamism.

The demotion of nature from a limitless extension of God to a limited, living machine had deep consequences for understandings of gender in science. Nature was now considered finite and, therefore, less than perfect. Echoing ancient Aristotelian gender categories, modern science marked nature as sexually feminine or, rather, as imperfect matter that hid the clarity of God's rational mechanism in the chaos of embodied life. For example, Newton believed nature to be brute (as in "mindless") matter, and Boyle described nature as a feminine automaton that stood between Man and God. From this perspective, veneration of God's perfection and power required that nature, as a lowly mechanism, be separated conceptually from God's being so as not to profane the image of God. Boyle wrote that "things corporeal" were created on the sixth day before God created Man. Man, being created on the seventh day and in God's image, was separate from nature. According to Boyle, to move closer to God, His sons had to move farther from nature by learning to control Her. To be a good son, Man had to be more like Father the clock maker and less like the clock. Man was meant to emulate God's perfection through the manipulation of female nature as, according to Londa Schiebinger, "ancient prejudices against femininity were not overturned but merely translated into the language of modern science."[14] The ancient categorical hierarchy of female as impassive substance, like clay, and male as spiritual ideation, like God, was refigured in a mechanistic context.

Similarly, the force of life that drives nature's mechanisms was feminized through its investment in female physiology. The most powerful investment of life's presence, especially in obstetrics and gynecology, has been the metonymic focus on the reproductive organs as the source of life. It is not a difficult connection to make, because the term nature is derived from nascitura, or birthing, such that "woman's pregnancy is the eminent analogy to nature's constant action." Accordingly, genetics and embryology have followed a trajectory toward understanding conception as *the* moment of life's truth, as Alice Adams remarks: "developments in mammalian embryology in the nineteenth century and the study of genetics in the twentieth describe a backward movement through the lifetime of the individual. Instead of focusing on the moment of death as the revelatory moment, now the clinical gaze focuses on the first moments of life. . . . In its search for the root of life, the clinical gaze shifts from the corpse to the living embryo."[15] For many early obstetricians and gynecologists, the site of memory for life's plan had become the womb, the presumptive place of each new life's first existence and the moment in human life deemed closest to nature's inner workings. In effect, life had been localized and gendered as a force whose swirls and eddies are most intense in women's reproductive systems. For Man to achieve reunification

Part II
Articulating a Memory of Life

Chapter Four
Organic Discourse

Fifty years ago, all that woman knew of herself was what man told her, and the definition of a woman might have read thus: 'a woman is a generative apparatus whose function *is* to perpetuate the species. She *has* a limited intellect contained in a frail body which is especially liable to be wrecked at the time of puberty and the danger is still greater at the menopause.'

— Anna Galbraith, "Are the Dangers of the Menopause Natural or Acquired? A Physiological Study"

If we are to think of early medical diagnostic practices as exegetical, as having produced somatic confessions of essential reproductive truths recently lost, what was in the archive of that truth? If women's bodily memory contained the truth about abortion and female destiny, then what was it that women's bodies said to physicians? Physicians articulated a natural memory of life through female physiology by textualizing corporeality, and this chapter is devoted to specifying the corporeal discourse of that memory. Rhetorical invention draws upon the context of available resources, and in the same act, memory takes its shape from the time in which it is recollected. In the context of race suicide fears, the transposition of the female body into words and images enabled antiabortion physicians to constitute a genealogy of cultural norms through biological reproduction, thus naturalizing those norms as given. I begin by tracing revelations of female anatomy and physiology that substantiated this extraordinary transformation, taking the uterus first, then the ovaries, menstruation, and finally the fetus.[1] Next, I examine the moral paradox female anatomy and physiology posed to early physicians: it is both life-giving and life-taking. Finally, I interpret the archive of life recalled from women's bodies in terms of a system of mnemonics, a means for reproducing cultural norms independent of reproducing children.

The extent to which the body can serve as a biological repertory of cultural norms depends not on a single message over which physicians debate, but a whole *organic discourse* that requires persistent attention to decipher. The various parts of the body speak to and with each other, in effect, and revelation of the meanings of that discourse requires a chiasmatic inversion of silent internal communication into perceptible external speech in the mode of descriptive realism. It is this simultaneity of meaning and matter that has enabled scientific medicine to produce its knowledge, an articulation of speech and body so tight and intimate that the motion of blood or the texture of tissue become voices of a sort. In terms of its meaning, physiology is as much about intrabody communication becoming extroverted as it is about corporeality achieving rational clarity. Given that the body is understood to be speaking not only to itself but also to culture in terms of health, the tight clasp of speech and soma in medical texts enables more than improvements in medical treatment. It enables our bodies to comment on civilization through recollection of our proper essence. I refer to the conjoined archive of life's truth between women's bodies and medical texts as a single, *organic discourse* that traffics between perception and language. Where must one attend, then, to catch the essential discourse of the female body and what does she say?

The Body Speaks

Until the 1850s, the uterus was treated as the center of woman's reproductivity, and until even the 1870s, it vied with the ovaries for the title of reproductive dictator.[2] Before ovulation became the defining characteristic of womanhood, a swelling uterus held that honor. As one doctor stated, "the uterine system [is] the great central characteristic of female life, around which moves the circle of all the mental, moral and physical phenomena." Another put it this way: "The womb, and its immediate tributaries, if I may call its appendages, are not only concerned [with], but they make a demand upon the heart, and through it the entire circulatory system—the spinal marrow, and through it the entire nervous structure—the brain, and through it the intellect and moral nature, *until all are forced into the work*." The uterus commanded all of a woman, including her mind and morality. The function of the uterus was more than physiological; it was essential in every way. As a result, a woman's being existed for her uterus: "In this function, likewise, it demands the sympathies of the entire being, of which it forms a part. . . . all bear an interesting and important relation to each other, *and each contributes its portion to maintain the uterus in its office*."[3]

This is the kind of uterine essentialism that prompted Warren Stone's comment about regular physicians' "uterine twist of mind."[4] Stone's comment highlights the metonymic trope intrinsic to forensic exegesis of the body in the beginnings of modern biomedicine: female pelvic anatomy and physiology are the source of truth about women. As numerous scholars have documented, the childbearing cycle of puberty to menopause dominated early biomedical understandings of women; a woman's body was understood as the larger apparatus of the cultural incubator within her. For example, anatomists of the eighteenth century depicted the female skeleton with wide hips and a proportionally small skull, thereby reflecting biological destiny. In the nineteenth century, phrenologists such as O. S. Fowler argued the smaller size of the cerebellum gave a woman a more passive sexuality, one more in line with her reproductive duty. The dainty size of her nerves that prevented a public life, the insufficient supply of blood to develop both brain and womb, and so on, all confirmed the maternal imperative.[5] In addition to seeming nearly monomaniacal, the early accounts of female structure seem senseless without the metonymic principle of woman's every fiber serving as a buttress to her reproductive system.

Two common justifications were offered for the centrality of the uterus to woman's generative core. One was that the uterus *was* the center. Spatially, the other organs were arranged around it like "tributaries" or "appendages," thus indicating its importance. Another justification was the singularity of uterine purpose. In 1855, for example, Thomas Massey argued that "[t]he uterus is more distinctly appropriated and confined, in our apprehension, to one specific end than perhaps any other organ of the human body, and characterized by greater complexity in its adaptation. Instead of enumerating here its peculiarities of structure, position, and functions, let them for a moment be recalled, and wonder will cease that its pathological state should assume expressions requiring special study." Therefore, in addition to being spatially reduced to a uterus and tributaries, the early modern female body was teleologically centered on the womb. The presumed end determined the appropriate use and structure of anatomy. In other words, the metonymic, even telescopic, anatomy and physiology of females logically was constituted through its spatial arrangement and telos. As Thomas Laqueur remarked, destiny is anatomy.[6]

By the 1860s, the dominance of the uterus began to fade as new understandings of the ovaries and ovulation spread and physicians reconsidered which part of a woman was most responsible for her predetermined end. W. H. Studley captured this shift perfectly: "With regard to the position that reproduction is the essential function of the uterus, I hold it to be false. If any one organ in the generative group has a right to claim superiority over another in that mixed process, undoubtedly it is the ovary." Tilt made it a career goal to argue that the ovary and not the uterus was the essence of woman. Interestingly, the ovary had been recognized as distinctly female only a century before; now it had become the core of her being. A particularly important moment in this transition was Theodor von Bischoff's demonstration of independent ovulation in dogs in 1843. Until that point, many had believed that sexual desire triggered ovulation. The new understanding of independent ovulation reversed this thinking—ovulation was controlling desire rather than desire controlling ovulation. F. A. Pouchet, an influential leader in biological studies, reiterated Bischoff's point and amplified it in 1847 by making independent ovulation his "eighth law" of reproductive biology. Keep in mind, an unfertilized human egg was not directly observed until 1930. Nonetheless, the principle was persuasive. Eventually, after years of ovulation theory disseminating through the rank and file, the ovary "became the driving force of the whole female economy, with menstruation the outward sign of its awesome power." Tilt expressed this as clearly as anyone: "the development of the pelvis, of the uterine system, and of the mammae, the function of menstruation, and all the peculiarities of the human female, depend upon the ovaria."[7]

As with the uterus, a teleological reason ruled anatomy and physiology. The ovaries' functional end was the reason for the female organism throughout nature, be it dog, human, or otherwise. Eliza Pettingill placed the ovaries in the broad context of all biological generation: "The most important of these organs, [sic] are the ovaries or germ preparing organs. Throughout the scale of creation, they are the ultima[te] ratio of generation." In an ode to sexual difference, "Sexual Peculiarities," the influential physician Charles Meigs remarked in awe at the teleological singularity of the female sex:

> Think, gentlemen, of such great power—and ask your own judgement whether such an organ can be of little influence in the constitution of the woman; whether *she* was not made in order that *it* should be made, and whether it may not on occasion become a disturbing radiator in her economy, and how much. You will answer yes, if you know that her ovary is her sex—and that she is peculiar because of, and in order that she might have this great, this dominant organ planted within the recesses of her body.[8]

An accessory to nature's plan, woman existed only for her ovaries' survival.

The spatial logic was flummoxing, however. The uterus was no longer at the center of reproductive telos. Rather than being discarded, the spatial argument was simply rearranged to accommodate the new master of generation. In an effort to depose the uterus, Tilt reconfigured the location of control from a uterine epicenter to an ovarian hierarchy:

> Moreover, in any series of organs constituting an apparatus, the middle organ is always placed between an organ anterior to itself, from which it derives it *ratio standi*, its final end,—and a third organ, whose development is posterior to its own, and from which it derives its appropriate stimulus. The uterus, therefore, derives its stimulus from the external organs of generation, and the reason of its existence from the ovaries.[9]

The female body was a flickering map of power on which the topography altered with the shifting balance of medical models.

Notwithstanding what such medicalized essentialism reveals about attitudes of the time, it also constituted a source of truth about sexuality through the sexing of the body. The body was indeed considered pregnant with a discourse of truth in need of exposition, as the following passage from Amos Nourse indicates:

> [T]he organs concerned almost seem to be endowed, not only with intelligence, but with forethought. Certain things, they perceive, are taking place in their as-

sociate organs, the result of which is to be that a new and laborious duty will shortly be thrust upon them, and they prepare for it. . . . the uterus feels herself called upon to prepare for the reception and nutrition of the product. . . . The ovary, she knows, is engaged, seriously and in earnest, in the great function of reproduction, the special office for which nature formed and fashioned it.

The body had a mind of its own, identifiable by virtue of an internal dialogue. It was a dialogue inaudible to the ears of the patient but entirely audible to a physician/translator, the "speaking eye" of medicine. As the intrabody communication network for this dialogue, nerves were analogically "the telegraph-wires of the system."[10] Like a telegraph operator, the physician could tap into cryptic and, therefore, privileged messages. Given voice in medical discourse, this dialogue was part of the archive about reproductivity that chronicled a biological memory of maternal instinct. I am not implying that the body is without internal communication, only that in the process of observing the body's interconnections, the perceiver is in the double position of "listening" and of "composing" that which he or she overhears.

Despite the centrality of the uterus or ovaries, it was the monthly cycle that physicians considered the most conspicuous effort by the female body to speak its essential purpose and to remind women of their responsibility to culture. As the sign of fertility, it was the natural notification of duty that enabled physicians to hypothesize about healthy female desire. The proper functioning of the organ of life required appropriate levels of use, neither too much nor too little. Smith-Rosenberg argues that two lines of thinking about menstruation were common: menstruation meant women were weak and "blighted," and/or menstruation was the apex of sexual appetite and the marker of optimal coitus. That is, menstruation, not woman's desire, was the sign of sexual arousal. Placing menstruation within a model of reproductive health and womanly completion, many physicians were countering a mythos about menstruation that was "age-old, varied, yet surprisingly consistent; it was a period of danger, of shame, of punishment." Bedford, like many of his contemporaries, saw menses as the flowering of womanhood:

> Closely allied with, and directly consequent upon these modifications of her *physique*, are to be observed certain changes in the *morale* of the individual. Before this, the girl was not only in reality a child, but she was conscious of the fact and hence all her thoughts and acts were those of a child—she was gay, sportive, wayward and without care. But now there is something, which tells her that she enters upon a new existence—new responsibilities devolve upon her—and, if I may be permitted to say, her sex is defined—hence we find her reserved—she feels that she is a woman, and instinct points out the modes bearing so emphatically the attribute of her character. When these various physical and moral developments have been completed, and even before, the most important function in the female economy commences—I mean menstruation.

Often termed the first "change of life," a woman's "sex is defined" in *body and virtue* by her menstrual capacity. Her instincts emerge from their slumber, tucked away in the memory of her "latent organ, hitherto inactive and apparently useless."[11] In Bedford's terms, her physical, reproductive attributes, once awakened, *emphatically* direct her being. The critical rhetorical point here is that at menarche, the female body signaled to early physicians that it possessed and acted on a knowledge of life independent of, and contrary to, bourgeois "fashion."

Menstruation established in women a cyclical pattern of health or sickness *and* of survival. Paradoxically, many obstetricians and gynecologists felt it was the primary source of debility in a woman's lifetime, while at the same time arguing it was essential to good health. Menstruation "made women weak, diseased, and dependent" by routinely leaving them incapacitated by the pains of the period, fragility from loss of blood, and a presumed susceptibility to monthly derangement. These signs of habitual sickness were offset by the necessity of menstruation to successful reproduction, often by "washing the menstrual blood white" in a revery of marriage and maternity, as Smith-Rosenberg put it. Tilt is paradigmatic of this contradictory standpoint. In *Diseases of Menstruation and Ovarian Inflammation*, he reasoned that, through the accumulation of days, a woman was "subject to this natural infirmity for about seven out of these thirty years" of child-bearing potential. Lamenting the prevalence of menstrual disease, he optimistically declared "there is no reason why the flower of woman's lifetime should be so blighted by intolerable misery." Physical blight clearly justified medical intervention. Nevertheless, he claimed "facts survive theories, and menstruation, however explained, must always be considered, if not absolutely as the *sine quâ non* of generation, at least as the meter of the conceptive power; and it will always be admitted, that during the whole of woman's life, it is the 'signum et praesidium sanitatis' [a sign and a ministration of health]." The "meter" of health for women, and for their incumbent debility, was entirely their power or capacity to conceive.[12] Further, the ability to relieve conceptive power of its blight made physicians indispensable to survival. Once chiasmatically inverted from an individual's interior change to a biopolitical event, the individual woman's menstrual cycle and its trials were of interest to everyone because they were directly implicated in the health of the social body.

Beginning with the first appearance of a theory of independent or spontaneous ovulation, the ubiquitous explanation for necessary levels of sexual congress was that a woman's period was analogous to estrus in animals and, thus, part of an economy of desire: "menstruation is the evidence, which nature furnishes that the female is susceptible of becoming impregnated, that is she is in a state to carry out the cardinal office of her sex, the procreation of her species."[13] Citing Bischoff and Pouchet, Gardner of New York's Northern Dispensary and Preparatory School of Medicine put it succinctly: "This season is in almost every respect analogous to the heat of animals. . . . The bitch in heat has the genitals tumefied and reddened, and a bloody discharge. The human female has nearly the same; and although she may possess sensual appetites at other periods they are notoriously heightened, somewhat anteriorly, and very manifestly immediately subsequent to this epoch." Supposedly rooted in common sense, it was a theory of sexuality based on, at best, casual comparisons of external signs and superficial similarities in histology. Laqueur carefully has documented the torturous evolution and persistent popularity of an estral theory of desire, from Bischoff through Pouchet, to Adam Raciborski and his epic *Traité de la Menstruation*, finally to Mary Putnam Jacobi's highly significant rebuttal that women's sexual desire and reproductive function were disparate.[14]

In 1877, in *The Question of Rest for Women During Menstruation*, Putnam Jacobi systematically argued against dominant theories that menstruation was a blight and distinguished the possibility of reproduction from the necessity of reproduction. She took pains to argue directly against physicians such as Edward Clarke, Storer, Tilt, Raciborski, and many others, that women were principally reproductive mechanisms in the service of species survival. Laqueur wrote that "Jacobi's task became one of severing the sexual from the reproductive life of women," although she, "like her opponents, tended to reduce woman's nature to woman's reproductive biology." More than that, Putnam Jacobi used a survey of women's experience as evidence, such that she "not only devised a new form of medical research . . . but also smuggled women's voices into the emerging scientific discourse of medicine," according to Wells. *A Question of Rest* did more than sever sex from reproduction because the treatise "foregrounds a sense of women's agency and consciousness. . . . Putnam Jacobi framed women's reproductive cycles within the context of their overall strength and mental energy, or what she called force."[15] Nonetheless, the estral theory lasted into the early twentieth century as it was buffeted about from claims that heat and menstruation were virtually identical, such as Gardner's, to claims that menstruation and heat were alike because their dissimilarities actually masked their similarities, such as Raciborski's.

The condition for the emergence of the cyclically aroused woman was the passage "of the sexually active woman of the seventeenth century to the passionless creature of the nineteenth." Based in Galenic theory, a woman's pleasure formerly was considered vital for conception. Likely beginning in the seventeenth century and bolstered by the observations of the obstetrician William Harvey, women's sexual satisfaction seemed less and less necessary to physicians and physiologists. By the mid-nineteenth century, women were motivated by a "desire for maternity" rather than pleasure, according to William Acton. Marion Sims, whose stature was unequaled in the United States, said that a woman's pleasure was irrelevant. The female orgasm had disappeared from the literature and the "frigid" woman had arrived. Of course, this dissolution of female passion was limited to the middle and upper classes of Europeans. Poor working women of any ethnicity or race still supposedly possessed a lascivious and dangerous sexuality, thus contributing to the threat posed by a weakened bourgeois sexuality.

The rigors of their daily labors were believed to toughen them for the trials of child-bearing far better than the delicate life of the bourgeois woman. The apparent conflict of frigidity of the well-to-do with an estral theory of desire was not resolved. In fact, Raciborski, who championed the theory, said three of four women had no sexual appetite. Instead, it was presumed most women of the "better" classes were relatively passionless, except for cyclical fits of arousal commensurate with ovulation and the bursting of their Graafian follicles. Therefore, female sexuality of the privileged was dutiful twice over. The banality of sex made it a requirement rather than a joy, *and* monthly lusts were nature's way of enforcing fertility. In craving or distaste, female organs acted on a maternal imperative independent of women's conscious desire.[16] As feminist critics have well noted, in appreciating the history of women's sexuality, one must account for not only the regulation and discipline of desire for bodies and pleasures, but also the desire for children and maternal duty, particularly how desire for children is set at odds with desire for bodies and pleasures.

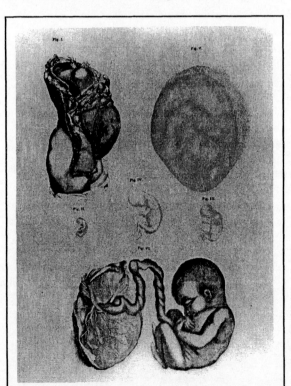

Figure 4.1. Plate VII depicting a fetus in various stages of development. From E. Martin and J. P. Maygrier's *Atlas of Gynaecology and Obstetrics.*

Even when pathologized in opposition to the estral theory, menstruation still indicated a woman's duty to replenish the race. In his essay, "A New Basis for Uterine Pathology," A. F. A. King, a one-time president of the Washington, D.C. Obstetrical and Gynecological Society, argued that menstruation was a sign of physical malfunction: "menstruation is the result of an interference with nature, of a thwarting of her design, of a violation of her laws, and is preventable by obedience to those laws. . . . No hemorrhage is natural." In response to the idea that menstruation is designed for coition, he argued that "the menstrual discharge . . . prevents coition . . . The menstrual *discharge of blood* has no analogue in other animals. Evidence is wanting to prove that menstruation is common to women belonging to the savage races of mankind, who live more strictly in accordance with nature, untrammelled in their reproductive function by the usages of civilization." The trick was to impregnate a pubescent girl just before menarche and maintain a level of pregnancy to prevent menstruation—until menopause. In this case, the *suppression* of menstruation formed the economy of desire such that as a negative incitement menses still led to high levels of fertility. Forgetfulness lurked behind his theory as well because supposedly more natural, "savage" cultures retained this wisdom. Again, the theme of civilized decline was struck, as only cultured people had seemed to have forgotten the truth of reproduction.[17] Whether as a sign of natural eroticism or pathologically civilized reproductive control, menstruation mandated copulation or at least the nourishment of the population's fecundity.

The product of the economy, the fetus, was an emblem of the cultural matrix, of the responsibilities of women and the future of the nation and race. In today's debates, the fetus is the icon of abortion; this was not so in the nineteenth century.[18] There were images of fetuses similar to those found today, such as the one in E. Martin and J. P. Maygrier's *Atlas of Gynaecology and Obstetrics*, published in 1881 (Fig. 4.1).[19] Notice the image of the dissected woman with her womb exposed in upper left-hand corner juxtaposed with the shaded image of the fetus presumably within her on the upper right-hand side. It is reminiscent of imagery today that presents the outline of a womb containing a fetus. However, images such as these were very rare. The life of the fetus was a justification, but it was not the dominant one, being packaged together with the life of the state and a commitment to God. Although fetal rights were justified in the language of individuality, it was an individuality that represented the future of society. The fetus was emblematic of the male citizen of the future state. The two common grounds, theological and biological, for granting the fetus the status of the next citizen were only faintly different. Although distinct from God as painting from artist, the body was part of God's canvas.

Nearly every physician resorted to Christian morality to demonstrate the inviolability of fetal life. In *Criminal Abortion*, Storer quoted from a letter by the late Bishop of Boston, who in turn invoked a 1588 bull of Pope Sixtus the Fifth:

> [B]ut [the fetus] has sacred rights, founded in God's Law, so much the more to be respected because it is helpless. . . . It affords me pleasure . . . to learn that the American Medical Association has turned its attention to the prevention of criminal abortion, a sin so directly opposed to the first laws of nature, and to the designs of God, our Creator, that it cannot fail to draw-down a curse upon the land where it is generally practised.

Also, in *Why Not?* he quoted from Percival's *Medical Ethics*. "To extinguish the first spark of life is a crime of the same nature, both against our Maker and society, as to destroy an infant, a child, or man." He concluded: "By that higher than human law, which, though scoffed at by many a tongue, is yet acknowledged by every conscience, 'the willful killing of a human being, at any stage of its existence, is murder.'" Similarly, A. E. Small, the chair of Medical Jurisprudence at the homeopathic Hahneman Medical College, delivered a lecture in which he cited several physicians, regular and irregular alike, all of whom invoked God's law to admonish abortion.[20] The very notion of a Christian physician, an explicit persona of many nineteenth-century doctors, meant the confluence of Christianity and medical practice. Physicians did not separate biology from theology; in fact, they relied on each to inform the other.

This was further illustrated by the biological proof offered in medical theories of life at conception. Often comparative anatomy was used to justify conception. In the following example from H. R. Storer, conception is redefined as birth: "The first impregnation of the egg, whether in man or in kangaroo, is the birth of the offspring to life; its emergence into the outside world for wholly separate existence is, for one as for the other, but an accident in time." Also, comparisons of fetuses to ex-utero beings justified conception as the beginning of life, as James Kelly presented in a lecture on abortion ethics. The difference between prenatal and postnatal life was a matter of degree, not kind:

> [I]mmediately after impregnation, vital phenomena are manifested in cell-proliferation, differentiation, nutrition, and organization. With the exception of respiration, all the functions are preformed early in fœtal life: the heart pulsates; the circulation is complete and independent of that of the mother . . . Consequently we may reasonably conclude that, at least after this period, abortion is a source of suffering to the fœtus proportionate to its age and the violence employed in the operation. The conclusion at which we must arrive, a conclusion corroborated by the teachings of religion, is that from the instant at which impregnation occurs and the ovum first receives life, the fœtus is human, and at all periods differs in degree and not in kind from the infant and the adult. Therefore, we must regard it as a "human being," with an inalienable right to life, and that its destruction is homicide.[21]

Comparative anatomy and degrees of humanity provide no biological reason for conception as the marker for life, except through equivocation. Bringing in kangaroos or birds or fish, as also was common, did not prove the point in question. Further, signs of fetal independence would lend more support to quickening than conception as the moment of first life. Firm biological proof was lacking because there were no criteria or organic tests available to measure "life." Physicians were not really sure what life was beyond Bichat's definition of "organization in action" or some similarly mechanical version thereof. Instead, authors typically just declared conception was life and fell back on ensoulment as their rationale. In that regard Kelly's piece is especially characteristic. In it he summarized the justifications for and against abortion, religious and biological, that were circulating in the late nineteenth century and then advanced a solid, conservative reading that supported the AMA position exactly. He offered no biological explanation that did not in some way rely on the simultaneity of conception and ensoulment.

Thus, divine, natural, and social law were understood conjointly, as the body, the state, and God were made one. Kelly seamlessly collapsed these together into a justification of fetal rights ratified by God:

> Abortion is an act which is directly antagonistic to reproduction, and as such, like suicide and other crimes which are unnameable, it is unnatural. Consequently it is a greater crime even than wilful [sic] murder. . . . The deed [conception] is ratified by being sealed with the image of God, which conveys to the fœtus the infinitely greater gift of the immortal soul. Consequently the life must be regarded as the inalienable and lawful property of the recipient, who can be deprived of it only by an unjust and despotic act.[22]

Small, in a typical listing of the offenses committed by abortionists, reiterates this condensation of law when he stated that abortion was a crime against the state, physiology, and morality.

Ratified by God with inalienable rights, the fetus was presumed to be male and to be the future of society, a habitual masculinizing of the fetus that Newman argues persists today. Smith-Rosenberg has demonstrated that in the nineteenth century female fetuses typically were not on the horizon, except when the occasional author might use a neutral pronoun. For example, in *Why Not?* Storer cites *Man Transformed,* published in 1653: "It is a thing deserving all hate and detestation that a man in his very originall, whiles he is framed, whiles he is enlived, should be put to death under the very hands and in the shop of nature." Further, a woman was believed to have no direct connection to the fetus because it was independent at conception; she was only a "spot" or "nidus" (nest) in the process of reproduction.[23] Paradoxically, the female body was both the generative apparatus of humanity *and* marginal to generation, which harks back to the Hellenic tradition that the mother only incubated man's seed and thus had no rights in reproduction. Indeed, critiquing Raciborski's theory of menstruation, Putnam Jacobi wrote: "Aristotle, to whom Raciborski attributes the first enunciation of his theory, calls the menstrual blood the marble, the sperm the sculptor, and the fœtus the statue." In the context of a decreasing fertility rate, the individual fetus was valued in terms of *his* potential contribution to society. Refuting Malthusian arguments for limitations on population, Storer argued that a nation could ill afford to lose any of its offspring, even "its frailer children, who oftenest, perhaps, represent its intellect and its genius." Less exclusive than Storer in her thinking, Mary Mitchell nonetheless echoed his biopolitical sentiment when she wrote that "every life is of political value and ought to be made a source of wealth to the country." Fetuses were more than individuals worthy of protection, they were the human resource generated within women. According to Newman, the (male) fetus "is the image *par excellence* of rights-bearing Enlightenment Man ferociously rendered in the fabled state of nature"; in the nineteenth century, he also was an emblem of a collective white future.[24]

As an archive of memory about reproductive truth, the organic discourse spoken by the body of the bourgeois, Anglo-Saxon, Protestant woman was that *her womb* was to be a matrix of culture, not just of infantile human bodies. As the anchor in a time of population crisis, her body became the locus of origin and demise on a scale far grander than that of the fetus, the mother, or even the family.[25] An old term for the womb, the matrix, accurately conveys the status of female reproductive organs and their corporeal discourse within the system of early medical rhetoric. In Latin, *matrix* historically referred to a "pregnant animal, a female used for breeding," but as time passed, it came to refer to the womb. Its root, *mater*, refers to mother and its suffix, *-trix*, refers to "a female who performs or is associated with an activity" (in this case, reproduction). Judith Butler explains that "the classical association of femininity with materiality can be traced to a set of etymologies which link matter with *mater* and *matrix* (or the womb) and, hence, with a problematic of reproduction." *Matrix* referred to the material generation of humanity. Over time, *matrix* also came to refer broadly to "that which gives origin or form to something enclosed within it, such as a mold for a casting."[26] The mother-function of generation was connected more broadly to the idea of forging anew anything material, such that generation was not necessarily limited to immediate offspring.

For example, Meigs, a writer of resplendent and expansive prose, reiterated the image of a matrix through the conjunction that duBois noted in ancient texts: "secrecy, female potentiality, the tempting, enclosed interiority of the body . . . with both treasure and death, with the mysteries of the other." He wrote:

> It is strange to think on the power of the race; and yet from what low beginnings! Even from the germiniferous tissue of the female! It is from her stroma that issues the generic as well as the genetic force! . . . notwithstanding the countless myriads of generations that from the remotest ages have reproduced individuals more numerous than the sands of the shore, or the stars in the firmament . . . every man and every woman go steadily, like the current of a river, down Time's flow, ever ending, ever beginning, always changing, yet immutably the same! . . . See, then, in this unobvious, apparently vile lump of animal texture within the inner court of the temple of the body, the very ark that contains the law which keeps the genera and the species unmixed from age to age. How *can* you study this subject sufficiently?

Note that Meigs locates generative force in the "stroma," or connective tissue, of the ovaries. As the connective tissue between generations, bourgeois women's bodies produced the genealogical effect of culture regenerated and molded anew in the womb; the matron quickened not just a child but a people.[27]

The uterus, ovaries, menstruation, and the fetus were the key elements that housed and renewed a memory of sexual truth in every girl upon the awakening of her body at the first "change of life." In every respect, these basic anatomical features and their physiology were presumed to store knowledge of women's true place in civilization, a machine of life whose every part and parcel was dedicated to the work of reproduction, which was commensurate with the very survival of civilization. The female body was a living record of truth that physicians made visible by meticulously doubling it in text and image, a hypomnesic supplement to a failing memory about maternal duty. Woman's sole duty was to heed her body's corporeal discourse, to recall it through each new birth. As a rhetorical accomplishment, the construction of the white, bourgeois woman's body as the central matrix in a system of cultural mnemonics was as phenomenal as it was complex.

Moral Physiology and Monstrous Pathology

There was an important difference to the reiteration of a maternal imperative from the classical epistemology of seeking truth in feminine recesses, however. Physicians were faced not with abstract, heterosexualized principles of generation, but with people, which made the alienation of women from their bodies more difficult and more important to sustain. Even though antiabortionists did not feel women were intended to have proprietary control over their bodies, women's bodies spontaneously or by induction could intervene in reproduction. Unlike Plato's philosophy, wherein the abstract, superplasticity of the feminine was its virtue, in the mechanistic models of early biomedicine, the plasticity and dynamism of woman's body was taken as both its virtue and its downfall.[28] Life was only as vital as the seat of its renewal, and in its feminized embodiment, life threatened itself. Or, rather, the "generative apparatus" of life was unreliably self-defeating. The narrative of biological destiny seemingly confessed by the female body was a benchmark of both health *and* illness, thereby establishing the parameters of judgments about normality in examination. It also established the parameters of judgement about the interruption of reproductivity, specifically abortion. Amy Allen points out that despite a clearly understood gender normativity, "these norms are in principle unrealizable and the very fact that they have to be cited opens up a space for their subversion."[29] Next to fears of race suicide and degeneracy, abortion was such a subversion and became a sign of the failure of bourgeois gender norms to produce the moral order the division of the sexes was believed to promise. Under observation, the female body revealed its *moral physiology* and *monstrous pathology*, its lawful functioning, its deviant transgressions.

In nineteenth-century medicine, morality and monstrosity were deeply imbricated in practice because "health" and "morality" were almost interchangeable terms. The good woman bearing children was well. Conversely, abortion became the conceptual center of female reproductive pathologies within body-machine epistemology. The teleological model subscribed to by early doctors made spontaneous abortion a linchpin of pathology, the apex of a horrible, natural debility in women. Criminal abortion was the result of cultural decay that ignited the monstrous fires within a suspect female nature. Consequently, the inherent abnormality of female reproduction justified obstetrics and gynecology as normalizing forces or, rather, as reiterative mechanisms for keeping alive a memory of maternity that was passing from existence. The criminality of induced abortion must be understood in relation to prevailing beliefs about health and sickness in women. The paradox of women's biology, that females were simultaneously construed as life-giving and life-taking, was a moral problem for early physicians. This placed women's bodies in the conflicted position of being the privileged storehouse of truth about life and also the greatest threat to the continued reanimation of that truth.

Of particular importance is that the organic discourse of women's bodies involved the reduction of divine, natural, and social law to three variants of one code made visible by forensic practices of medicalized exegesis. The moral physiology of nineteenth century was based on the continuity of morality, physiology, and legality. Ideally, divine and social law would come to mirror one another, but only through their linkage in physiology. Well-being was consonant with lawful virtue; conversely, lawful virtue translated into good health. These laws, based in a Cartesian logic, were theorized as mechanistic in their perfection. H. R. Storer's father, D. H. Storer of Harvard, wrote "that each organ has a law of its own . . . controlling the performance of its functions.—a law which cannot be broken with impunity. The Lawgiver is inexorable." The laws of the uterus "requires that a certain specified time be occupied in perfecting its most important work, this period is fixed, uniform, universal. In a state of perfect health deviation may be said to be unknown." If women succumbed to the machine-like laws of nature and God, all would be well. Hence, the morality of physiology was predicated on the assumption that body and soul were two planes, bound by similar dictates, that suffered alike from their transgression. Worrying over the state of women's health, A. F. A. King wrote,

> When I look over the armory of instruments that are daily used by the gynecologist, and regard the masses of medical lore crammed into our voluminous textbooks on gynecology, and when in the examination of women I so seldom find a perfectly healthy womb, I am often led to ask: Why is it that this unfortunate organ should be the subject of so many ills? And just as often am I disposed to give the same answer that the Divine does, when, looking into my face on a Sunday morning, he explains the reason of my spiritual deterioration. As with the transgressor metaphysically, so with the womb physiologically: it has left undone the things which it ought to have done, and has done those things which it not to have done; and (consequently) *there is no health in it*.[30]

In female anatomy and physiology, social and moral law were made coextensive.

However, even a "normal" reproductive life was suspect. As has been demonstrated with great force and clarity by many authors, man has been the norm of a healthy body since the days of Aristotle. In the Hellenic episteme, woman was defined as a deformed or incompletely formed male. In the Cartesian medical episteme, the unimpregnable male mechanism defined healthful functioning. The female was necessarily questionable by virtue of her dynamism. Rosi Braidotti argues in *Nomadic Subjects* that "[t]he woman's body can change shape in pregnancy and childbearing; it is therefore capable of defeating the notion of fixed *bodily form*, of visible, recognizable, clear, and distinct shapes as that which marks the contour of the body. She is morphologically dubious." Physicians held that the medical consequence of female morphology was an increased susceptibility to disease. Clarkson Collins stated that "the naturally delicate and susceptible constitution of the female is exalted to an acuteness not before known; the sudden transition of the sexual organs from a state of apathy to one of great activity, renders them *particularly liable to disease*." The engine driving female morphology, or the "female economy," was so forceful that it was often discussed as the special trial of woman, a cyclical marathon or natural gauntlet that had to be run. "The ovaries began their dictatorship of woman's life at puberty. They released her, often exhausted and debilitated, at menopause."[31] From a medical standpoint in the latter part of the nineteenth century, sickness became the normal state for bourgeois women.

Almost invariably, the normality of female maladies was attributed to the poor design of a woman's body. As one doctor lamented about the uterus, "what a pitiable piece of organization!" Not surprisingly, this made women "highly qualified clients" for a growing obstetrical-gynecological profession. Collins concisely summarized what came to be established medical knowledge:

> Such is their anatomical relation to each other and to the whole system, and the very important part they play in the animal economy, that were we merely to study them in the abstract we should readily conclude that such a delicate structure, governed by peculiar physiological laws, would become the seat of disease. Slight experience in the practice of medicine confirms us in the belief that no part of the human body is so liable to functional derangement and organic disease as the female genital organs. No class of diseases have remained in greater *obscurity*; and none, I affirm, are *more susceptible* of treatment.

This is a particularly rich passage. That assumptions about a woman's delicacy and her presumed duty in reproduction mandated that her body be inherently disease ridden, and that these premises were confirmed only by "slight experience," typifies what I mean by the "speaking eye" articulating the body. The physician, armed with the presumably self-evident truth of physical examination, reified preexisting cultural assumptions in the body of the patient. Also note Collins's subtext about a woman's place in the animal economy and the not so coincidental fact that her body was the perfect medical commodity. Easily stricken and easily treated, the nineteenth-century model of the diseased female body placed custody of reproductive power with physicians. In the name of pathology, Collins sewed

together the primacy and objectivity of anatomy and physiology as ways of knowing, the mechanical and economic assumptions undergirding that way of knowing,
and a patriarchal system of human capital.[32]

Within the framework of a mechanistic moral physiology, woman's inherently pathological, yet essentially moral body made her both malformed *and* miraculous. True to the ancient Greek term for monster (tera), which implied both
horror and wonder, female reproductivity was *monstrous*. Braidotti discusses sex
differences through the figure of the monster:

> Since the nineteenth century, following the classification system of monstrosity
> of Geoffrey Saint Hilaire, bodily malformations have been defined in terms of
> *excess*, *lack*, or *displacement* of organ . . . The monster is the bodily incarnation
> of difference from the basic human norm, it is a deviant, an a-nomaly [*sic*]; it is
> abnormal. As Georges Canguilhem points out, the very notion of the human
> body rests upon an image that is intrinsically prescriptive: a normally formed
> human being is the zero-degree of monstrosity.[33]

When the male form is the standard, females have no recourse to a "zero-degree"
of monstrosity.

Two commonly held beliefs illustrate this definition of "male as normal."
First, for centuries, women were believed to be able to deform their embryos and
fetuses by thinking evil thoughts or being subjected to horrible sights, great
shocks, and so forth. Scientists and physicians in the eighteenth century were extremely interested in the maternal genesis of the monster: persons with abnormal
growths, skin discolorations, and Siamese twins. In the late nineteenth century,
maternal impressions still were deemed decisive such that dreams of a brother in
shackles were used to explain the appearance of a "fibrous cord" on the hand and
foot of a miscarried fetus. A woman could produce a monster with the illusions of
her mind. Consider a plate of fetal monsters (one of two) in Martin's *Atlas of Gynaecology and Obstetrics* (Fig. 4.2). The legends for the figures describe a
"Double-Monster with One Head," a "Double-Monster with Two Heads," or
"Sympodia (Sireniform Monster)." For a number of medical observers, such
malformations could result from a pregnant woman's mental activity. Leading
gynecologists and obstetricians such as T. Gaillard Thomas rejected the idea;
however, a good deal of journal space in the nineteenth century was devoted to
woman's power to warp the very tissues developing inside her.[34]

Second, in a revisitation of Hippocratic medical beliefs, women's uteruses
became pathologically mobile. To mid-century physicians, who believed the improper alignment of the uterus to be the cause of all female maladies, there seemed to be an epidemic of uterine displacement.[35] W. O. Priestley referred to this as
the "displacement craze." Keep in mind that a prolapsed uterus, one that is
inverted or distended, is a painful and debilitating condition; however, physicians
had not paid much attention to prolapsus until the nineteenth century. The period
to which I am referring, roughly 1840-1860, was typified by a belief that defor-

mation of the uterus, even to a slight degree, could cause all of women's ailments. As W. E. Coale put it, the uterus, "of all the various viscera of the human body, [is] the one most liable to displacement." He argued that the uterus was normally abnormal: "considering the subject from a purely mechanical point of view, we would be surprised that a dislodgment of the uterus from its normal situation, upon the slightest assistance given to forces apparently continually at work, should not be the rule, and the cases where it resists these influences be the exception, in the history of woman's health." The flexibility and contractibility of the uterus became a source of habitual physical distortion, in labor and prolapsus, leaving the uterus pathologically suspect. Through the extreme contortions of her womb, woman was internally monstrous. Treatments, as a result, were directed at firming the uterine muscles, surgically repositioning the uterus, or immobilizing the uterus with pessaries that ranged from rubber balls to multi-arm, spring-loaded devices. During these years, a great amount of time was devoted to studying and rectifying uterine "deformation."[36]

These two beliefs give to support Braidotti's claim that "woman" as Other evokes a kind of misanthropic fear and awe. "Woman as a sign of difference is monstrous. If we define the monster as a bodily entity that is anomalous and deviant vis-à-vis the norm, then we can argue that the female body shared with the monster the privilege of bringing out a unique blend of *fascination* and *horror*." My choice of "misanthrope" is intentional because "misanthropy" literally refers to the distortion of Man. Divergence from a male norm of health is misanthropic, in effect. Further, as the liminal space of being

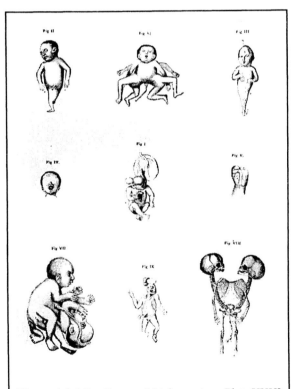

Figure 4.2. Nine figures of fetal monsters. Plate XXXI from E. Martin and J. P. Maygrier's *Atlas of Gynaecology and Obstetrics*.

or not being, woman's reproductive anatomy is especially evocative and threatening. Braidotti, elaborating on Julia Kristeva, has linked the double-meaning of the
monster "to the maternal body as the site of the origin of life and consequently
also of the insertion into mortality and death. We are all of woman born, and the
mother's body as the threshold of existence is both sacred and soiled, holy and
hellish; it is attractive and repulsive, all-powerful and therefore impossible to live
with."[37]

Susan Sontag wrote in *Illness as Metaphor* that, "in the nineteenth century,
the notion that the disease fits the patient's character, as the punishment fits the
sinner, was replaced by the notion that it expresses character." She argued that
illness was believed to be "the will speaking through the body." Of course, for
many doctors practicing under Victorian ideas of gender, a flawed, monstrous
fertility was the basis of a woman's character. This played out in the wholesale
convergence of health and illness in the "normal" female reproductive organ. The
contradiction arose from simultaneous use of fertility as a woman's glory and as
a model for her diseases. James Simpson was explicit about the parallels between
pregnancy and disease. He stressed the physical similarity between symptoms of
illness and pregnancy, arguing that

> Pregnancy is the same disease, if I may term it, in all. . . . It may be found that
> the patient is really not pregnant at all; the symptoms being sympathetic merely
> of some morbid state of the uterus and ovaries, but not sympathetic of the state
> of pregnancy, though very exactly similar to the symptoms which most com-
> monly accompany it. Observe . . . what important evidence these well-known
> facts afford. . . . first, that in pregnancy we have the same identical condition of
> the uterus . . . these symptoms varying greatly in different patients; and, sec-
> ondly, they show us that the most usual dynamic symptoms . . . which we see
> produced by pregnancy, may be present in other conditions of the uterus than in
> the pregnant condition.

Simpson equated pregnancy with pathology by presupposing the unimpregnated
state as the standard of health. Hence, he frequently described pregnancy as a
"disease" and considered it a medical problem subject to treatment. Similarly, Tilt
pathologized menstruation because menses are frequently accompanied by dis-
comforts of various sorts. In both cases, disease was mechanically defined as any
divergence from an effortlessly functioning, unimpregnated, female reproductive
system. Reproduction was paradoxically considered the biological burden of a
woman to continue the species and, at the same time, necessarily destructive to
her and, thus, to humanity. Both life-giving and life-taking, the middle- and
upper-class white woman was monstrously pathological in her frailty. Exemplify-
ing Sontag's insight that disease was seen as a bodily expression of character,
antiabortion physicians embodied women as suicidal threats to the community.[38]

To explain what I mean by "suicidal threat," consider that in the contradictory biological context of women as fecund *and* destructive, abortion became a

conceptual crux for reproductive pathologies. H. A. Ramsay declared that "probably no subject connected with the Science of Obstetricy is more important than Abortion, it is fearful in its progress, and hazardous in its results; while a proper knowledge of it distinguishes the man of true Science, from the vague routinist." Part of the reason for abortion's centrality to obstetricians and gynecologists was the perception that abortion caused, or was the product of, most uterine maladies. James Whitehead, in his influential monograph *On the Causes and Treatment of Abortion and Sterility*, reiterated the circularity prevalent in medical texts of the era: "The causes of abortion are, according to authors, exceedingly numerous, including almost every circumstance of life, *however trivial*, which happens in deviation from the ordinary quiet course of nature." This included the multitude of "female maladies" endemic to the presumably pitiable structure of woman's procreative system, malformations of the fetus, and situational conditions ranging from violent falls to "excessive grief, joy, fear, anxiety, and the like" or "the shock of the shower-bath." A refined woman's body was considered so delicate that any disturbance might upset its proper functioning. The opposite was also true. Virtually any illness could result from abortion, whether spontaneous or induced. "There is scarcely a phase of uterine or ovarian disease that may not stimulate, or be stimulated by, some form of abortion, common or extreme." One of the major lines of antiabortion argument, consistent with racialized biopolitics, was that it weakened the female population. In this construction, all roads potentially lead to or from abortion, making it a hub of reproductive pathology. As the final, ever-present threat for any illness or as the secret cause of disease, abortion was commonly viewed as the ultimate failure of a woman in her biological duty. In the dialectic of life-death that imbued antiabortion comment from physicians, this opposition is hardly surprising: as "life" is made an ultimate God term, "abortion" becomes an ultimate Devil term.[39]

Induced abortion, then, was the lurking monster within woman made fashionable. It was a moral failure that made a woman a criminal accessory to her body's inherently horrible potential. Often considered worse than murderers, women who aborted and abortionists habitually were described as "inhuman," "heinous," and "vile." One editorialist wrote,

> We refer to the felonious act by which a blow is aimed at the life of a human being, while yet in its foetal stage of existence, either for the purpose of concealing dishonor, or for the monstrous and more unnatural one of escaping the cares and responsibilities of maternity—an act which, three hundred years ago, subjected those convicted of the committal to all the penalties, civil and ecclesiastical, inflicted on murderers.

An 1847 image from the front page of the *National Police Gazette* represented popular medical condemnations of women who aborted and their abortionists. "The Female Abortionist" portrayed "a fashionably dressed and attractive woman whose arms were transformed into devil's wings. From her pelvis emerged a devil's head with fang teeth gnawing on a plump baby."[40] (Fig. 4.3) Abortion was evil incarnate in the popular press, as well as in the medical literature.

Of course, not all women were thought of as susceptible to or notable for such moral laxity. It was a certain class of white women, because of the influence of fashion, who were especially prone to abortion or whose perceived immorality simply counted more. The new gender norms discussed in chapter two (socializing, pursuing public life and career at the expense of fertility) were treated as a dangerous aesthetic of pleasure that obscured truth such that the "corporeal style" of the new bourgeois woman was rejected in Neoplatonic fashion as an ignorant semblance of true womanhood. Interestingly, gender performatives were attributed great constitutional power in culture, indicating the tension between the desire for a "timeless" body that binds culture through its laws and

THE FEMALE ABORTIONIST.

Figure 4.3. "The Female Abortionist" from the cover of *The National Police Gazette*, 1847.

the fear of a body that Butler would say has "the *appearance of substance* . . . A performative accomplishment that the mundane social audience, including the actors themselves, come to believe and to perform in the mode of belief."[41] The question was whether the new bourgeois woman would live out the truth of her sex through a properly reproductive heterosexuality or engage in the corruption of maternal instinct to the point of death. The biological Malthusianism of anti-abortionists was implicitly predicated on a critique of white bourgeois gender performativity. It was if gender norms had ruptured the essential connection of sexuality and sex by popularizing the female body's monstrosity, rather than its virtue.

In addition to femininity having latent monstrous potential, affluent whiteness was evidently sick from itself. There was an ambivalent attitude toward white supremacy among the antiabortionists. Contrasts of abortion practices in white Anglo Protestant communities to those of other communities seemed to rest on the conflicted sense of whites becoming other, of slipping into ways supposedly transcended or left behind by more "civilized" peoples. Bourgeois fashion promoted a selfishness and willful ignorance about procreation that was believed *not* to be as prevalent in other populations and cultures, from German and Irish immigrants to "Africans" and "Hindoos." "Enlightened" white culture was becoming inferior to these other groups in that it courted its own morbidity. At the same time, there was the feeling that ethnic and racial "others" were expected to abort because it was an ignorant thing to do; Christians were supposed to be more morally enlightened. In its apparent progress, affluent white Protestant culture had somehow devolved, somehow activated a savagery *more* degenerate than that believed to mark nonwhite, non-Christian others. Dominant whiteness had become ill with an insidious revitalization of its hidden other, brought on by changes in reproductive values of the middle and upper classes. Abortion demonstrated that the moral inferiorities ascribed by white Anglo Christians to other cultures and peoples, that were signs of their supposedly subordinate status, lurked within whites in a far worse form. Although "unmanaged sexuality was considered a threat" in the context both of a "Christian nation" of previous centuries and a more secular, bourgeois nation of the nineteenth, it was threatening for different reasons and so the U.S. antiabortion campaign was an attempt to "re-Christianize" the nationalist biopolitics of well-to-do whites.[42]

Thus, the bourgeois white woman's body was represented in medical discourse of the mid- to late nineteenth century as "suicidal." Inherently faulty, the female body-machine was prone to abort and, thus, kill the woman, the "infant," and by extension, even a white race. Worse yet, through the corruption fostered by modern life, white Christian civilization would aid and abet woman's undependable body in self-destructive behavior. In both of these scenarios, the woman was not afforded the full faculty of reason. Either her body was letting her down or she was too self-absorbed or weak-willed to carry the fetus to term. As such, the patient was seldom described as explicitly having suicidal tendencies, either personal or racial. Rather, she was constructed as unable to help herself, essentially forgetful in a Platonic sense: an untrustworthy, suicidal machine that needed the intervention of the doctor to carry out her function and avoid her shameful proclivity to kill. As a source of memory about reproductive truth, the female body was morally threatening. Hers was not a pure maternal instinct, but a flawed and untrustworthy one that the prevalence of spontaneous and induced abortions indicated. Women were embodied as undependable and prone to immorality down to the level of their tissues and organs.

Articulating A Genealogy of Ought

What, then, was the substance of the organic discourse confessed by women's bodies and documented by physicians in the language of medicine? The essence of life's memory was that *life is order*. Bichat argued life was organization in action. Antiabortion physicians' genealogical rhetoric effectively transformed this general definition from a description of what life *is* to a prescription for what life *ought* to be, from the existence of organization to the purpose of organization. I have stressed that Neoplatonic anamnesis is not a rhetoric that historicizes facts, but a rhetoric that establishes touchstones for normative principles. As such, early physicians did not constitute life as a series of facts but as a set of laws remembered, embodying as law moral prescriptions regarding the "civilized" order of things. The same exegetical practices which enabled them to recall a transgenerational memory of sexual truth simultaneously *placed* that truth in a corporeal and textual archive, a hypomnesic supplement that consigned immaterial verities to observable, accessible locations. This provided a home for normative discourse on the relation of reproductivity and culture to which one could return as a kind of anchor. The reliance on bodily law as a template of cultural order enabled antiabortion physicians to critique culture, ostensibly through the reported "speech" of women's anatomy and physiology. It was against this archive of how life ought to be ordered that antiabortionists treated abortion as an ignorant forgetfulness of truth. To use Derrida's notion of an archive, corporeal discourse was an *"external place* which assure[d] the possibility of memorization, repetition, of reproduction, or reimpression."[43]

As set forth in this chapter, the central facets to the articulation of life's memory were its law-like mechanization and its privileged placement in females—especially white, affluent females. Regarding mechanization, the embodiment of life as lawful organization in action was a key part of the genealogical effect of antiabortion rhetoric. The latent memory of reproductive ends was ostensibly tucked away in the laws governing its biological *means*. As such, life was constituted as the operation of three intersecting kinds of law: divine, natural, and social. The substance of life's memory was determined not by any *individual* body's tissues and organs, but by the laws governing female anatomy and physiology, the rules that physicians understood to undergird the body-machine. These laws were read from the relation of the uterus and/or ovaries to women's overall biology *and* morality, the function of the menstrual cycle in nature and in civilization, and the status of the fetus as an emblem of culture renewed. The memory of the truth of life resided in the operation of certain laws, not in the flesh *per se*. The body only served as a renewable repository of that knowledge, a working demonstration of presumably higher truths. Life was a set of normative abstract properties, whose memory resided in the regular action of laws that governed "concretes," to use Henry Howard's apt phrasing.

These intersecting laws were not on equal footing within physicians' rhetoric. Divine law mandated that life was sacred, expressed by the commandment "Thou Shalt Not Kill" and restated numerous times by physicians commenting on the sanctity of life. The natural law of female biology was understood to reflect this higher law so that a healthy body-machine was *intended* to work with precision to recreate life, not to contribute to death. If abortion was taken as murder because it ran counter to an intended natural purpose of maternity, then abortion was also necessarily unhealthy for individual women and for culture. In that sense, "not killing" meant not only the prevention of abortions but also the imperative to optimize the life of one's racial/ethnic group for reasons of survival: "be fruitful an multiply." The lawful functioning of the body-machine took on rhetorical purpose and motive when understood as the reflection of divine will among competing reproductive interests. It is here that remembrance shifted from the recollection of what life *is* to what life *ought* to be. Additionally, physicians judged social law against the natural and the divine, thereby finding social law proper only when concordant with higher laws. This hierarchical layering of law, with divinity expressing its will through nature and reaching toward the social, was crucial to the genealogical effect of medical antiabortionist rhetoric. Physicians constituted social law as derivative of divine law *by way of* its descent and emergence in the laws of the body. It is in this regard that physicians' diagnostic practices may be understood as forensic. Through exegetical means, the body itself confessed the laws by which not only its functional, but also its spiritual and criminal use ought to be judged. The present was given a transcendent origin, and thus a point of evaluation, by way of the body-machine's operation.

However, this hierarchy of laws looks different if one attends to the *performance* of medical body criticism, rather than to the genealogical effect produced by such work. In practice, natural law, not divine law, was in the dominant position in that physicians constituted divine will and civilized destiny through critical perception of regularities within female anatomy and physiology. In the name of survival, physicians *reiterated* a theological vision for white reproduction and a tradition of married sex practices through their exegetical work on the uterus, ovary, and menstruation. As a commonplace, the construct of biological life potentially encompasses almost everything, especially when broadly understood as "organized action." To metonymically locate one anatomical region of one sex as the privileged center of this vast force means that the whole of the construct may be construed from the vantage point of the part. The chiasmatic inversion of women's bodies so as to expose life's "truth" acts on this metonymy to prescribe the whole of life's purpose, whether in terms of God's will or of an implicitly white civilization, by attempting to bring before the eyes a particular knowledge of life's essence. It was not that the construct of life preexisted its articulation through biomedicine (the expression of the divine through nature), but that in their practices, physicians "quickened" theology and patriarchal culture through women's reproductive organs. The genealogical effect of the higher truths descending through the body to culture obscured the practices that created that very effect. A "true" body emerged from nature to speak to us, apparently existing outside the vicissitudes of biopolitical interest such that the privileged and dispassionate window on the knowledge of life was natural law. Rather than proceeding from the divine to the natural to the social, physicians reiterated established beliefs on the social and the divine in terms of an exposed biological nature.

The mechanization of the natural law of life, where woman is a "generative apparatus," is of special import for rhetorically capturing God's will and civilization's destiny within uteruses and menstrual cycles. The lawful quality of the body's mechanisms ostensibly revealed not only the body's intended purpose, but also something of the overall system it was "designed" to operate in. It was something like attempting to recreate the reason for and the blueprint of a building from one of the tools used to make it. The regularities of the natural world served as the source of rhetorical invention from which physicians materialized a wellspring of normative values regarding life. The use of laws to deduce what is not readily apparent is a simple principle of many exegetical practices. In this case, an intersecting hierarchy of laws meant that the operative patterns physicians perceived within women's bodies could be construed as discursive reiterations of the divine, natural, and social place of reproduction and abortion.

The genealogical effect of such discourse depended on more than the embodiment of certain organs as a mechanistic means to an end. It also depended on the embodiment of white, well-to-do women as the sacred yet troubled *context* for life's action, or rather, on the embodiment of a particular femininity of life's mechanism. The organic discourse of women's bodies was imbued with the sense that life descended through the uterus or the ovaries, that life's essential action was specially located there, for reasons *of* femininity. Women were to be more than biological reproducers, they were to be symbolic and ideological reproducers of order. Consider the interconnection of women's bodies and the concept of life as the context for organized action *that optimizes itself and so thwarts the "death" of certain populations*. The concatenation of a group's survival with the health of the ovary or the uterus liquidated the distinctively womanly, even as it reified gender with great specificity. Women's organs were conflated with the formation of nation and "race" such that the collective bodies of bourgeois matrons formed strategically ambiguous terminals through which white affluent life was promoted over other groups' lives. The boundaries of the female body were treated as distinct and special, as a sort of sacred matrix, yet they were penetrable and extremely porous. Another facet of the metonymic quality of the rhetoric was that female organs were accessible because they were everyone's organs, in effect, and they were also sacrosanct because they were the essence of "woman." Symbolically, the nation's life was synonymous with the life of certain women's reproductivity. H. R. Storer's comment that the nation's fate rested on women's loins epitomizes the symbolism of convergent biological and national order.

However, the conflation of bodily law with the proper cultural order meant that women need not reproduce more children to reproduce cultural norms. Rather, to reproduce norms, one need only oppose abortion on grounds that it was contrary to all law. The "dense ignorance" that had befallen the nation was to be remedied by education in forgotten truths such that whether women did or did not have more abortions, the memory work of recalling a nostalgic view of cultural order was accomplished. Thus, the rhetoric of anamnesis was reproductive on several levels. In terms of gender ideology, remembering the truth that life is an order that dictates a moral-biological duty to women and specifies the proper place of reproduction within a "civilized" nation certainly recites the gendered ideology of male superiority. What is more, the particular heterosexual relation between the female body as nature and the male observer as the midwife to God's reason, the complementary antagonism that I detailed in the previous chapter, was also recited. The female body was both the means to knowing the true order of life *and* the primary scene of its undoing so that the rational physician was professionally justified in seizing truth from the errors of womanly nature. The very act of "listening" to the organic discourse of the female body was a paradigmatic reiteration of the dynamic of masculine science lifting the feminine veil to perceive higher truth.

Further, ethnic, social boundaries and concomitant oppositions within a white, largely Protestant nation were asserted through the strategic ambiguity of the female body. Instead of compromising the presumed hierarchies of race and class, abortion as a sign of cultural and physiological infirmity prompted antiabortionists' call for purification by a return to origins. That is, if a dominant white civilization was perceived as degenerating from its own excesses, ostensibly there were resources for challenging the presumptive white superiority. If the sickness indicated by abortion was a form of rectifiable, feminized ignorance, however, then questions regarding superiority are sidestepped. The undependability of women's bodies and minds made a perceived threat to white superiority intelligible without fracturing the white ideal, in that women were a potential enemy to a white Christian way of life. As a measure of over-civilized savagery, abortion as degeneration and potential race suicide not only supported, but actually fueled a rhetoric of anamnesis, of recollection of "true" purpose and identity that only reinvigorated a sense of otherness regarding non-Christians and non-Anglo whites.

Rhetorically, the critical issue is not simply that a certain set of physicians took the opportunity afforded by increased abortion rates to claim some public authority and assert their vision of white Christian male superiority, although that is an important consequence. Amid the volatile changes of the nineteenth century, calls to reinvigorate traditional norms were common in numerous contexts, and health issues occupied many of those, making the fact that obstetricians and gynecologists participated in those calls significant, but not exhaustive in terms of abortion rhetoric. More than that, antiabortion physicians constituted a mechanistic formation of intersecting laws wherein the memory of life's order was the memory of culture's order. It was not just a moment when traditions were advocated in the face of change; it also was a moment when a medicalized system of rhetorical mnemonics was established.

Epistemically, in opposition to abortion, coming to *listen* to female anatomy and physiology was embodied as a *culturally* genealogical act, a point of articulation for the descent and emergence of normative order. Reproductivity has always been a commonplace for remembering the past but nineteenth-century medical antiabortionists accomplished something novel within that commonplace. As a matrix, the female body became a scene of remembrance wherein organs and cycles became discursive agents imbued with a kind of speech about *culture* that only physicians, as the privileged class of forensic exegetes, could reliably decipher. This mnemonic system did *not* depend on whether specific medical theories held true over time, as many did not even within the time frame of the late nineteenth century. Instead, it was the formation of memory that proved stable, wherein a return to the order of life, especially within female reproductive organs, could be counted on to quicken divisions and unities within culture when it was seen as losing its coherence, to produce an articulation of the way culture ought to be. Against life as a mnemonic system, abortion was cultural amnesia.

Chapter Five
Embodying a Matrix

> When there is not separation between the text to be inscribed and the
> body that historicizes it, the system no longer functions. It is precisely
> the tools that establish that difference. They mark the gap without
> which everything becomes a disseminated writing, an indefinite com-
> binative system of fictions and simulacra, or else, on the contrary, a
> continuum of natural forces, of libidinal drives and instinctual out-
> pourings. Tools are the operators of writing and also its defenders.
> — Michel de Certeau, *The Practice of Everyday Life*

Embodying a matrix of cultural memory from the order of life involved not only
the articulation of an intelligible discourse, but also the articulation of perceptual
tools and organs necessary to produce that discourse, in this case, the ligature of
patient and physician in diagnostic rituals of exposure. There must be a perceptual
interface between the normative codes to be embodied and the flesh through
which they will be embodied. The instruments of medical perception, the hand
and eye of the physician and related prostheses, were that interface. These organs
and tools were the medium of rhetorical invention, composing a set "of objects
whose purpose is to inscribe the force of the law on its subject," in this case, the
conflated code of physiological, divine, and social law, "in order to . . . demonstrate the rule, to produce a 'copy' that makes the norm legible," as Certeau put it.
This is necessary as bodies that are not perceived according to accepted norms do
not emerge as culturally recognizable entities; unmarked, illegible bodies are not
functional sources of memory within rhetorics of remembrance. In the passage
from mute *flesh* to a *body* that stored the genealogy of a *normal* cultural order, the
medical tools that extended the physician's senses become the "metallic vocabulary" of embodiment.[1]

In other words, articulating life's memory involved not only the consignment
of recovered sexual truth to an archive, but also the perceptual organs and rituals
involved in *making* that archive. The believability that the truths yielded by the

body are in fact prediscursive, given by nature and God, and not proffered by culture, depended as much on the physical acts of perception involved in making the body confess its knowledge as on the documentation of that body. Certeau explains in reference to the general act of embodying a believable referent for a discourse:

> The *credibility* of a discourse is what first makes believers act in accord with it. It produces practitioners. To make people believe is to make them act. But by a curious circularity, the ability to make people act—to write and to machine bodies—is precisely what makes people believe. Because the law is already "incarnated" in physical practices, it can accredit itself and make people believe that it speaks in the name of the "real." It makes itself believable by saying: "This text has been dictated to you by Reality itself."

In the case of abortion, archiving the truth of the female sex provided a reciprocal form of proof wherein expert discourse was generated from the same practices that incarnated the object of the discourse. The rituals of exposure by which physicians produced representations of the body helped "make real," in circular fashion, the body that was being represented. "The law requires an accumulation of corporeal capital in advance in order to make itself believed and practiced. It is thus inscribed because of what has already been inscribed: the witnesses, martyrs, or examples that make it credible to others."[2]

Perfomatively, physicians' body criticism established a particular division and interdependence between the body of the patient, the physician, and the texts generated from their interaction. This is not to say that early obstetric and gynecologic practice were essentially antiabortion. Rather, it is to say that the believability of the knowledge that abortion was a crime against the order of life ordained by God, nature, and society, *as established by medicine*, depended on a particular, normalized relationship between observer and observed. Paradoxically, the normalization of the modern pelvic examination connected patient and physician in the search for truths and also disconnected the physician from the formulation of those truths. Physicians were linked to the female body in acts of knowledge retrieval, not discourse creation. God and nature were the real rhetors, whereas female physiology, with the aid of medical tools and language, was the messenger. The regularity of how women's bodies were exposed and read was crucial to stabilizing women's *bodies*, not physicians' *practices*, as cultural memory sites. Regardless of the variations within the discourse remembered, the fact was medically naturalized that something within women's organs was to be remembered. In this chapter, I detail the perceptual rituals and tools necessary to produce a hypomnesic record of forgotten truths. Further, I consider how physicians and patients embodied their functions as "modest witness" and mute body "pregnant with discourse" within a culturally mnemonic system.

Materia Medica and Perceptual Prosthetics

"Prosthesis" was originally a term in rhetoric for adding syllables to the beginnings of words. It has come to mean "a foreign element that reconstructs that which cannot stand up on its own, at once propping up and extending its host. The prosthesis is always structural, establishing the place it appears to add to." Hypomnesis is essentially a memory prosthesis, a place external to the truth it documents that, in fact, establishes the memory "it appears to add to."³ In that regard, the doubling of the body of life's memory in female organs and medical texts was prosthetic twice over. The female body, as a living record of higher truths about reproduction, was already prosthetic, a natural extension of truths that made them visible in action. Except that the female body had become insufficient mnemonically as women rejected their bodies' "maternal instinct." The organs of perception of early physicians became additional prostheses to a forgotten knowledge of life, mnemonic devices that structurally "propped up" a failing biological archive of truth. The hands and eyes of physicians were the extensions of empirical observation and transcendent vision, points at which earthly substance and higher knowledge merged such that the greater social body might "see" the truth of sex.

In turn, the tools that extended those physicians' hands and eyes, the materia medica of body criticism, were pivotal links between the individual and the social. As women were conceptually collapsed into a small number of organs and their vital supports, physicians were conjoined to that small area by way of another reduction, the condensation of doctors' perceptual powers into highly developed sense organs. The character and significance of this physician/patient relationship was new to the nineteenth century and indicative of a broad transformation of observation practices that Jonathan Crary documents in *Techniques of the Observer*: "Very generally, what happens to the observer in the nineteenth century is process of modernization; he or she is made adequate to a constellation of new events, forces, and institutions." State biopolitical interest in abortion was part of a new constellation of events, forces, and institutions that required greater connection with women's bodies. The physician and patient were joined together through techniques of observation. Physicians' hands and eyes became the conjunction between various institutions and the womb. Crary argues that such reductive embodiment of observation into a function of the trained eye is a hallmark of the modernization of observation: "Beginning in the nineteenth century, the relation between eye and optical apparatus becomes one of metonymy: both were now contiguous instruments on the same plane of operation, with varying capabilities and features. The limits and deficiencies of one will be complemented by the capacities of the other and vice versa." Prostheses are metonymies, collapsing one body into another and yet another and in so doing, structurally articulating the space they appear to supplement. This transformation of modes of seeing directly impacted the order of culture and its ability to defend itself from internal sources of degeneration. It enabled the better incorporation of individuals into the collective project of "how to live": "at stake is how the human subject, through knowledge of the body and its modes of functioning, was made compatible with new arrangements of power: the body as worker, student, consumer, patient, criminal."[4]

In obstetrics and gynecology, this conjunction of patients' and physicians' bodies was accomplished by examination rituals that had supplanted patient testimony. These were gradually codified into palpation, taxis per vaginum or rectum, and specular application. In 1839, when William Jones "gave the first detailed description of the present day vaginal examination," the speculum was beginning to vie for diagnostic dominance. By mid-century, Jones's method was extremely common, although controversial, and by the end of the century it was doctrine. It was a method organized around the speculum as the final and most authoritative reading of the patient. Accordingly, there was heated debate over just what touch could indicate compared with what vision could indicate, and whether one could perceive accurately solely by touch.[5] In both cases, the female body posed problems because of its "deceptiveness," raising questions about how best to execute physical diagnosis.

Other senses were discussed in the early part of the century, but they were deemed less amenable than sight and touch to the growing emphasis on a visual-literate medicine. Smell, if considered at all, was considered too difficult to capture in language and, therefore, less helpful "because," remarked John Lever, "I am unable to describe the variety of scents attendant upon the several uterine diseases accompanied with morbid secretions." Hearing was much more "literary" and was widely praised for its efficacy in diagnosing thoracic maladies. In obstetrics and gynecology, auscultation of a heartbeat was taken as the only definitive proof that a fetus was alive. Given the symptoms of reproductive illnesses, however, hearing was of limited use beyond the determination of pregnancy and was of little use in doctoring abortions. Touch and sight were the most amenable senses. In fact, for centuries, "from Descartes to Berkeley to Diderot," sight had been explained analogically through touch.[6] During the eighteenth century, sight had become distinct from touch, smell, taste, and hearing, as observers of various stripes debated the relative merits of one sense over another. The senses were organized into new perceptual arrays with vision holding the principal position. In medicine, optics were surrounded and supplemented by the other senses because the physician's gaze had to do more than simply capture the appearance of the body's surface. According to Foucault, the gaze "had *to map a volume*; it deal[t] with the complexity of spatial data which for the first time in medicine [was] three-dimensional. Whereas clinical experience implied the constitution of *a mixed web of the visible and the readable*, the new semiology require[d] a sort of *sensorial triangulation* . . . the ear and touch [were] added to sight." To make the interior of the body and its various layers visible, the eye required a sense of touch and hearing, and obstetrics and gynecology were no exception. Whether perceived through the retina or the epidermis, these senses were converted to visual symbols as the body became language. Although opposition built on moral grounds, touch did not escape a system of visual representation; it simply achieved it though the fingertips. As Heidi J. Nast and Audrey Kobayashi state, "[i]nteriority and exteriority, then, are complexly refracted across social fields and change over time and in direction."[7]

The distinctions between touch and sight matter when considering the ways in which physicians employed and extended their senses. The womb encompassed a tricky, deceptive set of organs for early physicians, particularly regarding abortion. Even though doctors felt the patient's testimony was not to be believed, many, like Storer, felt the physician's interpretation of the body also was suspect. Anthony Todd Thomson, in his lectures pertaining to indicators of abortion in the *Northern Lancet*, was concerned about the difficulty of relying on bodily signs when determining whether an abortion had occurred and how. Similarly, Simpson thought female generative organs "very apt to deceive and mask the original and primary disease." Alfred Meadows explained the typical rationale for deception, stating "that a thorough sympathy both through the vascular and nervous system is established between [reproductive organs], the effect of which is, that . . . the specialty of the ovary is apt to be somewhat masked." Systemic connections between organs make an organ's function (in this case, the ovary) difficult to discern. Even in cases when a woman had died and been dissected, it was difficult to determine if she had aborted. Early pregnancies, because the fetus is so small and the woman's body is still so close to a nonpregnant state, gave few indicators of abortion to doctors. On the other hand, death during late pregnancy was confusing to the physician because signs of abortion paralleled those of parturition.[8] As Thomson's descriptions of the fetus and reproductive organs indicate, the answer was to habituate the senses through ever greater exposure thereby allowing greater precision in determining criminality. The answer was to parse the body into ever finer elements, chasing the horizon of exhaustive description. Within male dominant norms of early medical practice, physiology, no matter how deceptive, had supplanted the woman's testimony as the language of medical confession.

To achieve the precision physicians needed to authoritatively mimic the body in text, the hand and the eye of the physician had to be extended. The hand, although it provided a wealth of sensory data, was not always up to the task of unmasking the subterfuges arising from the confusing "sympathies" between reproductive organs. Ideally, the hand, with its remarkable sensitivity, became an exquisite sounding device as it entered the patient. Noticing each bump, each texture, measuring shape, position, and weight, digital exploration marked dimension and inner volume in the density of a woman's body. Similarly, palpation could sound inner density and became a standard procedure for tactile examination. Necessarily, the physician's touch inverted that inner space through the tip of a finger by bringing it into the outer world, opacity into structure. Great skill was required for such a deft chiasmus. Churchill admitted, "it is very true that a delicate sense of touch, and much experience, is necessary to the attainment of this degree of perfection; but it is equally certain, that perseverance in availing ourselves of every opportunity (both of the living and the dead body) will ultimately be crowned with success." In an effort to aid that training and normalize the sense of touch, Marion Sims provided a lengthy list of questions the physician should ask of the fingertips in his *Clinical Notes*. "As the finger passes, let it ascertain if there is anything abnormal about the ostium vaginæ. Is it contracted, rigid? Is the hymen present or absent? Is it irritable or tender? Then as to the vagina: Does it dip down towards the coccyx? Does it run more in the direction of the axis of the pelvis? Is it of normal temperature? Is it short? Is it deep? Is it narrow? Is it capacious?" The list continues, a text that falls between perception and language attempting to bridge the two.[9]

An ideal faculty was not always possible, even for a gifted and experienced physician, and the sound was developed to extend the hand's capacities. Three practitioners, P. C. Huguier and James Simpson in 1843, F. A. Kiwisch in 1845, "independently devised new sounds and forced their use upon the profession. All these were slender straight rods, but later they became curved." There were many different varieties, some longer, some shorter, many flexible. Simpson's sound, perhaps the most famous, was made with "a flat handle, to facilitate its manipulation; and terminates at its other extremity in a rounded knob or bulb, to prevent injury to the uterine textures" (Fig. 5.1). Many opposed the use of the sound because it took care to use properly and to avoid injury to the patient. For example, Theodore Gaillard Thomas described how to use a flexible sound in 1872:

Figure 5.1. James Simpson's sound. From the *Obstetric Memoirs and Contributions of James Y. Simpson, M.D., F.R.S.E.*

> The examiner then takes the probe, and with his fingers gives it the exact curve which he supposes the uterine canal to have and gently endeavors to pass it. Should he fail he withdraws the instrument, alters the curve slightly, and make other attempts until he succeeds, which will be very soon if has used this method so often as to have given himself experience. Every effort at introduction is made cautiously as if the probe were passing into the larynx instead of the womb, and no force whatever is exerted. Success is attained by properlly [*sic*] curving the probe, and by that alone.[10]

The introduction of a sound expanded tactility by allowing access to more remote parts of the body, as Simpson elaborated: "we can in succession bring within the range of tactile investigation different parts of this external surface and parietes, that are generally considered to be entirely beyond our reach." Nevertheless, the sound was not a suitable replacement to the increasingly popular speculum, as Sims indicated: "I should not omit to say that the mere touch by the vagina is not alone sufficient." John Balbirnie held a similar position, arguing that "the mere sense of touch will often afford but very insufficient and very imperfect notions, if the sense of *sight* be not had recourse to, to rectify its errors, and complete the diagnostic."[11]

The eye of the doctor, like that of the scientist, came to be an almost sacred organ that mediated the hidden world of nature's base matter with that of God. The moral weight invested in healing came to rest on the ability to diagnose a case properly. In turn, the keen vision of the healer, or the "lynx eye" as William Jones called it, became the key to the profession:

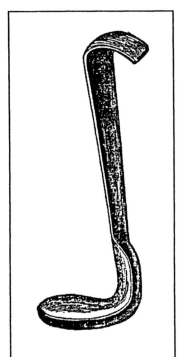

In the post-mortem examination, the eye is the organ by which is principally determined the nature of the disease which may have preceded, or produced dissolution; the eye is the organ which affords the clearest and most important indications, in every disease which can come within its scope in the living subject;— *the lynx eye it is which constitutes the great accomplishment of the physician*; and without an eye he would rarely be consulted even by the public, much less by his professional brethren. . . . Why then should we banish so important an organ as the eye from our service, or raise such an outcry against its assistance by the speculum?[12]

Historically, the trope of dissection was securely attached to vision during the Enlightenment. The eye, like the knife or the caustic with which Storer compared vision, peeled away the body. Whereas touch inverted space through a single point, vision completely turned the body inside out, making a hidden interior into a topographic map.

The speculum was believed by many to have ushered in a revolution in reproductive medicine: "an entire new face has been given

Figure 5.2. J. Marion Sims' "duck-billed" speculum. From his *Clinical Notes on Uterine Surgery*.

to the science: a new era has been created in its history; a new field of pathology altogether has been exposed to our view; lesions have been discovered that were formerly unsuspected; and efficacious modes of treatment had recourse to, formerly impracticable. These diseases have been in consequence all better analysed." Sims, whose speculum was one of the most popular of the century until the advent of T. W. Graves "combination" speculum in 1878, argued that visual examination was the most natural method: "many persons who have witnessed the use of my speculum, doubt the correctness of my explanation of its rationale as given above. But let such experiment for themselves, and give us a rationale more in accordance with the laws of natural philosophy, if they have one" (Fig. 5.2). Balbirnie, calling himself *the apostle of the speculum*," wrote: "the speculum we maintain, is for the diseases of the womb, precisely what the stethoscope is for the diseases of the chest. Without either, there is no accurate diagnostic. . . . Without these indispensable lights, we are often forced to grope entirely and literally in the dark." Gardner's comparison of the speculum to a telescope analyzing the Milky Way is equally telling. Even Churchill, a great believer in the accuracy of touch, felt that the speculum enabled perceptual options not available to touch. Little wonder that Tilt marked the beginning of gynecology with the reintroduction of the speculum by Récamier or that scores of modified specula appeared during the century. In all, Ricci found over two hundred versions of specula in the nineteenth century.[13]

The association of the speculum with the physician's eye was intense. Fervent advocates argued that no examination was complete until the speculum was used. In apostolic fashion, Balbirnie wrote: "The practitioner is not competent to give advice on the disease of the womb particularly, nor to undertake their treatment, till, by a speculum-examination, he has fully satisfied himself of the pathological condition of the organ he has to do with." The consequence of foregoing vision was death: "Without that, we expose ourselves to the most fatal errors." Visual acuity was actualized and reached its potential with the speculum. "The organs of vision afford us no small assistance in the detection and discrimination of uterine diseases . . . But the eye of the obstetric physician is more especially exercised in the employment of the speculum vaginæ."[14] As part of the transformation of vision in modernity, the speculum should not be neglected next to the stereoscope, kaleidoscope, and the photograph. It marked a radical gender break in the field of vision by opening the living female body, heretofore highly protected from view, to the eye of the expert.

Through the combination of touch and sight, sometimes more one than the other or in concert, the body might be made visible in text. Generally, the speculum required fair hand-eye coordination to be employed painlessly and with appropriate delicacy. Even after being introduced, coordinating the expansion and securing of the speculum required careful movements to keep the instrument in place, each speculum having different mechanisms for use. Further, a clear visual space opened greater opportunities for the use of touch via the sound. In fact, the sound was as much a tool for use after the introduction of the speculum as before. For example, discussing Smith's double speculum, the editors of the *American*

Journal of Obstetrics observed that "the passage of the uterine sound is rendered much easier than with the speculum of ordinary length, the uterus not being forced upward and backward and being allowed more of its natural mobility."[15]

Together, these two senses enabled the truths of the female body to become visible and legible in the indelible memory of medical texts. In the case of instrumental abortions, physicians searched for "wounds that had been inflicted upon the body" of the fetus such as puncture wounds to "the temples, the internal canthus of the eyes, and other parts," although this was much easier once the fetus was expelled. Also, they looked for punctures and scars from needles, sounds, and wires introduced into the uterus. More discreet features also were important, especially the appearance and feel of the womb as effected by chemical and herbal abortifacients. However, to be able to recognize features, either subtle *or* gross, knowledge of abortion was interwoven necessarily in obstetric and gynecologic practice as a whole, as I indicated in the last chapter. The pathological is merely an extreme of the normal and, thus, requires extensive mapping of the normal body to be recognizable to a trained observer. For example, menstrual blood and blood from an abortion differ in character, but only one trained to see the norm might notice the difference. Marking criminal abortions as separate from spontaneous abortions or

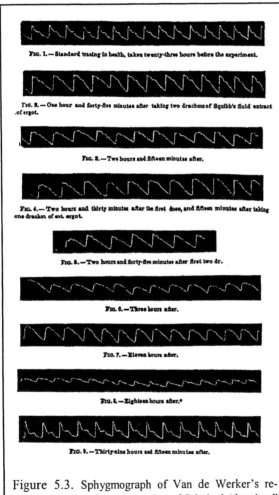

Fig. 1.—Standard tracing in health, taken twenty-three hours before the experiment.

Fig. 2.—One hour and forty-five minutes after taking two drachms of Squibb's fluid extract of ergot.

Fig. 3.—Two hours and fifteen minutes after.

Fig. 4.—Two hours and thirty minutes after the first dose, and fifteen minutes after taking one drachm of ext. ergot.

Fig. 5.—Two hours and forty-five minutes after first two dr.

Fig. 6.—Three hours after.

Fig. 7.—Eleven hours after.

Fig. 8.—Eighteen hours after.*

Fig. 9.—Thirty-nine hours and fifteen minutes after.

Figure 5.3. Sphygmograph of Van de Werker's response to ergot. From "Detection of Criminal Abortion."

other reproductive ailments required the full range of obstetrical and gynecological knowledge, thereby making general reproductive medicine mutually constitutive with antiabortion rhetoric. Consider that in *Scott v. People*, a criminal abortion trial in Illinois, expert testimony from physicians included educating the jury from medical texts, prompting the court to rule that "where extracts from medical books are introduced in evidence, counsel may read such extracts to the jury during the argument."[16]

Abortifacients troubled the mapping process, however, because they were especially dangerous and difficult to detect as they left very little interior evidence. In a series of articles written in 1871, Ely Van de Werker wrote that "the liability of an abortion induced medically to terminate fatally is largely in excess of the instrumental abortion" and that "the fœticidal drug forms the domestic expedient of the woman in difficulties. It is safe to say that every woman, married or single, when she suspects herself pregnant, resorts to the free use of drugs before she applies to the professed abortionist." These observations are consistent with Mohr's overview of abortion practice of the time.[17] Van de Werker focused on "the pharmacodynamics of the drug employed" to map the signs present on the exterior of the body. He looked at causation through time for the most common abortifacients (ergot, cotton root, savine, oil of tansy, and aloes) and any "peculiarity in the action of the exciting cause," such as physical responses of heart rate, temperature, pupil dilation, the smell of the particular drug, and characteristic "neuralgic" pain which was common to "ergotism" but not typical to a spontaneous abortion. To make his argument more believable, he tried these drugs on himself or a dog to observe the reaction and traced his own pulse at intervals up to a day and half after dosing himself. With his "sphygmograph," which measured heart rate, he visually represented characteristically irregular heart rates of various drugs, capturing the pulse in imagery: "When we take into consideration the marked power of ergot over the heart and its persistence of effects, we have in this instrument an unerring means for the detection of ergotism. *The pulse-tracing after ergot is so marked that when the sphygmographic pulse-wave is seen, it is simply a question of some grave pathological condition, or of ergotism*" (Fig. 5.3).[18] As with the interior of the body, the blood's pulse was moved into the visual-literate realm so as to speak of the body's normality and criminality.

Acts of medical perception articulated a bifurcation of the "seen" and the "said" that was treated as a redundancy: what was said was identical to was seen. To simply look at the body was not communicative, one had to look at it a certain way for believable bodies and discourses on life and abortion to become intelligible. Performatively, the female body and the medical texts that doubled it were coextensive effects of medical practices. Donna Haraway has remarked, "[t]here are all kinds of nonhumans with whom we are woven together," to which I would add "and through which we are woven to each other."[19] Those nonhumans include the texts and tools of medicine as well as the institutions of medicine, law, and family. For the prosthetic relations between body, text, materia medica, and institutions to hold, for modern body criticism to retain it validity and believability, both physicians and patients had to participate in normalized rituals of exposure.

The Observer Objectified

Antiabortion physicians needed to be both *disciplining* and *disciplined.* In addition to the fears of women turning to circles of friends or irregulars to abort, there was a growing realization that some regulars offered abortion services despite the AMA's position. In the early days of the official campaign, few would admit in print that regulars might be abortionists. For example, one anonymous practitioner, a certain "B.," questioned the conclusions of Storer's 1857 report on abortion and intimated that some regulars were abortionists. "B." was rebuked with vitriol, one author writing "we should be not a little, and most disagreeably surprised, did we think there was even *one,* in the profession or out of it, who could for a moment imagine that any honorable physician panders, ever so slightly, or even 'tacitly,' to the procurement of criminal abortion." However, it became conventional wisdom that a few quacks within the ranks were conducting abortions with full intent, whereas many others did so out of ignorance: "We have referred to an apparent disregard of foetal life, obtaining in the medical profession, as a prominent cause of the prevalence of criminal abortion."[20]

Physicians were exhorted to expose their unethical peers and make abortion visible to one another by discoursing about their observations. Asa T. Newhall, who was known as the "Lynn Abortionist," was expelled from the Massachusetts Medical Society and drew forth a call for purification from the editors of *Journal of the Gynæcological Society of Boston*:

> [H]is expulsion has purged our ranks of one dishonorable name. Are there any others? Let us look well to it! A ball has been set in motion which should not cease rolling; a movement has been inaugurated which should not be arrested until it has overthrown the grim Moloch to whom our children are being yearly sacrificed in numbers that would seem incredible to one not familiar with the statistics of the abominable rite.

For those who were "innocent abettors" in the crime, it fell to medical authors to educate them. "In view of the alarming extent of the evil, and the inefficiency of legal enactments, may not able tongues and able pens interest and instruct at least the medical philosopher; or has enough been said and written upon the subject?" Disciplined physicians would produce knowledge to discipline others. The following passage from an editorial is an excellent illustration of this point as it brings together the moral imperative of procreative sexuality, its implicit call for regulation, and the internalization of vigilance required by physicians accepting that imperative:

> With regard to the proposed remedies for this evil, we confess we have little con-
> fidence in mere legislative enactments. . . . It is rather to the medical profession,
> and to those more immediately entrusted with the morals of the community, that
> we are chiefly to look for the true remedy. The physician may do much by warn-
> ing his [*sic*] patients against the dangers and guilt of this awful crime, and using
> the "greater vigilance lest he become its innocent and unintentional abettor."

The disciplined doctor should be watched and watchful, in other words.[21]

Physicians, often peripatetic and trained in varied and inconsistent ways, were difficult to regulate in a dispersed system. The primary answer to this co-nundrum was to attempt to habituate or normalize the perceptions of physicians. In the medicine of the AMA, the perceptive power of the physician was what distinguished a regular from a quack. Meigs, while discussing the requisite qualities to be a physician in his *Females and Their Diseases,* argued that the faculties of perception were of prime importance:

> I think that, in order to be a physician, one ought to enjoy strong perceptive fac-
> ulties; he should be able to make nice discriminations; quickly perceiving the
> slightest shades of difference in all material forms, superficies, colours, weights,
> and resistance. The faculty of judging between the relations and differences of
> things should be of the primest quality; not sudden, hasty, and impatient in its
> operations, but slow, dispassionate, and attentive.

Expounding on this, Meigs related the morality and knowledge of the doctor to the prevention of deception. The doctor should not stray, "his mind should not deceive itself, and his heart should not suffer itself to be deceived and misled, by any earthly temptation, from the narrow and rugged way of duty and conscientiousness." Further, complete knowledge was necessary to perceive accurately: "Particularly should he be fully informed as to the nature of the Life-force, as displayed in the various tissues and organs of any animal economy . . . so thoroughly learned in medicine that he can detect the lesion of structure or function wherever it may hide."[22] The foundation of the physician's skill was true, morally unquestionable observation.

To regulate a decentralized medical practice required each to touch as others touched, to view as others viewed. Here, the vernacular reference to the "regular physician" is telling. Irregulars were those who perceived incorrectly or in ignorance. For example, in *Criminal Abortion*, Storer argued that the final determinant of the propriety of an abortion was in accordance with standard rules and in confirmation with another physician. "It will be evident that the plea of necessity can be made by none but a medical man. We shall show that cases where abortion is legitimated by the rules of science are extremely few, and that for safety's sake their applicability should in no instance be allowed to rest upon a single opinion." Antiabortion statutes throughout the nation required a second opinion to authorize an abortion, incorporating a mechanism of self-discipline to medical practice.[23]

Statutes requiring confirmation were only one attempt to regulate perceptions, however. Historically, the truthful observer of the Enlightenment became
autonomous through a normalized *objectivity* in the 1800s. The transformation of
observers' field of vision that Crary describes occurred between 1820 and 1840
as function of modern systems of representation and visualization. "A more
adaptable, autonomous, and productive observer was needed in both discourse
and practice—to conform to new functions of the body and to a vast proliferation
of indifferent and convertible signs and images. Modernization effected a
deterritorialization and a revaluation of vision." Prior to this transformation, authoritative vision was tethered to the metaphor of the camera obscura, a device
that produced images by controlling the passage of light into a dark, enclosed
space. It was not so much the apparatus itself that dominated understandings of
optics, as it was the metaphor of a geometrically coordinated vision regulated by
a stationary device. The eye itself did not control vision. "One feature of modernization in the nineteenth century was the 'uprooting' of vision from the more in-
flexible representational system of the camera obscura." Influenced by Bichat's
anatomy of bodily systems, vision was embodied in organs as theories of optics
passed from external devices to internal physiology. Ocular movement, retinal
after-images, peripheral and binocular vision, and the blind spot were all measured and quantified within a few short years as researchers began to rationalize
human vision. The result was that the observer, not a device, was now the apparatus. As with the camera obscura, the significance of the paradigm shift in optics
was not so much that vision became technically quantifiable, although that has
had profound consequences in science, as that the location shifted. Vision had
moved wholly within the human body and was a focus of regimentations within
modern systems of bodily discipline.[24]

The autonomy of the embodied observer allowed physicians to accommodate
the often domestic locale of his or her practice and still exercise some level of
coordinated observation. In particular, it removed the apparent connection between the mode of observation and the reading of the patient's condition. Lacking
an explicit structure that positioned the observer in relation to the body, the character of the physician's observations were deemed natural and not the result of an
observational device. "The autonomy of the eye suspends the body's complicities
with the text; it unmoors it from the scriptural place" thereby adding to the realism of the physician's observation—bodily knowledge seemed to emanate wholly
from the corpus because the observer was uncommitted to any particular body
through a device, free to roam from body to body. Thus, perception acquired a
new ideological punctuation in the appearance of a *free relation between perception and text*: what crossed the field of vision, and thus doubled in the field of
discourse, was not constituted by any prior commitments of the eye. Without a
device controlling vision, observation just "was." Extending Crary's thesis specifically to the nineteenth-century United States, Burbick analyzes the emergence of
the autonomous observer in moral, natural scientific, and popular contexts, such

as Ralph Waldo Emerson's musing on a "transparent eye-ball," which he imagined as spiritually restorative, or Oliver Wendell Holmes' fascination with the stereoscope.[25]

This notion of a free relation between "seen" and "said" supported objectivity by suppressing subjectivity in the dual act of examining and archiving. The regulation of the observer was actualized though a mechanistic perception in which "objectivity is related to subjectivity as wax to seal, as hollow imprint to the bolder and more solid features of subjectivity." Put differently, the idiosyncratic tactile and optical acumen of each physician was suppressed and normalized into a regular pattern. The body-machine of the physician was, in part, embodied as a perceptual device. This allowed coordination of physicians in two ways. First, it enabled the training necessary to habituate the senses to a new form of corporeal "reading." Doctors trained themselves to differentiate signs of abortions, labeling some criminal and others natural. In Thomson's lectures on the medico-legal aspects of reproduction, for example, he spent many pages detailing the nuances in texture, color, size, and weight of the fetus and of the womb at various stages of pregnancy in an effort to demarcate an illegal expulsion of the ovum from a legal one. Similarly, antiabortionists continually catalogued the sensate appearance of suspicious abortions so that the profession might not innocently abet the "crime." In this way, each physician's hands and eyes gradually became interchangeable with those of others. This replicable, interchangeable perception enabled physicians to coordinate with each other, and with other social institutions as the standardization of knowledge allowed medical expertise to traffic in other forums, such as the courts. Crary holds that "[t]he perceiver here becomes a neutral conduit, one kind of relay among others allowing optimum conditions of circulation and exchangeability, whether it be of commodities, energy, capital, images, or information."[26] The precondition for a mobile, diffuse system of medical documentation was a uniformity of perception across the bodies of physicians.

Such perceptual uniformity contributed to physicians becoming "modest witnesses" to truth and thus, "trustworthy agents" of truth telling. Well before the 1800s, suppression of idiosyncrasy in perception and ostentation in writing had become a form of gentlemanly modesty and a sign of credibility in science. In *Leviathan and the Air-Pump*, Steven Shapin and Simon Schaffer argue that Robert Boyle's experiments on the air-pump and his debates over proof with Thomas Hobbes in the 1650s and 1660s mark a paradigm shift in the scientific culture of objectivity. The natural philosopher's practices had to evince masculinized moral restraint to signify the validity of one's claims: "A man whose narratives could be credited as mirrors of reality was a *modest man*; his reports ought to make that modesty visible." U.S. physicians appropriated those conventions and, although experimental demonstration was still overwhelmed by the mechanistic rationalism of early medical theories, the morality of restraint through habituation of perception did become a marker of believability. In their methods of examining and recording cases, physicians created a self-effacing presence whose disciplined modesty was the predicate to uniformity of practice, and thus to valid documentation of sexual truth. More like the gentlemanly modesty of the idealized seventeenth-century natural philosopher than the depersonalized modesty of the twentieth-century scientific technician, nineteenth-century regulars cultivated the identity of a Christian physician who, ostensibly, enacted a restrained "virtue that guarantees that the modest witness is the legitimate and authorized ventriloquist of the object world, adding nothing from his mere opinions, his biasing embodiment."[27]

Second, the normalizing of physicians' perceptions enabled the documentation of a consistent bodily memory. The corporeal testimonies of thousands of women amassed a record of a racial destiny and biological threat in a hypomnesic memoir of abortions. Normalization enabled a "a vivid, indelible, memory" to be archived from many physicians, each of whom might have only a limited or partial experience with abortion. Shapin and Schaffer refer to this as a literary technology of witnessing, whereby the accounts of witnesses to truths can multiply their perceptions, virtually extending the numbers of witnesses to a readership. Literate witnessing, wherein spectacle is doubled in speech and circulated, becomes a mnemonic system such that the collective act of witnessing truths is an elaborate practice of collective memory work. The whole of the truth of life was housed in an archive that exceeded any single physician's knowledge. Taken as a whole, the austere, laconic imagery and language of biomedicine mimed nature so as to act as "a standing reproach to all who would, whether 'by their error or bad faith,' twist a fact to fit a theory." The memory of abortion, catalogued through a modest objectivism, functioned as a "sentinel" for culture, a reminder of duties greater than middle- and upper-class reproductive fashions.[28] The forensic exegesis of individual bodies was added to the pastiche of a racialized, genealogical memory because each individual case could be treated as objectively interchangeable and cumulative with others.

Physicians' perceptual practices brought with them a problem, however. The medical scene played out in the homes of patients was in conflict with norms of delicacy between the genders. The physical exam was literally obscene in its unobstructed intimacy.[29] The mobility of the healer enabled physicians some measure of access to the middle and upper classes, but effective surveillance depended "on a transformation of the social relationships that" connect the perceiver and the perceived. A new sexual politics had to be established for the documentation of the health of the bourgeois body to proceed. This involved reconciling the highly charged taboos of Victorian culture and the intrusiveness of repeated vaginal contact by, and exposure to, a man. Unlike physical experiment wherein modest witnessing involves a suppression of style and idiosyncracy, in early obstetric and gynecologic practice accurate witnessing involved sexual modesty as well. Meigs characterized the moral conflict as one of advanced civility and retrograde healthcare: "I say it is evidence of the dominion of a fine morality in our society; but nevertheless, it is true that a greater candor on the part of the patient, and a more resolute and careful inquiry on that of the practitioner, would scarcely fail to bring to light, in their early stages, the curable maladies, which, by faults on both sides, are now misunderstood and incurable." Regular physicians had to resolve the apparent impasse between modesty and health posed by reproductive medicine. The observer was to be ubiquitous, and even self-surveilling in his disciplined perceptions, and yet achieve a kind of "silence," meaning that the surveillance passed unobtrusively.[30] The challenge for male physicians was to establish a self-effacing presence *while* in intimate contact with women.

In the first half of the century, self-effacement seemed impossible. Critics of physical diagnosis were loudly opposed to such immorality. A typical objection to "Man Midwifery," as it was called then, was that men were prurient and not to be trusted; only female physicians could be entrusted with the care of female complaints. As a counterpart to the ideal of true womanhood, men were deemed inherently lascivious. Further, the supposedly passive and only periodically aroused female was considered sexually suspect as well. Caroline H. Dall, friend to H. R. Storer and moralist, claimed that "the presence of a physician in the chamber of 'even the purest' invalid female, must necessarily induce in that female's mind thoughts and longings of an improper kind."[31]

As Man Midwifery became obstetrics and gynecology, the debate over physical examination as the mode of perception became equally noisy. Many, especially in obstetrics, felt that touch alone was sufficient and less prurient than visual diagnosis. In contradistinction to French practice, where visual exposure for childbirth was more common, U.S. and English obstetricians prided themselves on minimal exposure, typically conducting examinations under the delicacy of a sheet or cloth and even keeping direct eye contact with the patient while touching her in order to assure absolute modesty of the gaze (Fig. 5.4). However, gynecologists more commonly used the speculum for cases of all kinds, including abortion, setting off a firestorm of moral outrage inside and outside the profession. In a more moderate tone compared with some of his contemporaries, Fleetwood Churchill felt that "there are, however, very considerable difficulties in the way of [the

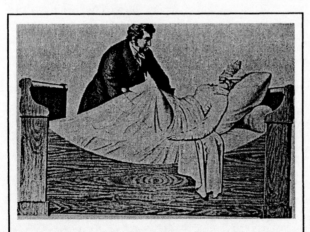

Figure 5.4. Tactile examination from J. P. Maygrier, *Nouvelles Dèmonstrations d'Accouchemens*.

speculum's] use becoming common. It requires greater exposure, and is more offensive to feminine delicacy than examination by the finger. In some cases, it is much more painful."[32]

Others were less diplomatic. Thomas Litchfield claimed, among other things, that the speculum was not only indecent, but also unnatural and that it harmed the budding relationship between the bourgeois matron and the regular ob/gyn:

> There is a perfect *furor* for its filthy and indecent application, though I confess there are many cases where it may be very serviceable in detecting inward mischief. . . . The fast hold our noble science yet has of the middle and thoughtful classes renders it highly necessary that we practice our art with decent propriety . . . depend upon it, the virtuous and delicate sensibilities once shocked by the medical attendant, he may find his position as the medical adviser of the family circle not so firm as previously. . . . neither can I believe organs so important for the furtherance of the great aim of creation can be so often diseased as to render personal examinations so generally made as they are in this our present day.

As an economic matter, the speculum was offensive to a clientele that the newly formed AMA desperately wanted to court, but this was only part of the risk. Specular examination could also harm the already delicate morality of women. Marshall Hall claimed a cumulative deterioration in the purity of women through specular intrusion:

> But, if there be no exposure of the person, and if the examination of the rectum be frequently made, is there, at first, no wounding of the feelings, and is there, afterwards, no deterioration and blunting of those feelings, by the repeated daily or weekly use of the speculum vaginæ in the virgin, and the very young, even amongst the married! I loudly proclaim that there is such deterioration, and that the female who had been subjected to such treatment is not the same person in delicacy and purity that she was before.[33]

Given the duality of morality and monstrosity invested in women's bodies, to harm female purity was to risk great evil.

In a single maneuver, the self-discipline that had been advocated to solve the logistical troubles of mobile observation and free the relation of observer and observed was extended to remedy the moral contradictions such observation created in reproductive medicine. Lorraine Daston and Peter Galison contend objectivity was "a form of self-control at once moral and natural-philosophical. . . . What began as a policing of others now broadened into a moral injunction for the scientists, directed both at others *and* reflexively at themselves." Physicians adopted the mantle of "heroic self-discipline" of scientific objectivity to argue that they could overcome what one physician termed the "disease of the doctor" and should be trusted to conduct examinations. By doing so, they balanced both sides of the contradiction, the morality of civilized women and the ritualized exposure necessary to science, in an attempt to preserve both. As Balbirnie wrote in advocacy of the speculum, "we may be said to opening a crusade against all the characteristic and praiseworthy delicacy of the sex. God forbid! No man can more highly appreciate than we do, this most amiable attribute of womankind. But there is moderation in everything." Regulars attempted to create a self-effacing presence within the very rituals of examination, performing their identity as modest witness under the most difficult circumstances.[34]

During specular examination, physicians were to act with conspicuous constraint, thus displaying the moral shield of their scientific objectivity against the necessarily indelicate matters in which they were engaged. William Jones wrote, "let it [specular exposure] be proposed with caution, circumspection, and delicacy; let the confidence of the patient be first gained, and then let the proper moment be taken for its employment." Through sensitive caution, a doctor might signal moral restraint. Further, to those who contended an unnatural affection grew between practitioner and patient, Jones retorted that it was a projection of their own uncontrolled libidos: "An objection to the employment of the speculum is sometimes raised by male relatives; an objection too frequently arising from their own sensuality, and from an unjustifiable want of confidence in the practitioner; but surely if a medical man be worthy of confidence in any case, he is worthy of all."[35] The morality of the male doctor is regular, as uniform as his practice. If he has the requisite self-discipline at one moment, he will have it in the next.

The most common injunction to protect delicacy and demonstrate discipline was the ritualized limitation of exposure in specular examination. The physician was literally to see nothing but the inside of the patient. Sims, in describing the use of his popular speculum, strongly advised the physician to avoid any unnecessary exposure. "I repeat, then, that we should never in our examinations allow any exposure of person, not even in hospital practice. When the touch is made, there can be none, of course, with the patient on the back and covered with a sheet. When the speculum is used, *we should see only the neck of the womb and the canal of the vagina.*" It became common practice to introduce the speculum with the aid of touch and under cover and only then to expose the genitals, as is illustrated by the image of a specular exam from Gardner's treatise on sterility (see Fig. 3.1). The surface of the patient was to remain unseen, even though for many another procedure a woman would be disrobed. Through the ritualized preservation of the physical mystery of the female body, of denying and therefore insisting upon its presence, the delicate doctor became self-effacing. Demanding a complete intimacy to view the reproductive organs, yet habitually maintaining sensual distance, the contradictions that riddled the vaginal exam remained morally irreconcilable, but rhetorically powerful. The precarious balance between health and modesty, at once synonymous and in opposition, created an opportunity for the physician to secure a much sought after clientele, as Balbirnie observed: "But we are persuaded the difficulties on this score have been magnified by practitioners. If the physician is firm in insisting on the necessity of such examination, and if he knows how to do his duty in this way properly, shewing a corresponding personal delicacy, and sympathy for their situation, the very pardonable scruples of the patient will give way to her good sense, and the natural timidity of the sex will yield to the sentiment of self-preservation."[36]

The Legible Patient

The rhetoric of embodying an archive involves the flesh behaving legibly. How, then, did the patient perform in relation to the physician? How was the female patient becoming a part of an archive about her biological destiny? As a choreographed ritual of investigation, archiving truth derives its power, not from other texts in endless circles of reference, but from readable bodies subject to perpetual scrutiny. It did so by placing the individual patient within a field of documentation, "a network of writing; it engage[d] them in a whole mass of documents that capture[d] and fix[ed] them." Each body was made a "case which at one and the same time constitute[d] an object for a branch of knowledge and a hold for a branch of power."[37] A particular rhetorical power of medicine is engaged when the patient or the cadaver become a "text" in a system of literacy. At mid-century, "neither the structure of the medical interview nor the form of the [medical] history had been stabilized," but the greater inclusion of bodies within medical literacy through direct examination brought with it, necessarily, a confluence of legibility and docility. As Foucault argued in *Discipline and Punish*, the modern body becomes productive through "the notion of 'docility', which joins the analysable body to the manipulable body." The disciplines by which bodily forces can be optimized and extended depends on the observation and analysis of the body's capacities within appropriate institutions. Only then can the behaviors that contribute to longevity, lethality, morality, or normativity generally be cultivated within populations. The ligature of observing bodies and bodies under observation within diverse institutional settings "outlines a meticulous meshing."[38] In medical examination, physician's hands and eyes were enmeshed with the object of observation, the female physique, to allow optimal legibility.

For two reasons, AMA physicians argued a woman could not be trusted to articulate the knowledge of her own body, and thus must enmesh herself in the system of medical literacy primarily as a patient. She already had demonstrated through increased rates of abortion that she had forgotten the cultural code, and she could not be trusted to speak for her body. Male doctors explained that female patient's testimony was insufficient for diagnosis. Of course, I would not assume that I understand a cancer that might be eating within simply because it is me that it is eating. However, in the context of a medical profession searching for status and place, women were completely detached from their own bodies in the male medical mind. They were presumed to be so thoroughly ignorant of their own bodies and so obsessed with modesty that, at best, a woman's verbal testimony would only replicate what the physician knew; at worst, it would contribute to malpractice. "But what mere random practice is that!" cried Balbirnie, arguing that the complex interactions of the uterus with other organs were only confounded "from the mere vague reports of the patient herself, whose modesty hardly dares reveal her sufferings, and who will point attention to every other quarter but the seat of the lesion?" Some called the reliance on verbal testimony "notorious," arguing that "daily experience demonstrates the futility, and in some cases the injury, arising to patients, from medicine prescribed upon such vague information." Physicians were admonished by the elders in the field, such as Simpson, to engage in greater physical contact:

> If we are to make comparisons between them, the physical symptoms, are assuredly, in most cases, by far the most valuable and trustworthy—and yet in the common course of medical practice, the testimony which they are capable of affording, is but too frequently neglected and overlooked—and the functional and much less faithful class of symptoms alone relied upon, as well in forming diagnosis, as in directing the measures of treatment.[39]

The newly embodied, modest hands and eyes of the male physician were the only faithful instruments for transcribing the body accurately.

Such insistence on the unreliability of women's testimony was contested by patients and by female physicians. Male physicians frequently commented about having arguments with female patients. Studying the rhetoric of the interview write up, marking the indications of contestation within the interview, Wells argues that "midcentury women did not simply comply with male physicians; they read medicine; they had opinions about their ailments and their treatment; they had something to say." Further, comparing the interview practices of male and female physicians, Wells demonstrates that women doctors partially resisted the model of the female body as only a corporeal text. Physicians at the Women's Medical College kept much more complete histories on each patient and provided greater, more sympathetic space to patients' voices within their records of examination. Yet, as noted previously, in the specific cases of unwanted pregnancies such sympathetic space did not translate into a more sympathetic attitude about abortion.[40]

Conceptualized as readable objects within male dominant body criticism, however, such resistance was stalwartly suppressed within rhetorically archival practices. Women's bodies primarily were brought into the network of medical literacy either as corpses or as docile patients. For centuries the legible body was the dissected cadaver, especially in the eighteenth and nineteenth centuries. An analogy between the dead body of the human and the body of the text is simple enough. However, physical diagnostics of the nineteenth century placed the living body in the same space as the corpse. Hence, Simpson's comment that diagnostics had become a necroscopic anatomy of the living wherein one attempted "to read and discover within the living body the actual morbid anatomy of the organ or organs that are affected." Jones compared the physical exam to the post-mortem, arguing that, like an autopsy, "evidence of the eye" was absolutely necessary. In many cases, cadavers were the only source physicians had regarding abortion, being called to women who had died or would soon die from a botched abortion.[41] The medical journals are filled with laconic records of a Mrs. S. or Mrs. N. whose story was converted to an autopsy report in case files or trial records. Similarly, living women under physical examination were converted to the austere testimony of somatic confessions, their verbal statements often reported with skepticism or ignored. As legible texts, the patient and the corpse were similarly constituted. It was the choice between autopsy and physical examination, death versus immodesty, that physicians offered as reason to subject oneself to a regular physicians' new methods.

To accommodate the perception of the physician during a vaginal examination the patient had to perform legibly, enacting an extreme docility that paralleled being the object of dissection. This begins, of course, with lying prone as Sims indicated: "for the digital examination, the dorsal decubitus [on her back] is preferable; but for the speculum, the left lateral semi-prone position is the best." Some physicians preferred that the patient lean, slightly flexed, for digital examination as Lever recommended: "Examination 'per vaginum' may be instituted either in the erect or recumbent position of the patient; by the former, we are more especially able to appreciate the relaxation of the uterine ligaments (from whatever cause such may have occurred)." In either case, she was to be relaxed and still so as to be optimally readable.[42] Note, I am *not* arguing physical examination is a form of symbolic death; rather, I am merely stressing the disciplined passivity one must carry out in becoming-patient.

As one might realize, the requirements for specular examination were much more detailed and required greater docility and discipline on the part of the patient. Here, Sims describes the positioning of the patient necessary for his duck-billed speculum:

> For a speculum examination the patient is to lie on the left side. The thighs are to be flexed at about right angles with the pelvis, the right being drawn up a little more than the left. The left arm is thrown behind across the back, and the chest rotated forwards, bringing the sternum very nearly in contact with the table, while the spine is fully extended, with the head resting on the left parietal bone. The head must not be flexed on the sternum nor the right shoulder elevated. Indeed, the position must simulate that on the knees as much as possible, and for this reason the patient is rolled over on the front, making it a left lateral semiprone position. The nurse or assistant standing at her back pulls up the right side of the nates with the left hand, when the surgeon introduces the speculum, elevates the perineum, and gives the instrument into the right hand of the assistant, who holds it firmly in the desired position.

She was made maximally visible with precision and care. Even so, she required an assistant to make her suitably docile. Edmond Souchon wrote of a self-retain-

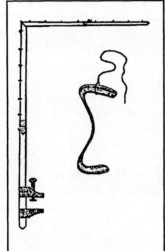

Figure 5.5. Edmond Souchon's self-retaining apparatus. From "Speculum Holder or Retainer."

ing version of Sims's speculum (Fig. 5.5), "if the patient stretches her limbs or 'draws in' and contracts the glutei muscles, we cannot conceive of any speculum that would remain in place and allow an examination. The patient will have to be replaced in proper position and the speculum reintroduced, before proceeding any further." Seeking a less cumbersome arrangement, J. C. Nott modified Sims' speculum to make it "perfectly self-retaining, without any arrangement external to the vagina" (Fig. 5.6).[43] To be legible, women needed to learn considerable restraint as patients.

However, I do not want to leave the impression that women simply lay still for medical treatments that were sometimes painful, suspect in their results, or of questionable necessity even from the lay perspective. Docility in treatment, as differentiated from diagnosis, could be induced by a number of means ranging from an assistant holding the patient, to the careful introduction of the speculum to relax the muscles, to the drugging and/or institutional commitment of a patient. As with A.G. Helmick's dosing of the anonymous slave woman, opium was often used in abortion cases to stop uterine contractions, whether the patient agreed to the treatment or not. Storer advocated quelling abortion symptoms by any means possible. Women might be remanded to lying-in institutions to ensure that their pregnancies came to term. One physician wrote that abortion could be prevented by "enjoining absence from home, or seeking an asylum in some well conducted Lying-in-Hospital."[44]

More than asking women to learn the docile regimens of being patients, or coercing them to do so, male physicians argued women were natural patients and unnatural doctors. One editorialist wrote, "The girls don't like to dissect." Against the idea that women should treat women, male doctors heterosexualized medical practice by citing the logic of complementarity. In the latter half of the nineteenth century, women pioneered allopathic medicine in greater and greater numbers. Madames Boivin and Lachapelle were well-respected gynecologists in France in the early part of the century. In England and the United States, female physicians made a presence for themselves in regular practice after Elizabeth Blackwell broke the gender barrier in 1848 when she entered the Geneva College of Medicine. The first U.S. medical school solely for women was the Female Medical School in Boston, which opened November 1, 1848. Women were admitted to medical schools or separate schools were created for them with increasing frequency as the decades progressed until, at the turn of the century, women comprised five percent of the profession. The entry of women into the profession was resisted mightily by male physicians, including on the job harassment and exclusion from medical societies.[45] The most enduring resistance, however, came in the way women were medicalized as natural patients. The male-dominated profession substantiated its objections to female practitioners primarily through biopolitics as well, further justifying the positions of women as cultural matrices and of men as their stewards.

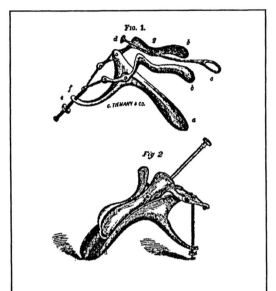

Figure 5.6. J.C. Nott's self-retaining speculum, from "On a New Duck-Bill Speculum, for Private Practice."

The belief that women disliked the realities of medical training is indicative of the justifications offered for an exclusively male profession. In the complementary logic of the Enlightenment, the cultural matrix housed in women was to be cared for, naturally and rightfully, by men. The female patient was to remain in the position of the interrogated, not the interrogator, as masculine science and feminine nature came to be antagonistic opposites in the wake of the Enlightenment. Schiebinger argues medical science established corporeally "a clear notion of causality: physical difference produced moral, and eventually social, difference."[46] The role of women's physical guardians that the AMA proudly championed was a pronounced aspect of the gendering of science. The attempt to cross the gender line was widely believed to ruin the female sex; as one commentator argued: "To initiate the mind to the ghastly mysteries of the dissecting-room and dead house, must blunt their natural refinement." Even with live subjects, the moral danger was too great for many an early physician. Referring to a clinical lecture attended by twenty women in a New York hospital, an editor wrote: "Several hundred young men were present, and he [the surgeon] thought it unfitting that the young ladies should remain. *They did not retire*, but occupied the *nearest seat*, while eighteen *male* patients were exhibited, necessarily *in a state of* NUDITY!" In Philadelphia, 1869, students from the Women's Medical College attended clinical lectures at the Pennsylvania Hospital, an event that devolved from jeering to a riot that spilled into the street. A petition subsequently was started to ban women from the lectures and eventually, in 1871, separate lectures began. "Nineteenth-century medicine depended on an economy of the visual in which women were to be seen by physicians." Naturally sick due to her moral vulnerability and habit of physical deformation, the female's healer was by rights male, as N. Williams claimed: "I had always supposed that the male sex was the legitimate and exclusive heirs [*sic*] to the 'healing art'; that its rights and obligations were emphatically and strictly our own and that we, as a sex, are better adapted to it than our fair competitors."[47]

Hence, opponents of female physicians couched their rationales in the naturalized biological destinies of the sexes. These rationales have been catalogued and critiqued elsewhere with great care. However, they have not been considered in the framework of gender difference operating within the newly emerging biopolitical paradigm of the nineteenth century. Keeping in mind the great fear for the white bourgeois body, how was the body of the physician gendered as the necessary remedy to a suicidal female organism? The same logic that placed women in a position of suicidal vulnerability was used to argue for an exclusively male custodian within reproductive medicine. The now infamous justifications, such as women's nerves being too frail to stand up to the demands of medicine, almost invariably were tied to the bodily threat posed by a loss of reproduction. More often than not, male doctors justified their sense of natural superiority by biologizing woman's inferiority. In a reflective posture, men were what women failed to be. It is important to revisit these arguments and examine how female and male physicians were embodied by the same medical practices that transformed a select group of women into unsound breeders.[48]

Three general kinds of explanations were offered by male physicians for the exclusion of women from medical practice: the natural order of complementary genders, the physical inadequacy of women, and the charlatanry of medical women. Each of these posited women as incapable of recollecting the sacred task with which their bodies were charged, with the result that their medical practice would actually worsen the biological threat to the middle and upper classes. The most general, complementarity, held that what kept civilization alive was the evolution into two distinct genders. This argument used *any* difference to ground conventional wisdom, as Williams illustrated in an assault on medical women: "had the office of the two sexes been identical, and the sphere of one the legitimate province of the other, then where would have been the necessity of any difference whatever? . . . *Marriage* is a natural and divine institution, and its duties by females incompatible with the practice of medicine." An editor of the *New Orleans Medical and Surgical Journal* expressed this fear biopolitically, claiming that transgression of this ostensibly natural boundary risked all that bourgeois society had cultivated:

> The plea of enlarging the sphere of woman's labor and promoting her independence is nothing but a subterfuge. Civilization, with its refinements and luxuries,

has multiplied the domestic duties of woman. Among uncivilized nations and in the lower grades of society, we find both sexes pursuing nearly the same avocations; while divergence of their respective spheres of action serves as an exponent of improvement in the social relations of our race, just as division of labor in the arts is inseparable from their protection.

The "race" was at risk without sexual complementarity. Rather than stealing medicine away from men, women needed men to help them through the special trials of pregnancy. "The fact is, however, that as a general rule, women in those hours of peril and suffering entailed upon them by an inscrutable Providence, feel the need of a stronger support and assistance than their own sex can afford, by a natural law, the weaker in those circumstances rely upon the stronger."[49]

Accordingly, physical difference, the second rationale, became a barrier too fragile to cross. The reproductive balance between the sexes was under too much strain, physicians argued, to allow the "New Amazons," as one observer called them, to educate themselves and risk their suspect physiology. The rigors of perception and the physical discipline necessary to sharpen one's faculties were supposedly beyond a woman's limited capacity:

> The practice of medicine is necessarily a *laborious* employment. . . . With the ease and comforts of life, or the healthful and agreeable occupation of the corporeal and mental faculties, which generally pertain to other pursuits, the medical man is comparatively a stranger. The path which he treads, although strewn with occasional flowers, is nevertheless a rugged and irregular one. The regulation of his habits, of his rest, his meals, and intercourses with others, are often circumstance over which he has little or no control. . . . if corporeal hardship and privation are the necessary consequences of the medical profession, that [*sic*] the *male* sex is better qualified in this respect to discharge its duties than the *female*.

Nor would women attempt such a rugged path, at least according to male physicians at mid-century.[50] This was disproved as women steadily entered the profession in greater numbers.

One of the classic demonstrations of the physical limitations of the female was the proposed dichotomy between her brain and her womb. Female physiology operated within a finely tuned, easily disturbed balance of forces, the greatest portion naturally being dedicated to birthing. Kathleen Hall Jamieson remarked on the constraints such a physiology presented: "The brain and the womb both required energy—so went the conventional wisdom of the day. A woman's intellectual activity cheated her uterus of the wherewithal to sustain her health and her ability to reproduce. Those who violated the natural order—by engaging in public or intellectual activities or by working in industry—supposedly paid a price." Harvard physician Edward Clarke is well known for his advocacy of this idea. Consistent with notions of moral physiology, "misuse" of the body threatened survival due to an overall degeneration of women's bodies. One editor opined:

> [T]he education of females among us is destructive to their health and happiness.
> Every effort in the school room is to cultivate their minds at the expense of their
> bodies. They consequently have a sickly life, if perchance it is not cut off in early
> girlhood; they make poor mothers, are unable to nurse their children in many
> instances, with a tendency to some of the most distress in complaints, and dis-
> ease is propagated to their children.

Henry Maudsley, a British psychiatrist, contended that "female education threatened to produce a lowering of the racial stock and even an eventual disappearance
of the species." Popular medical opinion was that too much blood to the brain left
"uteruses shriveled, their ability to conceive constricted, and, if they reproduced
at all, they risked bearing monsters."[51]

A natural reliance on wit and intuition rather than on rational intelligence was
another popular prejudice believed to naturally limit the feminine sphere of activity. In medical practice, a methodical surveyor was deemed preferable to a quick-
witted inventor. Intuition only fostered disaster by reading the patient's body too
hastily or improperly:

> Among the special qualifications of the masculine mind we place logical solid-
> ity, and a certain grasp which gives the power of surveying a wide range of
> facts, of classifying them so as to assign to each its proper place and bearing,
> and of passing upon them, as it were, judicially. The female intellect, on the
> other hand, we hold to be more suggestive, quicker and more acute in percep-
> tions, and perhaps more intuitive. . . . And in the diagnosis of a case we require
> not the sparkle of inventive wit, but the careful collection, sifting and compari-
> son of evidence indicative of the judicial mind.

Others were not so generous in assigning women wit. Were the "peculiar mental
powers" male obstetricians and gynecologists felt quite certain they possessed
shared by females? According to R. H. Whitefield, "with all due deference and
respect to the sex, we think not." The speaking eye of medicine, meditating as it
did on the transcendental hidden within the empirical, required a thoroughness
and depth beyond female capacity. As with a shriveled uterus, a woman stretching
her perceptive abilities too far only led to procreative ruin. Doctors frequently
recited horror stories of women practicing medicine, such as the supposed case of
a midwife trained at a London lying-in hospital who, "after the patient had been
delivered, dragged the womb itself out of the body and then, supposing that this
organ was something which out to be removed, *tore it away from the woman*,
causing her speedy death." Male doctors boldly claimed huge increases in the
number of live births and substantial decreases in maternal deaths, neither of
which is supported by statistics, and condemned women as medical disasters, particularly country midwives and "negresses." One fellow believed "the numerous
evils, injured mothers, protracted and loathsome diseases and even deaths, caused
by the unskillful management of ignorant women are enough of themselves to
condemn perpetually their employment."[52]

After years of women making inroads into medical practice, such arguments began to ring hollow. "What the medical societies and schools will do with their claims, is beginning to perplex the wise ones. It is not a matter to be laughed down, as readily as was at first anticipated," reflected one editor. Faced with the living proof that earlier, complacent attacks on female physicians had been wrong, male physicians turned to menstruation and pregnancy as final proofs of female physical inadequacy. Pregnancy's delicate management required a huge time investment from male doctors' standpoint, entailing by one man's estimate "a year and half or more of withdrawal from professional avocations." Menses functioned analogously, leaving women periodic invalids. Storer summed up what he considered a physical trump card:

> It is simply this, that granting that woman may have, in exceptional cases, all the energy, courage, patience, power of endurance, and opportunities for prelimi-nary instruction that are possessed by the average of medical men, she is yet physiologically unfitted, at very frequent and regular periods of her life, and whether she is married or single, for an equal or in any way commensurate exer-tion of body or mind; her mental as well as physical condition being for the time changed from what it may be at other seasons.

The menstrual economy of reproduction precluded women from medically treat-ing difficulties with reproduction. Whether because of underdeveloped organs, a lack of intellectual rigor, or the simple shackles of maternity, women's bodies were not as capable of doctoring the reproductive organs as men's bodies were.[53] Females were designed to be treated, evidently.

A third line of argument, pertaining specifically to abortion, was that women physicians were charlatans who would help one another abort in a kind of con-spiracy to harm the body politic. That they wished to subvert their maternal des-tiny by doctoring was prima facie evidence of their corruption. The very phrase "female physician" connoted "quack" in the nineteenth century and was a com-mon term used to refer to abortionists like Madame Restell. Many male doctors believed "there is an especial liability of women physicians becoming principals in that guilt." In *Criminal Abortion*, Storer argued that among the most common abetters of abortion were female friends who themselves had aborted, "perhaps endeavoring to persuade an uneasy conscience" by having others share in their guilt; nurses who might be "approached with less hesitation" than a physician; and female midwives and doctors whom he claimed kept fetuses "preserved in jars" in morbid collections.[54] Women were morally as well as physically weak and were not to have their bodies entrusted to their safe keeping. That was a man's job.

Over and over again, male physicians portrayed female physicians as sloppy butchers, conniving assassins, or fair-weather debutantes. By contrast, what made man the rightful heir of the medical arts was that he was *not* these things. If women were to live out their biological duty and remember the natural order, they could not be trusted with medicine. Any attempts by women to walk in stride with male doctors raised fears of further debilitating a weakened racial progeny. Consistent with the narrative of dangerous physical defects, the bottom line was that women killed life; they did not protect it unless held under direct male supervision. "Imagine the world with its medical cares in the hands of female physicians. Medical science, like the withering leaves of Autumn, would fade and fall into everlasting oblivion. Empiricism would stalk abroad though the earth, and disease and death, uncontrolled would have their sway." Marking the threshold of life and death, woman was depicted as a fearful reaper and man as the bulwark against her morbid forgetfulness. Positioning women physicians as bringing death and furthering race suicide was another "*tactic* in the internal fission into binary oppositions, a means of creating 'biologized' internal enemies, against whom society must defend itself."[55]

Women refuted these arguments in the latter part of the century, claiming male opposition was nothing more than outdated, uncharitable custom. In 1867, an anonymous "Female Medical Student" wrote to the *Boston Medical and Surgical Journal*, a bastion of opposition to female physicians: "Every year proves more clearly that women will study medicine, will receive qualifications to practise, and will be employed by the public. On these points the gentlemen of the medical profession have no choice whatever." Florence Nightingale contended that adequate education, both preparatory and medical, would lead to a class of women physicians from which no ailing female would turn. She supported her claims by proposing a clinical training ward specifically for thirty female midwives, including floor plans and a curricular outline. Others like Sophia Jex-Blake, a physician trained in Edinburgh, argued that medicine was an extension of the nurturing domestic sphere and rightly woman's place: "if a child falls down the stairs and is more or less seriously hurt, is it the father or the mother (where both are without medical training) who is most equal to the emergency, and who applies the needful remedies in the first instance?" Further, to refute notions of female incapacity, Jex-Blake also wrote a history of women healers from the *Iliad* through Alice Massy (the midwife to Elizabeth of York), to Anna Mazzaloni (a professor at Bologna), to contemporaries such as Mary Putnam Jacobi.[56] Beyond the modes of explicit contention, resistance to male dominance within medicine also was couched in what Wells calls "invisible writing." One form, an institutionalized "cross-dressing," is exemplified by Ann Preston, dean of the Women's Medical College, who enacted a wholesale congruence with masculine professional norms while expanding women's presence in medicine. The other form, a kind of parodic "travesty" of gender, is exemplified by Hannah Longshore, who appropriated masculine discursive forms and then "offered them as conventional performances," while challenging the legitimacy of male medical dominance.[57]

As far as women physicians operating in a kind of conspiracy to abort and subvert the growth of scientific medicine, male physicians were nothing if not a little hysterical. Women physicians contributed substantially to early scientific medicine. The subversive power of these modes of resistance (direct argument, subtle mimesis, and gender parody) was directed at misogyny and exclusivity of early medicine in an effort to make science more "porous and accessible." The inequality of medical institutions was subverted, not the basic modes of perception and practice. Through comparison of the male-run Boston Lying-In Hospital with the female-run New England Hospital, Morantz-Sanchez confirmed what reviews of the early medical literature indicate: "although women physicians had a greater awareness and sensitivity to women's issues than men, their overall medical opinions tended to reflect professional and scientific trends and their divergences among themselves often appeared to be similar to those of male doctors." Amid the rebuttals, performative appropriations, and demonstrated successes, women practitioners did not undercut the scriptural system through which male physicians articulated the reproductive body, nor largely the racial project that supported it. Attacking the misogyny of male doctors overtly and covertly did not weaken the biopolitical commitments of a bourgeois body politic. Alice Stockham, Elizabeth Blackwell, Annetta Kratz, Charlotte Whitehead Ross, Lydia Hunt, and many others opposed abortion, although many favored voluntary motherhood. At the turn of the century, Jennie Oreman expressed the era's biopolitics regarding abortion as clearly as anyone, reiterating the education of desire toward how to live and the motif of anamnesis: "Women, ignorant of the right way to live resort to different means of procuring criminal abortion. in [*sic*] order to escape the responsibilities and duties of maternity."[58]

The apparent opposition to abortion by physicians in favor of voluntary motherhood underscores the importance of abortion as a unique aspect of biopower that must be studied in its specificity and not grouped with birth control unless historical reasons so warrant. How abortion rhetorically shifts in and out of configurations of acceptable fertility management is a singularly important indicator of the interests of biopower within a given historical moment. The point of resistance marshaled by these medical pioneers was *within* a rhetoric that constructed them as needy machines and men as wise mechanics. In effect, by demonstrating they were not prone to derangement, weak, or sympathetic to abortion, women physicians argued that, as professionals, they were not biological enemies of the state. Although some favored fertility control, women physicians largely concurred with the men that abortion was a threat to white civilized society.

Chapter Six
Prenatal Space

The past is reconstructed from a moment in the present to convince ourselves of something we wish to be or have been. The objects of memory, then, become a *spatial annex* to the mental images, that voluntarily or involuntarily, are projected into consciousness.
— Jennifer A. González, "Autopographies"

To articulate life's memory means to produce and to maintain a biological-cultural repertory of human truths, that entails the orderly embodiment of practices by which memory can be constituted, as well as the consignment to an archive of an intelligible discourse about the substance of that memory. This involves an important manipulation of space, in both the material and the semiotic senses. Manipulation of space is particularly relevant when discussing abortion and cultural memory because womanhood has historically has been used to reiterate normative boundaries through female reproductivity. As women's reproductive capacity is managed for a collective purpose, space is managed. Women's bodies are represented in public forums to be regulated; their organs are opened to scrutiny for debate on proper reproductive practice. With a recollection of the purpose and significance of life comes the delineation of frontiers: who is one of us, who is a threat; who is bound by life's dictates, who is free from them. In an age dominated by biopolitical justifications for legal and cultural norms, when optimal health and well-being are deployed to constitute ideological interests, normalizing life *inside* the womb is a high priority for organizing boundaries of individual and collective identities *outside* of the womb. The practices that make possible discourse about fetuses, organs and cells create a *prenatal* space in and around women's bodies that is an important terminal within a network of public and private spaces.

To clarify, I do not mean space-as-thing, a measurable object that can be numerated by one science or another. Nor do I mean space-as-transparent, which Gillian Rose critiques as "the public space of Western hegemonic masculinities" that zeroes out difference and contradiction. Instead, I understand space as a dense, dynamic, heterogeneous configuration of material and semiotic elements, which is the result of ordered, collective action. Space is not empty; no single person creates space, nor is it ready-made and self-contained. Space forms and reforms, it moves, and it has its history. Space is a consequence of everyday performance, as Certeau described in *The Practice of Everyday Life*:

> [A] *space* exists when one takes into consideration vectors of direction, velocities, and time variables. Thus space is composed of intersections of mobile elements. It is in a sense actuated by the ensemble of movements deployed within it. . . . On this view, in relation to place, space is like the word when it is spoken, that is, when it is caught in the ambiguity of actualization . . . In short, *space is a practiced place*. Thus the street geometrically defined by urban planning is transformed into a space by walkers. In the same way, an act of reading is the space produced by the practice of a particular place: a written text.

Place is static, whereas space is the dynamism of time and action incorporated with place. Lefebvre, who offers a conceptualization of space sympathetic to Certeau's, uses the analogy of waves: any wave is the collective result of a dynamic, dominant tendency in the water's action, but is run through by counter-tendencies, and any wave eventually breaks. Hence, the "wave-like" dynamics of spatial formation emerge from the rhythms of practice. Doreen Massey remarks, "'Space' is created out of the vast intricacies, the incredible complexities, of the interlocking and the non-interlocking, and the networks of relations at every scale from local to global. . . . Space is not a 'flat' surface in that sense because the social relations that create it are themselves dynamic by their very nature." As a result, "space is by its very nature full of power and symbolism, a complex web of relations of domination and subordination, of solidarity and co-operation."[1] What makes a space unique is the historical, performative configuration of practices that compose it.

Women's bodies, as places, become dynamic spaces of recollection when the elements of time and the practices of biomedical body criticism (understood as *spatial practices*) are accounted for. To the extent that memory is the reiteration of another time in the present, remembrance *is* the element of time and action that I am concerned with accounting for. One can call attention to the spatial consequences of any practice, but Certeau points out that memory work is a vital component of spatial rhetoric: "Memory mediates spatial transformations." Generally, remembrance is a practice that unfolds at specific moments in time, in more or less improvised or ritualized behaviors, and the insertion of one time into another alters space through the implantation of memory in a foreign place. He asks, "how does time articulate itself on an organized space? How does it effect its 'breakthrough' in the occasional mode? In short, what constitutes the *implantation of memory in a place* that already forms an ensemble?" Memory is not recalled in a vacuum; it is recalled in already-existing spaces that have directions to them, pur-

poses, goals, and motives to them. Memory has no space of its own, it must oc-
cupy and reorder that space to which it is introduced. Jennifer González explains:

> Memory, like identity, is a process not unlike placing within an architectural
> model for our perusal those rooms, objects, events, and landscapes, that we have
> encountered again and again in pacing through time. . . . The past is recon-
> structed from a moment in the present to convince ourselves of something we
> wish to be or have been. The objects of memory, then, become a *spatial annex*
> to the mental images, that voluntarily or involuntarily, are projected into con-
> sciousness.

Thus, whatever cultural work memory does, it must do so by intervening in an
existing order. "Like those birds that lay their eggs only in other species' nests,
memory produces in a place that does not belong to it."[2] That is why forensic exegesis and the genealogical effects it produces must also be considered for their
impact on space. Recollecting the provenance of an ideal, entity, or practice alters
the space in which the memory of that thing is recollected.

What is peculiar to the anamnesis and hypomnesis of early medical practices,
the "unforgetting" and archiving of ostensibly higher truths, is that the memory
here is not specific to another time—it is transgenerational and ubiquitous, not
fixed and local in its prior existence. As a result, the transcendent world of divine
and natural law was afforded a space within the immanent world of biology and
culture. The Godly was made humble, the miraculous was made normal by the
fact that a mysterious higher order of being had a dynamic flesh and blood field
of action on which to work its intent. By reifying that which properly has no time
(because it is for all time) within the corporeality and customs of human beings,
physicians transformed the eternal into the historical and in the process, appropriated the space of women's bodies for the purpose of affecting cultural order. As
an implantation of memory in a new space, white patriarchal ideals of motherhood and reproduction became culturally productive in a place that was not theirs
before: uterine tissues, blood flows, ovarian cells.[3] Yet because these ideals were
understood as transcendent and without fixed location in the past, more than taking their form from the space of implantation, they easily became the cause behind that space. Although the occupation was new, it was already very, very old.
It is not as if women's bodies at one time were divine works and now were not.
Rather than recreating a past moment again, to accept that a divine order of life
made itself manifest in the space of women's bodies meant that it had always
been and would always be that way. Certeau's imagery of an egg in a foreign nest
is especially appropriate. The real power of physicians' antiabortion rhetoric was
that they held women's bodies were impregnated not only with fetal individuals,
but also with a memory of life as normative order. Biological reproductivity was
folded back onto itself to reproduce culture through the very action of female fertility cycles, irrespective of numbers of pregnancies. To be more precise about my
thesis: culture, alongside and through the *possibility* of the fetus, quickened itself.

But *where* is this prenatal space located in relation to other spaces, both concretely and abstractly? To assume that it is simply wherever a woman's body exists is to undercut analysis of the womb as a cultural as well as a physical object by collapsing the way a thing is made intelligible with the thing itself, to confuse place (being there) with space (action incumbent to a place). The space of the womb has become as complex to identify as the spaces of the private and the public. These spaces are at least partially coincident due to the story which actively marks out their contiguous boundaries. The genealogical effect of women's bodies remembering the story of maternal destiny, and by extension racial/national entitlements, serves to delimit boundaries and modes of action. Certeau writes: "'every description is more than a fixation,' it is 'a culturally creative act.' It even has distributive power and performative force (it does what it says) when an ensemble of circumstances is brought together. Then it founds spaces. . . . the primary function is to *authorize* the establishment, displacement or transcendence of limits . . . This founding is precisely the primary role of the story. It opens a legitimate *theater* for practical *actions*." Yuval-Davis and Anthias argued that woman, or rather the story of being woman, has been used to reproduce the racial/ethnic boundaries of the state ideologically, symbolically, spatially, and in terms of identity.[4] A memory of "life as proper order" within female bodies serves the purpose of a founding narrative, articulating prenatal space as a legitimate theater of cultural rejuvenation. Because it is more than a simple set of images of woman's body and because it involves collective as well as individual life and death, the delimitation of this space is an ongoing activity that incessantly establishes a theater of practical actions regarding procreativity, identity, and cultural order.

Spaces of Representation

The spatial effects of remembrance, of the spatial practices of medical body criticism, play out in the convoluted intersection of two distinct elements: *spaces of representation* and *representations of space*. Taken from Lefebvre, the former term refers to the spaces in which one goes about constituting a memory, and in particular to the spatial alterations brought about in the immediate location of mnemonic practices. The consequences to space from acts of representation are partially or wholly independent of the space represented in the memory. The medical scene of examination and documentation carried out in the clinic and in the home, or the chronicling of medical investigations in journals, court rooms, and legislatures enact spaces of representation. Representations of space refers to space symbolically portrayed. The depiction of a population within the womb, the city as a threatening environment to the womb, or the national landscape as coincident with the womb would be representations of space.[5]

Spaces of representation were important in the nineteenth-century articulation of life's memory because of the emphasis placed on archiving the truth about life and educating the public about the contents of that archive. With the AMA's 1859 charge to be "the physical guardians of women . . . of their offspring in utero" ringing in their ears, physicians routinely declaimed "it was the duty of physicians to expose and denounce" criminal abortion, or as Storer put it, "to strip down the veil, and apply the searching caustic or knife to this foul sore in the body politic." By way of the ligature of patient to physician, antiabortion doctors envisioned themselves in the role of a relay between the community and possible criminals, a liaison between the pregnant body and the body politic. The AMA's National Code of Ethics, under the responsibilities of the physician to the community, specified that "it is the duty of physicians to be ever vigilant for the welfare of the community, and to bear their part in sustaining its institutions and burdens; they should also be ever ready to give counsel to the public in matters especially appertaining to their professions, or on subjects of *medical police, public hygiene, and legal medicine.*" By documenting for the body politic the corporeal discourse of maternal duty, physicians simultaneously established a medicalized space of cultural remembrance *and* linked the body politic to the female body through the exegetical practices that produced that memory. Hypomnesis, in establishing an external, supplementary space to the memory it records, establishes not only the *space of witnessing* (the body perceived and the subsequent texts about that perception), but also the *space of virtual witnessing* (the forums which rely on the texts of those perceptions), wherein the archive is made available to others.[6]

In the nineteenth century, the space of witnessing women's reproductive organs principally involved the hospital and the home. The delineation of who was examined where and under what conditions constituted early class boundaries within prenatal space. A woman's participation and consent in this newly emerging medical space depended greatly on her status, as is evident in the development of the hospital versus the home as a site of medical treatment. The medical experience of the Civil War spurred drastic changes in hospitals, starting them on the road to becoming modern, hygienic clinics and learning centers. Gradually, hospitals left behind a care-taking ethos signified by hot meals and charitable stewardship, and took on a curative ethos signified by the introduction and increased use of thermometers, stethoscopes, microscopes, chemical treatments, urine tests, temperature charts for each patient, and so forth. By the 1870s and 1880s, pathologists were appointed to most hospitals and modern clinical training of interns was gaining momentum. In addition, there were structural changes, many recommended by Florence Nightingale, that accommodated greater and more careful observation. Her plans included placing "the nurse's room so that she [*sic*] might observe all its inmates from a single vantage point." Further, "closets and stairwells where 'skulking' might occur or where convalescents might 'play tricks' must be avoided. These were to be eliminated by the enlightened hospital architect, just as he [*sic*] avoided corners in which dust might accumulate or sewers that allowed the escape of dangerous fumes." These changes were implemented rapidly in the latter part of the nineteenth and in the early twentieth century as hospitals proliferated. According to an official survey, there were fewer than 200 hospitals in 1873; in 1910, more than four thousand were extant; and in 1920, more than six thousand existed.[7] The infrastructure for centralized medical observation and treatment was not available until after the antiabortion campaign had completed its work, nor were hospitals in possession of the aura of medical expertise they would come to have.

Early hospitals, especially those of the antebellum era, served the poor, not the bourgeoisie. Hospitals were impractical for many, poor and well-off alike, and were considered dangerous and pitiable places. Logistically, reaching a hospital was a time-consuming endeavor. Great distances and the lack of hard roads meant that "in an unmechanized rural society, the general hospital [was] inaccessible in most cases of short-term acute illness," such as complications from an abortion. Even in emerging urban contexts, where transportation might be better, however, the long-standing stigma of hospitals as "lower-class institutions" was only reinforced. They were considered indelicate, unrefined places, wherever they might be, rampant with the disease of the poor and the sickly. Before the advent of antiseptic methods, hospitals were as much sites of death as healing, making the home preferable for safe recovery. More than that, from their beginnings, hospitals were conducted under the auspices of Christian charity and intended by their benefactors as places of respite for society's wretched souls. According to historian Charles Rosenberg, in the antebellum United States, "both physicians and trustees saw the hospital in similar terms; its wards were dominated by people and behaviors alien and unsettling." As cities grew, the ethos of stewardship expanded the charity for the working classes, especially women and children. Unlike rural communities, cities were disproportionately populated with "unattached individuals living alone," eventual charity cases who had no one to turn to in times of illness. "The different loci of medical care had different moral connotations. Treatment in hospitals and offices was generally regarded as a mark of lower status," whereas a mark of

Figure 6.1. William Jones' speculum table, from his *Practical Observations of Diseases of Women*.

social worth was the ability to afford home care by a physician. Paul Starr wrote in *The Social Transformation of American Medicine*, "[a]lmost no one who had a choice sought hospital care."[8]

This gradually changed as hospitals and the offices of physicians became more scientific in their management and the regular medical community grew in stature, as compared to alternative or irregular communities, to become the only medical choice for ever greater numbers of people. Also, improvements in transportation, along with the installation of telephones beginning in the 1870s, made physicians more affordable and more accessible, thereby helping to bring the sick to doctors, rather than the other way around. Starr noted that "[t]he space in which the physician worked became steadily more compressed. The doctor of the nineteenth century was a local traveler who knew the interior of his [*sic*] patients' homes and private lives more deeply than did others in the community. By the early twentieth century, many physicians went to work at hospitals or offices and had little contact with the homes or living conditions of the patients they treated."[9] Before the turn of the century, then, the typical physician did not have the possibility of a "compressed" clinical practice because of a lack of infrastructure and, especially with well-to-do patients who eschewed clinical spaces, had to enter the home to have contact with patients. For the brief transitional moment in which the antiabortion campaign was conducted, the peripatetic doctor played an important role as liaison (or relay) in a diffused system of observation and management.

Within the home, to carry out the exegetical rituals necessary to the new obstetrics and gynecology a suitable work space was required. The space of the modest witness and legible patient required that the patient's body lay properly, for example. Sims observed, "I have said that for a speculum examination there is nothing better than a table covered with a quilt or blankets folded, and this is literally true; but for the consultation-room I have a chair which has served such a good purpose that I introduce it here, that others may profit by it." He then described a chair that folded out into a table to assist in diagnosis. The home, like the consultation room, required the furniture necessary for the patient to participate properly. Hence, the doctor's office and the home paralleled one another in the use of space. The first speculum table was made by William Jones and it had many features, such as forerunners of today's gynecological stirrups:

> It consists of a frame supported on four legs, to which a cushioned top is attached by hinges at one extremity: by means of these hinges and a rack placed beneath it, the top of the table may be made into an inclined plane, so as to give to the pelvis the requisite elevation; by means of the cushion for the head, those inconveniences may be obviated, which might result from retaining the head in the dependant position. To prevent the legs of the patient getting in the way of the operator, two iron rods with semi-circular cushions are attached to the table, over which the legs are placed;—these rods are moveable, and are capable of giving different lengths, to correspond with the varied extent of the *femora* of different females. (Fig. 6.1)

Ricci noted that the greater use of the speculum "led to the development of special examining tables" ranging from rocking-chair types to exam stools. Still others worked on portable varieties or devices, like Souchon's, to make the home more like the office.[10]

Along with a suitable position, the patient had to be properly illuminated. In the days before electrification, this meant using candles or daylight. Nott felt that "[t]o get at the cervix uteri they [specula] all require either the semi-prone position or that on the knees; they consequently require an elevated table, and a light horizontal with the table, to give a good view, all of which conditions are inconvenient in private houses." The home environment posed challenges to an efficient use of space for examination as well as the moral difficulties detailed in the previous chapter. Whereas some had advocated the use of a candle to illuminate the body cavity, many found this to be insufficient. Thomas R. Mitchell of Dublin advocated the positioning of the patient to allow natural light: "the patient shall lie in such a position, that a ray of light can be directed through the speculum, and a correct view of the parts be obtained. This is far superior to the use of a candle, which although it enables the operator to see the disease, prevents him forming a correct opinion of the colour and condition of the parts. The use of a crystal I have found of no practical value." Many a speculum was polished so as to catch and reflect what light there was into the vagina, making a woman's interior as bright as possible.[11] Through lighting and equipment of the requisite practices of body criticism, the home could be transformed into a medical space.

As I have mentioned, perceptual prosthetics and rituals of exposure were not always employed, and not always because of situational difficulties, such as excessive pain or bleeding. "Despite these details about the method of conducting a vaginal examination, quite frequently in these decades a gynaecological patient was treated from a study of symptomatology and a palpation to the abdomen without any attempt at a vaginal examination." Amid the growing prevalence of the direct exam, bourgeois women often were able to avoid exposure because of their class privilege and the morality of "civilized" people. Ironically, although much of the antiabortion commentary of physicians stressed the special character of the bourgeois woman, the order of life physicians staked their opposition in was founded substantially on the bodies of the less fortunate. Fearing the loss of a paying client or simply finding the indelicacy too much, some physicians relied on the testimony of the refined patient to make their diagnoses.[12] The uneven success of securing a fully compliant middle- and upper-class clientele meant that the normative female body found in the medical treatises and journals was more a collective representation of charity cases in hospitals and lying-in institutions than of bourgeois matrons.

Poor women and women of color who sought regular medical care had fewer opportunities to affect their care-givers' practices. Beginning with the move toward clinical medicine, charity patients began to turn their bodies over to medical education in return for medical services. This was based on doctors' demands for access to hospital patients for teaching purposes, as with clinical midwifery. "The arguments of physicians who sought unfettered access to patients for teaching were strikingly similar to those justifying demands for liberal autopsy regulations. The particular patient, they emphasized, was not as important as the lesson his [*sic*] illness might impart to students." To learn medicine, there must be a supply of bodies. Wertz and Wertz note:

> [T]aboos against revealing the body retarded clinical training in obstetrics until medicine learned to exchange with lower-class women the gift of treatment for the right to expose them to students. In time doctors devised rituals and a rationale for medical intimacy with more 'refined' women, although some women were so acutely discomforted by male doctors that they chose continued illness over exposure or sought female attendants.[13]

Although clinical treatment of charity cases sharply increased after the Civil War with the rationalization of hospitals, the exchange of education for treatment was common even before the great hospital reforms. Leading authors in obstetrics and gynecology, both U.S. and European, for example, relied on extensive access to clinical patients. Storer was a surgeon at the New England Hospital for Women. Sims' famous *Clinical Notes* were based on his years at the New York Woman's Hospital, his experiments with slave women, and his observations of European hospitals. Gunning Bedford, a professor at the University of New York, lectured on his clinical experience years before the war. Augustus Gardner worked in New York's Northern Dispensary and taught at the New York Preparatory School of Medicine. Whitehead of the Manchester and Salford Lying-in Hospital said that he had conducted more than 2000 specular exams.[14]

As spaces of representation, specifically of witnessing, the home and the hospital, of course, were central components of the archive of knowledge about life that physicians were building. To know the truth about pregnancy, the space to investigate female bodies had to be established. Rhetorically, a distinction between well-bred women and poor women was founded spatially in the conditions of witnessing for the two locations. The pregnancies of affluent women simply counted more and, thus, bourgeois clients were able to command in-home care and to garner exceptions to diagnostic rituals (whether that was advisable or not). The same hierarchy that considered the fate of affluent, white Anglo-Saxon Protestant women's pregnancies of greater interest grounded both physicians' specific fears of race suicide and a raced, classed difference in the space of witnessing bodies. That is, the same logic that said that abortion among this group of women was a threat to the civilized world also established a functional boundary within exegetical practices that attempted to document that threat. The practices which helped produce a knowledge of race suicide also enacted, in their very operations, the vital difference that made that threat intelligible. These practices constituted in the space of their enactment what they asserted in the space of their texts.

Spaces of representation also included legislatures and law courts, wherein abortion law was crafted and applied based on the testimony of physicians. Dissemination of medical texts into judicial and deliberative forums produced still other representations of women's bodies in law and legislation. The practice of virtual witnessing thus delimited prenatal space in medico-legal contexts. The criminalization of abortion was one of the first legislative successes won by the AMA, marking an important connection of law and medicine through the management of procreativity. Also, the participation of physicians in prosecuting abortions was of considerable significance to many in the medical community. It was an important way for physicians to assist in the clampdown on abortion and a way that some authors felt physicians could intervene in a judicial system that they did not trust to enforce the law. However, many physicians were increasingly dissatisfied with their roles as medical experts generally, especially on the point of disagreement and error, which made "physicians look scientifically weak."[15]

In medico-legal discourse, examination reports, autopsy reports, general medical texts, as well as expert testimony on the state of abortion practices regionally or nationally replicated the observations of physicians and thus extended the perceptions of direct examination to legislative and judicial audiences normally separated from the inner workings of women's bodies. Medical texts were representations of space themselves and I will discuss some of the spatial work done by them as representations in a moment. First, however, consider the womb as the representational ground of interconnection, regardless of the specific text in a given instance. Assemblies and courts were now joined to women's bodies by way of physicians' observations, either written or oral. Just as the physician became a prosthetic extension of the inner discourse of women's bodies into legal contexts, replacing the authority of women's personal testimony, physicians also became prosthetic extensions of the law into women's bodies. Once more, my point is not that physicians were successful as enforcers of the law, but that they were successful at establishing a network. Despite conflicts of opinion and risks to the professional image of the AMA, physicians' body criticism became the practice by which the intimate space of women's bodies, the private space of the home, and the public space of the law were linked prenatally.

For instance, in court cases prosecuting abortionists and their clients, the medical testimony as to the condition of the woman's body was crucial to the success of the prosecution. Proof that she had been treated by instruments or chemicals meant that the female body had become a principal space of legal dispute, a place of practiced contestation. The presentation of post-mortem and live-examination reports were a central feature of abortion trials, often with conflicting expert testimony. This required physicians to enter their perceptions into the record visually in diagrams, orally, or in writing. Juries occasionally needed to be educated as to the terrain of dispute, as in *Scott v. People*, wherein Freeman J. Scott appealed his conviction as an abortionist. In his case, the Supreme Court of Illinois ruled that a lawyer could read from and show medical books to educate the jury about women's bodies.[16] Although court records are often sparse in terms of the details of medical testimony, it was common for physicians to publish their autopsies and examinations after the fact, particularly when the jury acquitted either the abortionist, the woman who aborted, or both.[17] The general failures of prosecutors to produce convictions on abortion charges, regardless of the medical evidence, lead many physicians to argue the courts were underwriting abortion practice. Whether or not the number of convictions satisfied antiabortion advocates, in abortion trials, prenatal space was established as the terrain of dispute about the proper regeneration of life and law. Interpreting state laws that limited abortion (and maximized a particular vision of life), debating such law on the medicalized ground of women's bodies, meant that the biopolitics of life now spanned forums of law and the home by way of women's medical biology.

In like fashion, women's bodies became sites of legislative debate concerning abortion. James Mohr points out in a survey of legislation of the nineteenth century that state level initiatives to tighten or add antiabortion statutes usually were prompted by pressure from state medical societies and individual physicians, particularly after the end of the Civil War. A post-war political climate that favored greater use of state power, increasing scientific prestige for regular physicians, and public support for antiabortion measures by homeopathists (the leading competitors of AMA regulars) meant that medical pressure had achieved a previously unknown level of influence. State legislatures were not always enthusiastic supporters of antiabortion laws, often passing law on simple, rather than super, majorities but the ground of dispute was firmly established as the medicalized female body, regardless of enthusiasm. In 1867, Ohio, for example, Storer's arguments about reproductive risk to the nation and scientific evidence about pregnancy were offered to support the passage of antiabortion legislation. Citing Storer's essay *Why Not? A Book for Every Woman* explicitly, State Senators L. D. Griswold, Toland Jones, and Henry West paraphrased the central ideas of Storer's influential tract:

> It has been ascertained, by statistics carefully prepared, that in one of the Eastern States [Massachusetts] the number of children born alive of native American parentage is less than the deaths of the same class of persons, and that the small increase of population which the census shows is the result of immigration and of the larger number of children born of foreign parentage. Your committee believe that if the facts could be ascertained, the statistics of Ohio would not show a much better state of things.

The report goes on to discuss the inviolability of life at conception due to divine as well as natural law, "any interference" of which results in "evils innumerable, among which are alarming and dangerous hemorrhages, inflammation of the womb and its appendages, displacement or prolapsus of the organ." The demographic of and rationale offered for abortion was strictly according to medical opinion:

It is a melancholy fact that this crime is more frequent among the educated, the fashionable and the wealthy, than among the poor and illiterate. The demands of society and fashionable life; the desire of freedom from care and home duties and responsibilities; and the absence of a proper understanding of the dangers and criminality of the act, lead our otherwise amiable sisters to the commission of this crime. Do they realize that in avoiding the duties and responsibilities of married life, they are, in effect, living in a state of legalized prostitution? Shall we permit our broad and fertile prairies to be settled only by the children of aliens? If not, we must, by proper legislation, and by the diffusion of a correct public sentiment, endeavor to suppress a crime which has become so prevalent.[18]

Notice that the public, suffering from fashionable, ever-growing ignorance regarding maternal duty must be called to obey the truths exhibited by the body. The framework of a natural memory of life's true order being recalled to prevent a racial calamity is clearly operative. What is more, physicians' perceptual practices are the key in that they record and make visible the female body's inner truth.

Rather than focus on specific moments wherein juries or legislators were convinced to enforce or enact law, I want to call attention to the establishment of the prenatal as a theater of action within homes, hospitals, courts, and assemblies. Medical body criticism enacted spaces of representation, both of witnessing and virtual witnessing, that connected sites of medical care with arenas of dispute. When deliberating on the value of life or its violation, medical discourse about women's bodies had become not just vernacular for argument, it had become the terrain. Setting aside the relative persuasiveness of physicians' growing expertise or the increasing importance of statistical quantification in biopolitical argument, the apparatus of the law had become contiguous with the private sphere by virtue of women's bodies being transposed into medical testimony. That spatial arrangement is a function, not of an image of the body *as* space, but of the *practices of witnessing* the body that constitute a shared space. In the process, a shared, medically constituted environment performatively articulated medical and legal institutions through prenatal space.

Representations of Space

From another perspective, one more comfortably familiar in studies of biomedical discourse, the increasingly complex map of women's bodies was itself a *representation of space*. As a representation, the womb was open to many uses, including the articulation of reproductive health with state interest. The reification of populations, institutions, and territories in female generative organs made the womb a terminal for linking diverse areas of the cultural topography, principally the private and the public.

Feminists have studied and debated the relationship of female reproductive organs to the state for centuries, contesting the manner in which social structures are organized through procreative sexuality. A prime explanation for these intersections has been that biological structures are part of the political theories of a sexually complementary society, meaning that modern sexed bodies and political models materialize together in the flesh. "Complementarians articulated a vision of men and women not just as opposites but as interdependent parts of a physical and moral whole in which their complementary opposition (and not sameness or equality) was important to the smooth working of society." The reproductive organs of women were to be the focal point of their identity and, therefore, the identity of society as envisioned by some of its elite architects.[19]

The spatial organization of modern sexual complementarity is familiar to all: the private and public spheres. Here, I refer to the traditional feminist distinction of private versus public, rather than the model of a civic space common to political philosophy where individuals collectively form various publics between a private world and the state. From a feminist perspective, the public and private spheres are amorphous, convoluted spaces, tenuously different in practices, everchanging in their boundaries, that exist in ideational and physical realms. They are less given realities than they are principles used to demarcate gender norms, ways of life, and punishments for poorly executed gender performances. As Nancy Duncan argues, "[b]oth private and public spaces are heterogeneous and not all space is clearly public or private. Space is thus subject to various territorializing and deterritorializing processes whereby local control is fixed, claimed, challenged, forfeited and privatized."[20] Together they function as markers of gendered enactments, grounded in sexual essence, that supposedly enable a civilized society to exist harmoniously and efficiently. Londa Schiebinger explains:

> In setting the public sphere of the professions against the private sphere of the home, complementarians envisioned two distinct ways of living: each sphere had its own logic, ethic, and *modus operandi*. The purposes and activities of the public realm differed essentially from those of the home. As one complementarian put it, in the state, everything originates in abstraction, in concepts; while in the home everything originates in the physical needs of the heart and soul.

No doubt these observations are familiar. What I would emphasize is that spatial structure was given form by its investiture in sexual materiality.[21] What gave the public and private spheres their contours were not only the markets, forums, and homes that make acts public or private, but also the hips and shoulders, the cranial circumferences, differing musculatures, and sex organs over which public and private life were draped. These complementary spaces were not intelligible without sexed bodies to cling to. Being places of cultural practice, these spaces are not empty vacuums but outgrowths of the flesh and blood that enact their norms.

Although there are multiple intersections of public and private space, and many thresholds we pass through, medical science has spanned the confused, slippery domains of the public and the private by fashioning a prenatal space that exists in a tremulous and uneven manner with them. In the context of the late twentieth century, one incisive way of conceptualizing this spatial articulation was to argue that medical imagery absents women, negates them, by virtue of representing the fetus. It is now common to consider the transformation of women into environments for fetuses as disembodiment. For example, in her classic critique of *The Silent Scream*, Rosalind Petchesky argues, "we have to restore woman to a central place in the pregnancy scene. To do this, we must create new images that recontextualize the fetus, that place it back into the uterus, and the uterus back into the woman's body, and her body back into social space." Since the 1980s, one of the most vital and active lines of feminist scholarship, analyses of fetal imaging, has established the disappearing woman as the condition of a fetal individual. As Duden argues in *Disembodying Women*, for example, fetal imaging connotatively erases any humanly female presence from reproduction in the atomistic, mechanical rhetoric of medical description.[22] It is a point of departure for a contest between individuals, fetus versus woman, that can be understood in terms of who is and who is not materialized by medical rhetoric. Hence, the private property of a woman, her body, is negated as it is made into a transparent public viewing space for fetal individuals.

However, in earlier biomedical theory, a more significant effect of representation of women's reproductive capacity was to spatialize women not as absences but as fertile grounds, the "woman-as-womb" idea according to Nancy Theriot. As a regenerative commonplace, the representation of female reproductive organs has different implications for the complementary relation of the public and the private. From the standpoint of early medicine, reproduction generated other individuals, not mothers by choice. Women had to be naturally preformed and given as mothers by virtue of their wombs or society's very being would be forgotten, lost. Without a preformed mandate for procreation, society dies figuratively and literally. Mary Poovey describes the stakes for individual rights of representing women as naturally maternal:

The metaphysics of substance . . . in the discourse of rights is historically related to the basic tenets of individualism, from which the discourse of rights is derived. A cardinal feature of individualism as it was elaborated in the late seventeenth century and institutionalized in the eighteenth and nineteenth centuries was the constitution of maternity as the essence of the female subject. . . . For, if the normative woman is a mother, then the mother-nature of woman is one of the linchpins of sexed identity and therefore, by the oppositional logic of gender, one ground of the intelligible masculinity for men. If women are allowed to question or to reject their maternity, then not only is the natural (sexed) basis of rights in jeopardy, but so is the natural basis of female identity and, by implication, of masculine identity as well. From this perspective, in other words, the abortion debate is about what it means to accept—or reject—the notion that there is a "natural" basis for individual identity and therefore for individual rights and sexual identity.

From a natural rights point of view, prenatal space is that space in which the maternal body *ratifies* fetal individuality. It is, in a sense, a contractual space wherein ratification of the contract confesses sexually differentiated terms hidden within the flesh. "That is to say, a body is postulated as the signifier (the term) in a *contract*. This discursive image is supposed to inform an *unknown* 'reality' formerly designated as 'flesh.'"[23] The sexual differentiation underlying individual rights grounded social structure in naturalized contracts of masculinity and femininity, thereby establishing sexually differentiated public and private spaces.

The prenatal sat as a terminal between both private and public, being neither in and of itself. Both intimate and thoroughly externalized, prenatal space became an intermediate theater between the mother and the state. Physicians were fairly explicit about this relationship, arguing that women were distinct from society, yet impressed on it like a mold. Meigs contended:

> The medical man, surely, of all men, ought to be best able to appreciate the influence of the sex in the social state; because, more than other men, he is by his vocation of closer observation of those influences that bind together members of families that compose the social compact. He more clearly than others can recognize the power of woman in the family—and thus in all society, which he sees to be moulded and controlled by the gentler sex. But for the power of that female influence, which one of you would doubt the rapid relapse of society into the violence and chaos of the earliest barbarism?[24]

Reprising the theme that a civilized nation can only exist if it respects sexual complementarity, notice that Meigs situates the witness to this concatenation of family and state from a third position. Not seeing the family from the point of view of the state or vice versa, he stands back from both private and public to observe their conjunction through women as mothers. The female body, in its inverted, exposed form, became a space in which the bourgeois body, with its nuclear family, professions, legal statutes, and social structures, could anchor itself. Meigs' comment and similar ones from other early physicians strongly illustrate the argument, forwarded variously by feminist scholars such as Luce Irigaray, Julia Kristeva, and Judith Butler, that the feminine functions in the patriarchal imagination as that which shapes substance, but which never shares in that substance.[25] The womb, and thus woman by extension, is nothing except by virtue of that which is shaped by it/her. The power to mold is the power of a matrix and many early medical practitioners envisioned themselves as the privileged protectors of this arrangement.

Prenatal space, then, represented the visual field of the physician as a relay/regulator of discourse between the family and the public. Medical rhetoric

about reproduction, particularly abortion, articulated organic communication between the life of the family and the life of the state by effectively reconfiguring
space such that the prenatal sat at the crossroads of public and private affairs.
Consider that physicians went into homes to try to ensure that pregnancies were
not terminated for reasons of civil, as well as individual, well-being. Also, the
ratification of individuality within the womb dictated that the collective public
interest traversed reproductive space. Through women's bodies, physicians could
portray the sex life of the family as clearly as they could portray the life of the
body politic.

The spatial relationship of public and private, mediated prenatally, relied on
two different scenes: the larger scene of a national struggle over fecundity and the
more personal scene of female anatomy, both embodied in terms of reproductive
capacity. At the national level, different races, ethnicities, and classes were pitted
against one another, en masse, in a warlike competition of breeding. Each population became a reproductive agent in itself, with the white bourgeoisie losing its
edge in part from a pathological tendency to abort. At the anatomical level,
women's wombs were scenes of reproductive pathology, scenes within a scene,
so to speak. What made this relationship even more convoluted is that women,
"carriers" of wombs, were materialized within the larger body politic as prag-
matic, functional spaces, or, collectively, a matrix. The womb was simultaneously
a space and a tool, a context and a means.[26] It is the functional capacity of the
womb to foster life that led physicians to treat it as a "generative apparatus." The
perceived national struggle over fecundity was carried into the bodies of women
so that their bodies became not only instruments, but also corporeal contexts for
managing the life of the body politic. The "woman-as-womb" rhetoric of many
nineteenth century antiabortionists construed prenatal space as the workshop of
life for the social body in its struggle to survive. In this way, the functional capacity of "women's loins" began to coincide with the landscape of a nation apparently lacking a sufficient white population, as Storer claimed in *Why Not?* and
which numerous other physicians, legislators, and commentators seconded.

As represented in the act of archiving life's memory, prenatal space articulated the sexualized private/public dichotomy by means of a simultaneous conjunction and disjunction. As a terminal, a threshold, between public interest and
private decisions, the prenatal was a representation of ligature: the life of the body
politic and the life of the family were one in the organic discourse of antiabortion
physicians. At the same time, the relationship of the public and private was distinguished by means of biomedical representation. The physician, with his or her
reading of the female body, was the proper point of access both to sex life of the
family and the life of the white public, thereby constituting a spatial cleavage by
the same acts that provided the connection between the two. The prenatal was an
"in-between" that established the theater of action for physicians as biopolitical
conservators of the memory of life's true order. This reiteration and modification
of a complementary spatial grammar meant that the scheme of unequal individual

rights underwritten by such a grammar was also reiterated. The representation of the womb as a space of cultural regeneration and even national expansion performatively brought into being the spatial order it described—especially in light of criminalization, where states declared their collective interest in the outcome of individual pregnancies throughout the United States. By "remembering" in biological terms that the essence of woman was motherhood, physicians renaturalized not only the sexual differentiation within individual rights, but also a spatial order incumbent to such a sex-segregated society that was crosscut by hierarchies of race, ethnicity, religion, and wealth. Once more, physicians' rhetoric enacted spatially what it claimed discursively.

The conjunction and disjunction of the private and the public through the prenatal had the additional capacity to articulate spatially the moral threat that bourgeois culture was believed to pose to itself. In the nineteenth century, pollution of the body and soul commonly was believed to be a result of the moral environment in which one lived. No longer quite human, an aborting woman was a willful creature, yet her immorality was not typically considered a deliberate evil. A woman's decision to abort was construed as the result of contamination by the degrading social milieu of modern civilization, as I stated when delineating physicians' organic discourse on life and abortion. The morality and monstrosity of the aborting woman's body, therefore, needs to be considered within nineteenth-century moral environmentalism and the anti-urban sociology that bolstered it. The fear of environmental contamination of the soul and the body indicates the way in which life in the pregnant woman (and any threats to it) were tied to the conditions of social life. Although anti-urban thinking has long roots in Judeo-Christian faiths, the extraordinary growth of cities in the 1800s and the severe contrast between life in the modern city and traditional patterns raised urban phobia to a crescendo. For many social ills, urban moral corruption became causative fact. "Especially from the early 1830s on, urban reformers attacking a host of different social problems increasingly relied upon environmental explanations of the causes of human degradation. . . . Moral environmentalism suffused the social vocabulary of the new urban culture taking shape in antebellum America." Seduced by the temptations of the city, a young woman was considered monstrous yet victimized by a harsh and dangerous city landscape.[27]

A parallel with the sociology of suicide is instructive. Historically, suicide, abortion, and euthanasia have been linked together in popular discourses on ethics. Howard Kushner, writing about nineteenth-century explanations for suicide, reveals how early explanations for suicide correspond with those for criminal abortion. "Because self-destructive behavior became a *prima facie* example of the corrupting effects of urbanization, the incidence of suicide developed into a barometer of social health." Amid nostalgic visions of home and hearth, "both religious and secular assertions that modernity led to suicide were founded on the shared belief that humans were unable to negotiate the variety and choice that urban life offered." Informed by moral physiology, it was believed that "health depended upon the combination of diet, atmosphere, climate, work, and life style; disease, even lesions of the brain, resulted from imbalance of these elements." Further, responses to suicides and to the population threat they posed were largely disciplinary. "Fed by a belief that, like the environment, individuals were malleable, suppressive modes of control were de-emphasized in favor of more repressive behaviors. Reflecting wider cultural, economic and political developments, the moral treatment stressed self-discipline as an alternative to external authority." The best treatment for suicide was a return to the male-dominant, traditional family and a retreat from the changes associated with urban, industrial life. Conflicts between older traditions and the anxieties of a modern culture permeate the broad spectrum of nineteenth-century "somatic politics" that Burbick analyzes, such as Walt Whitman's "biodemocracy" or Harriet Hunt's "history of the heart."[28]

Operating within conventional terms of moral environmentalism, antiabortionists initially located the threat to life's true order in the moral toxicity of urban life, but later contended that the threat had radiated outward across the country. As with suicide, induced abortion was considered the result of a breakdown in traditional values. Abortion was a moral contagion, not an act, and its etiology was mapped across an urban/rural division as well as a public/private one. As the bourgeois public life of cities became models for smaller communities, the moral sickness of cities spread as well. "'[C]ivilization' became a metaphor for modern urban society" and to be civilized was to play havoc with the natural order of sex. Bedford, a proponent of urban contamination theory regarding female health, argued that the city was a morass of temptation, over-excitement, and decay:

> Child-bearing, unrestrained sexual intercourse, abortion, precocious nervous excitement from the perusal of prurient books, the lascivious Polka, and the various exciting scenes of City life are so many influences, which are constantly exhibiting their destructive results on the frail girl of the gay Metropolis; add to these the uninterrupted rounds of excitement consequent upon balls, parties, the opera, etc., the liability to cold imposed by these amusements, and more than all, the fact that these disastrous influences—disastrous to health and happiness—are exercised on a *physique* too often without a single attribute of solidity—and you will at once have explained why it is that the females in the higher classes of our large cities decay long before they have attained the meridian of life.[29]

In addition to the wear from her natural duty to bear children, the additional stresses of a metropolis put the young woman at risk. The city was widely held to be extremely dangerous to female health and, therefore, to culture generally. As I have indicated, among antiabortionists specifically, bourgeois "fashion" was the leading explanation for the increase of induced abortions.[30]

The stories of Mary Rogers and Madame Restell, one apparently a victim of a botched abortion, the other the most notorious abortionist of the 1800s, highlight the anti-urban moral environmentalism that surrounded discussions of criminal abortion. Amy Srebnick, in her wonderfully detailed *The Mysterious Death of Mary Rogers*, recounts the ways in which a young New York woman's death in 1841 was used to support abortion and police reform, sensationalize the dangers of the city, and generally to demarcate the place of sex in modern urban culture. Mary Rogers was a young woman who worked at a cigar shop, "the beautiful cigar girl" as she was called. She died during an attempted abortion, her second, and was evidently dragged to the river and left there. Although her death was one of very few within the city that year, she became a symbol in the press, in fiction, and in social reform discourse of the dangers of the city. "Following Mary's death the tenor and intensity of the rhetoric of crime and danger increased dramatically ... fostering hysteria over crime and social disorder. Masking other concerns, the unsolved and particularly sensational death seemed evidence enough of a 'savage state of society—without law—without order—and without security of any kind.'"[31]

Although she was never connected to Mary Rogers' death, in the popular imagination Madame Restell was held responsible. Calling herself Madame Restell, Ann Lohman was referred to in guidebooks as "the Wickedest Woman" in antebellum New York City. She was a very successful, high-profile abortionist who practiced out of her well-appointed home at 148 Greenwich Street. Her flamboyance earned Restell a place as *the* symbol of the criminal abortionist from 1839, when she first came under public scrutiny, until 1878, when she committed suicide after being indicted under the Comstock Law. "The quintessential antitype of domestic literature and mid-nineteenth-century social ideology, she was depicted as brash, vulgar, audacious, and duplicitous, a woman, 'tricked out in gorgeous finery.' Always reviled, she was known alternatively as 'madam killer,' a 'she devil,' a 'hag,' and the keeper of a 'bloody empire.'" Coupled with the image of a seducer, Restell was an icon of the urban decay that threatened moral reproduction.[32] Mary was seduced by city life, as the popularizers of her fate described her, and suffered at the hands of urban vampires like Madame Restell, whose evil practice culled profit from immorality and corruption.

Two common profiles of females criminally contaminated by civilization were "the selfish young woman" and "the addict." In a prevailing climate of compulsory motherhood, efforts to establish voluntary motherhood, whether by regulation of sex, contraception, or abortion, routinely elicited charges of selfishness. For example, the elder Storer wrote that "the fashionable young bride," was unwilling to be "shackled" by married life and thus was selfish. Similarly, others blamed the affluent classes' desire to maintain economic advantage through planned families. Generally, the association of pregnancy with bondage captures the tone of numerous entries from the texts I reviewed and replicates the conclusions of other historians.[33] Women also were described as addicts, unable to control the abortive habits pushed on them by unscrupulous physicians, as J. P. Leonard observed: "Irregular practitioners, and the women themselves, are addicted to this kind of criminality; but as a general thing, they have learned their art of some unprincipled doctor, who either purposely or accidentally let slip the secret to the vulgar." Whether the motivation was selfishness, addiction, or otherwise, the routine lament of medical authors was that women's abortive practices were threats to the family and hard to control. One anonymous commentator put it simply: "The immorality and the danger of the proceeding are but slight drawbacks to women who are determined not to have families, and the profession have not yet discovered the means of preventing criminal abortion."[34]

The moral contamination of modern life eventually escaped the city limits, however. "By the 1860s, the vast majority of writers on abortion, even those who estimated the total incidence of abortion rather conservatively, reinforced the belief that the practice was common to 'every village, hamlet, and neighborhood in the United States.'" The arguments before the Ohio Senate in 1867 are typical examples. What was once considered an urban, East-Coast problem had spread like a pestilent virus. Further, although it was now apparent that abortion was practiced at all levels of society throughout the nation, concern for the consequences of such a contagion was still disproportionately focused on white Protestant women. What had at first seemed like a moral lapse among the middle and upper classes of the city, now appeared to contemporary observers to be a wholesale moral failure resulting from the civilized customs of modern life, particularly of the wealthier classes. Thus, the threat of abortion, although intensified in an urban context, could touch any community in the entire country.[35]

The spatial articulation of abortion as moral contagion was a justification for the physician to become an environmental as well as bodily custodian. Prenatal space specified the appropriate habitat for the woman's reproductive organs to perfectly execute its duty; it was a blend of nature and culture as morality, education, climate, literature, lifestyle, entertainment, race, and class became "environmental factors" in the healthy functioning of a woman's reproductive system. All of these factors were thought to influence the degree to which a woman was fecund or fragile and whether or not she would menstruate in healthy fashion and her "economy" would be adequately utilized. Only those conditions that allowed for optimal procreativity were considered natural, as A. F. A. King explained: *"First,* as to the *natural environment of the womb.* This can be ascertained, and with considerable exactness, by searching out the precise functions which the organ is naturally adapted by its anatomical construction and physiological power to perform. The environing conditions that elicit from the uterus these, and only these, particular functions, will, it is evident, constitute its *natural* environment."[36] Combined with the physiological "weakness" of females, a constricting link formed between concentric environments of life: the internal, potentially monstrous environment of the reproductive organs was aggravated by the external, morally toxic environment of modern life. In a generative irony, life threatened itself inside and outside the body. As a justification of obstetric and gynecologic expertise, the determination of what constituted the natural environment again placed the physician in a crucial third position, prenatal space. In antiabortion rhetoric, the synergistic tendency of the environment and the pregnant body to produce self-immolating "monsters" established a threatening connection between the individual and the social.[37] Physicians, legitimated medical power over the cultural environment by extending the limits of the pregnant body to include its cultural context. What else quickens with the fetus? Anything that is considered at present to be a relevant influence on prenatal space as a fragile environment: fear, stress, unwomanly behavior, moral laxity, etc.

The Regenerative "In-Between"

Prenatal space does not refer to the womb in a strictly corporeal sense, but to a layered set of practices that create a space that is at once physical (the womb and the medical practices of representation that make it intelligible) and imagined (the vision of life in the womb and the life of culture). As a space, it is not stable or given, but forms and reforms performatively according to articulatory practice. It forms in a courtroom when medical texts are used to educate a jury. It forms when images of fetuses are used to represent humanity, individualism, or as the condensation of a specific collective. I am arguing that prenatal space has become part of the cultural topography, a part of the complex network of spaces that are discursively constituted and provide a biopolitical landscape.[38] It is performatively enacted in diverse ways according to historical patterns of citation and transformation, and those patterns can be understood as unique rhetorics in the embodiment and arrangement of life, collectively and individually.

As a result, prenatal space is a quintessential *heterotopia*. In Foucault's lecture, "Different Spaces," he famously defined heterotopias as "places that are designed into the very institution of society, which are sorts of actually realized utopias [no-places] in which the real emplacements, all the other real emplacements that can be found within a culture are, at the same time, represented, contested, reversed, sorts of places that are outside all places, although they are actually localizable." They are "spaces which are linked with all the others, and yet at variance somehow with all the other emplacements." As it was operationalized in the nineteenth century, prenatal space was neither causative, nor prior to, nor imitative of the private or public spheres. It was the "permanent and unchangeable condition of both" within a system of sexed complementarity, as a mold is to the molded. It was not causative in that the principle, the efficient cause, of life was not a woman's, or reproduction would have been considered a woman's choice. After the 1880s, a woman did not own what was in her womb. As a matrix, life was formed *within* her but not *of* her. Prenatal space was not prior to the public and the private because it was present in both as a condition of their continued existence. Life is in constant renewal. And prenatal space was not like nor did it resemble the public and the private, although it was coincident with both. When the physician examined a patient in her home, prenatal space occupied the home and transformed it. When the images and texts of medicine were employed in a trial to convict a woman of abortion, the public sphere was likewise occupied and transformed, although in a different way. Life in prenatal space was connected to life in the private and public spheres, regenerating both, but it did not resemble those spheres.[39]

Prenatal space existed *with* the public and the private as a permeable, interconnected site in which social arrangements were memorialized as normal life forces. "Heterotopias always presuppose a system of opening and closing that isolates them and makes them penetrable at the same time." Given that I take space as a functional or practiced place and not a quantified volume, the medical practices that constituted prenatal space occurred within any environment, public or private, and were necessarily articulated with those environments. That is why I have pointed to the concentric environments of life, in- and ex-utero, that were used to justify medical stewardship of reproduction. Where cultural life was being invested in women by medical professionals, prenatal space was the rhetorical venue articulated by and necessary for such investments. The memory work that constituted prenatal space was a condition of the social spheres that surrounded it and passed through it as their true order was remembered in the body's order. "[A] society can make a heterotopia that exists and has not ceased to exist operate in a very different way."[40] The woman-as-womb had become functionally reproductive in a new mode.

Prenatal space, thus, may be characterized as a regenerative "in-between" that is both semiotic and material. Situated at the cusp of life, between a transgenerational memory of supposedly higher truths and their worldly manifestation, in prenatal space one witnessed the signification of the transcendent through the immanent. As thresholds, "heterotopias are connected with temporal discontinuities." In the process of articulating life's memory, physicians also established the grounds of action appropriate to protect life and to prevent abortion—the relation within and between spaces of witnessing truth, the complementary arrangement of the public and the private by way of the prenatal. They also, necessarily, reiterated boundaries of privilege, of warlike opposition, and of identity. In its articulation, this space continually regenerated the topography of white patriarchal cultural order. Heterotopias also can be compensatory in that they create "a different real space as perfect, as meticulous, as well-arranged as ours is disorganized, badly arranged, and muddled."[41] Whether or not there were fewer abortions, in coming to remember what truths about life women's bodies held, a normative spatial arrangement of culture was also remembered. Prenatal space is not just a *product* of a traditional male dominant ideology, it is an important theater for its regeneration, a factor that can be understood in two ways.

First, given that prenatal space is neither public nor private, for it can certainly be both given the right context, it is more useful to refer to prenatal space as a terminal for divergent institutions to articulate their common interests. As a location involved in the invention of rhetoric, the womb connects the "spatial institutions" of the family, medicine, law, religion, and politics in the generation of authoritative discourse on life and its appropriate management.[42] Women's bodies, as biological storehouses of maternal truths, become a crossroads for institutional discourses that are directed toward managing life. Prenatal space is a point of articulation for divergent interests in "life" with biomedical nomenclature and imagery in the privileged position of common vernacular. The arrangement of these institutions, to each other and to individuals, can be understood by their connection though prenatal space. Whether it is a reductive rhetoric that condenses women into birthing apparatuses or a rhetoric of erasure that effaces women from reproduction, medical body criticism has helped transform women's bodies into culturally inventive spaces for embodying the body politic and the individual. As Foucault observed, medicine became the common denominator in biopolitics.[43] Whereas studies of public space link institutions by their relationship to the public, one can argue in an age of biopolitics that institutions linked to life have the potential to link prenatally.

Second, the scope of prenatal space can vary widely, rather than being limited to a singular physical location. Prenatal space can subsume and be subsumed by public space. Considered as a corporate entity, the reproductive capacity of the white affluent classes could encompass all of a civilization in its matrix. Similarly, the public could be swallowed by the vision of a single fetus. Conversely, the public can contain the individual womb of a woman on trial or in the public eye. Or each woman's body can be contained within the body politic's "womb," thereby justifying intervention. Hence, there is a reversibility of prenatal space, the scene of the corporeal body and the scene of the collective body, equally capable of containing the reproductive action of the other. The grand form, wherein the prenatal contains the public, is frequently used to inspire awe and respect, I have observed. Its diminished form, the public containing the prenatal, is often used to exercise control over reproductive capacity. Because it is represented as well as representational, prenatal space has a plasticity to its articulation that must be appreciated at the level of its "doing." We should ask of each manifestation, be it in the home, hospital, or senate floor, how was prenatal space done? The *possibility* of the fetus has been used to reproduce culture, not just in terms of ideals, not just in terms of roles, but in terms of the basic spatial arrangements between all kinds of entities.

Conclusion
In Living Memory

... sexuality *is* a somatic fact *created by* a cultural effect.
— Anne Fausto-Sterling, *Sexing the Body*

It is a somewhat startling, and to the moralist must be a disheartening fact, revealed by the statistician, as well as by the experience and observation of the medical practitioner, that a crime, in itself one of the foulest, and against which in times past the severest penalties have been attached, should, at this moment, be one of the most frequent not only in the older portions of the civilized world, but here, in our very midst, where it has been supposed, from the character of the population and of the institutions under which we live, a higher and more healthy moral tone must necessarily prevail. . . . It is rather to the medical profession, and to those more immediately entrusted with the morals of the community, that we are chiefly to look for the true remedy.
— *Boston Medical and Surgical Journal* editorial

This relationship of domination is no more a "relationship" than the place where it occurs is a place; and, precisely for this reason, it is fixed, throughout its history, in rituals, in meticulous procedures that impose rights and obligations. It establishes marks of its power and engraves memories on things and even within bodies.
— Michel Foucault, "Nietzsche, Genealogy, History"

On February 16, 1860, when the editors of the *Boston Medical and Surgical Journal* began a commentary on "Criminal Abortion" with the above quotation, they no doubt were little aware of the complex rhetoric necessary to substantiate a genealogy of abortion in the United States as a perverse detour from the moral order of life, much less that medicine was the means of moral restoration. The editors presented abortion as an aberrant disturbance in the history of reproduction. The United States of the nineteenth century was supposed to be a special time and place, one with "a higher more healthy moral tone." Yet, it was no longer clear when or where the United States was, given that "one of the foulest" crimes common to "older portions of the civilized world" was now common here as well. As the editorialists clarify in the full text, three hundred years prior, abortion, being "a violation of the positive laws of God" and "a total indifference to the most sacred privileges with which a woman is endowed," was treated as murder both civily and ecclesiastically. The emergence of this abnormality was demonstrated by measuring the descent of abortion practice, its evolution through myriad events, against a normative ideal of what should have been the *proper* descent of abortion practice, which would have been no descent at all. For the authors, had the order of life been respected, abortion practices would never have emerged in the nineteenth century as they did. The broader community of physicians, particularly regular obstetricians and gynecologists, did indeed attempt a remedy: a return to apparently forgotten truths located in the female body. Tracing the genealogy of culture through fetal life involved the forensic inspection of the body as the repertory of memory, a text in which a moral biological history of "civilization" might be inscribed.[1] To be sure, the biological age of "life" had been upon us for many decades already, but early medical antiabortion rhetoric was a significant episode in the larger project of transforming life into a mnemonic commonplace. Viewed in this light, we should resist the temptation to bracket issues other than individual rights when considering the interests of rhetoric about abortion.

Working from the premise that culture quickens itself alongside and through the possibility of the fetus, I have sought to illustrate how physicians successfully articulated the confluence of reproduction and remembrance over and above any impact the campaign had on abortion practice. Early antiabortion rhetoric invested fetal life with rights; it also invested fetal life with cultural survival. It is ironic that the antiabortion campaign did not stop abortion, but instead made it very difficult and contributed to the danger of the procedure. As Smith-Rosenberg argued, criminalization "effectively created the deadly underground of illegal abortions that thrived between the 1870s and the 1970s—an underground that took the lives of thousands of women annually." In 1936, Frederick Taussig, a leading authority on abortion at the time, estimated nearly 700,000 abortions annually in the United States, with "not less than 4000" deaths, deaths that were so often grisly, lonely, and slow.[2] However, it would be a mistake to see the campaign as singularly unproductive, horribly counterproductive in fact, relative to its theme of regenerating life. As a form of mnemonics, despite increasing numbers of abortions, early antiabortion rhetoric enabled the *opposition* to abortion to recuperate and reconfigure divisions of race, class, and gender in the form of medical truth about procreative sexuality.

When understood as a practice of anamnesis and hypomnesis, medical body criticism was the method by which antiabortion physicians constituted life's memory as a dialectical counterweight to a perceived cultural amnesia regarding life. Women's organs and medical texts about them functioned as a living memory and as a representational simulacrum of memory, a double-bodied archive that materialized higher truths. Through the metonymic and chiasmatic functions of body criticism, female organs and cycles were imbued with an organic discourse that only physicians could translate from spectacle to speech. In other words, cultural memory was made intelligible in terms comfortable to its biomedical home. Exegetical practices also linked the female body to public bodies by way of physicians. As privileged witnesses to the organic discourse about maternity embodied in women, physicians became prosthetic relays to the truth. The very acts that made cultural memory intelligible as biomedicine also conjoined physicians simultaneously to the womb and to the public. A network was formed between the source of memory, archivists, and those who wanted to remember. Finally, coincidental to these effects, the complementary spaces of the public and private were reformed through an intersection with an "in-between" prenatal space, as was the antagonistic space of the "bourgeois moral environment" and "civilization." In the context of a new medicine, the rhythm and order of space was reworked as physicians produced from reproductive custom a mnemonic system about human truth. Rhetorically, turnover in medical theory and failures in the battle against abortion practice did not interfere with this mnemonic system. On the contrary, they fed the drive to recall life's "truth."

Despite a clear articulation of an idealized normative order, full remembrance, full restoration of that order in the present is "in principle unrealizable," and the necessity of reciting norms to sustain them creates the condition of their perpetual subversion. The condition of possibility for memory is the inevitability of amnesia. In fact, Derrida argues that "right on that which permits and conditions archivization, we will never find anything other than that which exposes to destruction, and in truth menaces with destruction, introducing, *a priori*, forgetfulness." At the moment a memory of life's order formed, its dialectical counterpart, forgetfulness, did also. The resulting tensions formed the landscape of a rhetoric, as González explains: "The dialectic of remembering and forgetting maps the path of internal revisions and debate. Memory is never fixed."[3] According to physicians, abortion was caused principally by women's ignorance of their maternal instinct; they represented women as inherently monstrous and configured the female body as a source of death as well as life. The possibility that abortion resulted from knowing deliberation, not forgetfulness, was made incomprehensible. To consider maternity inessential to woman was a sign of possible madness or immature fashionability. Hence, cultural amnesia was made intelligible too, in terms comfortable to its biomedical home. Further, because women's bodies were a source of truth, whereas women's statements might not be, women as speaking subjects largely were separated from the archival process. Female testimony, whether as patient or physician, systematically was treated as suspect within emerging rituals of exposure, for fear of deceit or threat to virtue. A network of disjunctions formed that excluded women, placing them in an "untruthful" relation with the female body; women were to be witness*ed* more than to do any witness*ing*. Finally, spatially, the presence of abortion itself was a moral pathology within the very womb of a "civilized" nation. The proper rhythm and order to the United States would continue to be corrupted so as long as abortion lingered. As antiabortionists called for a restoration of moral order, the cultural amnesia indicated by abortion was constituted not as an outside threat, but one inherent within privileged women and within modern culture. Forgetfulness welled from the same spring as memory.

A mutual reinforcement of belief and action across interrelated performativities, *taken collectively*, reincarnated cultural norms in living memory. As noted from Certeau previously, the truth value of a rhetoric is contingent on the tangibility of that truth's embodiment: "Because the law is already applied with and on bodies, 'incarnate' in physical practices, it can accredit itself and make people believe that it speaks in the name of the 'real.'"[4] With abortion, expert practices of recuperating and recording sexual truth formed a reciprocal proof wherein the discourse and its object, conjoined through mutually dependent embodiment, each demonstrated the believability of the other. A traditional maternal imperative became a medical "reality" in that physicians embodied it within their models of health and in their practices regarding pregnancy. As physicians began to proceed as if parturition was the only healthy outcome to a pregnancy, the "as if" in their actions gave reality to a maternal imperative. That large number of pregnancies miscarried or that childbirth was very deadly only demonstrated the flaws of the female body, not possible flaws in physicians' assessment of abortion. The reality of a maternal imperative was physiologically "accredited" by the cumulative acts of antiabortion medical practice. The female body seemed to speak on behalf of women, with the aid of physicians. This effect is particularly powerful because two bodies, one biological and one discursive, were articulated together such that they shared the burden of recording "truth" about abortion for future use. As an archival process, the interplay of representational and perceptual practices produced a *citable reality*, a tangible truth available for various reiterations.

As a rejection of the maternal imperative, the act of abortion was in a mutually constitutive relationship with the medical assessment of women's reproductive nature. Bourgeois women were taking greater control of their reproductive capacity by interrupting pregnancy, and doing so in contrast to previous generations' practice and against religious narratives of God's plan for women. The Malthusian couple was a performative redefinition of heterosexual normality against past practice, a contrast that enabled physicians to find in physiology and tradition a lost truth incarnate. Because women could reproduce more and had done so in the past, the maternal imperative had a reality that physicians could claim to rediscover in female organs and cycles as a natural memory of what ought to be. Nor was there an immediate precedent for bodily control among women. Apparently lacking or refusing other incarnations to point to, archives to cite for emerging bodily sovereignty among women, physicians could couch abortion as untrue to God and nature. Every death from abortion, every complication could be used to reinforce the maternal imperative: following the laws of life would not cause injury. As a kind of "joint performance," the interaction of new bourgeois fertility norms and physicians' critical exegesis of the nature of maternity created a circular reinforcement between what was deemed natural and unnatural. We can appreciate the normative power of memory embodied "when . . . everyday life is envisaged as a structure of exemplary recurrence" wherein the force of belief "is wrought through what may be called *a rhetoric of re-enactment*."[5] Life's memory, *through* opposition to abortion, had become an archive about procreative normality regarding nation, race, class, and gender.

Consequently, in medical antiabortion rhetoric, articulating life's memory ultimately is about reproducing order through maternity, and the mnemonics of early antiabortionists did just that. Certainly, the order of white patriarchal ideology was reproduced, as Smith-Rosenberg has noted. Women were mothers by nature, dutiful by divine intent, and white women counted more than nonwhite women because their wombs held the future of the nation. Any divergence from this script was taken as probably deviant. However, medical practice was more than a *reflection* of this ideology. Symbolically, materially, and spatially, it helped rhetorically *constitute* the order of white Victorian gender ideology. Symbolically, white nationalism was made synonymous with women's reproductivity, making changed fertility norms symbolic threats to white entitlement. Materially, the practices of medicine reiterated the gendered truth seeking of early science, wherein the feminine was a threatening, mysterious source of higher truth that must be unveiled to the masculine mind to prevent danger. Further, medical practice established connections by which such revelations regarding life could circulate. Spatially, hierarchies of privilege and the geography of reproductive threats were demarcated biologically and environmentally as the prenatal assumed national importance. Narrowing Yuval-Davis and Anthias's argument by way of Butler, life as a "sex and sex-related construct" was deployed to regenerate the nation ideologically, symbolically, materially, and spatially. Accounting for the articulation of life's memory is an attempt to "delimit and describe the mundane manner in which these constructs are produced, reproduced, and maintained within the field of bodies."[6]

To articulate cultural memory is to do something other than give voice to ghosts from time's past, something more than render an intelligible story about yesterday's happenings, but something less than recreate a lost world. It is to disarticulate the contemporary order so as to transform it by incarnating some prior, or higher, order in its place. It is a kind of action that sunders the "here" from the "now," leaving a cleft that can only be sealed by a "then." Consequently, *where* is "here" and *when* is "now" come to be understood by their triangulation through some recollected "then." Memory produces in a place that is not its own, Certeau says of memory's cryptic nature. Memory has no home and, thus, must make room for itself elsewhere but not before transforming its new context. With memory, articulation is the performative enactment of a culturally productive relationship between anamnesis and hypomnesis.

These effects were lateral and unintended to the stated purpose of early antiabortionists. Antiabortionists did not set out to produce a mnemonic system for culture within the parameters of biomedical practice, nor did they anticipate that such a system might transcend the vicissitudes of medical theory. Instead, in the practice of attempting to learn the truth of life in the womb, which was set against the practice of abortion, they unavoidably constituted memory. The establishment of a functional mode of rhetoric requires sources of memory to be effective to the extent that each rhetorical act mnemonically "calls up" some knowledge, remembers some knowledge in a way that is meaningful to collectives, rather than just individuals. That is, sites of memory and protocols for access are substantiated, normalized. It can be the knowledge of shared experience, the knowledge of experiment, the knowledge of story, but for any performative act to reach the rhetorical horizon of intelligibility and communicability, remembrance of some sort must be practiced. To the extent that knowledge gains the force of seeming prearticulate and given by *way* of its articulation, knowledge is embodied, located as memory. In the case of nineteenth-century antiabortionists, to constitute life as a source of truth about reproductive practice also meant that death became a sign of forgetfulness. Without apparent design, cultural knowledge and the biology of reproduction were linked; therefore, negating life was negating culture, not just aborting a single individual.

To appreciate the mnemonic work of medical antiabortion rhetoric, then, we should not consider the articulation of cultural memory a rare or necessarily deliberate action; it is habitual and monotonous, a ubiquitous reassertion of past theses into contemporary compositions. The evidence of memory is always with us, it is always right here in our hands, before our eyes, in our thoughts as we scrutinize its contours. Yet, from a simultaneity of evidence and perception comes a rift through which other times enter and dwell in the present. González says "[i]t is possible, for example, to think of two different movements that make up the work of reviewing the past: *memory* which is an intrusion of the past into the present, and *remembrance*, which is a retrogressive movement from the present into a reconstruction of the past."[7] Memory work creates the diachronic *from within* the synchronic and does so relentlessly. Why? Because invention requires it.

Rhetorical invention is not about creation from whole cloth, but about the sometimes predictable, sometimes novel reformulation of recognizable forms and themes; it is about the tension of determinism and voluntarism, or "archaism and neologism." Certeau writes that, "In order to engender the future by reinscribing the present within the past," we "depend on the archaeology of gesture, objects, words, images, forms, and symbols, a repertory with many entrances from which are composed a landscape of communication and are invented the propositions of innovation." González has this activity in mind when she writes that "memory is less 'found' than fabricated. Consciousness is a patchwork rather than a seamless web." Invention is intricately interwoven with the patchwork production of an exterior perspective, both backward and forward looking, on the present moment, *within the present moment*. Producing an exterior from which to view the present is not limited to the relation of "speaker and audience as a form of persuasion or goal oriented activity." Cultural practices, as performative acts, have "rhetorical effectivity" through the "process of world disclosure," or the unfolding of social theses that are embedded in everyday enactment. The "multi-form presence of memory can be found everywhere, even in our most ostensibly theoretical inquiries." Memory work is the ancillary effect to the rhetorical tension between normativity and creativity within cultural practice. As Paul Connerton writes, "[a]ll beginnings contain an element of memory."[8] All rhetorically creative effort is necessarily, in part, *re*creative effort.

Rhetorical invention, then, is more than the articulation of some*thing* that is said; it is, as Foucault recognized in so many contexts, the articulation of parameters for what is intelligible and communicable. On a broad scale, it is not the invention of specific texts, but the limits of inventing culture that are at stake. Butler argues that constraint "impels and sustains" the reiteration of cultural norms, setting forth possibilities and fostering the compulsive recreation of past precedents. George Lipsitz addressed such compulsion in terms of memory and form: "Cultural forms create conditions of possibility, they expand the present by informing it with memories of the past and hopes for the future; but they also engender accommodation with prevailing power realities, separating art from life, and internalizing the dominant culture's norms as necessary and inevitable." Memory formation is a paramount concern for understanding how those limits and possibilities of reiteration are set. From where are past iterations of norms drawn? Where is cultural memory located? How is it accessed? Who is trusted to archive its contents? These all are questions that speak to the search for inventional limits. From this perspective, what is of interest rhetorically is not so much that early physicians articulated memory; it was where, how, and for whom that is of interest and "how the fixity of such constraints is established."[9]

If memory places constraint on invention, then the memory ensconced in reproductive life constrains the invention of anything dependent on it. At a time and place increasingly marked by population management through the optimization of the body's life forces, where control of "life" has become a nexus of power and politics, all things potentially are dependent on life. The nineteenth-century "invention of sexuality as the repository of human truth" made sex and sex-related constructs privileged, biologized repertories of memory, mnemonic commonplaces for cultural normativity. However, the reproduction of normativity through sexual truths depends not just on the centrality of sexuality in power relations, but also on the materialization of a *mnemonic system* that helps stabilize the performative order in which such truths are produced and circulated. At a performative level, life's memory impels and sustains institutions that link themselves to the "truth" about procreative sexuality. Studying the relationship of anamnesis to hypomnesis, truth to archive, allows one to conceptualize not only what those performative constraints are, but also how they achieve stability. The intangible "truths" of white patriarchal heteronormativity become citable as they were made concrete in archives, conjointly corporeal and discursive. These archives are themselves also maintained performatively in the ritualization of memory work, particularly in forms of body criticism that reify unseen, essential truths. In regard to the rhetorical history of abortion, we can delineate "what sexual (im)possibilities have served as the constitutive constraints" of procreative sexuality, "and what possibilities of reworking those constraints arise from within its own terms."[10] More than that, we can understand rhetoric about abortion against the grain of individualism and ask what other work is being accomplished. We can widen our focus from how the "individual" is created biomedically within normalizing institutions and begin to appreciate *how institutions are dependent on normalized bodies as sources of living memory*.

Within nineteenth-century antiabortion rhetoric, life in its very laws was to remember culture for us, if only we were able to listen and record the truths of that memory. To the extent that knowing the truth about reproduction produced cultural memory, the maternal imperative became an imperative to regenerate culture. In this way, cultural memory was necessarily gendered in its production because the conditions of remembrance instituted the ancient relation of the feminine as the medium for creation and the cache of potentiality.[11] Ironically, because all imperatives fail to some degree, hence requiring them to be continually cited, abortion became culturally productive even as it was cast as an essential forgetfulness. The early antiabortion campaign, although not stopping abortions, did bring abortion within a medicalized system of cultural mnemonics that, always working against its inherent failures, fueled still greater efforts to document the truth about reproductive sexuality. The persistence of abortion as a metaphor for cultural amnesia is part of the persistence of "life" as a metaphor for the true memory of sexual normativity and cultural order. To archive the truth of sex is not so much to freeze the past as it is to anticipate and constrain the future life of culture.

Notes

Notes for Preface

1. I use "semiosis" in the broad sense of "meaning-making" through metaleptic sub-stitution, rather than the more narrow structuralist sense which might exclude symbols, for example. My purposely imprecise use of the term includes all forms of textual and im-agistic representation, including symbolic, iconic, ideographic, and emblematic forms, as well as those that might be considered signs. The reason for such a broad definition stems from my understanding of articulation, which posits a wavering and flexible division be-tween the discursive and the nondiscursive, and the fact that I am not following a structuralist method, therefore obviating the need to follow such conventions. Further, although I invoke materiality and semiosis through separate terms, that is for analytical clarity and emphasis. As becomes clear by chapter 4, I consider materiality to be meaning-ful and, likewise, meaning to be material. How the confluence of materiality and semiosis are configured within a given rhetoric is the focus of this study.

2. For instance, it occurs to me that some might consider this volume as undecided about whether it is an archaeology or a genealogy, as if it were a flaw, and that is not accu-rate for several reasons. I do share an abiding interest in the basic thematic of each of these methods, the "processes of recuperation, of the distillation of earlier discursive imprints, remodeled in new forms." However, the scope of the project is simply not broad enough and the focus of my arguments make it inaccurate for me to adopt such labels. Although I do analyze a "local discursivity," I am not mapping a discursive formation, its full disper-sion of statement-events and all the strategic possibilities created by its principles of rarity or grids of intelligibility. I apply some aspects of biomedical discursivity, but only as they relate to appropriating the commonplace of biological life as cultural memory, specific to abortion in the United States, for the rules of biomedical discourse. In fact, the intercon-nectivity of different discursive formations through women's medicalized bodies would point to the porous margins of various discursivities, where purposeful heteroglossia and fungibility of rules become vectors of power relations. I am thinking about how different discursivities attempt to link to one another through certain kinds of bodies and how one formation comes to dominance as the privileged vernacular in such promiscuous locations. This work is certainly archaeological, but hardly an archaeology. Similarly, I am tracing the descent and emergence of discursive norms as they attach themselves to the body, but again the scope and direction of what I write is not a genealogy as Foucault describes. My

appropriation of his Nietzschean method is to remove it from its place as an alternative historiographic *method* and to think through genealogy as a common *factor* in discourse. To the extent that memory is always formed by articulatory practices, genealogy is traced. Academics engaged in writing a genealogy are, in effect, critically appraising a collective memory formation and reconstituting it. This does not mean rhetors do not make genealogical claims on their own; they are simply not using Foucault's methodology. Hence, here I look for the descent and emergence of culture as it is attached to the body by specific medical practices and texts. I am not writing a genealogy per se, I am tracing others' genealogical rhetoric. Finally, archaeological and genealogical tactics are "organically dependent and *complementary* tools of analysis," not mutually exclusive theoretical commitments (Ann Laura Stoler, *Race and the Education of Desire: Foucault's* History of Sexuality *and the Colonial Order of Things* [Durham, N. C.: Duke University Press, 1995], 68, 60). See Michel Foucault, *Archaeology of Knowledge*, trans. A. Sheridan (New York: Pantheon Books, 1972); idem, "Nietzsche, Genealogy, History," in *Language, Counter-Memory, Practice: Selected Essays and Interviews*, trans. Donald F. Bouchard and Sherry Simon and ed. Donald F. Bouchard (Ithaca: Cornell University Press, 1977), 139-64; idem, "Two Lectures," in *Power/Knowledge: Selected Interview & Other Writings, 1972-1977*, trans. Colin Gordon et al. and ed. Colin Gordon (New York: Pantheon Books, 1980), 78-108. Also see Gilles Deleuze, *Foucault*, trans. Seán Hand (Minneapolis: University of Minnesota Press, 1988); Hubert L. Dreyfus and Paul Rabinow, *Michel Foucault: Beyond Structuralism and Hermeneutics*, 2nd ed. (Chicago: University of Chicago Press, 1983); Elizabeth Grosz, *Volatile Bodies: Toward a Corporeal Feminism* (Bloomington: Indiana University Press, 1994), chs. 5 and 6; Michael Mahon, *Foucault's Nietzschean Genealogy: Truth, Power, and the Subject* (Albany: State University of New York Press, 1992).

Notes for Chapter One

1. I came across reproductions of these signs in Karen Newman, *Fetal Positions: Individualism, Science, Visuality* (Stanford: Stanford University Press, 1996), 9.

2. For examples see Alice Adams, *Reproducing the Womb: Images of Childbirth in Science, Feminist Theory, and Literature* (Ithaca: Cornell University Press, 1994); Monica Casper, "Operation to the Rescue: Feminist Encounters with Fetal Surgery," in *Fetal Subjects, Feminist Positions*, ed. Lynn Marie Morgan and Meredith W. Michaels (Philadelphia: University of Pennsylvania Press, 1999), 101-12; Celeste Condit, *Decoding Abortion Rhetoric: Communicating Social Change* (Urbana: University of Illinois Press, 1990); Barbara Duden, *Disembodying Women: Perspectives on Pregnancy and the Unborn* (Cambridge: Harvard University Press, 1994); idem, "The Fetus and the 'Farther Shore': Toward a History of the Unborn," in *Fetal Subjects, Feminist Positions*, ed. Lynn Marie Morgan and Meredith W. Michaels (Philadelphia: University of Pennsylvania Press, 1999), 13-25; Sarah Franklin, "Fetal Fascinations: New Dimensions to the Medical-Scientific Construction of Fetal Personhood," in *Off-Centre: Feminism and Cultural Studies*, ed. Sarah Franklin, Celia Lury, and Jackie Stacey (London: HarperCollinsAcademic, 1991), 190-205; Donna J. Haraway, *Modest_Witness@Second_Millenium.FemaleMan©_Meets_OncoMouse™: Feminism and Technoscience* (New York: Routledge, 1997); Valerie Hartouni, "Fetal Exposures: Abortion Politics and the Optics of Allusion," *Camera Obscura* 29 (1992): 131-49; Emily Martin, *The Woman in the Body: A Cultural Anal-*

ysis of Reproduction (Boston: Beacon Press, 1992); Meredith W. Michaels, "'Fetal Galaxies': Some Questions About What We See," in *Fetal Subjects, Feminist Positions*, ed. Lynn Marie Morgan and Meredith W. Michaels (Philadelphia: University of Pennsylvania Press, 1999), 113-32; Newman, *Positions*; Rosalind Petchesky, "Foetal Images: The Power of Visual Culture in the Politics of Reproduction," in *Reproductive Technologies: Gender, Motherhood and Medicine*, ed. Michelle Stanworth (Minneapolis: University of Minnesota Press, 1987), 57-80; Barbara Katz Rothman, *Recreating Motherhood: Ideology and Technology in a Patriarchal Society* (New York: Norton, 1989); and Carole Stabile, "Shooting the Mother: Fetal Photography and the Politics of Disappearance," *Camera Obscura* 28 (1992): 179-205.

3. Mary Poovey, "The Abortion Question and the Death of Man," in *Feminists Theorize the Political*, ed. Judith Butler and Joan W. Scott (New York: Routledge, 1992), 239-56. For an early example of analysis that argues the creation of woman as machine, see Gena Corea's *The Mother Machine: Reproductive Technologies from Artificial Insemination to Artificial Wombs* (New York: Harper & Row, 1986). Also see Dion Farquhar, *The Other Machine: Discourse and Reproductive Technologies* (New York: Routledge, 1996).

4. Duden concludes *Disembodying Women* by discussing the environmental linkages between fetal images and planet Earth, the pink disk and the blue disk of life. Haraway, in *Modest_ Witness*, discusses the rhetoric of the fetus in terms of its contribution to articulating a new world order in addition to the disembodiment of women accomplished through its imaging. Similarly, Dion Farquhar argues that the discourse of artificial reproductive technologies produce culture not just fetuses (*Other*).

5. See Carroll Smith-Rosenberg, *Disorderly Conduct: Visions of Gender in Victorian America* (New York: Oxford, 1985), 218, 219. Degler also writes that it was not until 1869 that "American Catholic bishops make a general pronouncement on abortion" (Carl N. Degler, *At Odds: Women and the Family in America from the Revolution to the Present* [New York: Oxford University Press, 1980], 239). Also see Zoila Acevedo, "Abortion in Early America," *Women & Health* 4, no. 2 (1979): 159-67; Janet Farrell Brodie, *Contraception and Abortion in 19th-Century America* (Ithaca: Cornell University Press, 1994); Charles R. King, "Abortion in Nineteenth Century America: A Conflict Between Women and Their Physicians," *Women's Health Issues* 2 (1992): 32-39; Michael A. La Sorte, "Nineteenth Century Family Planning Practices," *Journal of Psychohistory* 4, no. 2 (1976): 163-83; James Mohr, *Abortion in America: The Origins and Evolution of National Policy, 1800-1900* (New York: Oxford University Press, 1978); Leslie Reagan, *When Abortion Was Crime: Women, Medicine, and the Law in the United States, 1867-1973* (Berkeley: University of California Press, 1997), ch. 1.

6. Smith-Rosenberg, *Disorderly*, 219.

7. Haraway argues that to articulate is to produce both bodies and language from the same acts ("The Promises of Monsters: A Regenerative Politics for Inappropriate/d Others," in *Cultural Studies*, ed. Lawrence Grossberg et al. [New York: Routledge, 1992], 295-337; also see Bruno Latour, *Pandora's Hope: Essays on the Reality of Science Studies* [Cambridge, Mass.: Harvard University Press, 1999], 140-53). I would argue that such a production, "always already" embodied, also forms and manipulates social space of necessity. As I look at how a rhetoric constrains the invention of discourse, I want to understand how that rhetoric provides itself with an ancestry and makes room for itself in the future.

8. Barbara Maria Stafford, *Body Criticism: Imaging the Unseen in Enlightenment Art and Medicine* (Cambridge: MIT Press, 1993), 17. Stafford does not argue that the *female* body was the basic figure of a hidden truth, so much as the body generally. However, Page

duBois has traced the feminization of truth (*Torture and Truth* [New York: Routledge, 1991], ch. 14). As for ritualized exposure, Stafford's remarkably detailed *Body Criticism* is dedicated to outlining these practices and their justifications. It is a record of how the body was rejuvenated as the literal and metaphorical site of inquisition, as it had been with the Greeks.

9. I take up themes from his history of medical perception in chapters 3 and 5. For more detail, see Michel Foucault, *The Birth of the Clinic: An Archaeology of Medical Perception*, trans. A. M. Sheridan Smith (New York: Vintage, 1973), chs. 3-5. For a survey of the changes involved in U.S. hospitals, from almshouses to sites of knowledge production, see Paul Starr, *The Social Transformation of American Medicine: The Rise of a Sovereign Profession and the Making of Vast Industry* (New York: Basic Books, 1982), 149-62.

10. Foucault's morbid but insightful commentary is from *Birth*, 144-45, 125. Also see Adams, *Womb*.

11. Foucault, *Birth*, 166. Simpson's words appeared in an anthology published in the United States by H. R. Storer and W. Priestley, *Obstetric Memoirs and Contributions of James Y. Simpson, M.D., F.R.S.E.*, vol. 1, ed. W. Priestley & H. Storer (Philadelphia: J. B. Lippincott, 1855), 46. Alfred Meadows, "Remarks on Ovarian Physiology and Pathology," *American Journal of Obstetrics* 6, nos. 2-3 (1873): 215-47, 371-404. Also see Jonathan Sawday, "The Fate of Marsyas: Dissecting the Renaissance Body," in *Renaissance Bodies: The Human Figure in English Culture, c. 1540-1660*, ed. Lucy Gent and Nigel Llewellyn (London: Reaction Books, 1990), 111-35.

12. Simpson's quotation is from his anthology (*Obstetric*, 46). Storer and Priestley felt that Simpson's contributions were so significant, they wanted him to be read in the States. Tilt's comments are directed at the importance of the perceptual methods pioneered by the French in accessing the truth about reproductive pathology (*On the Diseases of Menstruation and Ovarian Inflammation* [London: John Churchill, 1857], xi, emphasis mine).

13. For the full address to the Association, see "Opening Address," *Peninsular Journal of Medicine* 1 (1853): 139-40. Many U.S. physicians studied in Paris as well, attempting to keep pace with the French revolution in medical practice (Starr, *Transformation*, 54-55). Lecture series by European clinical physicians were regularly published in U.S. journals. For instance, a multitude of lectures on uterine displacement by M. Valleix were published in the United States. ("Displacements of the Uterus," parts 1-7, 9-16, trans. L. Parks, Jr., *Boston Medical and Surgical Journal* 48 [1853]: 169-72, 229-34, 269-74, 318-22, 351-56, 392-96, 456-61; 49 [1853]: 89-93; 50 [1854]: 269-77; 334-39, 412-18; 51 [1855]: 15-20, 129-35, 236-41, 335-42); similarly, M. Jobert, "the first surgeon of the Emperor of France" was held up as an example of how to employ cautery in the treatment of the uterus (W. E. Johnson, "The Actual Cautery of Diseases of the Uterus," *New Orleans Medical and Surgical Journal* 10 [1854]: 397).

14. Tilt's proclamation opens a history of gynecology contained in his *A Handbook of Uterine Therapeutics and of Diseases of Women*, 4th ed. (New York: William Wood & Co., 1881), 1; T. Gaillard Thomas, *Practical Treatise on the Diseases of Women*, 3rd ed. (Philadelphia: Henry C. Lea, 1872), 46. Récamier's colleague, Madame Boivin, was also a great advocate of the speculum. Specula were used in Roman times, but exactly when early modern physicians resuscitated the instrument is open to debate (see Richard A. Leonardo, *History of Gynecology* [New York: Froben Press, 1944], 282-96). There also is debate about the hierarchy of perception in obstetrics and gynecology of the nineteenth century. Richard W. Wertz and Dorothy C. Wertz argue that touch was the preferred mode of perception for several reasons, not the least of which was a sense of morality and deco-

rum (*Lying-In: A History of Childbirth in America*, exp. ed [New Haven: Yale University Press, 1989], 90). This might have been the case with parturition proper in the earlier half of the century, which is the emphasis of their study. However, there is evidence for the emergence of a visual mode of perception in the latter half of the century, as argued by Jane Donegan, *Women & Men Midwives: Medicine, Morality, and Misogyny in Early America* (Westport, Conn.: Greenwood Press, 1978), 156-57. I demonstrate in chapters 3 and 5 that Donegan's observations are more accurate.

15. J. C. Nott, "On a New Duck-Bill Speculum, for Private Practice," *New Orleans Journal of Medicine* 22 (1870): 146. Information on Churchill's ambivalence about the speculum is from Donegan (*Women*, 157). Gardner was enthusiastic about the speculum, but not alone ("The Speculum and Its Modifications," *The Peninsular Journal of Medicine* 2 [1854]: 39). Also see Nott, "Duck-Bill"; Edmond Souchon, "Speculum Holder or Retainer, an Apparatus for Keeping in Place Sims' Duck-Bill Speculum, Without an Assistant," *New Orleans Journal of Medicine* 23 (1870): 81-84. The first commonly used speculum was designed by J. Marion Sims, the much lauded "father of gynecology." For more information on Sims, see James V. Ricci, *The Development of Gynaecological Surgery and Instruments* (Philadelphia: Blakiston Company, 1949), 313-315; Diana Scully, *Men Who Control Women's Health: The Miseducation of Obstetrician-Gynecologists*, rev. ed. (New York: Teacher's College Press, 1994), 40-48.

16. Warren Stone, "Observations Upon Disease of the Uterus," *New Hampshire Journal of Medicine* 5 (1855): 75. Stone was not without his own assumptions, however. He claimed that inflammation was the real cause of most diseases and that married women who engaged in proper behavior hardly suffered from disease (read true womanhood). Illegitimate sex practices caused most "uterine disease," then.

17. Many texts attest to this. Indeed, Edward Tilt argued in 1881 that the turn to the visual was the great advance in obstetrics and gynecology (*Handbook*, 1-3). Prior to the nineteenth century, direct examination was not the norm. For example, Barbara Duden has documented the medical practice of a doctor Johannes Storch in the eighteenth century, who relied generally on a method of question and answer to diagnose his patients (*The Woman Beneath the Skin: A Doctor's Patients in Eighteenth-Century Germany* [Cambridge: Harvard University Press, 1991]). In the United States in the early nineteenth-century, customs of physical modesty made it difficult for physicians to implement full bodily access to the patient both in education and in practice (Wertz & Wertz, *Lying-In*, ch. 3). For more background on direct examination in medicine, see John Balbirnie, *The Speculum Applied to the Diagnosis and Treatment of the Organic Disease of the Womb* (London: Longman, Rees, Orme, Brown, Green, and Longman, 1836); Donegan, *Midwives*; William Jones, *Practical Observations on Diseases of Women* (London: H. Bailliere, 1839); Charles D. Meigs, *Females and Their Diseases* (Philadelphia: Lea and Blanchard, 1848); Roy Porter, "The Rise of Physical Examination," in *Medicine and the Five Senses*, ed. W. F. Bynum and Roy Porter (Cambridge: Cambridge University Press, 1993), 179-97; Stanley Joel Reiser, *Medicine and the Reign of Technology* (Cambridge: Cambridge University Press, 1978); Ricci, *Development*; J. Marion Sims, *Clinical Notes on Uterine Surgery* (New York: William Wood & Co., 1866).

18. Maurice Halbwachs, *On Collective Memory*, ed., trans. Lewis A. Coser (Chicago: University of Chicago Press, 1992), 53, 169. Elizabeth Grosz argues "the exploration of conceptions of space and time as necessary correlates of the exploration of corporeality" (*Space, Time, and Perversion: Essays on the Politics of Bodies* [New York: Routledge, 1995], 84). Only after determining the space-time frameworks that schematize bodies can we change them or even debate the politics of the body.

19. Barbie Zelizer, *Remembering to Forget: Holocaust Memory Through the Camera's Eye* (Chicago: University of Chicago Press, 1998), 3. Zelizer is not referring to the specific view of memory as performative (in contrast to the view of memory as transcendent within medical epistemology), but the larger notion of collective memory as social, cultural, political, and I would add necessarily rhetorical, action is applicable.

20. Jacques Derrida discusses the connection between medicine, writing, and anamnesis in Platonic texts in his essay on the *pharmakon* (*Dissemination*, trans. Barbara Johnson [Chicago: University of Chicago Press, 1981], 105); also see Evelyn Fox and Christine R. Grontkowski, "The Mind's Eye," in *Feminism & Science*, ed. Evelyn Fox Keller and Helen E. Longino (Oxford: Oxford University Press, 1996), 187-202.

21. The idea of wresting hidden truths from nature by means of rational inquiry is characteristic of scientific discourse since before Descartes, although the Cartesian influence is important. After Descartes, the Platonic imperative to discern divine essences was reinvigorated in monistic, mechanistic form, wherein one rediscovered the universal rationality of God by abstracting true principles from the world's mechanisms.

22. See Bedford's lengthy "Clinical Lectures on Diseases of Women and Children," *Nelson's American Lancet* 7, no. 3 (1853): 101-19; 8, no. 1 (1853-1854): 3-22; 9, no. 1, 3 (1854): 3-12, 85-92; 10, nos. 3-5 (1854): 99-106, 147-64, 186-96; J. B. W. Nowlin, "Criminal Abortion," *The Southern Practitioner* 9, no. 5 (1887): 179-80. Storer's essay was originally written in the early 1850s, but not published until H. R. Storer had editorial control over his own periodical and printed it as "Two Frequent Causes of Uterine Disease," *Journal of the Gynecological Society of Boston* 6 (1872): 197-98, emphasis mine.

23. Hugh Hodge, *On Criminal Abortion* (Philadelphia: T. K. and P. G. Collins, 1854), 18. For the others referenced, see Edwin M. Hale, *The Great Crime of the Nineteenth Century. Why Is It Committed? Who Are the Criminals? How Shall They Be Detected?* (Chicago: 1867); Elizabeth Blackwell, *Counsel to Parents on the Moral Education of Their Children*, 4th ed. (New York: Brentano Bros., 1883); Andrew Nebinger, *Criminal Abortion: Its Extent and Prevention* (Philadelphia: Collins, 1870); Nowlin, "Criminal"; Annetta Kratz, "An Essay on Criminal Abortion," (M.D. thesis, Women's Medical College of Pennsylvania, Special Collection on Women and Medicine at Allegheny University [hereafter SCWM], 1870-71); Lydia M. Hunt, "Thesis," (M.D. thesis, Women's Medical College of Pennsylvania, SCWM, 1880); Helen M. Miller, "Foeticide," (M.D. thesis, Women's Medical College of Pennsylvania, SCWM, 1884); Mary Mitchell, "Infanticide: Its Moral and Legal Aspects," (M.D. thesis, Women's Medical College of Pennsylvania, SCWM, 1884); For other examples, see J. S. Andrews, "Infanticide," *Massachusetts Eclectic Medical Journal* 4, no. 7 (1884): 289-97; T. W. Hurley, "The Prevention of Conception—Abortions, Justifiable and Criminal," *Transactions of the Arkansas Medical Society, Twenty-Eighth Session* (Little Rock: Thompson Litho. and Printing, 1904): 268; Joseph Taber Johnson, "Abortion and Its Effects," *American Journal of Obstetrics* 33 (1896): 92; Jennie G. Oreman, "The Medical Woman's Temptation and How to Meet It," *The Woman's Medical Journal* 11, no. 3 (1901): 87-88.

24. H. R. Storer, *Why Not? A Book for Every Woman* (Boston: Lee and Shepard, 1868), 70, 37-38. His book, originally an essay, was awarded the AMA's gold medal by his colleagues in 1865, but it is not at all clear that the contest was not rigged. His father chaired the committee that awarded the prize. Storer mentioned instinctual repugnance many pages before the "traces of regret" and in relation to all people and physicians specifically (*Why Not?*, 17 and 43, respectively). However, his theme of instinctual knowledge is so pervasive, I do not think this condensation of prose is misrepresentative. For more information on the gold medal prize, see Mohr, *Abortion*, 158.

25. Storer, *Why Not?*, 48, 49, 15.

26. Ibid., 74-75. Storer also wrote a piece explicitly on uterine-based madness, an early form of the "hysterical woman" that would permeate discourse about bourgeois women in the late nineteenth and early twentieth centuries. For background on women and insanity in this period, consider Barbara Ehrenreich and Deidre English, *For Her Own Good: 150 Years of Experts' Advice to Women* (Garden City, N.Y.: Anchor Books, 1978); Charlotte Perkins Gilman, "Why I Wrote 'The Yellow Wallpaper,'" in *The Captive Imagination: A Casebook on "The Yellow Wallpaper,"* ed. Catherine Golden (New York: Feminist Press, 1992), 51-53; Elaine Showalter, *The Female Malady: Women, Madness, and English Culture* (New York: Pantheon Books, 1985); and Ann Douglas Wood, "'The Fashionable Diseases': Women's Complaints and Their Treatment in Nineteenth-Century America," *Journal of Interdisciplinary History* 4 (1973): 25-52.

27. The nostalgic call for "olden times" is from Storer, *Criminal Abortion: Its Nature, Its Evidence, and Its Law* (Boston: Little, Brown, 1868), 46; Alice B. Stockham, *Tokology: A Book for Every Woman*, 2nd ed. (Chicago, 1883), 231. My style is glib but these rationales are present in the medical literature and in popular tracts of the time. For example, Storer quotes from "A Woman's Thoughts About Women," in which the author mentions women boasting of abortions as they did of social climbing (*Why Not?*, quotation from 42, 81).

28. G. Maxwell-Christine, "The Medical Profession vs. Criminal Abortion," *Transactions of the Twenty-Fifth Session of the Homeopathic Medical Society of the State of Pennsylvania* (Philadelphia: Sherman Co., 1890), 73, 69. For examples of the "civilization in decline" narrative, see Andrews, "Infanticide," 297; Kratz, "Criminal," 12; Mitchell, "Infanticide," 3-4; Nowlin, "Criminal," 179-80; A. M. Longshore-Potts, *Discourses to Women on Medical Subjects*, 12th ed. (National City, San Diego Co., Calif.: Longshore-Potts, 1897), 297; "Criminal Abortion," *The Colorado Medical Journal and Western Medical and Surgical Gazette* 9, no. 3 (1903): 170-71; E. F. Fish, "Criminal Abortion," *Milwaukee Medical Journal* 17, no. 4 (1909): 107; H. C. Ghent, "Criminal Abortion, or Foeticide, and the Prevention of Conception," *The Texas Courier-Record of Medicine* 23, no. 5 (1906): 1-16; John M. Grant, "Criminal Abortion," *Interstate Medical Journal* 13 (1906): 514; William Asbury Hall, "Criminal Abortion and Its Treatment," *Northwestern Lancet* 8 (1888): 113; Johnson, "Abortion"; Mary Parsons, "The Written Law in Reference to the Unborn Child," *Washington Medical Annals* 9 (1910/11): 153-60; Edmund J. A. Rogers, "The Attitude of the Profession Toward Abortion," *The Colorado Medical Journal and Western Medical and Surgical Gazette* 9, no. 3 (1903): 149; James Foster Scott, "Criminal Abortion," *American Journal of Obstetrics* 33 (1896): 73, 77.

29. Nebinger, *Criminal*, 19; Oreman, "Temptation," 88. The number of physicians is legion who claim education about abortion's truth is the only real remedy. For a few examples, see Andrews, "Infanticide," 290; "Discussion of Criminal Abortion," *American Journal of Obstetrics* 33 (1896): 132; Kratz, "Criminal"; Ghent, "Criminal"; Hale, *Great Crime*; Hodge, *Criminal*; Hurley, "Prevention"; Hunt, "Thesis," 8-9; Miller, "Foeticide"; Mitchell, "Infanticide"; Nowlin, "Criminal," 180; Charlotte Whitehead Ross, "Abortion," (M.D. thesis, Women's Medical College of Pennsylvania, SCWM, 1875), 8-9; Scott, "Criminal Abortion"; Stockham, *Tokology*; Storer, H. R. et al. "Report on Criminal Abortion," *Transactions of the American Medical Association* 13 (1859).

30. I have adapted Derrida's discussion of the dynamics of memory from his discussion of Freud's "impression" (*Archive Fever: A Freudian Impression*, trans. Eric Prenowitz [Chicago: University of Chicago Press, 1995], 11, 68, 67). The performative character of memory work is what I am after. I have done so because, although I am informed by

158 Notes for pages 17-19

the "processes of recuperation" that mark Foucault's work, his notion of an archive in the *Archaeology* is about the "system of enunciability" and the "system of functioning" of statement-events; "it is the first law of what can be said" (129). As I mentioned in note 2 of the preface, the scope of my work is simply not that broad. What is more, his emphasis on the abstract system of rules over the material performance in the *Archaeology* is at odds with the focus I am taking. So, although my work broadly resonates with a Foucauldian notion of archive, the performative dynamics of memory work are poached from Derrida. I feel it necessary to appropriate and modify both to be able to attend to the materialization of a rhetorical commonplace in medical practices.

31. Smith-Rosenberg argues that within fictional literature, women developed a symbolic discourse that "paralleled and opposed the male antiabortion discourse" (*Disorderly*, 243).

32. Wife of a Christian physician, "'Why Not? A Book For Every Woman.' A Woman's View" *Boston Medical and Surgical Journal* 75, no. 14 (1866): 274-75, emphasis in original. Linda Gordon describes the convergence of a promotherhood ideology of fertility control in her chapter on "Voluntary Motherhood" (*Woman's Body, Woman's Right: Birth Control in America*, rev. ed. [New York: Penguin Books, 1990], 106). Degler provides the information on contraception advocates opposing abortion (*At Odds*, 245). The quotation on moral forgetfulness is from "'Why Not?'," 274. I have forgone any lengthy discussion of sex drives and morality because the complexity of sexuality in the medical scene and views on women's frigidity prohibits a fair treatment at this moment. For a more specific analysis of Storer's text and the letter, see Nathan Stormer, "*Why Not?* Memory and Counter-Memory in 19th-Century Abortion Rhetoric," *Women's Studies in Communication* 24, no.1 (2001): 1-29.

33. Rachel B. Gleason, *Talks to My Patients: Hints on Getting Well and Keeping Well* (New York: M. L. Holbrook Co., 1895), 159, 162, emphasis in original. Elizabeth Blackwell, *Pioneer Work in Opening the Medical Profession to Women* (London: Longmans, Green, and Co.), 30. Regina Morantz-Sanchez, *Sympathy and Science: Women Physicians in American Medicine* (New York: Oxford University Press, 1985), 218, quotations from 220, 225. Information on Sarah Dolley is from Ellen S. More, *Restoring the Balance: Women Physicians and the Profession of Medicine, 1850-1995* (Cambridge, Mass.: Harvard University Press, 1999), 13, 35-36. Degler characterized women physicians as expanding the blame, but not refuting the indictment (*At Odds*, 245). Also see Susan Wells, *Out of the Dead House: Nineteenth-Century Women Physicians and the Writing of Medicine* (Madison: University of Wisconsin Press, 2001), 32.

34. The distinction of "official" from "vernacular" memory is adapted from John Bodnar, *Remaking America: Public Memory, Commemoration, and Patriotism in the Twentieth Century.* (Princeton, N.J.: Princeton University Press, 1992). For a discussion of how historiography might affect the play of "official" versus "vernacular" memory, see Yael Zerubavel, *Recovered Roots: Collective Memory and the Making of Israeli National Tradition* (Chicago: University of Chicago Press, 1995).

35. For example, Foucault indicates in "Nietzsche, Genealogy, History" that counter-memory also begins in the body. Walter Benjamin writes that "calenders do not measure time as clocks do; they are monuments of a historical consciousness" (*Illuminations: Essays and Reflections*, trans. Harry Zohn, ed. and intro. Hannah Arendt [New York: Schocken Books, 1968], 261-62). The calendrical marker here is not some holiday, but the "healthy" reproductive cycle as monument to civilization. I discuss the counter-memory of the anonymous letter in greater detail in "*Why Not?* Memory and Counter-Memory in 19th-Century Abortion Rhetoric," *Women's Studies in Communication* 24, no.1 (2001): 1-

29. There is an argument, however, that remembrance is *essential* to revolt. Herbert Marcuse invested anamnesis with revolutionary potential, holding that forgetfulness (in its more essential meaning) was a consequence of bourgeois society (*The Aesthetic Dimension: Toward a Critique of Marxist Aesthetics* [Boston: Beacon Press, 1978], 64-69, 73; *One Dimensional Man: Studies in the Ideology of Advanced Industrial Society* [Boston: Beacon Press, 1964], 99). In an unexpected parallel, like early antiabortionists, he found bourgeois culture had eroded the past and he argued for the utopian possibilities in recollection (*Eros and Civilization: A Philosophical Inquiry into Freud* [Boston: Beacon Press, 1966]). Yet, Marcuse explicitly dismissed "remembrance of a Golden Past (which never existed), of childhood innocence, primitive man, etc. Remembrance as epistemological faculty rather is synthesis, reassembling the bits and fragments which can be found in the distorted humanity and distorted nature" (*Counter-Revolution and Revolt* [Boston: Beacon Press, 1972], 70). As Martin Jay argues, Marcuse's anamnesic theory lacks a working explanation of "mnemonic praxis," "that recollection is too close to repetition" in its form, and that, via Marcuse's appropriation of Freud, he "smuggled an a priori philosophical anthropology into Critical Theory" (*Marxism & Totality: The Adventures of a Concept from Lukács to Habermas* [Berkeley: University of California Press, 1982], 237, 236). Agreeing with Jay, I reject this understanding of memory on grounds of its essentialism because, as I will demonstrate, bourgeois culture was also in the game of remembering. Memory and counter-memory have everything to do with one's political relation to the past. Rather than posit an a priori within memory, which leads back to Neoplatonic tendencies, I understand remembrance as culturally performative, thereby explaining how collective memory is constituted from individual acts. The normative force of remembrance is not always on the side of dominance because, as a performance, it is caught in the prospects of its failures (Amy Allen, "Power Trouble: Performativity as Critical Theory" *Constellations* 5 [1998]: 456-71). The tension of remembrance and forgetfulness is equally at issue whether one is attempting to produce a Golden Past, a hidden legacy of brutality, or any other collective memory. Remembrance does not serve the left or the right; always working within and against the limits of prevailing power asymmetries, it is a kind of action that is continually, simply made to serve.

Notes for Chapter Two

1. Dilip Parameshwar Gaonkar, "Rhetoric and Its Double: Reflections on the Rhetorical Turn in the Human Sciences," in *The Rhetorical Turn*, ed. Herbert Simons (Chicago: University of Chicago Press, 1990).

2. James Mohr has written the most comprehensive and sweeping history of abortion in the nineteenth century, *Abortion in America* (148). Information on Storer's ambition and the block quotation are from Mohr, *Abortion*, 149-51, 152. Smith-Rosenberg provides the details about legislation in the 1840s (*Disorderly*, 220). The most extensive biography on Storer is by Frederick N. Dyer; although he seems unaware of or unconcerned by the race, class, or gender ideology in Storer's discourse, Dyer's attention to factual details is very helpful (*Champion of Women and the Unborn: Horatio Robinson Storer, M.D.* [Canton, Mass.: Science History Publications, 1999]).

3. Smith-Rosenberg provides the summary of legislation (*Disorderly*, 221). Brodie's work is a fascinating and extensive history of the popular discourse around contraception and abortion from the nineteenth century (*Contraception*, 286).

4. For a discussion of the animosities between specialists and general practitioners, see William G. Rothstein, *American Physicians in the Nineteenth Century: From Sects to Science* (Baltimore: Johns Hopkins University Press, 1972), 207-11. For an example of the debate, see G. E. Herrick, "Specialties," *Michigan Medical News* 4/5 (1881-1882): 40-41. A voluntary motherhood advocate, Herrick critiqued the antiabortionists after they had gained centrality in medical discourse, arguing no "woman should be forced to become and unwilling mother" ("Abortion and Its Lessons," *Michigan Medical News* 4/5 [1881-1882]: 7-10.) Also, for more on regional and sectarian conflicts, see James H. Cassedy, *Medicine in America: A Short History* (Baltimore: Johns Hopkins University Press, 1991), ch. 2; Mohr, *Abortion*, ch. 6; Starr, *Social Transformation*, 79-144.

5. Brodie (*Contraception*), Mohr (*Abortion*), and Smith-Rosenberg (*Disor-derly*) all make note of the pervasive nativistic population politics of early abortion opponents and the fear for white racial superiority, but none of them makes more than a small sidebar out of the issue. Further, Degler seems to give all the force of the rhetoric to the persuasive-ness of the idea that life begins as conception (*At Odds*). Their projects were not devoted to understanding the aspects of whiteness and white superiority involved in reproductive control. I consider this a significant perspectival limitation and one I would like to redress after examining the literature with a different eye. I believe biopolitics now provides an indispensable lens for understanding the rhetoric of early opponents.

6. Smith-Rosenberg provides a quick analysis of gendered argumentative assump-tions and metaphors in early physicians' rhetoric (*Disorderly*, 239-244). She argues, in effect, that physicians' ideas of women were deeply incorrect. However, to pursue a rhe-torical analysis within the confines of traditional notions of rhetoric and to focus on whether or not science gets the right picture of women prevents us from appreciating the magnitude of the rhetorical work done by early physicians.

7. Stoler quoting Foucault in *Race*, 79. Stoler's project is to reread Foucault in light of modern imperialism, paying particular attention to his College de France lectures re-garding the emergence of state racism. She argues that technologies of sexuality were in-volved, not only in constituting a bourgeois self, but also in struggles over who would be allowed to live and flourish in society, making class and race conflict modes of perpetual struggle rather than as causative conditions of identity and power. Complicated admixtures of race and class are produced by modern states as part of this struggle and are strongly informed by the experience of race and sexuality in imperial contexts, the Dutch East In-dies serving as her exemplar. Normative gender performances, as they relate to regimens of sexuality, thus are central technologies of struggle, whereby "a fundamental division between those who must live and those who must die" is produced and regulated (Stoler quoting Foucault, *Race*, 84). Hence, race becomes a means of normatively educating de-sire as to its functional role within social struggle. Also see Michel Foucault, "Society Must be Defended" and "Security, Territory, and Population," in *Ethics: Subjectivity and Truth; Essential Works of Foucault, 1954-1984*, vol. 1, ed. Paul Rabinow (New York: New Press, 1997), 59-71.

8. For more background on these social changes, see Mary H. Blewett, *Men, Women, and Work: Class, Gender, and Protest in the New England Shoe Industry, 1780-1910* (Urbana: University of Illinois Press, 1990); Sara M. Evans, *Born for Liberty: A History of Women in America* (New York: Free Press, 1989), 73, 130-138; Gordon, *Woman's Body*, 11, 16, 95, 134-35, 145-47; Matthew Frye Jacobson, *Whiteness of a Different Co-lor: European Immigrants and the Alchemy of Race* (Cambridge, Mass.: Harvard Univer-sity Press, 1998); Raymond Mohl, ed., *The Making of Urban America* (Wilmington, Del.: SR Books, 1988); Raymond A. Mohl and Neil Betten, eds. *Urban America in Historical*

Perspective (New York: Weybright and Talley, 1970); Eric. H. Monkkonen, *America Becomes Urban: The Development of U.S. Cities and Towns 1780-1980* (Berkeley: University of California Press, 1988); David Roediger, *The Wages of Whiteness: Race and the Making of the American Working Class* (London: Verso, 1991), 1-163; Stanley K. Schultz, *Constructing Urban Culture: American Cities and City Planning, 1800-1920* (Philadelphia: Temple University Press, 1989); Smith-Rosenberg, *Disorderly,* 167-81; Christine Stansell, *City of Women: Sex and Class in New York, 1789-1860* (New York: Alfred A. Knopf, 1986); Alan Trachtenberg, *The Incorporations of America: Culture & Society in the Gilded Age* (New York: Hill and Wang, 1982), 36-139; Barbara Welter, *Dimity Convictions: The American Woman in the Nineteenth Century* (Athens, Oh.: Ohio University Press, 1976); Howard Zinn, *A People's History of the United States 1492-Present* (Rev. ed., New York: HarperPerennial, 1995), 206-289.

9. Republican motherhood, stemming from Enlightenment political philosophy, presumed a social contract within the family that placed maternity within the political structure rather than within the kinship system of an aristocracy. For a discussion of republican motherhood, the idea that the proper citizen was morally cultivated within the home (a stark contrast to classical notions of cultivated citizenship), see Evans (*Born,* 63-5, quotation from 95), Linda K. Kerber (*Women of the Republic: Intellect and Ideology in Revolutionary America* [Chapel Hill, N.C.: University of North Carolina Press, 1980], especially ch. 9), and Nancy F. Cott (*The Bonds of Womanhood: "Woman's Sphere" in New England, 1780-1835,* 2nd ed. [New Haven, Conn.: 1997]). True womanhood, as Welter termed it, is now infamous within feminist circles. The idea of that a true woman naturally embodied the virtues of domesticity, piety, purity, and submissiveness can be found throughout nineteenth-century literature, religious prose, medical discourse, and political tracts. See Welter (*Dimity,* 21-41, 57-70), Smith Rosenberg (*Disorderly,* 129-216), and Evans (*Born,* 95-101).

10. In the final chapter of the first volume of *The History of Sexuality: An Introduction* (trans. Robert Hurley [New York: Vintage, 1990], quotation from 124), Foucault argues that the bourgeois body entered relations of power through the vulnerability of sex which resulted in the intense regulation of the body's sexuality through medicine and law. Gayle Rubin makes parallel arguments through Marx, Freud, and Levi-Strauss in her now classic piece, "The Traffic in Women: Notes on the 'Political Economy' of Sex," in *Toward an Anthology of Women,* ed. Rayna Rapp Reiter (New York: Monthly Review Press, 1976), 157-210. Stoler stresses that class war and race war are contingent vectors of an underlying dynamic of a society at war with itself (*Race,* 84).

11. Susan Bordo quoting Barbara Johnson in *Unbearable Weight: Feminism, Western Culture, and the Body,* (Berkeley: University of California Press, 1993), 17; Foucault, *History,* 138, emphasis in original; Stoler, *Race,* 96-97, 83.

12. Michel Foucault, "Body/Power," in *Power/Knowledge: Selected Interviews & Other Writings, 1972-1977,* trans. Colin Gordon et al. and ed. Colin Gordon (New York: Pantheon Books, 1980), 62; idem, *History,* 125. In addition to Stoler (*Race*), numerous authors from different vantage points have directly and indirectly explored the thesis that racial categories are constituted by multiple factors including ethnicity and class. For an assortment of examples, see Sander L. Gilman, *Difference and Pathology: Stereotypes of Sexuality, Race, and Madness* (Ithaca, N.Y.: Cornell University Press, 1985); David Goldberg, "The Social Formation of Racist Discourse," in *Anatomy of Racism,* ed. David Goldberg (Minneapolis: University of Minnesota Press, 1990), 295-318; Jacobson, *Whiteness;* Frank Livingstone, "On the Nonexistence of Race," in *The Racial Economy of Science: Toward a Democratic Future,* ed. Sandra Harding (Bloomington: Indiana Uni-

versity Press, 1993) 133-41; Gloria A. Marshall, "Racial Classifications: Popular and Scientific," in *The Racial Economy of Science: Toward a Democratic Future*, ed. Sandra Harding (Bloomington: Indiana University Press, 1993), 116-27; Ann McClintock, *Imperial Leather: Race, Gender and Sexuality in the Colonial Contest* (New York: Routledge, 1995); Radhika Mohanram, *Black Body: Women, Colonialism, and Space* (Minneapolis: University of Minnesota Press, 1999); Roediger, *Wages*, 133-63; Michael Omi and Howard Winant, *Racial Formation in the United States: From the 1960s to the 1990s*, 2nd ed., (New York: Routledge, 1994); Edward Said, *Orientalism* (New York: Pantheon Books, 1978).

13. In addition to discussing population, C. W. Gleason presented lectures on digestion, respiration, blood circulation, the skin, musculature, and the brain and nerves in *Seven Lectures on the Philosophy of Life and the Art of Preserving Health* (Columbus: Scott & Bascom, 1852), 10-11. Other equally representative examples reflecting a wide variety of biopolitical variation include, Blackwell, *Counsel*; idem, *The Human Element in Sex* (London: 1884); idem, *A Medical Address on the Benevolence of Malthus, Contrasted with the Corruptions of the Neo-Malthusianism* (London, 1888); P. C. Dunne and A. F. Derbois, *The Young Married Lady's Private Medical Guide*, trans. F. Harrison Dunne (1854); M. L. Holbrook, *Stirpiculture; or, the Improvement of Offspring Through Wider Generation* (New York: M. L. Holbrook, 1897); Prudence B. Saur, *Maternity: A Book for Every Wife and Mother*, rev. ed. (Chicago: L. P. Miller & Company, 1888); Sarah Hackett Stevenson, *Physiology for Women* (Chicago: Fairbanks, Palmer, 1882); George H. Taylor, *Health for Women* (New York: American Book Exchange, 1880). For more information on the kinds of modern hygienic and health based discourses, Brodie, *Contraception*, 57-86; Joan Burbick, *Healing the Republic: The Language of Health and the Culture of Nationalism in Nineteenth-Century America* (Cambridge: Cambridge University Press, 1994); Gilman, *Difference*; Gordon, *Woman's Body*, 72-90; Ronald Walter Greene, *Malthusian Worlds: U.S. Leadership and the Governing of Population Crisis* (Boulder, Colo.: Westview Press, 1999); Kathleen Hall Jamieson, *Beyond the Double Bind: Women and Leadership* (New York: Oxford University Press, 1995), 54-66; Ludmilla Jordanova, *Sexual Visions: Images of Gender in Science and Medicine between the Eighteenth and Twentieth Centuries* (Madison, Wisc.: University of Wisconsin Press, 1989); Thomas Laqueur, *Making Sex: Body and Gender from the Greeks to Freud* (Cambridge: Harvard University Press, 1990); idem, "Orgasm, Generation, and the Politics of Reproductive Biology," in *The Making of the Modern Body: Sexuality and Society in the Nineteenth Century*, ed. Catherine Gallagher and Thomas Laqueur (Berkeley: University of California Press, 1987), 1-41; Susan Poirer, "The Weir Mitchell Rest Cure: Doctors and Patients," *Women's Studies* 10 (1983) 13-40; Smith-Rosenberg, *Disorderly*, 182-196; Welter, *Dimity*, 57-70; and Wood, "'Fashionable Diseases.'"

14. Stoler, *Race*, 92, 67, 79; Foucault as quoted by Stoler, *Race*, 67.

15. Ibid., 69. For a rich contextualization of race from a Foucauldian perspective, see Alexander Butchart, *The Anatomy of Power: European Constructions of the African Body* (London: Zed Books, 1998).

16. Gould provides an authoritative account of craniometric racism and Galton's place within it in *The Mismeasure of Man* (New York: W. W. Norton & Co., 1981), 75. See Reggie Twigg's analysis of Riis' photo-documentary rhetoric and the state of bourgeois anxiety over large numbers of undesirables, "The Performative Dimension of Surveillance: Jacob Riis' *How the Other Half Lives*," *Text and Performance Quarterly* 12 (1992): 305-28. Mohr lists nine different signs of the increase in great detail (*Abortion*, 50-93). Gordon volume is an invaluable piece for understanding the conflict over fertility

and its social consequences. See her work for a discussion of demographics, fertility rates, and abortion practices (*Woman's Body*, 48 for quotation, 49-60). Also see Stewart E. Tolnay, "Black Fertility in Decline: Urban Differentials in 1900," *Social Biology* 27, no. 4 (1980): 249-60.

17. Smith-Rosenberg explains that the "True Woman/bourgeois matron" was caught in a Catch-22, wherein social expectation demanded that she use her skills and resources publicly and that she stay at home and bear children (*Disorderly*, 225). Dennis Hodgson, "The Ideological Origins of the Population Association of America," *Population and Development Review* 17, no. 1 (1991): 5. For examples of reactions against new norms of womanhood, see Hugh Hodge, "Marriage" (Lecture, MS C98, National Library of Medicine, Bethesda, Md., 1857); idem, "On the Rights of Women" (Lecture, MS C98, National Library of Medicine, Bethesda, Md., 1851); John P. Reynolds, "The President's Annual Address," *Transactions of the American Gynecological Society* 15 (1880): 3-24.

18. For examples of implicit critique of the new bourgeois woman's performativity, see Nebinger, *Criminal*; Horatio Robinson Storer, *Is It I? A Book for Every Man* (Boston: Lee and Shepard, 1868); Storer, *Why Not?*.

19. E. M. Pendleton's essay was reprinted from the *Charleston Medical Journal* as "The Comparative Fecundity of the Black and White Races," *Boston Medical and Surgical Journal* 44, no. 19 (1851): 365. The letter to Channing evidently was not anonymous to him, but the author was not disclosed in the journal article in which this portion was reprinted ("Criminal Abortion," *Boston Medical and Surgical Journal* 63 [1860]: 66). The letter is also a perfect example of Roediger's arguments about the construction of an Irish race (*Wages*, 133-163). Additionally, the increase in abortion was frequently characterized as a threat to women and as infanticide, as J. P. Leonard illustrated: "I need not remark on the evil consequences of this mischief upon health—the health of American women" and "*the massacre of infants*" (in "Quackery and Abortion," *Boston Medical and Surgical Journal* 43 [1851]: 480, emphasis in original).

20. Horatio R. Storer, "Contributions to Obstetric Jurisprudence." *New York Medical Journal* 3, no. 18 (1866): 423. Clarkson T. Collins, "Diseases of Females," *Boston Medical and Surgical Journal* 47, no. 23 (1853): 477. T. Gaillard Thomas, *Practical Treatise on the Diseases of Women*. (Philadelphia: Henry C. Lea, 1868), 60. On the "sickening" of bourgeois women, see Smith-Rosenberg, *Disorderly*, 186. Diane Price Herndl calls this an "invalid ideology." Her work is a good guide to the dynamics of invalidism in the United States (*Invalid Women: Figuring Feminine Illness in American Fiction and Culture* [Chapel Hill: University of North Carolina Press, 1993], 12). Wayne Glausser indicates that in the eighteenth-century idea of biologically weaker affluent classes, especially women of those classes, was already present in the writings of John Locke ("Locke and Blake as Physicians: Delivering the Eighteenth Century Body," in *Reading the Social Body*, ed. Catherine Burroughs and Jeffrey David Ehrenreich [Iowa City, Ia.: University of Iowa Press, 1993], 218-43). See Barbara Ehrenreich and Deidre English, *Complaints and Disorders: The Sexual Politics of Sickness* (New York: Feminist Press, 1973), 17-30; idem, *For Her,* for early work on the topic. Also see Gilman "Why I Wrote"; Jamieson, *Beyond*, 89-91; Poirer, "Weir; and Wood, "'Fashionable Diseases.'"

21. Mohr provides the quotation on white Anglo protestant women (*Abortion*, 46). Andrews, "Infanticide," 297. Kratz, "Criminal Abortion," 12. For more examples, see Collins, "Diseases," 477; "Criminal Abortion," *The Colorado Medical Journal and Western Medical and Surgical Gazette* 9, no. 3 (1903): 170-71; W. J. Fernald, "A Sociological View of Criminal Abortion," *Illinois Medical Journal* 5, no. 2 (1903): 57-65; Fish, "Criminal Abortion," 107; Ghent, "Criminal Abortion"; Grant,"Criminal Abortion," 514; C. K.

B., "Marriage in America," *Boston Medical and Surgical Journal* 77 (1867): 153-57; Longshore-Potts, *Discourses*, 297; Mitchell, "Infanticide," 3-4; Nowlin, "Criminal Abortion," 179-180; Parsons, "Written Law"; Rogers, "Attitude," 149; Ely Van de Werker, "Detection of Criminal Abortion," parts 2 and 3, *Journal of the Gynæcological Society of Boston* 5 (1871): 229-45, 350-70. Also see Mohr, *Abortion*, 86-94, 101-103.

22. Robert J. C. Young, *Colonial Desire: Hybridity in Theory, Culture, and Race* (London: Routledge, 1995), 93, 98. The quotation on internal enemies is from Stoler, *Race*, 92. In the U.S. medical community, a particularly vivid example of the racialized production of hostile juxtapositions within biopower comes from S. B. Hunt of Buffalo, New York:

> It is now a received opinion with ethnologists, that the large-headed Teuton is the domi-
> nant race of all the earth. Wherever climate will permit his existence, his passion for dis-
> covery leads him. The negro, the Hindostanee, the Malay, the Aborigines of America,
> have all fallen before him; and now he knocks at the door of the Japanese Mongol, and
> demands admission there. One by one the lesser tribes have owned his sway. The lively
> Celt of Ireland has yielded his long-fought battle with the English Teuton; the high-spir-
> ited Hungarian, and the wily Italian, feel the yoke of the Austrian Teuton; and still another
> family of this great group is pressing down up on the Turk. The stream of emigration has
> filled the United States with unceasing additions of Teutonic blood. Before them has fled
> the Indian, and beneath their iron rule is bowed the unfortunate African. ("The Cranial
> Characteristics and Powers of Human Races," *Boston Medical and Surgical Journal* 51,
> no. 4 [1954]: 74)

Hunt speaks generally of cranial capacity, and is not within the anxious dialogue regarding abortion. Nonetheless, his racist biopolitics are of a piece with Storer, for example. For more background on early scientific racism, see Stephen H. Browne, "Counter Science: African American Historians and the Critique of Ethnology in Nineteenth-Century America," *Western Journal of Communication* 64, no. 3 (2000): 268-84; Burbick, *Healing*; Gilman, *Difference*; Greene, *Malthusian*; Gould, *Mismeasure*; Uli Linke, *Blood and Nation: The European Aesthetics of Race* (Philadelphia: University of Pennsylvania Press, 1999); Marshall, "Racial Classifications"; Londa Schiebinger, *Nature's Body: Gender in the Making of Modern Science* (Boston: Press, 1993), 211-13; Nancy Stepan, *The Idea of Race in Science: Great Britain, 1800-1960* (London: Macmillan, 1982); Stepan, Nancy, and Sander Gilman, "Appropriating the Idioms of Science: The Rejection of Scientific Racism," in *The "Racial" Economy of Science: Toward a Democratic Future*, ed. Sandra Harding (Bloomington, Ind.: Indiana University Press, 1993), 170-93; Kirt H. Wilson, "Toward a Discursive Theory of Racial Identity: *The Souls of Black Folk* as a Response to Nineteenth-Century Biological Determinism," *Western Journal of Communication* 63, no. 2 (1999): 193-215.

23. Gordon provides a thorough overview of the connection between race suicide and fertility in her chapter "Race Suicide" (*Woman's Body*, 135). Hodgson, "Ideological," 3. Smith-Rosenberg notes the presence of race suicide in the medical literature, but does not link it to larger concerns regarding the population (*Disorderly*, 238).

24. Joseph J. Spengler, "Notes on Abortion, Birth Control, and Medical and Socio-logical Interpretations of the Decline of the Birth Rate in Nineteenth Century America," *Marriage Hygiene* 2, nos. 1-3 (1935): 299; 42-53, 158-69, 288-300. Hodgson, "Ideological," 5. Although Spengler's analysis is older, it is still an invaluable review of the literature. Further, his work supports the argument that the population was a new phenomenon that recasted issues of social power (Foucault, *Sexuality*, part 5).

25. H. R. Storer's comments (*Why Not?*, 84-85), though noisome to many today, are not the least bit out of tune with the discourse of biological Malthusians of the late nineteenth century, as a few hours with the writings of Thomas Nelson Page or Francis Galton will demonstrate. Another example comes from James Kelly in a lecture to the Gynecological Society of Boston. He said, "I marvel at the prevalence of a horrible crime which is devastating this fair land, and curtailing by the million the development of its population and its power," in "The Ethics of Abortion as a Method of Treatment in Legitimate Practice," *Transactions of the Gynecological Society of Boston* 1 (1889): 25. It is striking, I think, that we have failed as yet to take the powerfully biopolitical practices of early antiabortionists as principal to the substance of their efforts. Interestingly, U.S. arguments are the reverse of arguments in Ireland and the British Isles, where overpopulation was a greater concern than underpopulation. For example, a report of Mr. Lawrie to the Dialectical Society in Dublin transcribes a debate that replicates Malthusian arguments for limiting population to decrease poverty, indicating abortion might be a useful tool for effective decrease in poverty if health to mother and offspring could be improved in the procedure ("New Views on Abortion," *Boston Medical and Surgical Journal* 79 [1868]: 156-58).

26. The editors were reviewing Storer's *Why Not?* when making this claim in "*Why Not? A Book for Every Woman*. The Prize Essay to Which the American Medical Association Awarded the Gold Medal for 1865," *Boston Medical and Surgical Journal* 75 (1865): 104.

27. See Foucault, *Sexuality*, 104-5. Gordon's work on reproductive freedoms substantiates Foucault's argument in a U.S. context although her work is centered around individual liberty, rather than systems of disciplined heterosexuality (*Woman's Body*, 47-155). Likewise for Smith-Rosenberg, although her work is grounded by gender as an ideology (*Disorderly*, 245-296).

28. Storer, "Contributions," 426.

29. Frederick J. Taussig, *Abortion, Spontaneous and Induced: Medical and Social Aspects* (St. Louis: C. V. Mosby, 1936). Mary Steichen Calderone, ed., *Abortion in the United States: A Conference Sponsored by the Planned Parenthood Federation of America, Inc. at the Arlen House and the New York Academy of Medicine* (New York: Harper and Brothers, 1958). Reagan, *Abortion*; Carol Joffe, *Doctor's of Conscience: The Struggle to Provide Abortion Before and After* Roe v. Wade (Boston: Beacon Press, 1995). Rickie Solinger, *Wake Up Little Susie: Pregnancy and Race Before* Roe v. Wade (New York: Routledge, 1992).

30. Stoler, *Race*, 91. Nira Yuval-Davis and Floya Anthias, introduction to *Woman-Nation-State*, ed. Nira Yuval-Davis and Floya Anthias (New York: St. Martin's Press, 1989). Mohanram, *Black Body*, 85. Also see Carole Pateman, *The Disorder of Women: Democracy, Feminism and Political Theory* (Cambridge: Polity Press, 1989); McClintock, *Imperial Leather*; George L. Mosse, *Nationalism and Sexuality: Respectability and Abnormal Sexuality in Modern Europe* (New York: Howard Fertig, 1985).

31. Burbick, *Healing*, 302. Mary Douglas, *Natural Symbols: Explorations in Cosmology* (London: Routledge, [1970] 1996), 69.

32. Max Horkheimer and Theodor Adorno, *Dialectic of Enlightenment*, trans. J. Cumming (New York: Continuum Press, 1993), 3; also see "Excursus I."

33. Mohr has related the emergence of antiabortion efforts to the professionalization efforts by the AMA (*Abortion*, 147). Paul Starr documents the conflict between the great variety of medical practitioners popular in the nineteenth century and members of the AMA (*Transformation*, 58). For more information, see Mohr, *Abortion*, chs. 1 and 2; also

see H. Coulter, "Political and Social Aspects of Nineteenth Century Medicine In the United States: The Formation of the American Medical Association and Its Struggle with Homeopathic and Eclectic Physicians," (Ph.D. diss., Columbia University, 1967); Francis R. Packard, *History of Medicine in the United States*, vol. 2 (New York: Hafner Publishing, 1963), 1121-239.

34. Reviewing journal entries demonstrates a legion of articles on the evils of quackery—especially in the 1850s when the AMA was only beginning its campaign for medical dominance in earnest. For examples, see Honestus, "Quackery in the Regular Profession," *Boston Medical and Surgical Journal* 43, no. 15 (1850): 280-81; Dan King, "Quackery—Its Causes and Effects, with Reflections and Suggestions," *Boston Medical and Surgical Journal* 48, no. 11 (1853): 209-40; "Profits of Quackery," *Boston Medical and Surgical Journal* 46, no. 20 (1852): 406; "Quackery," *New Hampshire Journal of Medicine* 1 (1850): 128-13; "Quackery, Versus the Regular Medical Practice," *Boston Medical and Surgical Journal* 44, no. 12 (1851): 239-40. In particular, articles in *The Boston Medical and Surgical Journal* expressed the viewpoints of midwifery and homeopathy as quackery; see the editorial "Female Practitioners of Medicine," 76, no. 13 (1867): 272; for arguments on midwifery, an anonymous letter entitled "Female Physicians," 54 (1856): 171-74; for claims about homeopathy, also see a letter from H. Cocles, "Homeopathic Interference with Regular Practitioners," *Boston Medical and Surgical Journal* 50, no. 7 (1854): 136-41. For examples of pieces that describe all women as quacks by birth, see two editorials from *The Boston Medical and Surgical Journal*, "A Question Which Should be Settled," 72, no. 25 (1866): 481-83; "Our Editorial Last Week," 73, no. 26 (1866): 504. For an in-depth look at early women's medical education and the obstacles physicians like Blackwell faced, particularly establishing hospitals and gaining favor with male medical societies, see Morantz-Sanchez (*Sympathetic*, chs. 3 and 4). Information on women's medical societies, as well as the quotation about Sarah Hackett Stevenson is from More (*Restoring*, 45, 63). Also see Mary Roth Walsh, *"Doctors Wanted: No Women Need Apply": Sexual Barriers and the Medical Profession* (New Haven, Conn.: Yale University Press, 1977).

35. In particular, Coggeshall was concerned about the sullying of pharmacy's reputation by druggists "collaborating" with quacks (George D. Coggeshall, "Connection of Druggists with Quack Medicines," *Boston Medical and Surgical Journal* 50 [1854]: 340). Randall's letter expressed a sentiment held by many, as evidenced by a large number of letters to journals in the 1850s decrying malpractice against regulars as unethical, almost by definition (O. W. Randall, "Suits for Mal-Practice," *Boston Medical and Surgical Journal* 45, no. 7 [1851]: 137). Keep in mind that there was great competition between various medical sects and many did try to weaken the strength of the AMA, but there is not evidence to indicate the plotting of a "small portion" to use malpractice laws to demolish the regulars. The sense of persecution more likely grew out of the bitter feuding that characterized medical practice in the latter half of the nineteenth century (Starr, *Transformation*, ch. 3). For more background on malpractice, see James C. Mohr, *Doctors and the Law: Medical Jurisprudence in Nineteenth-Century America* (New York: Oxford University Press, 1993), ch. 8.

36. Leonard was one of many who vilified the abortionist as the worst of quacks (J. P. Leonard, "Quackery and Abortion," *Boston Medical and Surgical Journal* 43 [1851]: 478, emphasis in original). Also see G. E. Herrick, who found the debate over the quackery of specialists to be wrongheaded ("Specialties," 40-1). Mohr also substantiates that abortionists were first and foremost "quacks" from the AMA's perspective and that some regulars indeed did perform abortions for additional funds because it was one of the only

procedures that paid well (*Abortion*, 161-64).

37. Storer et al., "Report," 75-76, 76-77. Concerning the National Code of Ethics, the journal cited contains only a portion of whole code ("Code of Medical Ethics," *Peninsular Journal of Medicine* 1, no. 2 [1853]: 138).

38. Rudolph E. Seigel, *Galen's System of Physiology and Medicine* (Basel, Switz.: S. Karger, 1968); Owsei Temkin, *Galenism: Rise and Decline of a Medical Philosophy* (Ithaca: Cornell University Press, 1973). For an example of how this Aristotelian and Galenic tradition might be deployed, see Duden's *The Woman Beneath the Skin*, a detailed history of a particular eighteenth-century physician, Johann Storch, working within an "old-world" medical paradigm. Also, see her *Disembodying Women* for information on quickening and a woman's power in former days to announce her pregnancy (ch. 12). Paul Starr has called the various traditions I have summarized the "medical counter-culture," and the practice of home remedy "domestic medicine" after William Buchan's well-liked home manual, *Domestic Medicine* (*Transformation*, 32-37, 47-54).

39. Jane Donegan surveyed English midwifery guides and, even setting aside misogynist denigrations of women's abilities, found them lacking in many respects due to their empiricism (*Women & Men Midwives: Medicine, Morality, and Misogyny in Early America* [Westport, Conn.: Greenwood Press, 1978], 15). Ulrich's *A Midwife's Tale* is an valuable study of how early midwives conducted themselves and a history of incredible skill (*A Midwife's Tale: The Life of Martha Ballard, Based on Her Diary, 1785-1812* [New York: Vintage Books, 1991], 11-12).

40. Walsh writes that Samuel Gregory was in fact an opportunist of sorts and documents his opposition, direct and indirect, to meaningful medical education for women (*"Doctors"*, ch. 2). Coupled with Donegan's more general remarks on midwifery guides and comments from Litoff, and Wertz & Wertz (*Lying-In*), it is possible to get a sense of the tutelage of midwives. Judy Barrett Litoff surveyed the state of midwife education in the United States (*American Midwives: 1860 to the Present* [Westport, Conn.: Greenwood Press, 1978], 9,12). The Medical College for Women is an example of a homeopathic school open to midwives (Wertz and Wertz, 52-53).

41. Coulter offers an overview of "irregular" methods and practices ("Political and Social"). The information on homeopathy, botanics, and eclectics is from Wertz & Wertz, *Lying-In*, 51-52; also see Brodie, *Abortion*, 143-46. Wertz & Wertz also discuss hydropathy (*Lying-In*, 53-54); also see Brodie, *Abortion*, 147-50. For background on bloodletting and purgatives see Rothstein, *American*, 41-54. For more information on irregular medicine, see Susan E. Cayleff, "Gender, Ideology, and the Water-Cure Movement," in *Other Healers: Unorthodox Medicine in America*, ed. Norman Gevitz (Baltimore: Johns Hopkins University Press, 1988), 82-98; Martin Kaufman, "Homeopathy in America: The Rise and Fall and Persistence of a Medical Heresy," in *Other Healers: Unorthodox Medicine in America*, ed. Norman Gevitz (Baltimore: Johns Hopkins University Press, 1988), 99-123; and William G. Rothstein, "The Botanical Movements and Orthodox Medicine," in *Other Healers: Unorthodox Medicine in America*, ed. Norman Gevitz (Baltimore: Johns Hopkins University Press, 1988), 29-51.

42. Brodie, *Contraception*, 107, 108 for quotations; see 106-19 for general information on lecturers. Also see Degler, *At Odds*. For information on Paulina Kellog Wright Davis, see Lynne Derbyshire, "Paulina Kellog Wright Davis," in *Women Public Speakers in the United States, 1800-1925: A Bio-Critical Sourcebook*, vol. 1, ed. Karlyn Kohrs Campbell (Westport, Conn.: Greenwood Press, 1993), 309-12.

43. Brodie (*Contraception*) credits Knowlton and Owens with inciting much of the public literature on contraception and abortion in the nineteenth century. Mauriceau was

actually Joseph Trow, the brother of Ann Trow Lohman or Madame Restell (ibid., 64). Ashton's argued Trow's "female pills" were innocuous powders, hinting at the level to which these texts were in dialogue (ibid., 186-87). Douching was a common method of contraception and Becklard advocated douching within the first two months to abort (ibid., 69). Certainly not all of those discussed supported abortion, Hollick being a prime example (Degler, *At Odds*, 229). See Frederick Hollick, *The Matron's Manual of Midwifery and the Diseases of Women During Pregnancy and in Child Bed* (New York: T. W. Strong, 1848), 409-18; Charles Knowlton, *The Fruits of Philosophy*, in S. Chandrasekhar, *"A Dirty Filthy Book": The Writings of Charles Knowlton and Annie Besant on Reproductive Physiology and Birth Control and an Account of the Bradlaugh-Besant Trial: With the Definitive Texts of Fruits Philosophy, by Charles Knowlton, The Law of Population, by Besant, Theosophy and the Law of Population, by Annie Besant* (Berkeley: University of California Press, 1981); A. M. Mauriceau, *The Married Woman's Private Medical Companion* (New York, 1848).

44. Coulter claims that the difference between regulars and irregulars (especially homeopaths) was initially more a difference of politics than a difference of kind. My own survey of literature demonstrates little if any "experimental data" on cautery, for example, and more simple testimonial ("Political"). For an example, see W. E. Johnson, "The Actual Cautery of Diseases of the Uterus," *New Orleans Medical and Surgical Journal* 10 (1854): 397-99. Information on early innovations in medical education is from Kenneth M. Ludmerer, *Learning to Heal: The Development of American Medical Education* (New York: Basic Books, 1985), 20, 45, 47-71. Ludmerer demonstrates that French methods of observation were preferred in the United States over the emerging scientific methods of early German medicine (ch. 2). Regarding AMA antiabortion influence on irregulars, Mohr discusses how homeopaths came to oppose abortion, furthering their cause. Edward Hale, a leading homeopath, is a principal example (*Abortion*, 173-176). For more on the pseudo-scientific days of early medicine, see Morantz-Sanchez, *Sympathy*, ch. 9; Starr, *Transformation*, book 1.

Notes for Chapter Three

1. Ulric Neisser, "Remembering as Doing," *Behavioral and Brain Sciences* 19 (1996): 204. Also see Aaron Ben-Ze'ev, "The Alternative to the Storehouse Metaphor," *Behavioral and Brain Sciences* 19 (1996): 192-93; Judith Butler, *Bodies that Matter: On the Discursive Limits of "Sex"* (New York: Routledge,1993), ch. 1; Barbie Zelizer, "Reading the Past Against the Grain," *Critical Studies in Mass Communication* 12, no. 2 (1995): 214-39.

2. Foucault, "Nietzsche." The quotation about spatial relationships is from Michel de Certeau, *The Capture of Speech & Other Political Writings*, trans. Tom Conley and ed. Luce Giard (Minneapolis: University of Minnesota Press, 1997), 129; on that point, also see Zelizer, "Reading," 227, 222-23.

3. Haraway, "Promises," 298. The definition of "embody" is from the *Thesaurus of Traditional English Metaphors*, s.v. "embody." Haraway, *Simians, Cyborgs, and Women: The Reinvention of Nature* (New York: Routledge, 1991), 208. Also see idem, *Modest*; idem, *How Like a Leaf: An Interview with Thyrza Nichols Goodeve* (New York: Routledge, 2000). The quotation on identity formation and power is from Zelizer, *Remembering*, 3. I am not pursuing the figure of the "cyborg" for which Haraway is so well

known, or the "posthuman" body that readers might know from Katherine Hayles (*How We Became Posthuman: Virtual Bodies in Cybernetics, Literature, and Informatics* [Chicago: University of Chicago Press, 1999]) because I feel those are proper to studies of technoscience. It does not mean questions of boundary confusion and the articulation of shifting arrangements between different kind of historical bodies are reserved only for a post-World War II chronology. That said, "body" is a contingent category for me that is not finally about the human frame per se. For an excellent discussion on the historicity of the corporeal body, see Duden, *Woman*, ch. 1; Anne Fausto-Sterling, *Sexing the Body: Gender Politics and the Construction of Sexuality* (New York: Basic Books, 2000), ch. 1.

4. duBois, *Torture*, 91, 90. Also see Jordanova, *Sexual Visions*; Evelyn Fox Keller, *Secrets of Life, Secrets of Death* (New York: Routledge, 1990); Londa Schiebinger, *Nature's Body: Gender in the Making of Modern Science* (Boston: Beacon Press, 1993); Adams, *Reproducing*; Newman, *Fetal*; Duden, "Fetus." For information on alternative classical models of cultural memory, see Ekaterina V. Haskins, "Rhetoric between Orality and Literacy: Cultural Memory and Performance in Isocrates and Aristotle," *Quarterly Journal of Speech* 87, no. 2 (2001): 158-78.

5. Plato, *Phaedrus*, trans. Alexander Nehemas and Paul Woodruff (Indianapolis, Ind.: Hackett Publishing, 1995). Keller and Grontkowski, "Mind's Eye," 190. Keller and Grontkowski argue that knower and known are one in Western epistemology from classical times to Descartes and Newton, although with substantial modifications in modes of perception and practices for achieving communion between the knower and the known. Michel Foucault argues in *The Order of Things* that the epistemological shift of the Enlightenment placed Man as the object and subject of inquiry such that all that is possible in knowledge is located in the ideal of Man (*The Order of Things: An Archaeology of the Human Sciences* [New York: Vintage Books, 1994], 303-43).

6. In his dazzling analysis of the pharmakon in Plato's *Phaedrus*, Derrida deconstructs the inseparability of anamnesic memory and truth and the pathologization of hypomnesis, or writing (Derrida, *Dissemination*).

7. duBois, *Torture*, 122. Stafford's chapter on "Conceiving" in *Body Criticism* is a sweeping survey of the Neoplatonic emphasis on ideational prototypes in the Enlightenment. Of course, there were numerous debates about the epistemological and ontological nuance of such a belief, but few were out and out dissenters from the historical primacy granted the mind over the body (*Body*, 10; also see ch. 3 for an overview). Keller and Grontkowski present the metaphorical placement of truth in a vision of God's work for both Descartes and Newton ("Mind's Eye," 192-98).

8. René Descartes, *Meditations on First Philosophy*, 3rd ed., trans. Donald A. Cross (Indianapolis: Hackett, 1993), 54. Paraphrased parts of *Treatise of Man* were included in *Discourse on Method* (René Descartes, *Treatise of Man*, trans. Thomas Steele Hall [Cambridge: Harvard University Press, 1972], 2). Pierre Gassendi (1592-1655) and Marin Mersenne (1588-1648) were also part of this intellectual community. They were not a uniform voice, as evidenced by disputes over the fundamental character of a mechanistic universe, although these debates are not relevant for my claim and so I leave these details aside. For example, Gassendi came to believe that only a probable understanding of mechanistic principles was possible (a position that would later influence Robert Boyle and Isaac Newton in England), whereas Descartes is notorious for his belief in the certainty of the abstract (Carolyn Merchant, *The Death of Nature: Women, Ecology and the Scientific Revolution* [New York: HarperCollins, 1983], 194-205). However, I am concerned with the Cartesian legacy of a mechanistic rationality superseding the physical, a viewpoint that haunts early obstetrics and gynecology of the nineteenth century.

9. Bedford, "Clinical," 10 (1854): 99. Martin, *Woman*, 56. Mary Shaw Kuypers cites George Berkeley, Peter Browne, and Isaac Waats in addition to Hume, as the foremost critics of rationalism (*Studies in the Eighteenth Century Background of Hume's Empiricism* [New York: Garland Publishing, Inc., 1983], 41-44). However, Stafford argues that we should separate the immateriality of Berkeley as Neoplatonic from Hume's skepticism (Stafford, *Body*, 379-384). For more information on the positivist challenge to rationalism, see Wayne Waxman, *Hume's Theory of Consciousness* (Cambridge: Cambridge University Press, 1994); John P. Wright, *The Sceptical Realism of David Hume* (Manchester: Manchester University Press, 1983); John W. Yolton, *Thinking Matter: Materialism in Eighteenth-Century Britain* (Minneapolis: University of Minnesota Press, 1983). For more on mechanistic thinking and Cartesianism in the life sciences, see Georges Canguilhem, *Ideology and Rationality in the History of the Life Sciences*, trans. Arthur Goldhammer (Cambridge, Mass.: MIT Press, 1988), 87-94, 128-38.

10. I summarize Descartes's *Meditations* here. Of particular interest to me are Meditations Five and Six, which deal with the etherealness and doubtfulness of material things. For a discussion of rationality as the only means to apprehend the rational plan of God, also see his *Discours de la méthode/Discourse on the Method*, trans., ed., and intro. George Hefferman (Notre Dame: University of Notre Dame Press, 1994). Merchant (*Death*) argues that the rational emphasis of the Enlightenment can be traced to Platonic emphasis on the mathematical. However, I do think that the shift from the Forms of beauty, justice, and honor to the austerity of a Cartesian logic is a rupture that should not be smoothed over. The unity of One Logic reduces the Forms to the Form. Horkheimer and Adorno argue that the deployment of rationality as a universal method effects the dissolution of all things if they are to be knowable. Descartes's view on the physical epitomizes their contention (*Dialectic*, 13). Stafford documents the extent of a liquidating abstraction in her chapter on "Abstracting" in *Body Criticism* (ch. 2). For more on Descartes' view on memory, see Peter A. Schouls, *Descartes and the Possibility of Science* (Ithaca: Cornell University Press, 2000), ; Dennis L. Sepper, "*Ingenium*, Memory Art, and the Unity of Imaginative Knowing in the Early Descartes," in *Essays on the Philosophy and Science of René Descartes*, ed. Stephen Voss (New York: Oxford University Press, 1993), 142-61.

11. Foucault argues in *The Order of Things* that the beginning of modern knowledge is at that point when then human body becomes finite; modern thought begins when "the human being begins to exist within his [*sic*] organism, inside the shell of his head, inside the armature of his limbs, and in the shallow structure of his physiology. . ." (318). I think when taken in conjunction with Merchant's work on the death of nature, the gendering of the finite body of the feminized earth allows one to argue the antagonistic character of science toward the feminine is an enabling condition of its discourse.

12. Duden discusses the transformation of nature's force (*Disembodying*, 103, emphasis in original). Foucault also discusses Cuvier as a key figure in the transition (*Order*, 278). I choose Lamarck, following Duden, because of the marker of biology. It is a somewhat arbitrary, but useful, choice. The "moment" of the transition was years and years in the happening. Also see W. D. Ian Rolfe, "William and John Hunter: Breaking the Great Chain of Being," in *William Hunter and the Eighteenth-Century Medical World*, ed. W. F. Bynum and Roy Porter (Cambridge: Cambridge University Press, 1985), 297-319; John L. Thornton, "William Hunter (1718-1783) and His Contributions to Obstetrics," *British Journal of Obstetrics and Gynecology* 90 (1983): 787-94.

13. Bichat is quoted in the anonymous article by "A Midland Surgeon," "The Genesis of Life," *Journal of the Gynecological Society of Boston* 7, nos. 5-6 (1872): 389. The sur-

geon's arguments clearly are influenced by the expansionist technological landscape of the mid-nineteenth century, where the life of the nation and the life of the body were barely distinguishable (ibid., 378). Canguilhem traces the presence of mechanical metaphors in Western life sciences in the eighteenth- and nineteenth-centuries, noting that "[m]etaphors from economic management and steam-engine technology were widely accepted in physiology for reasons having to do with the history of physiology itself" (*Ideology*, 89). In should be noted that, including "organization in action," Bichat defined life in many ways, such as: "Life consists in the sum of the functions, by which death is resisted" (Xavier Bichat, *Physiological Researches on Life and Death*, trans. F. Gold [Boston: Richardson and Lord, 1827], 10). For greater background on Bichat's influence over life and anatomy, see Foucault, *Birth*, ch. 8. For a review of medical opinion on life from antiquity, see Robert Etienne, "Ancient Medical Conscience and the Life of Children," *Journal of Psychohistory* 4, no. 2 (1976): 131-61; G. E. R. Lloyd, *Science, Folklore and Ideology: Studies in the Life Sciences in Ancient Greece* (Cambridge: Cambridge University Press, 1983).

14. Keller rereads Boyle in *Secrets of Life, Secrets of Death* to demonstrate the gendered character of his view on nature, God, and Man. She also illustrates how Newton followed suit (60-67). Merchant recapitulates Bacon's story of a brute, female nature in detail (*Death*, ch. 7). I quote form Londa Schiebinger's discussion of complementary views of gender that date back to Aristotle and Pythagoras (*Mind*, 234). Also see Lloyd, *Science*; Schiebinger, *Nature's Body*.

15. Duden, *Disembodying*, 105; Adams, *Reproducing*, 136-37.

16. The quotation comes from Schiebinger, *Nature's*, 40. Also see the chapter on sexual complementarity in *The Mind Has No Sex?* wherein she traces complementarity in anatomy, political theory, and education (ch. 8). For Carole Pateman's work, see *Disorder*; idem, *The Problem of Political Obligation* (Berkeley, Calif.: University of California Press, 1986); idem, *The Sexual Contract* (Stanford, Calif.: Stanford University Press, 1988).

17. I rely on Keller's summary of feminist historians and philosophers (namely Harding, Keller, and Merchant) who have documented the "death of Nature" in the formation of modern scientific principles (*Secrets*, 59). Foucault, *Order*, 323, emphasis in original. He is talking generally of man here, but I believe his arguments are more properly is understood as referring to Man in the advised sense of the masculinized pursuit of knowledge through the impregnated feminine.

18. In addition to popular and scientific fears of racial degeneracy discussed in the previous chapter, in biological studies, an important point in the rise of theories about human mutability was the triumph of epigeneticism over preformationism. In the early half of the eighteenth century, the preformationist theory had great currency and "presented an image of a mono-prenatal embryo in which conception implied simply an enlargement of what was already there. There was no 'creation' *per se*." Preformationism was inaugurated in the 1660s by Regnier de Graaf, who located what are now known as Graafian follicles, in which eggs are stored in ovaries. God was believed to have created all beings long ago in the form of minuscule, immaterial germs in the reproductive organs awaiting the necessary excitation to begin enlargement. This perspective was eroded by criticism, and in the latter half of the eighteenth century, epigeneticism emerged as the dominant theory of generation. Under this model, life unfolded in "the physical and *ad seriatum* development of a seemingly undifferentiated mass of matter into organs and, finally, into an exquisite structure" (Angus McLaren, "The Pleasures of Procreation: Traditional and Biomedical Theories of Conception," in *William Hunter and the Eighteenth-Century Medical World*, ed.

W. F. Bynum and Roy Porter [Cambridge: Cambridge University Press, 1985], 334-35, emphasis in original). Life was materially elaborated through time via linear development. Rather than being ideationally generated ages ago, life was generated and embodied within the cauldron of nature, such that the living body was subject to environmental conditions in its development. Consequently, the progress of the fetus became important. Angus Mc-Laren ("Pleasures") discusses the relative theoretical weaknesses of preformation as a model of generation. Note there were two branches of preformationists, the animiculists who believed the preformed embryo was in the sperm and the ovists who held that the ovary held the preformed being. Also, mammalian follicles were not identified until 1827.

Duden identifies a threshold with the 1799 publication of *Icones Embryonum Humanorum* by Samuel Thomas Soemmering (*Disembodying*, 41-42; "Fetus"). In two plates in this atlas, Soemmering presented twenty discontinuous images of fetal development, although he did not argue for an unfolding fetus. Nonetheless, the shift to staged fetal growth was beginning. Fears of fetal malformation began to change as well. In the eighteenth century, it was believed looking at a black cat or witnessing something grotesque might result in a blemish on the child's skin. Worse, a mother filled with evil or base thoughts might birth a monstrosity. In the latter nineteenth century, environmental influences on the fetus were still thought important, although some of the more sensational fears were subsiding. Stafford discusses the ad seriatum unfolding of life in *Body*, 242; also see 242-47.

19. Henry Howard, "The Somatic Etiology of Crime," *American Journal of Neurology and Psychiatry* 2, no. 2 (1883): 235. Samantha S. Nivison, "Priest of Nature and Her Interpreter" (M.D. thesis, Women's Medical College of Pennsylvania, SCWM, 1855), 6-7.

20. Derrida, *Archive*, 11; Certeau, *Writing*, 3.

21. duBois, *Torture*; Foucault, *History*, 63; Greene, *Malthusian*, 17. duBois's thesis is straightforward enough but her argument is brilliant. In an almost Nietzschean fashion, she traces the etymology of the word truth and the practices developed to locate it. Foucault's discussion of the confession is the perfect complement to duBois's argument. Foucault made a distinction between the study of reproductive biology and the study of sexual pleasure, claiming they are two different fields, conducted according to different rules. The medical antiabortion rhetoric of the nineteenth century bridges these two fields and should rightfully complicate any discussion of sex as basically pleasure for one simple reason: women's sexuality was discussed within the regular medical community in terms of duty, not pleasure.

22. Foucault, *History*, 61-62.

23. Halbwachs, *Collective*, 43. For a broader discussion of the relation or normativity and memory, see A. Radley, "Artefacts, memory and a sense of the past," in *Collective Remembering*, ed. David Middleton and Derek Edwards (London: Sage, 1990), 46-59; James Fentress and Chris Wickham, *Social Memory* (Oxford: Blackwell, 1992).

24. Jackson, "Gravid Uterus," *Boston Medical and Surgical Journal* 61 (1859): 239. A. G. A Helmick, "Case of Threatened Abortion," *Nelson's Northern Lancet* 10, no. 1 (1854): 12, emphasis mine. Gleason, *Talks*, 159. Helmick was treating a slave, but the use of drugs and coercion was not limited to those whom physicians might have seen as inferior beings. Women of higher station were treated with more care and respect, but they were still "confessed" by their bodies as a survey of court records and medical cases indicates.

25. Storer is describing the almost clerical confidentiality of the patient-doctor relationship (*Why Not?*, 18, 54, emphasis in original). Nonetheless, as I argued with Foucault's limitation to the spoken confession, women's bodies spoke for them and there-

by induced spoken confessions. For examples of medical testimony in court cases, see *Commonwealth v. Follansbee*, 155 MA Rep 274 (MA Sup Ct 1891/92); *Commonwealth v. Parker* 63 Am Dec 396 (MA Sup Ct 1845); *Hatchard v. State*, 79 WI Rep. 35 (WI Sup Ct. 1891); *Mitchell v. Commonwealth*, 39 Am Rep 227 (KY Sup Ct 1879); *People v. McGonegal*, 17 NY Sup 147 (NY Sup Ct 1891); *People v. Sessions*, 58 MI Rep 594 (MI Sup Ct 1886); *State v. Cooper*, 51 Am Dec 248 (NJ Sup Ct 1849); *State v. Leeper*, 22 IA Rep 748 (IA Sup Ct 1887); *State v. McIntyre*, 19 MN Rep 65 (MN Dup Ct 1882); *State v. Smith*, 53 Am Dec 578 (ME Sup Ct 1851). Examples from medical cases are legion. For a healthy sampling, see "Abortion and Murder," *Boston Medical and Surgical Journal* 42, no. 13 (1850): 275; "Alleged Manslaughter by Procuring Abortion," *Boston Medical and Surgical Journal* 44 (1851): 288; C. H. Cleveland, "Poisoning by Oil of Cedar," *Boston Medical and Surgical Journal* 44, no. 17 (1851): 336-38; R. G. Curtin, "Pelvic Cellulitis from Abortion," *American Journal of Obstetrics* 8, no. 2 (1875): 330; John Doe, "A Case of Abortion," *Boston Medical and Surgical Journal* 42, no. 15 (1850): 313-14; T. C. Finnell, "Chorea a Cause of Abortion," *Nelson's Northern Lancet* 2, no. 4 (1852): 170; M. Godfray, "Unusual Case of Abortion," *Nelson's American Lancet* 7, no. 1 (1854): 44; H. S. Hendee, "Attempted Abortion by the Use of Veratrum Veride," *Boston Medical and Surgical Journal* 57 (1857): 299; Jacobi, "Case of Abortion in the Third Month," *American Journal of Obstetrics* 6 (1874): 632; Mackenzie Johnston, "Case of Retained Ovum after Death of the Fœtus," *American Journal of Obstetrics* 7, no. 4 (1875): 679-89; Francis Minot, "Morbid Adhesion of the Placenta After Abortion," *Boston Medical and Surgical Journal* 53, no. 2 (1855): 35-38; Charles Palmer, "Attempted Abortion by American Hellebore," *Boston Medical and Surgical Journal* 57 (1857): 436; Thomas, "Attempted Criminal Abortion with a Long Wire—Penetration of the Right Lung," *American Journal of Obstetrics* 6, no. 1 (1873): 103-5; Tower, "Pelvic Viscera from a Patient Dead of a Criminal Abortion," *Journal of the Gynæcological Society of Boston* 1 (1869): 202-3; J. B. Treadwell, "Case of Criminal Abortion with Retained Placenta, Followed by Metritis, Pelvic Cellulitis, and Pyæmia. Recovery," *Boston Medical and Surgical Journal* 78/79 (1, no. 7 New Series) (1868): 97-99.

26. Wells, *Dead*, 32, 33 with ellipsis to 55-56. Wells compares several women physicians' records of medical histories against leading men physicians' records to conclude that women generally were better listeners and more respectful of patient testimony.

27. Foucault writes of this paradox in *Order*, ch. 9. Also see Keller and Grontkowski, "Mind's Eye."

28. Foucault is discussing the relationship between the disjointed world of observation and the ordered world of reflective thought (*Order*, 322-23). Stafford, *Body*, 467.

29. Keep in mind, Stafford argues that body criticism is the general model for all attempts to know influenced by the eighteenth century. Thus, to use metaphors of dissection in high-energy physics is the transposition of the body onto particles. In Burkean terms, the human body became the "terministic screen" for all objects of knowledge (Kenneth Burke, *Language as Symbolic Action: Essays on Life, Literature, and Method* [Berkeley: University of California Press, 1966], 44-62). In *The Order of Things*, Foucault describes the enabling condition of corporeal finitude as a principal fact in the connection between a transcendental truth and an empirical reality (323-27). Also see Keller, *Secrets*, ch. 3. Martin Jay has also addressed the double-vision I describe, but not in the same manner. He questions the negative value attached to vision by such French theorists as Foucault in Jay's fascinating volume *Downcast Eyes: The Denigration of Vision in Twentieth-Century French Thought* (Berkeley: University of California Press, 1993). To respond to his thesis would be far beyond the scope of this work; however, I would note that the productive

capacity of vision, in and of itself not negative, deserves critique when used to reinforce social inequality. On the other hand, the nature of an endemic ocularphobia in French thought is a compelling argument. Leave it to say, my point is not to demonize vision, but rather to specify the means by which modes of perception have been employed for purposes of social power.

30. duBois, *Torture*, 122. Also see Keller and Grontkowski, "Mind's Eye."

31. Henri Lefebvre discusses the very problem of the speaking eye in terms of the illusion of transparency and the realistic illusion. These illusions are coded into the social production of space (*The Production of Space*, trans. Donald Nicholson-Smith [Oxford: Blackwell, 1995], 26-33); also see Foucault, *Birth*, ch. 7.

32. Foucault, *Birth*, 114, 115, emphasis in original. Michel de Certeau, *The Writing of History*, trans. Thomas Conley. (New York: Columbia University Press, 1988), 3. Also see Jordanova, *Sexual*.

33. Duden, *Disembodying*, 17-20. I draw from Foucault when he discusses the work of Condillac and principles of perception in the French clinical and educational system at the end of the eighteenth century (*Birth*, 117). Although the situation is not identical to general medical practice of ob/gyn's in the nineteenth-century United States, I have argued that regulars endeavored to follow suit with French practices, via the great English obstetricians and gynecologists and directly. Given the attitude of linguistic transparency of the physicians I have read, I have little doubt this postulate of perfect reversibility of word and vision was in operation.

34. Lorraine Daston and Peter Galison, "The Image of Objectivity," *Representations* 40 (1992): 82-83. Gardner, *Causes*, opening plate after title page. Treadwell, "Case," 97. Daston and Galison describe pictorial objectivism ("Image," 103).

35. Foucault is describing the kind of "chemical action" the clinical gaze has on the body in that it seemingly provokes a revelation by the body about itself (*Birth*, 120). I am adapting this point to the process of separating true from false medicine, which came down to a knowledge of what counted as true for regulars. Foucault discusses mapping the body as a projective matter: "to establish these signs, artificial or natural, is to project upon the living body a whole network of anatamo-pathological mappings: to draw the dotted outline of the future autopsy. The problem, then, is to bring to the surface that which is layered in depth; semiology will no longer be a *reading*, but the set of techniques that make it possible to constitute a *projective pathological anatomy*" (*Birth*, 163, emphasis in original).

36. The quotation regarding a "social language" is from Michel de Certeau (*The Practice of Everyday Life*, trans. Steven Randall [Berkeley: University of California Press, 1984], 148, emphasis in original). Remarks regarding perception and social structure are from Donald M. Lowe (*History of Bourgeois Perception* [Chicago: University of Chicago Press, 1982], 1, emphasis in original). Certeau is not referring to medical perception per se, but as I understand the process, his remarks about machining bodies are describing precisely that operation. Also, Certeau describes the corollary of the scriptural economy of knowledge production: *removal* of "something excessive, diseased, or unesthetic from the body" and *addition* "to the body what it lacks" (*Practice*, 147). Also see Richard Leppert's *Art and the Committed Eye: The Cultural Functions of Imagery* for a discussion of the epistemic function of perception (Boulder, Colo.: Westview, 1996).

Notes for Chapter Four

1. For an introduction to medical attitudes toward women in the nineteenth century, see Jordanova, *Sexual*; Poovey, *Uneven Developments*; Cynthia Eagle Russett, *Sexual Science: The Victorian Construction of Womanhood* (Cambridge, Mass.: Harvard University Press, 1989); Nancy M. Theriot, *Mothers & Daughters in Nineteenth-Century America: The Biosocial Construction of Femininity* (Lexington, Ky.: University Press of Kentucky, 1996).

2. Ricci states that, "The uterus as a *central* organ of the female genital system dominated the field of gynaecology for fully the first half of the nineteenth century" (*One Hundred Years of Gynaecology, 1880-1900* [Philadelphia: Blakiston Company, 1945], 33, emphasis in original). Also see Ehrenreich and English, *Complaints*, 30-32; Laqueur, *Making Sex*, 175-81; Smith-Rosenberg, *Disorderly*, 184-87.

3. "'Change of Life' in Women; With Remarks on the Periods Usually Called 'Critical,'" *Boston Medical and Surgical Journal* 50, no. 3, 18 (1854): 349, 56, 350. The overwhelming interest in uterine therapeutics and treatments until the 1870s bears witness to the centrality of the uterus at the time. The number of guides based on uterine treatment itself is daunting. The author of "Change of Life" continued at length about the radical metonymy of woman/uterus: "The hidden uterus, aroused from its long lethargy, grows, and developes the whole being, first giving evidence of its power to execute the ommcand [*sic*] to 'Be fruitful and multiply,' and then, by the same inherent *vis vitale*, spreading out and affording shelter for a living being, and bearing it into the world" (351-52, emphasis in original); and:

> A new organ—a womb. For twelve years it has lain it its pelvic bed without alteration, except a very gradual increase of size, to maintain its progressive relation with other parts of the economy. A trunculated conoid body, flattened somewhat upon its surface, nearly an inch in thickness, about twice that length, and in breadth perhaps midway between the two. It has a body and a neck, with a slight fissure or cavity occupying its interior, and of the same shape, terminating below in a corresponding opening, called its mouth, or *os uteri*. Its appendages—Fallopian tubes . . . The ovaries . . . the vagina . . . The entire system sympathizes with the effort, and there is rapid change in the whole being (55-56, emphasis in original).

4. I have remarked on this passage before. I think his comment is very revealing of the state of medical faddishness of the time, not to mention being downright funny (Stone, "Observations," 75).

5. This is a commonly stressed and central facet of early biology and medicine. For earlier work, see Ehrenreich and English, *Complaints*, 26-32, and *For Her*; Smith-Rosenberg, *Disorderly*, 185; and Welter, *Dimity*, 57-63. Also see Stephen Jay Gould, "American Polygeny and Craniometry before Darwin," in *The Racial Economy of Science: Toward a Democratic Future*, ed. Sandra Harding (Bloomington: Indiana University Press, 1993), 84-115; Laqueur, *Making Sex,* 208-210 for cranial capacity; Schiebinger, *Mind,* 191-200, for female skeletal anatomy. See Edward Clarke, *Sex in Education* (Boston: James R. Osgood & Co., 1873) for an excellent illustration of this line of thinking at work, especially the "limited blood supply" argument.

6. Thomas E. Massey, "Observations Upon Disease of the Uterus," *New Orleans Medical and Surgical Journal* 11, no. 1 (1855): 473. Laqueur, *Making Sex*, 25-62.

7. For a thorough and fascinating tour of the labyrinthine changes in female repro-

ductive biology, see Laqueur, *Making Sex*. Also, he details the spread of ovariotomy as the outgrowth of Bischoff's discovery. Information about Bischoff, Pouchet, and the distinction of the ovary from the teste (178-79, 210-11, 213), as well as the quotation regarding ovaries and the female economy (213) are from Laqueur. W. H. Studley's remarks in "Is Menstruation a Disease?," *American Journal of Obstetrics* 8, no. 3 (1876): 491, are indicative of a vast majority of authors. Consider Alfred Meadows' comments: "The physiology of the ovaries is a very central point in the generative system, and they are, if I may so say, masters of the situation, from the very commencement of puberty up to the decline of the procreative period" ("Remarks," 215); or Tilt's: "In woman it has been amply shown, by the successful experiments of modern observers, that the ovaria are the essential organs of reproduction and that in them originate the greater proportion of those sympathies which have been so long called uterine . . . These may consequently be considered the essential organs of the generative system, for they are always present, what form of organization they assume" (*Diseases*, xxx, inclusive of his quotation in the body of the text).

8. Eliza F. Pettingill, "A Thesis on the Ovaries" (M.D. thesis, Women's Medical College of Pennsylvania, SCWM, 1864), 3. Charles Meigs, *Woman: Her Diseases and Remedies* (Philadelphia: Blanchard and Lea, 1854) 64-65.

9. Tilt, *Diseases*, xxix, emphasis in original.

10. Amos Nourse, "Menstruation and Its Connection with Utero-Gestation," *Boston Medical and Surgical Journal* 71, no. 25 (1864): 492, emphasis in original. The comparison to telegraph wires is from a journal entry adapted from a private letter of a Dr. Cleaveland, Cincinnati physician and editor of the homeopathic *College Journal* ("The Powers of Life," *College Journal of Rational Medicine* 1, no. 9 [1856]: 336). The similarity between Cleaveland's telegraph metaphor and those of allopathic doctors reinforces H. L. Coulter's and James Mohr's argument that homeopaths and allopaths had many similar assumptions about bodies and medical practice. Note, I do not contend that bodily organs do not respond to one another. However, given the gendered manufacturing process depicted and the Victorian morality of the passage, I wonder whose intellect was reflected in the anthropomorphized uterus?

11. Smith-Rosenberg, *Disorderly*, 190, 189. Bedford "Clinical Lectures," 10 (1854): 148, emphasis in original. Bedford preceded this comment by arguing that menstruation was the sign of womanly completion: "Puberty in the female is characterized by certain physical developments, the most prominent and remarkable of which is *menstruation*. Indeed, it may be said that the appearance of the menstrual function is the positive evidence afforded by nature that the various physical modifications of developments, more or less directly connected with the advent of puberty, have been completed" (ibid., 147, emphasis in original). Another example, from "Change of Life": "The peculiarities of childhood already noticed, are natural to both sexes; but the first great *change* to which the human female is subject, is menstruation. . . . Its office is to transform the girl, from girlhood to the estate of woman. It performs its office by developing a latent organ, hitherto inactive and apparently useless. Power is exhibited by the transformation—power to conceive and to mature a living human being" (55, emphasis in original). For interesting insights as to how menstrual blood has been associated with nationalism, see Linke, *Blood*.

12. Tilt, *Diseases*, xxiii, xxii, xxviii, emphasis in original, Latin translation by Michael Tiffany. Smith-Rosenberg cites Henry C. Wright's *Marriage and Parentage* (Boston: Bela Marsh, 1854) and Alice Stockham's *Tokology*, rev. ed. (Chicago: Sanitary Publishing Co., 1887) for evidence of menstrual health (*Disorderly*, 189).

13. Augustus Gardner, *The Causes and Curative Treatment of Sterility with a Prelim-*

inary Statement of the Physiology of Generation (New York: De Witt & Davenport, 1854), 17.

14. Ibid. Laqueur provides a thorough discussion of the subject, particularly regarding Putnam Jacobi's introduction of a new governing metaphor of *nutrition*, rather than *sexual appetite*, regarding menstruation (*Making*, 210-17, 222-24). See Mary Putnam Jacobi, *The Question of Rest for Women During Menstruation* (New York: G. P. Putnam's Sons, 1877). Bedford provides an example of a mid-ground between Gardner and Raciborski, in which surface similarities are less important than spontaneous ovulation:

> There is, indeed, a striking similarity in this respect between the menstrual period in woman, and what is termed the period of *heat* in animals. . . . [If] it be argued that during the period of *heat*, certain animals do not have any sanguineous discharge, no matter how slight or for how short a time, then I object to the doctrine for it is against the evidence furnished us by accurate observation. Examine, for example, the slut at the time she is about to take the dog (her period of *heat*) and you will find not only congestion of the parts, but also a slight sanguineous secretion; and during this time of *heat* the same thing is observed which is so characteristic of the menstrual function in women, viz.: the spontaneous maturation and subsequent escape of ovules." ("Clinical Lectures," 10 [1854]: 148-49, emphasis in original)

Also see Anna M. Galbraith, "Are the Dangers of the Menopause Natural or Acquired? A Physiological Study," in *Transactions of the Twenty-Fourth Annual Meeting of the Alumnæ Association of the Women's Medical College of Pennsylvania* (Philadelphia: Alumnæ Association of the Women's Medical College of Pennsylvania, 1899), 39-64; Smith-Rosenberg, *Disorderly*, 190; Wells, *Dead*, 172-78.

15. Laqueur, *Making*, 222, 223. Wells, *Dead*, 176, 174. Wells rightly critiques Laqueur on characterizing the female body in Putnam Jacobi as passive. On the contrary, menstruation became a source of strength. Hence, Wells and Laqueur differ on how they see nutrition as it relates to agency in Putnam Jacobi. Laura H. Satterthwaite ("Thesis: Menstruation," M.D. thesis, Women's Medical College of Pennsylvania, SCWM, 1888) makes an argument for viewing menstruation as part of a healthy life and refutes the idea of menstruation as a sign of weakness.

16. Angus McLaren traces the connection of pleasure to theories of conception in his essay ("Pleasures," 339). Acton's quotation was taken from McLaren (ibid., 338), as was the reference to Sims, although I have cross-checked it for accuracy. Laqueur provides the tidbit about Raciborski (*Making*, 190). For perspective on feminine sexuality of the working class, see Griselda Pollack, "The Dangers of Proximity: The Spaces of Sexuality and Surveillance in Word and Image," *Discourse* 16 (1993-94): 3-50; Stansell, *City of Women*. Also see Degler, *At Odds*; Laqueur, "Orgasm."

17. A. F. A. King, "A New Basis for Uterine Pathology," *American Journal of Obstetrics* 8, no. 2 (1874): 243, emphasis in original. King's argument was singular in its brazenness, although the equation of high fertility and health of the race was shared by the community at large. In fact, Studley published a response to King that supported reproduction, but called King's logic faulty: "I would affirm, as he does not, that 'every female on attaining the age of puberty ought to marry and perform the reproductive office.' But inasmuch as he avowedly does not allow this (again applying the practical teaching of his proposition), the legitimate inferences would be, as the other horn of the dilemma, that we should cause femaledom to retrograde from civilization—to get back to its ancient and typical normality by uncivilizing as fast as possible" ("Menstruation," 509). Notice the

opposition *within* the civilizing necessity of reproductive norms.

18. I use *emblem* and *icon* advisedly here. As I use the terms, an emblem is a sign of something else in a more superficial sense, like the patch on a uniform. An icon is a fetishized sign, in my usage.

19. This atlas is a compendium of images from other atlases. For instance, the figure in the upper-left corner is from William Hunter's *Gravid Uterus*. E. Martin and J. P. Maygrier, *Atlas of Gynaecology and Obstetrics*, trans. and ed. Wm. A. Rothacker (Cincinnati: A. E. Wilde, 1881).

20. Storer used comparative biology as an explanation of fetal life at conception, but his strongest plea, I believe, was theological (*Criminal*, 73; *Why Not?*, 28, 29). Small's lecture, "Jurisprudence of Abortion," was reprinted in Edwin Hale's *A Systematic Treatise on Abortion and Sterility*, rev. ed. (Chicago: C. S. Halsey, 1868), 313-37. Yet another example of *theo-medical* discourse comes from an editorial: "No sophistry can do away with the fact, that whether the lamp of life is extinguished in the womb or at any period after birth, with an avowed and wilful [*sic*] intention to taking the life of the fœtus or infant, it is murder, and the perpetrator of it cannot expect to escape the vengeance of offended heaven," in "Procuring Abortions," *Boston Medical and Surgical Journal* 51, no. 10 (1855): 205. There is no better illustration than an editorial in the *Boston Medical and Surgical Journal* in which, after reviewing a copy of *The Northwestern Christian Advocate*, the editors wrote:

> Quotations are also freely made from the writings of Drs. Hodge, Taylor, Stewart, H. R. Storer, and others. The medical press, generally, has for several years faithfully done its work in exposing the prevalence, the criminality, and the pernicious effects of this sad business; and in its pages may be found all the data our theological journalists and teachers may require in filling their bills of indictment, and addressing their instructions to their readers. (Editors, *Boston Medical and Surgical Journal* 76, no. 7 [1867]: 145)

Also see Hodge, *Criminal*; D. H. Storer, "Two Frequent."

21. In *Why Not?*, Storer removed birth as a beginning (31). Indeed, he found the biological argument positively obvious: "That the fœtus is *alive* from the commencement of pregnancy cannot be gainsaid" ("Contributions," 431, emphasis in original). Kelly's synopsis was responded to heavily by his audience ("Ethics," 28). Their reactions were generally confirming.

22. Ibid., 30-31.

23. Newman, *Fetal*, 67 (for both references). Smith-Rosenberg, *Disorderly*, 241-42. Storer, *Why Not?*, 28 (he was fond of locating historical authors to indicate the depravity of his contemporaries). The reference to a "spot" or "nidus" comes from Hodge, *Criminal*, 9-10. Smith-Rosenberg cites Hodge and Storer to argue that females have no rights over their fetuses. Quoting from a note in Smith-Rosenberg: "Storer went so far as to argue that the father's genetic influence on the fetus was far greater that the mother's" (*Disorderly*, 341, n. 67).

24. Putnam Jacobi, *Question*, 7. Storer, *Criminal*, 62. Mitchell, "Infanticide," 8. Also see William J. Curran, "An Historical Perspective on the Law of Personality and Status with Special Regard to the Human Fetus and the Rights of Woman," *Health and Society* 61, no. 1 (1983): 58-73; Michael R. Harrison, "Unborn: Historical Perspective of the Fetus as a Patient," *The Pharos* Winter (1982): 19-24.

25. Note, I am not claiming that antiabortion advocates in contemporary times do not attend to abortion on a grand scale. Rather, I am arguing that the greater focus of today's

discourse is not on the population as a whole, but on a mass of individual tragedies. The fetal icon and the millions of individual "murders" is the dominant figure in today's antiabortion discourse, whereas the suicide of the race is not a central trope, although I would contend it has a strong presence.

26. See *Oxford Dictionary of English Etymology*, s. v. "matrix," for original Latin and the root *mater*. See *Suffixes and Other Word-Final Elements of English*, s. v. "-trix." Butler, *Bodies*, 31. Barnhart's, s. v. "matrix," for "origin" definition. Note, *Barnhart Dictionary of English Etymology*, s. v. "matrix," fixes the usage of matrix as womb in Late Latin, as well as Old French, and dates usage prior to the fifteenth-century. It also fixes the first usage of matrix as a place of formation in 1555. Also see *Concise Oxford Dictionary of English Etymology*, s. v. "matrix," *Funk & Wagnall's New Comprehensive International Dictionary of the English Language*, deluxe ed., s. v. "matrix," and *Oxford Encyclopedic English Dictionary*, 3rd ed., s. v. "matrix." I have attempted to reserve the term "matrix" for the aggregate of reproductive organs of the bourgeoisie and "womb" or "reproductive organs" for the bodies of individuals, although there are times when the latter two are used collectively.

27. duBois, *Torture*, 91; Meigs, *Woman*, 56.

28. See Butler, *Bodies*, ch. 1.

29. Allen, "Power," 464.

30. D. H. Storer, "Two Frequent," 200. King, as I have stated, was extreme in the tenor of his arguments, but he did reflect the line of thinking common to many antiabortionists ("New Basis," 256, emphasis in original). For more background and examples of a mechanistic model of moral physiology, see Brodie, *Contraception*, 57-86; Edward H. Dixon, *Woman and Her Diseases* (New York: Edward H. Dixon, 1846); J. H. Kellog, *Ladies' Guide in Health and Disease* (Battle Creek, Mich.: Modern Medicine Publishing, 1895); Laqueur, "Orgasm"; Meigs, *Woman;* Nourse, "Menstruation"; H. Pomeroy, *The Ethics of Marriage* (New York: Funk & Wagnalls, 1888); Smith-Rosenberg, *Disorderly*, 182-91; Stone, "Observations"; H. R. Storer, *Why Not?*; idem, *Is It I?*; Studley, "Menstruation"; and Wilson Yates, "Birth Control Literature and the Medical Profession in Nineteenth Century America," *Journal of the History of Medicine and Allied Sciences* 31 (1976): 42-54.

31. Rosi Braidotti, *Nomadic Subjects* (New York: Columbia University Press, 1994), 80. Collins is discussing the onset of menstruation in "Diseases," 477. Smith-Rosenberg provides the comment on ovarian dictatorship (*Disorderly*, 184). For information on the male standard of anatomy and physiology, see Duden, *Woman*, 31-35, 112-19; Ehrenreich and English, *For Her*; Laqueur, *Making*, 25-43; Lloyd, *Science*; Schiebinger, *Mind*, 160-213, and *Nature's Body*.

32. N. Hastings, "Inflammation of the Uterus," *College Journal of Medical Science* 4, no. 6 (1859): 269. Ehrenreich and English discuss the professional advantages of female maladies (*For Her*, 99-100). Collins, "Diseases," 477, emphasis in original.

33. Braidotti argues that we should study how discourses on monstrosity function in culture to explain bodily difference (*Nomadic*, 78-79, emphasis in original).

34. For a historical overview of eighteenth-century theories of maternal impressions and physical oddity, see Stafford, *Body*, 254-79, 306-29. The case of the shackled brother is contained in C. O. Wright, "Maternal Impressions Affecting the Fetus in Utero," *American Journal of Obstetrics* 11, no. 3 (1878): 635. Also see H. A. Gerby, "Maternal Influence on the Fœtus," *Boston Medical and Surgical Journal* 44, no. 7 (1851): 137-38; James M. Hartwell, "Maternal Influence on the Fetus as Exhibited in a Cat," *Nelson's American Lancet* 8, no. 8 (1853): 126; "Influence of a Mother's Mind on the Fetus,"

Boston Medical and Surgical Journal 55 (1856): 85-86; "Maternal Impressions and the Fetus," *Boston Medical and Surgical Journal* 44, no. 7 (1851): 148; M. J. M'Cormack "Influence of Maternal Impressions on the Fetus," *Boston Medical and Surgical Journal* 44, no. 4 (1851): 79-80; "On the Reciprocal Agencies of Mind and Matter," *Boston Medical and Surgical Journal* 45, no. 9 (1851): 169-201; L. Slusser, "Influence of the Imagination of the Mother upon the Fœtus," *Medical Examiner* 8 (1852): 344-46; T. J. Williamson, "Influence of the Mother's Mind on the Embryo in Utero," *New Orleans Journal of Medicine* 23 (1870): 94-96; Ellwood Wilson, "Death of a Fetus Caused by Fright of the Mother," *American Journal of Obstetrics* 10 (1877): 340.

35. This is reminiscent of Hippocratic writers who believed that women's uteruses moved about: "several gynaecological treatises develop elaborate theories about how the womb wanders all around the body and thereby causes diseases" (Lloyd, *Science*, 84).

36. Ricci discusses the displacement craze in *One Hundred Years* (36, 269-97). Priestley's opinion is described by Ricci (ibid., 36). Coale's remarks begin a lengthy serialized treatise on displacement, "A Treatise on the Causes, Constitutional Effects and Treatment of Uterine Displacements," *Boston Medical and Surgical Journal* 47 (1852): 41, 42. Also see "Case of Procidentia Uteri," *Boston Medical and Surgical Journal* 50, no. 4 (1854): 80-82; W. E. Coale, "Woman's Disease a Cause of Uterine Displacements," *Boston Medical and Surgical Journal* 45 (1852): 14-17; H. S. Hender, "Chronic Prolapsus Uteri," *Boston Medical and Surgical Journal* 52 (1855): 197; McClintock, "Mechanical Tendency of Uterine Therapeutics," *Boston Medical and Surgical Journal* 77, no. 4 (1867): 87; "Uterine Displacements," *New Orleans Journal of Medicine* 12 (1856): 98; Valleix, "Displacements."

37. Braidotti (*Nomadic*, 81) is citing Julia Kristeva's *Pouvoirs de l'horreur* (Paris: Seuil, 1980).

38. Susan Sontag, *Illness as Metaphor and Aids and Its Metaphors* (New York: Anchor Books, 1990) 43-44; Simpson, *Obstetrical Memoirs*, 38-39; Tilt, *Diseases,* xxii.

39. H. A. Ramsay, "Abortion in the Earlier Months, and in Fever," *Nelson's American Lancet* 7 (1853): 77. James Whitehead, *On the Causes and Treatment of Abortion and Sterility* (Philadelphia: Blanchard and Lea, 1854), 203, 252-53. H. R. Storer describes the reflexivity of disease and abortion ("Studies," 17). For a few examples of abortion being treated as the cause of other illnesses, see the unattributed letter to Walter Channing, "Criminal"; Curtin, "Pelvic"; Leonard, "Quackery"; Minot, "Morbid"; Storer, *Why Not?*, 36-61; and Treadwell, "Case." For a discussion of terministic screens and ultimate God and Devil terms, see Burke, *Symbolic Action*, 44-62.

40. "Criminal Abortion," *Boston Medical and Surgical Journal* 62 (1860): 65. See the AMA's "Report," 75; Kelly, "Ethics," 25, 30. The description of the *Gazette* image is from Smith-Rosenberg (*Disorderly*, 226). Copies of the image are available in Mohr, *Abortion*, 127, and Amy Gilman Srebnick, *The Mysterious Death of Mary Rogers: Sex and Culture in Nineteenth-Century New York* (New York: Oxford University Press, 1995), 100.

41. Judith Butler, *Gender Trouble: Feminism and the Subversion of Identity* (New York: Routledge, 1990), 139, 141. For examples of limited fertility being taken as a dangerous aesthetic, see Storer, *Why Not?*; Nebinger, *Criminal*; Stockham, *Tokology.*

42. Discussion of Christian nationalist biopolitics and bourgeois nationalist biopolitics is from Stoler, *Race*, 41-42. There was not the kind of iconography of otherness within antiabortionists writing, the scientific specification of the black body's difference, that Sander Gilman (*Difference*, 76-108) has noted in his essay on the Hottentot Venus or Robert Gordon has noted about the Bushman penis ("The Rise of the Bushman Penis:

Germans, Genitalia and Genocide," *African Studies* 57, no. 1 [1998]: 27-53). Rather, there was a diffuse reference to bodily and cultural difference as a condition of specifying an ailing white body. The revitalization of suicidal primitavism within whites is a paradigmatic case of constituting the other within the self, as variously discussed in psychoanalytic literatures or critical Derridian works. Mohanram suggests that we consider the racialization of the body as a function of the "rhetorical strategy of displacement" by which the body "functions as différance, especially in the tiresome way it lingers on after it has been expunged. On the one hand it lends itself to the construction of hierarchies body/consciousness, body/mind and further differences, yet, on the other, the very effects of these differences refer to a point of origin" (*Black Body*, 50-51). Blackness is a spatial locator of displacement, relative to an idealized white body, that seems unmarked and transcendent of its physicality. In terms of abortion related fears of race suicide, the body of whiteness lingers on in its vulnerability relative to the dark bodies that have been marked and placed as both internal and external threats. Blackness is the result of the displacement of the body from the mind, but the displacement is never complete and functions to create a racialized topography of hostile social juxtapositions.

43. Derrida, *Archive*, 11. Note, I am not relying on Foucault's notion of the archive because I want to stress the materiality of the performance of archivization more so than the rules that enable one to speak, the first general law of statements. As such, in his effort to dematerialize his meaning of archive in the *Archaeology*, I prefer how Derrida discusses the process. However, as for the recuperative, reiterative aspect of archivization, I am very much influenced by Foucault (*Archaeology*). For different insight on life as order, see Karl M. Figlio, "The Metaphor of Organization: An Historiographical Perspective on the Biomedical Sciences of the Early Nineteenth Century," *History of Science* 14 (1976): 17-53.

Notes for Chapter Five

1. Here, Certeau is describing the tools that add to and remove from the body inscribed. "In order for the law to be written on bodies, an apparatus is required that can mediate the relation between the former and the latter. From the instruments of scarification, tattooing, and primitive initiation to those of penal justice, tools work on the body. Formerly the tool was a flint knife or a needle. Today the instruments range from the policeman's billy club to handcuffs and the box reserved for the accused in the courtroom" (Certeau, *Practice*, 141). I contend that perceptual tools accomplish this task in conjunction with those operations that might physically mark the subject more directly, such as surgery or torture. Tools, he argues, call for their use: "A necessity (a destiny?) seems to be indicated by these steel and nickel objects: the necessity that introduces the law into the flesh by means of iron and that, in a culture, neither authorizes nor recognizes as bodies flesh that has not been written out by the tool" (Certeau, *Practice*, 143). Instruments of bodily manipulation "represent in concrete form the tortuous knowledge, sharp sinuosities, perforating ruses, and incisive detours that penetration into the labyrinthine body requires and produces. In that way, they become *the metallic vocabulary* of the knowledge that they bring back from these expeditions" (ibid., 145, emphasis mine).

2. Ibid., 148, emphasis in original. Certeau is talking about how social law is inscribed in bodies, but the analogy is sound. Social law in the garb of nature and divinity were inscribed in women's organs in order to fabricate a lineage of norms.

3. Mark Wigley as cited by Jennifer A. González, "Autotopographies," in *Prosthetic Territories: Politics and Hypertechnologies*, ed. Garbriel Brahm, Jr. and Mark Driscoll (Boulder, Colo.: Westview, 1995), 135.

4. Jonathan Crary, *Techniques of the Observer: On Vision and Modernity in the Nineteenth Century* (Cambridge: MIT Press, 1990), 9, 129, 147. Braidotti observes that "*homo sapiens* was never more than a crafty *homo faber*. No one can tell how long ago the human hand picked up the first stone and shaped it so as to multiply its strength, so as to strike better. This elementary principle of prosthesis and prosthetic projection animates the whole technological universe" (*Nomadic*, 42-43).

5. After an extensive review of diagnostic practices, Ricci concluded Jones was the first. He also provides the most detailed overview available of nineteenth-century uses and development of specula (*Development*, 303, 294-319).

6. John C. W. Lever, *A Practical Treatise on Organic Diseases of the Uterus* (Newburgh, N.Y.: David L. Proudfit, 1846), 13-14. Lever also discusses the primacy of hearing for determining pregnancy (ibid., 14-15). Also see Whitehead, *Abortion*. Crary, *Techniques*, 59.

7. Ibid., 94. Heidi J. Nast and Audrey Kobayashi, "Re-corporealizing Vision" in *Bodyspace*, ed. Nancy Duncan (New York: Routledge, 1996), 89. One aspect Crary does not acknowledge is the interrelation of the newly distinguished senses in hierarchies of perception, which, as Foucault indicates, was necessary to modern medical perception (*Birth*, 163). For more information on the separation of the senses, see Stafford, *Body*, ch. 6.

8. Anthony Todd Thomson, "Lectures on Medical Jurisprudence," *Nelson's Northern Lancet* 1, no. 5 (1852): 248 (in the series of lectures XIII, XIV, XV, XVI, XVII, *Nelson's Northern Lancet* 1, nos. 1, 3-4 (1851): 95-107, 156-63, 208-15; 1, nos. 5-6 (1852): 246-53, 289-97; 2, nos. 1-2 (1852): 49-52, 88-97). Simpson, *Memoir*, 28. Meadows, "Remarks," 225. For an example of habituating description, consider Thomson's description of parturition: "about a week after delivery, the [uterus] is as large as two fists; at the end of a fortnight, it is five inches long, generally lying obliquely on one side; the inner surface is still bloody; and covered with a pulpy substance, like decidua" ("Lectures," 1 [1851]: 161). For an example of the standardization of oral histories as supplement to physical diagnosis, see William H. Baker and Francis H. Davenport, "Methods of Gynæcological Examination and General Outlines of Differential Diagnosis," in *Clinical Gynæcology: Medical and Surgical for Students and Practitioners by Eminent American Teachers*, ed. John M. Keating and Henry C. Coe (Philadelphia: J. B. Lippincott, 1895), 26-32.

9. Churchill, *Diseases*, 33. Sims, *Clinical*, 7-8. Touch could determine "any dislocation of the uterus . . . the existence or non-existence of inflammation or irritability, whether the os uteri is preternaturally firm or hard; whether there are any polypoid growths . . . whether the os uteri is even and smooth, or corrugated, or scabrous" (Lever, *Organic*, 8). Similarly, Churchill argued that the hand could give indications "as to caliber, heat, moisture, and sensibility; the condition of the pelvic cavity, whether unusually empty or filled . . . the elevation of the os uteri, its patency, sensibility, and integrity; the density of the cervix, its sensibility, and freedom from morbid growths or ulceration; the position and volume of the womb, its mobility and sensibility" (*Diseases*, 35). Ricci cites Frederic Boyd as one of the first to argue palpation was a valuable practice in diagnosis (*Development*, 311). Also see Thomas, *Practical*, 66-7.

10. Information on invention of the sound is from Ricci, *Development*, 322. Description of Simpson's sound is from Simpson, *Memoirs*, 57. Thomas as quoted in Ricci, *De-*

velopment, 325-26. The first text on the sound was written in 1865 by Huguier and included descriptions of "thirty different types of sounds" from Hyppocritean physicians to contemporaries. The curette, a sound with a scoop for scraping, was introduced by Récamier in 1843 (ibid., 322, 326). For an example of an abortion case in which a sound was used for diagnosis, see Thomas, "Attempted Criminal Abortion." For examples of how the sound was being standardized within practice by the end of the century, see Baker and Davenport ("Methods," 55-60) and Thomas (*Practical* 1868, 76-80).

11. Simpson, *Memoirs*, 61. Sims, *Clinical*, 8. Balbirnie, *Speculum*, 42, emphasis in original. See Ricci for more information on the use of the sound (*Development*, 322-28).

12. Jones, *Practical*, 90, emphasis mine. For information on the valorization of vision, see Francis Barker, *The Tremulous Private Body: Essays on Subjection* (London: Methuen, 1984), 73-84; Crary, *Techniques*; Daston and Galison, "Image"; Deleuze, *Foucault*; Foucault, *Birth*; idem, *Discipline and Punish: The Birth of the Prison*, trans. Alan Sheridan (New York Vintage, 1979); Keller and Grontkowski, "Mind's"; Porter, "Rise"; Jonathan Rajchman, "Foucault's Art of Seeing," *October* 44 (1988): 89-117.

13. Balbirnie, *Speculum*, 2-3. Sims, *Clinical*, 13. Gardner, "Speculum," 67. Balbirnie, *Speculum*, 13, 14, emphasis in original. Churchill was ambivalent about the use and abuse of the speculum. I think he represents as close to a middle ground on the debate of taxis versus opsis as one might find (*Diseases*, 34, 35-36). Ricci, *Development*, 294-319. Also see Lever, *Organic*.

14. Balbirnie, *Speculum*, 12-13, 9, emphasis in original. For examples of the standardization of specular application, see Baker and Davenport, "Methods," 46-55; Thomas, *Practical* (1868), 70-75. Lever explained the benefits of vision: "for by the eye we recognise the waxen hue of amenorrhæa or chlorosis, the shrivelled and wasted features attendant upon carcinoma, as well as the pale and flabby appearance of patients suffering from long existing hemorrhages. The eye, moreover, assists us in discrimination between the several secretions or discharges from the vagina . . . it distinguishes also tumours . . . it recognizes inversio uteri . . ." The speculum, however, was not a perceptual panacea. "It must not, however, be forgotten that there are many circumstances which prohibit the employment of a speculum, such as a hymen, membranous bands traversing the vagina, contractions of the upper part of the vagina into a funnel-like tube, vaginal tumours, deep ulcerations of the vagina, extreme irritability" and complications from abortion, among others (*Organic*, 9-10). For example, Mackenzie Johnston initially relied on the patient's report of how she felt. Only after she had complications from her abortion did he conduct a digital exam ("Case"). In another example, a woman (whose name was not revealed) was examined digitally, rather than with a speculum because of extensive hemorrhaging after an abortion induced by a sharp instruments (Minot, "Morbid," 36-38). Another, Mrs. S., was so swollen from complications of her abortion that the physician could hardly pass a single digit for examination. In other situations, visual perception could be had only days after the fact, as in a criminal trial (Doe, "Case," 313).

15. "New Vaginal Speculum," *American Journal of Obstetrics* 2 (1869): 545. Also see Lever, *Organic*, 13. Jones provides an excellent description of the dependence of the speculum on touch: "the index finger having reached the cervix uteri, points out the locality of the uterus, and serves as a guide for the speculum, while it makes pressure on the lower part of the vagina, and dilates its cavity; meanwhile, the speculum held in the other hand of the operator, is gradually conducted on the upper surface of the finger, along the vagina, till it reaches the cervix uteri;—the finger being gradually withdrawn as the speculum advances" (*Practical*, 67-68). Nott offers an example of the careful use of the hands to operate his modified Sims' speculum: "The depressor being extracted, and the instru-

ment closed, the palm of the hand is placed over the outer opening of the instrument; the end of the thumb is placed on the back of the duck-bill, and the index and middle fingers curved over the heels of the feet—the blades are all thus firmly compressed together. Pass the instrument into the vagina as *far as it will go* . . . Then turn the button on the screw until the perineum is pushed sufficiently out of the way, and the ostium vaginæ is opened" ("New," 150, emphasis in original). See Ricci for a discussion of the use of the sound (*Development*, 322-28).

16. Description of instrumental abortions is from Thomson, "Lectures," 1, no. 6 (1852): 294, 291. *Scott v.People*, 329; also see 334. When determining criminality, only the fetus was positive proof of abortion (Thomson, 1, no. 5 [1852]: 252), because "for the traces it [abortion] leaves behind are very obscure, the hæmorrhage is seldom profuse, sometimes scarcely perceptible; and no judgement can be grounded on the condition of the uterus. If it take place in the middle or towards the termination of pregnancy, the same signs are to be looked for as I have already described as those indicative of recent delivery." The same is true about a recently fatal delivery in the case of finding a corpse (ibid., 252). Knowing what a normally aborted fetus looks like is also important, then. For more discussion of norms and extremes, see Thomson (ibid., 1, no. 3 [1851]: 156-63). Also see *People v.Sessions*, 603-4 when medical books are shown to the jury.

17. Van de Werker, "Detection," part 2, 223, 229; he notes two varieties of abortifacients, 230. Ibid., 234. For an earlier, less-detailed discussion of abortifacient symptoms, see Thomson who also describes the effect of purgatives such as vomiting, bloody stools, and convulsions ("Lectures," 1, no. 5 [1852]: 249-250). Also see "Attempt to Produce Abortion with Oil of Tansy, Followed by Death," *Boston Medical and Surgical Journal* 44, no. 19 (1851): 306; Charles E. Buckingham, "Two Cases of Labor in the Same Patient," *Boston Medical and Surgical Journal* 63, no. 8 (1860): 207-13; Cleveland, "Oil of Cedar"; A. I. Cummings, "Tannin, As a Medical Agent," *Boston Medical and Surgical Journal* 47 (1850): 36-40; "Effects of Quinine on the Uterus," *Boston Medical and Surgical Journal* 54, no. 26 (1856): 528; "Ergot and Galvanism as Ecbolics," *New Hampshire Journal of Medicine* 4 (1854): 225-27; "Ergot vs. the Tampon in Puerperal Hemorrhage," *New Orleans Journal of Medicine* 23 (1870): 843-44; "Galvinism as a Substitute for Ergot," *Peninsular Journal of Medicine* 2, no. 2 (1854): 134; Hendee, "Veratrum Veride"; Adolph Kessler, "A Contribution to the Hypodermic Ergot Treatment of Uterine Myomata," *American Journal of Obstetrics* 13, no. 3 (1880): 548-62; Mohr, *Abortion*, 50-73; Palmer, "American Hellebore"; "Quarterly Report on Obstetrics," *American Journal of Obstetrics* 7, no. 2 (1874): 286-89; R. L. Scruggs, "On the Use of Ext. Belladonna in the Treatment of Obstinate Vomitings in Pregnant Women," *Peninsular Journal of Medicine* 1, no. 4 (1853): 165-69; "Standards for Drug Inspectors," *Boston Medical and Surgical Journal* 45, no. 12 (1851): 246-47; "Use of Ergot in Abortion,"*American Journal of Obstetrics* 11, no. 3 (1878): 772-73; W. S. C., "Preparation and Sale of Domestic Medicines," *Boston Medical and Surgical Journal* 45, no. 22 (1852): 447-49.

18. Van de Werker, "Detection," part 2, 235, 234, 239, emphasis mine.

19. Haraway, *Leaf,* 87. Also see idem, *Simians,* ch. 8; idem, *Modest.*

20. The response to "B." is from "Report of the Committee Upon Criminal Abortion," *Boston Medical and Surgical Journal* 56 (1857): 386, emphasis in original. The quotation on ignorant physicians is from Storer, *Criminal,* 104. Also see Storer et al., "Report." For more information on the flap over Mr. "B.," see "Criminal Abortion," *Boston Medical and Surgical Journal* 57 (1857): 45-46; Mohr, *Abortion,* 152-54; "Report upon Criminal Abortion," *Boston Medical and Surgical Journal* 57 (1857): 67. For an example

of the presumed rarity of the "quack among us," see Storer, *Criminal*, 102-3.

21. "Editorial Notes," *Journal of the Gynæcological Society of Boston* 3 (1870): 269. The anonymous letter to Walter Channing is quoted in "Criminal Abortion," *Boston* 63, 66. The call to medical professionals to remedy abortion is from "Criminal Abortion," *Boston* 62, 67.

22. Meigs, *Females*, 21. He argued that to be successful, a doctor should "be endowed with a clear perceptive power, a sound judgement, a real probity, and a proper degree of intelligence, and a familiarity with the doctrines of a good medical school" (ibid., 20).

23. Storer, *Criminal*, 90. Also see A. Cabot, "Survey of Abortion Law: History of Abortion Law," *Arizona State Law Journal* (1980): 73-127.

24. Crary, *Techniques*, 149, 113. Crary explains further:

> It is a shift signaled by the passage from the geometrical optics of the seventeenth and eighteenth centuries to physiological optics. . . . One result of the new physiological optics was to expose the idiosyncrasies of the "normal" eye. Retinal after images, peripheral vision, binocular vision, and thresholds of attention all were studied in terms of determining quantifiable norms and parameters. The widespread preoccupation with the defects of human vision defined ever more precisely an outline of the normal, and generated new technologies for imposing a normative vision on the observer. (ibid., 16)

Thus, "by the beginning of the nineteenth century the camera obscura is no longer synonymous with the production of truth and with an observer positioned to see truthfully. The regularity of such statements ends abruptly; the assemblage constituted by the camera breaks down and the photographic camera becomes an essentially dissimilar object, lodged amidst a radically different network of statements and practices" (ibid., 32). Referring to Gustav Fechner, whose law of sensation to stimulus mathematically quantified human perception, Crary argues: "Vision may well be measurable, but what is perhaps most significant about Fechner's equations is their homogenizing function: they are a means of rendering the perceiver manageable, predictable, productive, and above all consonant with other areas of rationalization" (ibid., 147). Nast and Kobayashi have complicated Crary's thesis, arguing that the break between a mobile observer and the camera obscura is not absolute historically, that they work interdependently across different configurations. Hence, visual activities "depend upon a geometrical optics only partially captured by the camera obscura. . . . it is important to recognize the socio-spatial unevenness of the regimes and their interconnectedness in contemporary social relations" ("Recorporealizing," 87). Their point is well taken. My use of Crary is not to insist on a complete historical break, signified by medical observers, but to stress the autonomy of vision regarding judgment and exegesis in liberating memory from hidden recesses. The presumed autonomy of observation added to the genealogical effect of medical rhetoric. However, by insisting on the prosthetic relation between materia medica and the observer's eye, I am acknowledge that optical apparatuses are crucial to visuality. What is worth exploring is how such a material apparatus can become invisible within its own visual field.

25. Certeau, *Practice*, 147. Burbick, *Healing*, chs. 13 and 14.

26. Quotation on objectivity is from Daston and Galison, "Image," 82. Thomson, "Lectures." Crary, *Techniques,* 94. Daston and Galison explain the habituation of vision through atlases: "To acquire this expert eye is to win one's spurs in most empirical sciences; the atlases drill the eye that present images from new instruments, such as the X-ray atlases of the early twentieth century, everyone in the field addressed by the atlas must

begin to learn to 'read' anew. Because atlases habituate the eye, they are perforce visual, even in those disciplines where other sensations play a significant role" ("Image," 85). Also see Maria Minnis, "Disquisition on Medical Jurisprudence," (M.D. thesis, Women's Medical College of Pennsylvania, SCWM, 1853); Storer, *Criminal*, 82-86; Van de Werker, "Detection." For examples of abortion cases that describe the appearance of the patient, see A. I. Cummings, "Use of the Tampon in Abortion," *Boston Medical and Surgical Journal* 49, no. 5 (1853): 98-99; Doe, "Case"; Helmick, "Case"; Johnston, "Case"; Minot, "Morbid."

27. Steven Shapin and Simon Schaffer, *Leviathan and the Air-Pump: Hobbes, Boyle, and the Experimental Life* (Princeton, N. J.: Princeton University Press, 1985), 65. Haraway offers the "ventriloquist" remark in *Modest_Witness*, 24. Note, Haraway is discussing modest witnessing generally; I have adapted her statements to a particular kind of performance of modest witnessing. The importance of replicability in early experimental philosophy and method is paralleled in the importance of habituated perceptual techniques, although medical case histories are not "experimental." Shapin and Schaffer argue three technologies are necessary to multiply witnesses and create believable truths: material, literary, and social (25). I will not adopt their vocabulary in full, although certainly each of these technologies is at work in nineteenth-century medicine. Also see Steven Shapin, *A Social History of Truth: Civility and Science in Seventeenth-Century England* (Chicago: University of Chicago Press, 1994).

28. Daston and Galison are discussing imagery in diverse medical atlases, but the textual imagery of case reports and collected treatises of the nineteenth century function similarly ("Image," 86). Crary describes the process of transforming the visual field into a surface of inscription for the observer:

> [T]he empirical sciences of the 1830s and 1840s had begun to describe a comparable neutrality of the observer that was a precondition for the external mastery and annexing of the body's capacities, for the perfection of technologies of attention, in which sequences of stimuli or images can produce the same effect repeatedly as if for the first time. . . . It was the remaking of the visual field not into a tabula rasa on which orderly representations could be arrayed, but into a surface of inscription on which a promiscuous range of effects could be produced. (*Techniques*, 96)

29. The physical exam is comparable to Crary's discussion of the technical obscenity of the stereoscope. "The stereoscope as a means of representation was inherently *obscene*, in the most literal sense. . . . The very functioning of the stereoscope depended, as indicated above, on the visual priority, of the object closest to the viewer and on the absence of any mediation between eye and image" (ibid., 127, emphasis in original).

30. Quotation on the relationship of surveillance is from Certeau, *Practice*, 173. Description of the moral conflict between modesty and health is paraphrased from Donegan, *Women*, 152-153. Meigs, *Females*, 19. Also see Wertz and Wertz, *Lying-In*, ch. 3. Foucault describes the paradoxical self-effacing presence of surveillance:

> By means of such surveillance, disciplinary power became an 'integrated' system, linked from the inside of the economy and to the aims of the mechanism in which it was practised. It was also organized as a multiple, automatic and anonymous power, for although surveillance rests on individuals, its functioning is that of a network of relations from top to bottom, but also to a certain extent for bottom to top and laterally . . . This enables the disciplinary power to be both absolutely indiscreet, since it is everywhere and always alert, since by its very principle it leaves no zone of shade and constantly supervises the

very individuals who are entrusted with the task of supervising; and absolutely, 'discreet', for it functions permanently and largely in silence. (*Discipline*, 176-177)

31. William M. Cornell discusses the relative morality of men and women physicians treating female patients in "The Medical Education of Women," *Boston Medical and Surgical Journal* 49, no. 21 (1854): 419-22. Dall's comments were reported by H. R. Storer in response to William Lloyd Garrison ("The Gynæcological Society of Boston and Women Physicians; A Reply to Mr. Wm. Lloyd Garrison," *Journal of the Gynæcological Society of Boston* 2 [1870]: 95). Also see Regina Markell Morantz, Cynthia Stodola Pomerleau, and Carol Hansen Fenichel, eds., *In Her Own Words: Oral Histories of Women Physicians* (New Haven: Yale University Press, 1982), chapt. 1; Welter, *Dimity*, 37-41.

32. Wertz and Wertz discuss the issue of modesty in obstetrics of the nineteenth century (*Lying-In*, chapt. 3). Churchill, *Diseases*, 35.

33. Thomas Litchfield, "On the Use and Abuse of the Speculum," *New Orleans Medical and Surgical Journal* 7 (1850): 377. Marshall Hall, "Assumed Frequency of the Ulceration of the Os Uteri," *New Orleans Medical and Surgical Journal* 7 (1850): 229-30. In 1883, the editors of the *Massachusetts Eclectic Medical Journal* claimed specular applications, once "enthroned king among the implements of torture," had declined in usage. However, looking to all standard obstetric and gynecologic handbooks at the end of the century, it is clear that specular application was vital and normal, although it is likely unsystematic and unskilled experimentation was on the decline ("Vaginal Speculum," *Massachusetts Eclectic Medical Journal* 3, no. 6 [1883]: 268-69).

34. Daston and Galison, "Image," 103-104, 83, emphasis in original. Referring to the excessive use of both the speculum and the caustic, an anonymous contributor wrote, "the *disease of the doctor* is an unmanageable one, and one that every practitioner dislikes to encounter" ("Ulceration of the Cervix Uteri," *Boston Medical and Surgical Journal* 43 [1851]: 286, emphasis in original). Balbirnie, *Speculum*, 18. Daston and Galison provide a general explanation of the connection between mechanistic objectivity and moral irreproachability ("Image," 82-84). Also see Meigs, who argued there was a need to overcome the delicacy surrounding the speculum to help alleviate maladies (*Females*, 21).

35. William Jones, *Practical Observations on Diseases of Women* (London: H. Bailliere, 1839), 92, 94.

36. Sims, *Clinical*, 20, emphasis mine. Balbirnie, *Speculum*, 19. Earlier in his *Clinical Notes*, Sims advised: "The patient once on the back with the extremities properly flexed and fixed, must be assured that there is to be neither pain nor exposure of person; this last being more dreaded than the most intense suffering" (7). Note also arguments that the speculum, when properly used was not painful were common, but not the focal point of my analysis. For example, Jones stated: "Women readily take alarm, and the bare name of an instrument is frequently sufficient to fill their minds with horror; but let them be made to understand that no pain can possibly be inflected by the speculum (except in the hands of a rude operator)" (*Practical*, 91). He continued advising physicians to convince the patient that resistance only prolongs the agony as one "might exhaust the whole range of the materia medica in our fruitless efforts to relieve her" (ibid., 97).

37. Foucault is discussing the institutional setting, such as the clinic, but I argue the basic principles are still viable in early U.S. medical practice with some allowances (*Discipline*, 184, 189, 191). Discipline, through its endless observations, made penality normal: "The perpetual penalty that traverses all points and supervises every instant in the disciplinary institutions compares, differentiates, hierarchizes, homogenizes, excludes. In short

it normalizes." As Foucault put it, "this discipline could now abandon its textual character and take its references not so much from the tradition of author-authorities as from a domain of objects perpetually offered for examination." In short, discipline "imposes on those whom it subjects a principle of compulsory visibility" (ibid., 183, 186, 187).

38. The quotation on medical interviews is from Wells, *Dead*, 20. Foucault is discussing the man-machine discipline of a docile individuality of the classical age, through LaMettrei's *L'Homme-machine* (ibid., 137, emphasis in original). Foucault argues throughout *Discipline* that regulated extraction of a body's potential is a productive form of power, rather than a negative prohibition, as is associated with more juridical forms of power. This is accomplished, in part, through the partitioning of time within a disciplinary space: a time-table; a temporal elaboration of the act or a routine/habitus; gestures and body are correlated such that "[a] disciplined body is the prerequisite of an efficient gesture" (ibid., 52-153).

39. Balbirnie, *Speculum*, 15-16. Quoting Sir Charles Clarke, Jones, *Practical*, 33. Simpson, *Memoirs*, 47. For an example of patient's testimony attributed as cause in abortion, see "Accidentally Produced Abortion," *American Journal of Obstetrics* 13 (1880): 405-8.

40. Wells, *Dead*, 27-28; also see idem, ch. 2. My analysis complements the work Wells has done in the sense that I am concerned with the visual perceptual rituals, rather than the modes of conversation. I consider medical conversation extremely important, but in the context of early antiabortion medicine, physicians of all stripes strongly favored seeing over listening when documenting "the truth of life." Patient testimony, although resistant, did not have the impact it would in the twentieth century in contesting a medicalized cultural memory of life. During the first half of the twentieth century, patient testimony would become much more important in a contest over cultural memory than in the latter half of the nineteenth century. Hence, although medical conversations are an important moment for contests of power within early medicine generally, they are of less centrality when considering abortion specifically.

41. Simpson, *Memoirs*, 46. Paraphrasing Jones, *Practical*, 90.

42. Sims, *Clinical Notes*, 10; Lever, *Organ*, 8. Another example: "the female is placed in the same position as already described, half sitting, half lying, and if the operator stand on the right side of the bed or couch, on which the patient is lying, with the right leg semiflexed, the index finger, or the second finger of his right hand, previously oiled, are carefully insinuated within the vagina until they arrive at its uterine extremity" (Jones, *Practical*, 35). Also see Wertz & Wertz, *Lying-In*, 90; Donegan, *Women*, 156-57.

43. Sims, *Clinical*, 23-24; Souchon, "Speculum," 82; Nott, "Duck-Bill," 148. S. N. Harris, in "Case of Stricture of the Cervix Uteri," *Boston Medical and Surgical Journal* 42 (1850): 507, explained how the speculum could be used to ease the cervix: "The blades being closed and well oiled, should be passed through the stricture, either with or without the use of a speculum, and, when introduced, expanded by means of the screw. By proceeding gradually and gently, it is probable that the spasm will be ultimately fatigued into relaxation, and the end accomplished."

44. The writer advocating institutional stay was the editor of "Criminal Abortion," *Nelson's American Lancet* 7 (1853): 184. Storer wrote: "and here I affirm that the *duty of the physician* is in most cases not, as is generally attempted, to complete the abnormal process as soon as possible, but *to arrest it*; for I am satisfied, from my own experience in very many cases were there no other reason, that this can often be done even in cases apparently desperate as far as the foetus is concerned, and yet its life be saved" ("Studies of Abortion," *Boston Medical and Surgical Journal* 68, no. 1 [1863]: 18, emphasis mine).

The S. Weir Mitchell rest cure was often used in a similar fashion (to break women of resistance to birthing) in the latter part of the century (Poirer, "Weir Mitchell").

45. The "dissection" comment is from "Female Physicians," *Boston Medical and Surgical Journal* 54, no. 9 (1856): 173. The figure on the composition of women to men is from Morantz, Pomerleau, and Fenichel, eds., *Her Own*, 21. Blackwell was advised by her mentor, Dr. Warrington, and a friend, Dr. Pankhurst, to go to France and learn in drag to get her education, but she stayed in the United States. Once at school, Blackwell reported no obstacles, but as an intern, she received opposition from other residents, who would not post case histories on the beds of patients thus hindering her ability to treat them. Other residents also routinely left the room when she entered (*Pioneer*, 61, 65-73, 74, 80-81). Women became doctors in Finland, France, Russia, Germany, Holland, Italy, Denmark, Sweden, Great Britain (most notably Sophia Jex-Blake), as well as in the United States. Schools in the United States that had opened to women included Geneva College (1848), where Blackwell received her first instruction, Female Medical College of Philadelphia (1850), Women's Medical College of New York (1865), Department of Medicine and Surgery of the University of Michigan (1871), Syracuse University (1870), and the very first, the Female Medical School in Boston, Nov. 1, 1848 (James R. Chadwick, *The Study and Practice of Medicine by Women* [New York: A. S. Barnes & CO., 1879], 452-63). Despite these changes, no woman was recognized by the Massachusetts Medical Society, for example ("Our Editorial," 504).

46. Schiebinger, *Mind*, 220-37; the quotation is from 221-23. Pertaining to moral causation of physical difference, in the eighteenth century, Soemmering, who also developed a staged model of fetal development, naturalized difference in skeletons: "The medical community thus established a clear notion of causality: physical differences produced moral, and eventually social, differences. Soemmering, the German anatomist who drew one of the first female skeletons, believed that gender differences were to be traced to nature, not to nurture" (ibid., 222-23).

47. The remark on a blunted refinement is from "Female Practitioners," *Boston*, 274. The alarmed editor is quoted from "What Female Medical Students Are Capable Of," *Boston Medical and Surgical Journal* 76, no. 26 (1867): 503, emphasis in original. The quotation on visual economy is from Wells, *Dead*, 199. N. Williams, "A Dissertation on 'Female Physicians,'" *Boston Medical and Surgical Journal* 43, no. 4 (1850): 69. Wells (*Dead*, ch. 7) provides an excellently detailed account of the Pennsylvania Hospital incident in the context of women and vision in nineteenth-century medicine.

48. For reviews of the exclusion of women from science generally and medicine specifically, I recommend Schiebinger's *Mind*; Blackwell, *Pioneer Work*; Chadwick, *Study*; Virginia G. Drachman, "Women Doctors and the Women's Medical Movement: Feminism and Medicine, 1850-1895" (Ph.D. diss., University of New York at Buffalo, 1976); Sophia Jex-Blake, *Medical Women: A Thesis and History* (Edinburgh: Oliphant, Anderson, & Ferrier, 1886); Morantz, Pomerleau, Fenichel, *In Her Own Words*, 1-33; Morantz-Sanchez, *Sympathy*; Walsh, *"Doctors"*. The argument that women lacked nerve or were too hysterical is one of the most powerful folkloric explanations for gender difference. Medicine was at the forefront of naturalizing this argument. Consider this example from R. H. Whitefield: "She is too apt to throw aside her reason and judgment, and to be guided by a mistaken observation and badly formed experience, and to forbid them entrance into her practice of any thing like the principles of science. What could the delicately nerved females do in a case of severe uterine hemorrhage, rupture of the uterus, or placenta prævia, when, often the mere sight of venesection, or the simplest surgical operation makes her sicken and faint?" ("The Practice of Midwifery," *New Orleans Medical and*

Surgical Journal 7, no. 2 [1855]: 199). Similarly, N. Williams felt "the *temperament* of females is less favorable for the medical profession than that of males. . . . the *nervous* or *excitable* temprement" ("Dissertation," 73, emphasis in original).

49. Ibid., 70-71, emphasis in original. "Female Practitioners of Medicine," *New Orleans Medical and Surgical Journal* 23 (1870): 394-96. The comment on "inscrutable Providence" is from "Females as Physicians," *Boston Medical and Surgical Journal* 53, no. 14 (1855): 293. The categories of objections to women physicians are intended for convenience, not as a firm typology. One could easily reframe them in different categories for a different purpose. Occasionally women were accused of stealing medicine from men in Roman times and in early Christendom ("Female Practitioners of Medicine," *Boston*, 272).

50. On the "New Amazons," see "Female Doctors," *Medical Examiner* 8 (1854): 703. On the labor of medicine, see Williams, "Dissertation," 70. Women also were deemed too fickle to dedicate themselves to such a regimented process: "to be well qualified for the practice, requires a thorough knowledge of anatomy and physiology, especially of those parts connected with the gestation and parturition. This can only be acquired by diligent study, deep research, and a frequent attendance upon the dissection table. Are such opportunities offered to women? Would she avail herself of them? We think not. Men engage in these labors who know and feel their importance and necessity" (Whitefield, "Practice," 199).

51. Jamieson, *Double*, 55; see Clarke, *Sex*. The editorial comment is from "Female Education," *Boston Medical and Surgical Journal* 49, no. 9 (1853): 187. The quotation about Maudsley and remarks on bearing monsters is from Jamieson, *Double*, 55.

52. Remarks on intuition and reason are from "Female Practitioners," *Boston*, 274. Whitefield, "Practice," 198; ibid. the comment on "loathsome diseases," 197. The story of a botched delivery is from "Female Physicians," *Boston* 54, 172. Even success by some was turned into negative confirmation of supposed intellectual limitations: "These very exceptions, however, only serve to prove the rule, that by far the greater amount of intellectual superiority is found in the male sex" ("Females as Physicians," 293). On replacing midwives with accoucheurs: "The *results* of this change were, a diminution of the mortality incident to childbirth, in the course of a half century, *to half its former amount.* . . . This reason was, the *notorious harshness of the midwives.* With all the desire to display their importance and their skill which belongs to half-cultivated minds, they sacrificed the comfort and even the safety of the patient to the endeavor to make a brilliant impression of their own ability" ("Female Physicians," *Boston* 54, 171, emphasis in original). Also see Storer, "Studies,"16.

53. "Female Physicians," *Boston* 48, 66. The calculation of menstrual incapacity if from "Female Physicians," *Boston* 54, 273. Storer, "Gynæcological," 96-97. "During the menstrual period, Michelet declares that the woman is an invalid, and should be treated as such. . . . During, then, from one ninth to one fourth of the active period of life, it is imprudent for the female to be exposed to those inclemencies of weather which, by night and by day, and for seven days in a week, it is the business of the medical practitioner to encounter" ("Female Practitioners," *Boston*, 273). Also see "Females as Physician": "In the physical conditions of women, also, we find much in support of our views. The weaknesses of her bodily organization renders her less fit to undergo the incessant fatigue, the loss of sleep, the exposure to weather at all hours of the day and night, which are the lot of the active medical practitioner" (293).

54. "Medicine, ever peculiarly exposed to the inroads of charlatanry, was the first profession to tempt the zeal and the ambition of the New Amazons" ("Female Doctors,"

703). Referring to The Female Medical School of Boston: it "is no better than a school of irregular practitioners. We refer, of course, to the Female Medical School, and its associate hospital" ("Question," 481). Women physicians as abettors to abortion is from Storer, "Gynæcological," 98. Idem, *Criminal*, 98-100. Also see "Female Medical Colleges," *Boston Medical Surgical Journal* 45, no. 5 (1852): 106-7.

55. Whitefield, "Practice," 199. Stoler, *Race*, 59.

56. The editors printed the student's letter so as to raise the question of whether women should have co-educational access rather than same-sex education. Female medical student in "Female Physicians," *Boston Medical and Surgical Journal* 76, no. 1 (1867): 43. Florence Nightingale wrote: "Here is a branch so entirely their own, that we may safely say that no lying-in would be attended but by a woman if a woman were as skillful as a man—a physician accoucheur. Yet, instead of the ladies turning all their attention to this, and organising a midwifery school of the highest efficiency in both science and practice, they enter men's classes, and lectures, and examinations, which don't wish to have them, and say they want the same education as men" (*Introductory Notes on Lying-In Institutions* [London: Longmans, Green, and Co., 1871], 105). Jex-Blake, *Medical Women*, 5-6 for quotation; 9-38 for history of women in medicine. For another example of the natural domesticity of medicine, see the introductory lecture to the New England Female Medical College, November 2, 1853 (Cornell, "Medical Education").

57. Wells offers a careful examination of the discursive performance of "invisible writing" through the professional biographies of Preston and Longshore (*Dead*, chs. 3 and 5).

58. "Porous" quotation, ibid., 145. Morantz-Sanchez, *Sympathy*, 222. Blackwell, *Counsel*; Stockham, *Tokology*; Kratz, "Essay"; Hunt, "Thesis"; Ross, "Abortion." For other examples of women physicians biopolitically opposed to abortion, see Longshore-Potts, *Discourses*; Miller, "Foeticide"; Mitchell, "Infanticide"; Parsons, "Written Law"; Saur, *Maternity*. Oreman's remarks are from "Temptation," 87. Morantz-Sanchez argues that "although women physicians had a greater awareness and sensitivity to women' issues than men, their overall medical opinions tended to reflect professional and scientific trends and their divergences among themselves often appeared to be similar to those of male doctors" (*Sympathy* 222). For general discussions of the mode and tenor of women physicians resistance to a male-dominant profession, see Drachman, "Women Doctors"; Regina Morantz-Sanchez, "The Making of a Woman Surgeon: How Mary Dixon Jones Made a Name for Herself in Nineteenth-Century Gynecology," in *Women Healers and Physicians: Climbing a Long Hill*, ed. Lilian R. Furst (Lexington, Ky.: University Press of Kentucky, 1997), 178-220; idem, *Sympathy*; Morantz, Pomerleau, and Fenichel, *Her Own*.

Notes for Chapter Six

1. Gillian Rose, *Feminism & Geography: The Limits of Geographical Knowledge* (Minneapolis: University of Minnesota, 1993), 62. Certeau, *Practice*, 117. Lefebvre, *Space*, 87. Doreen Massey, *Space, Place, and Gender* (Minneapolis: University of Minnesota Press, 1994), 265 (also see 2-13). Also see Shirley Ardener, "Ground Rules and Social Maps for Women: An Introduction," *Women and Space: Ground Rules and Social Maps*, ed. Shirley Ardener (Oxford: Berg, 1993), 1-30; Linda MacDowell, "Spatializing Feminism: Geographic Perspectives," in *Bodyspace: Destabilizing Geographies of Gender and Sexuality*, ed. Nancy Duncan (London: Routledge, 1996), 28-44.

2. "Spatial practices" is Lefebvre's term, *Space*. Certeau, *Practice*, 85, 86; the quotation about memory nesting also is from Certeau, *Practice*, 86. Jennifer González, "Autotopographies," 135-36. Note, for three reasons, Massey critiques views of space as being in opposition to time: the indictment of static space made by radical geographers; the need to escape gender duality with space/femininity juxtaposed against time/masculinity in a contest for power; and the importance of making space a constituted/constitutive element in social relations, rather than a given (*Space*, 251-63). I agree completely, and have explored the intersection of cultural performance and memory in relation to spatial formation as a way of keeping space and time as interdependent, rather than opposed, concepts.

3. When I say "a space that was not its before," I do not mean that women's bodies had been free from the sway of patriarchal ideology, but that the female body of the nineteenth century was new and required a reterritorialization. One might argue that patriarchal ideals always had a hold on women's reproductive organs because children have for millennia been the property of men and not women, and that the womb has been discussed as a kind of incubator for men's potency since antiquity. This reduces the dynamism of space to the inertia of place. In other words, patriarchy was and just is. I am arguing that with each successive formation of a space it is recreated anew. The relatively biologically sophisticated womb of the nineteenth century with its epigenitically unfolding fetus and successive stages of pregnancy is not the same as that of, say, the late middle ages with its homunculous squatter inside a rather mysterious pear-shaped bladder. Although the nineteenth century saw the reiteration of male-dominant ideology within early obstetrics and gynecology, to set aside the new practices by which women's bodies were transformed from a passive location into a dynamic space where life begins is to set aside all the work necessary for patriarchal notions of reproductivity to recreate themselves from one age to the next. It is, in short, to ignore the very work by which traditions make themselves anew and make room for themselves in each successive moment of their remembrance.

4. Certeau, *Practice*, 123, 125, emphasis in original. Yuval-Davis and Anthias, "Introduction." Also see Ardener, "Ground."

5. The three elements of the production of space (spatial practice, spaces of representation, and representations of space) are crucial to Lefebvre's project (for an overview, see Edward W. Soja, *Thirdspace: Journeys to Los Angeles and Other Real-and-Imagined Places* [Cambridge, Mass.: Blackwell, 1996], 26-52; for a critique of sexism in spatial theorizing, see Massey, *Space*, 212-48). I have dealt largely with medical rituals as practices to this point, and so now specify more exactly their effects on space.

6. Storer et al., "Report," 76. "Denunciation" quotation in "Criminal Abortion," *Boston Medical and Surgical Journal* 56 (1857): 283. Idem, *Why Not?*, 34. "Code," 137, emphasis mine. For discussion of witnessing and virtual witnessing, see Shapin and Schaffer, *Leviathan*, ch. 2.

7. Charles Rosenberg presents an expansively researched history of hospital transformation in *The Care of Strangers: The Rise of America's Hospital System* (Baltimore: Johns Hopkins University Press, 1987), 97-121, 142-65. He argues that "the Civil War hospital represented a triumph of scientific rationality. . . . Cleanliness, order, and ventilation were the requirements for a modern hospital and, as Florence Nightingale had dramatically contended in the 1850s, these requirements could be guaranteed by proper design and a newly professional internal order" (98). The quotation of Florence Nightingale is also from Rosenberg (ibid., 133). For an example of Nightingale's recommendations, see her *Introductory Notes on Lying-In Institutions*. Information on the growth of hospitals is from Starr, *Transformation*, 72-73.

8. Ibid., 75. Information on the social status of hospitals is from Rosenberg, *Care*,

133, 47, 100-14. Starr documents the demographic effect of urbanization in an industrial economy: "Industrialization and urban life also brought an increase in the number of unattached individuals living alone in cities. In Boston between 1880 and 1900, boarding and lodging house keepers rose in number from 601 to 1,570, almost double the rate of population growth for the city" (*Transformation*, 74). Generally speaking, "in the early nineteenth century, there was little demand for the services of general hospitals in A-merica. Almost no one who had a choice sought hospital care. Hospitals were regarded with dread, and rightly so. They were dangerous places; when sick, people were safer at home . . . (ibid., 72).

    9. Ibid., 76. Starr explained the role of the telephone:

> The telephone made it less costly to reach a physician by greatly reducing the time for-merly spent tracking down the peripatetic practitioner on foot. Phones first became avail-able in the late 1870s. Curiously the first rudimentary telephone exchange on record, built in 1877, connected the Capital Avenue Drugstore in Hartford Connecticut, with twenty-one local doctors. (Drugstores often served as message centers for physicians). The first telephone line in Rochester, Minnesota, set up in December 1879, connected the farm-house of Dr. William Worall Mayo with Geisinger and Newton's drugstore downtown. (ibid., 69-70)

    10. Sims, *Clinical Notes*, 19. Jones, *Practical*, 71, emphasis in original. After Jones, many produced alternate versions. F. Jagger, Jr. and E. Mauke had examination/operating tables. "A rocking-chair type appeared in 1850." French models were more comfortable in the latter part of the century being designed for use in a parlor, "after 1860." Mathew Berkeley Hill had an exam stool, "not unlike a chair in a shoe shine in parlor." Ricci pro-vides a nice synopsis of table developments in *Development*, 319.

    11. Nott, "Duck-Bill Speculum," 148. Lever employed a candle, for example: "a lighted candle or taper should be applied to the external extremity of the cylinder, by the aid of which we shall distinctly see the os uteri, and be able to notice any deviation from the normal state" (*Organic*, 13). Mitchell was quoted in Ricci, *Development*, 311, from *Practical Remarks on the Use of the Speculum*, 1849, Dublin, 16.

    12. Ricci, *Developments*, 311. Women used this to "subvert the sick role" as Ehrenreich and English called it. Ehrenreich and English are discussing the use of hysteria by women, not abortion, but the idea of "poaching" as best as one can is similar (*Com-plaints*, 38-44).

    13. The history of using the bodies of the disempowered for medical testing and ad-vancement is extensive. I do not allude to a larger pattern here, although it would be war-ranted. The quotation on "unfettered access" is from Rosenberg, *Care*, 57. Wertz and Wertz, *Lying-In*, 78. Wertz and Wertz explain further:

> After the Civil War doctors realized the maternity hospitals provided occasion for clinical obstetrics; students might learn and professors teach and research. Doctors therefore struck a bargain with the charity patients in such hospitals; in exchange for medical treat-ment, the women would allow themselves to be exposed to the eye of medicine. Doctors could do this because respectable women patrons supported such institutions for the de-serving poor, who were valuable to the patrons as object lessons about the redeemability for the poor and the value of charity. (ibid., 89)

Rosenberg confirms this, writing that "charity patients did not relish being used in such clinical exercises. Despite frequent medical reassurances that patients welcomed the attention, I have found no institutional data to question the abundant evidence that patients did in fact fear the invasion of their bodies and privacy by student hands and eyes" (*Care*, 207).

14. Storer, *Why Not?*. Sims, *Clinical*, v-vi. Bedford, "Clinical Lectures." Gardner, *Sterility*. Similarly, Simpson worked in Edinburgh's great hospital and Tilt worked in London's hospital. Whitehead used a conical speculum that he called a "prolapsus tube" (*Abortion*, xi). For more information on "demonstrative midwifery" (the vernacular for clinical training of midwifery) and the use of bodies in medical schools, see "Demonstrative Midwifery," *Boston Medical and Surgical Journal* 42 (1850): 257-58; "Multiplication of Medical Schools," *Boston Medical and Surgical Journal* 76 (1867): 203-4.

15. For an example of debate over fetal staging, relative to the medico-legal status of the fetus, see the discussion of W. F. Brown in "Report of Medical Societies," *Boston Medical and Surgical Journal* 79, no. 13 (1868): 200. Mohr offers four reasons why doctors felt a "crisis of the expert witness": risk to personal reputation, unscientific image, unscrupled witnesses for hire, and a corresponding reduction in morale for more civic-minded physicians (*Doctors*, 197-200). For an example of debate over the problems of expert testimony specific to abortion, see F. A. Harris, "A Case of Abortion with Acquittal," *Boston Medical and Surgical Journal* 104, no. 15 (1881): 346-50. For discussions on medico-legal aspects of abortion and expert testimony, see "Abortion," *Medico-Legal Journal* 7 (1890): 170-187; Everett W. Burdett, "The Medical Jurisprudence of Criminal Abortion," *New England Medical Gazette* July (1883): 200-14; Robert Christison, "On the Present State of Medical Evidence," *Boston Medical and Surgical Journal* 46, no. 9 (1852): 176-81; "Criminal Abortion," *Nelson's*; F. W. Draper, "Criminal Abortion, with a 'Dying Declaration,'" *Transactions of the Massachusetts Medico-Legal Society* 3, no. 2 (1900): 35-42; William W. Porter, "A Discussion of the Medico-Legal Aspect of Criminal Abortion," *Medical and Surgical Reporter* 48 (1893): 655-60; Sherman Hoar, "On the Duties of a Medical Examiner as a Witness," *Transactions of the Massachusetts Medico-Legal Society* 2 (1898): 328-30; E. G. Hoitt, "Criminal Abortion," *Boston Medical and Surgical Journal* 135, no. 22 (1896): 541-43; Reamy, "Reply to Dr. Underhill," *American Journal of Obstetrics* 3, no. 2 (1879): 392-93; Small, "Jurisprudence"; D. H. Storer, "An Address on Medical Jurisprudence," *Medical Examiner* 7 (1851): 572-73; Thomson, "Lectures"; J. W. Underhill, "The Female Generative Organs in Their Medico-Legal Relations," *American Journal of Obstetrics* 12, no. 1 (1879): 91-111.

16. 30 NE Rep 329 (IL Sup Ct 1892). This was part of the nineteenth-century wrangle over expert testimony generally and forensic medicine specifically. I am not claiming only that reproductive medicine was brought into court, but that, given the special status of the womb in society, the introduction of prenatal space into legal forums deserves separate recognition. Also see *Commonwealth v. Follansbee* (155 MA Rep 274 [MA Sup Ct 1891/92]); *Commonwealth v. Blair* (126 MA Rep 40 [MA Sup Ct 1883]); *Hatchard v. State* (79 WI Rep 35 [WI Sup Ct 1891]); *Moody v. State of Ohio* (17 OH Rep 111 [OH Sup Ct 1887]); *People v. M'Gonegal* (17 NY Sup 147 [NY Sup Ct 1891]); *People v. Sessions* (58 MI Rep 594 [MI Sup Ct 1886]); *State v. Leeper* (22 IA Rep 748 [IA Sup Ct 1887]); *State v. Smith* (53 Am Dec 578 [ME Sup Ct 1851]); Thomson 1851-52.

17. For examples, see "Abortion and Murder"; W. S. Birge, "A Case of Abortion with Peculiar Features," *Boston Medical Surgical Journal* 138, no. 17 (1895): 412-14; J. Foster Bush, "Medical History of a Case of Abortion, With a Synopsis of the Criminal Trial," *Boston Medical Surgical Journal* 107, no. 9 (1882): 205-6; "Conviction for Criminal Abortion," *Boston Medical and Surgical Journal* 106, no. 1 (1882): 18-19; Stephen Crowe, "Report of a Case of Septic Peritonitis Following a Criminal Abortion," *Maryland*

Medical Journal 227, no. 21 (1892): 1013-14; Thomas M. Durell, "The Leach Case," *Boston Medical and Surgical Journal* 130, no. 16 (1894): 382-83; W. W. Gannett, "A Case of Criminal Abortion Resulting in Death from Air-Embolism," *Boston Medical and Surgical Journal* 106, no. 2 (1882): 28-31; J. C. Gleason, "A Medico-Legal Case of Abortion, Followed by Conviction of the Accused Abortionist," *Boston Medical and Surgical Journal* 101 (1879): 185-92; F. A. Harris, "Case"; Jackson, "Gravid Uterus"; Samuel B. Ward, "Criminal Abortion by Inflation of the Uterus With Air," *Albany Medical Annals* 10, no. 1 (1889): 1-8.

18. For an overview of antiabortion legislation, see Mohr, *Abortion*, 200-25. Ohio General Assembly, *General and Local Laws and Joint Resolutions, Passed by the Fifty-Seventh General Assembly 1867* (Columbus, Ohio: L. D. Myers & Bro, 1867); idem, *Journal of the House of Representatives of Ohio of the Fifty-Seventh General Assembly, 1867* (Columbus, Ohio: L. D. Myers & Bro, 1867); idem, *Journal of the Senate of the State of Ohio for the Adjourned Session of the Fifty-Seventh General Assembly Commencing on January, 2 1867* (Columbus, Ohio: L. D, 1867).

19. Schiebinger, *Mind*, 224.

20. Nancy Duncan, "Renegotiating Gender and Sexuality in Public and Private Spaces," in *Bodyspace: Destabilizing Geographies of Gender and Sexuality*, ed. Nancy Duncan (London: Routledge, 1996), 129. Duncan provides a more thorough, descriptive account of public/private geography:

> It is clear that the public-private distinction is gendered. This binary opposition is employed to legitimate oppression and dependence on the basis of gender; it has also been used to regulate sexuality. The private *as an ideal type* has traditionally been associated and conflated with: the domestic, the embodied, the natural, the family, property, the 'shadowy interior of the household', personal life, intimacy, passion, sexuality, 'the good life', care, a haven, unwaged labour, reproduction and immanence. The public, *as an ideal type* has traditionally been the domain of the disembodied, the abstract, the cultural, rationality, critical public discourse, citizenship, civil society, justice, the market place, waged labour, production, the polis, the state, action, militarism, heroism and transcendence. (ibid., 128, emphasis in original)

Further, Daphne Spain contends that "women and men together create spatial segregation and stratification systems. Both sexes subscribe to the spatial arrangements that reinforce differential access to knowledge, resources, and power: men because it serves their interests, and women because they may perceive no alternative" (*Gendered Spaces* [Chapel Hill: University of North Carolina Press, 1992], 18). For an interesting example of the superfluity of pubic/private territorialization, see Lynne Walker, "Home and Away: The Feminist Remapping of Public and Private Space in Victorian London," in *New Frontiers of Space, Bodies and Gender*, ed. Rosa Ainley (London: Routledge, 1998), 65-75. For a discussion of spatial metaphors in theory as it relates to bodies, gender, and separate spheres, see Kerstin W. Shands, *Embracing Space: Spatial Metaphors in Feminist Discourse* (Westport, Conn.: Greenwood Press, 1999), ch. 3.

21. Schiebinger, *Mind*, 235. For more information on the simultaneity of political theory and sexed bodies, see Susan Bordo, *Unbearable*, 71-97; Laqueur, *Making Sex*, 194-207; Pateman, *Sexual*; Poovey, "Abortion"; Gayatri Chakrevorty Spivak, "French Feminism Revisited," *Feminists Theorize the Political*, ed. Judith Butler and Joan W. Scott (New York: Routledge, 1992), 54-85. Also see Evans, *Born*; Karlyn Kohrs Campbell, *"Man Cannot Speak for Her"*, vol. 1, *A Critical Study of Early Feminist Rhetoric* (New York: Greenwood Press, 1989); Cott, *Bonds*; Kerber, *Women*; Rose, *Feminism*, 34-

38; Smith-Rosenberg, *Disorderly*.

22. Petchesky, "Foetal Images," 287; Duden, *Disembodying*, 50-55. For other writings on the same point, see Adams, *Reproducing*; Casper, "Operation"; Duden, "Fetus"; Arthur Kroker and Marilouise Kroker, "Theses on the Disappearing Body in the Hyper-Modern Condition," in *Body Invaders: Panic Sex in America*, ed. Arthur Kroker and Marilouise Kroker (New York: St. Martin's Press, 1987), 20-34; Elizabeth Manion, "A Ms.-Managed Womb," in *Body Invaders: Panic Sex in America*, ed. Arthur Kroker and Marilouise Kroker (New York: St. Martin's Press, 1987), 183-200; Rothman, *Recreating*; Stabile, "Shooting"; Nathan Stormer, "Prenatal Space," *Signs: Journal of Women in Culture and Society* 26, no. 1 (2000): 109-44. Hartouni ("Fetal") argues that the fetus, too, is necessarily disembodied because it has been removed, rhetorically, from the woman's body. Meredith Michaels ("Fetal") argues that the call to re-embody women can produce a disappearing fetus.

23. Poovey, "The Abortion Question," 243. Certeau, *Practice*, 145.

24. Meigs, *Woman*, 54-55.

25. Butler, *Bodies*; Luce Irigaray, *Speculum of the Other Woman*, trans. Gillian C. Gill (Ithaca, N.Y.: Cornell University Press, 1985); Julia Kristeva, *Revolution in Poetic Language*, trans. Margaret Waller (New York: Columbia University Press, 1984). Also see duBois, *Torture*; Grosz, *Space*.

26. Kenneth Burke, *A Grammar of Motives* (Berkeley: University of California Press, 1969). Burke does not discuss possible grammatical relationships of scene to agency but in this case, the scene is an agency making it a metaphoric substitution.

27. The history of anti-urban thinking is long. Andrew Lees argued "The anti-urban impetus carried over strongly into early Christianity" (*Cities Perceived*, 7). Stanley K. Schultz provides an overview of urban environmental thinking in the nineteenth century (*Constructing Urban Culture: American Cities and City Planning, 1800-1920* [Philadelphia: Temple University Press, 1989], 113-114). Also see Ruth Glass, *Clichés of Urban Doom and Other Essays* (Oxford: Basil Blackwell, 1989).

28. Howard I. Kushner, "Suicide, Gender, and the Fear of Modernity in Nineteenth-Century Medical and Social Thought," *Journal of Social History* 26 (1993): 461, 463. Burbick, *Healing*. The parallels between suicide and abortion are powerful. They are still common today in popular debates about medical ethics. The foremost and still authoritative treatment of suicide, according to Kushner, is Emile Durkheim's *Suicide: A Study in Sociology* (trans. John A. Spalding and George Simpson, ed. and intro. George Simpson [Glencoe, Ill.: Free Press, 1951]).

29. "Thus, 'civilization' became a metaphor for modern urban society, while 'education,' 'ennui,' and the breakdown of social distinctions were its signifiers. . . . Modernity ('civilization') led to suicide because it subverted traditional forms of deference" (Kushner, "Suicide," 463-464). In fact, in 1859, *The New York Times* warned against "A New Epidemic" of suicides caused by "the conditions fostered by urban life" (ibid., 465). Bedford, "Clinical Lectures," 7 (1854): 103.

30. For example, Christine Stansell explains the urban environmental explanations offered for prostitution and vagrancy among working-class women and how these phenomena constituted social "ruin" (*City of Women*, 171-192).

31. In the wake of the hysteria, although certainly not the direct result, the Police Reform Act and the New York Abortion Law were passed in 1845. Srebnick's is a work of great care, thorough research, and insightful historical analysis. She traces the telling and retelling of Mary Rogers' story from the *Police Gazette*, stories by Ned Buntline, ratiocinations by Poe, court records, and government documents (*Mysterious*, 94).

32. Undaunted by public opinion, Restell and her husband advertised abortion services openly and did not hide the wealth they accrued from her practice. To many, she was an inhuman villain after whom the *Police Gazette* image of a well-to-do woman devouring a baby was modeled. Restell was tried several times for abortion and was always under attack in popular literature. Although there are other recountings of Restell's life, I am fond of Srebnick's because she connects Mary Rogers and anti-urban hysteria with Restell (*Mysterious*, 99). Also see Clifford Browder, *Madame Restell the Abortionist* (Hamden, Conn.: Archon Press, 1988); Alan Keller, *Scandalous Lady: The Life and Times of Madame Restell* (New York: Antheneum, 1981). For information on Anthony Comstock and Comstockism, see Brodie, *Contraception*; Smith-Rosenberg, *Disorderly*, 222-23. For a discussion of changes in urban space, gender and morality through the turn the twentieth century, see Sarah Deutsch, *Women and the City: Gender, Space, and Power in Boston, 1870-1940* (New York: Oxford University Press, 2000), particularly ch. 3.

33. D. H. Storer ("Two Frequent," 197-198). For more information and examples, see Gordon, *Woman's Body*, 72-113; Brodie, *Contraception*, 57-86; Dixon, *Woman*; Kellog, *Ladies' Guide*; Laqueur, "Orgasm"; Meigs, *Woman;* Nourse, "Menstruation"; Pomeroy, *Ethics*; Smith-Rosenberg, *Disorderly*, 182-191; Stone, "Observations"; Storer, *Why Not?*; idem, *Is It I?*; Studley, "Menstruation."

34. Leonard, "Quackery," 480. "Two Cases," 212-213.

35. Mohr, *Abortion*, 100. Keep in mind, I am not arguing about demonstrable fertility rates. I am discussing the perceptions of nineteenth-century doctors about fertility rates.

36. Bedford cites climate, education and mode of life, temperament and constitution, and race as determinants of first menstruation. He cites Raciborski to argue race limits the age of first menstruation (Bedford, "Clinical Lectures," 10 (1854): 149-150). King, "New Basis," 240, emphasis in original. Of course, the discussions of bourgeois women's frailty and civilized physical debility play a part in this as well. Susceptibility to abort was physically a result of increasingly sickliness and sickening behavior. Abortion, spontaneous or induced, was an environmental issue.

37. I have discussed the environmental linkages of antiabortion discourse and biology elsewhere; see Stormer, "Embodying Normal Miracles," *Quarterly Journal of Speech* 83, no. 2 (1997): 172-91.

38. By discussing prenatal space as in-between the private and public and as generative and changeable, I am aware one could mistake my analysis as exploring "thirdspace," which Edward Soja has termed the "trialectic" analysis pioneered by Lefebvre (*Thirdspace*). In Soja's terms, a trialectic of *being* breaks the dialectic of historicality and sociality within the study of spatiality. A trialectic of *space* involves perceived, conceived, and lived space (ibid., 70-82). I have decided not to inhabit Soja's vocabulary for several reasons but two are sufficient. First, Soja treats "thirding-as-othering," by which he means "thirding" breaks the constricting habits of dialectical ontologies and epistemologies and, thus, "is radically open to additional otherenesses, to a continuing expansion of spatial knowledge" (ibid., 61). Such openness (with the connotation of liberating radical potentialities) is not historically viable if one considers the material in question in this book. The "thirdspace" of the prenatal, as established by physicians' practices is not "radically" open, nor is it about harnessing the disruptive power of marginality and difference. Emancipatory insurgency imbrues Soja's thirdspace, but he is unclear as to whether that is apparent only from the point of view of the scholar who sees "thirdspace" or from within the space being analyzed. An a priori "radicalness" is not tenable: some "thirdspaces" are powerful conservators of hegemonic relations. Second, the "aleph" (a term Soja borrows from Borges' story) of "thirdspace" decidedly takes "thirdspace" into the aesthetics of

sublimity, which will become highly problematic in later work on prenatal space (the floating fetus as a vision of the sublime). Further, the unexamined enthusiasm for sublimity within Soja's figure (the aleph) is problematic because of the historical gendering of the sublime. Although my language (the prenatal as a third position) might sound like I am either poaching or extending Soja's notion of "thirdspace," I am, in fact, rejecting it.

39. Michel Foucault, "Different Spaces," in *Michel Foucault: Aesthetics, Method, and Epistemology*, ed. James B. Faubion, *Essential Works of Foucault, 1954-1984*, vol. 2, series ed. Paul Rabinow (New York: New Press, 1998), 178. Adjusting Judith Butler's words to accommodate the medical transformation of the feminine into a cultural matrix, prenatal space "will be entered, and will, give forth a further instance of what enters [it], but [it] will never resemble either the formative principle or that which it creates" (*Bodies*, 42). Butler is discussing Irigiray's rereading and ironic mimesis of Plato. My use of her language is not intended to invoke that specific discussion, if such a theft is possible. Rather, like a stone skipping on water, the buoyancy of her description of the feminine carries the clumsy weight of my notion of prenatal space.

40. Foucault, "Different," 183, 180.

41. Ibid., 182, 184.

42. "Spatial institutions" is a concept from Spain, *Gendered*, 10-15. I have expanded her list of the family, school, and workplace, however.

43. Foucault, "Body/Power."

Notes for Conclusion

1. An expanded version of this chapter has been published previously (Nathan Stormer, "In Living Memory," *Quarterly Journal of Speech* 88, no. 3 (2002): 265-83; used by permission of the National Communication Association). "Criminal Abortion," *Boston*, 62, 65. Language of bodily inscription from Foucault, "Nietzsche," 148. Also see Grosz, *Volatile*, 148-59.

2. Smith-Rosenberg, *Disorderly*, 223. Taussig, *Abortion*, 26-7. Also see Reagan, *Crime*.

3. Allen, "Power," 464. Derrida, *Archive*, 12, emphasis in original. González, "Autotopographies," 139.

4. Certeau, *Practice*, 148.

5. Paul Connerton, *How Societies Remember* (Cambridge: Cambridge University Press, 1989), 65, emphasis in original. Also see Butler, *Bodies*; Bernard Rimé and V. Christophe, "How Individual Emotional Episodes Feed Collective Memory," in *Collective Memory of Political Events: Social Psychological Perspectives*, ed. James W. Pennebaker, Darí Páez, and Bernard Rimé (Mahwah, N.J.: Lawrence Erlbaum Associates, 1997), 131-46.

6. Judith Butler, "Performative Acts and Gender Constitution: An Essay in Phenomenology and Feminist Theory," in *Writing the Body: Female Embodiment and Feminist Theory*, ed. Katie Conboy, Nadia Medina, and Sarah Stanbury (New York: Columbia University Press, 1997), 407-8.

7. González, "Autotopographies," 136. Also see Halbwachs, *Collective*, 52-53, 140-43, 175-76.

8. Certeau, *Capture*, 129. González, "Autotopographies," 137. Connerton, *Societies*, 6. The explanation of rhetorical effectivity as world disclosure is adapted from Ronald

Walter Greene, "The Aesthetic Turn and the Rhetorical Perspective on Argumentation," *Argumentation & Advocacy* 35, no. 1 (1998): 19. The comment about the ubiquity of memory work is from Certeau, *Capture*, 129-30. Also see Zelizer, *Remembering*, 4.

9. Butler, *Bodies*, 95, including the "fixity of constraints" quotation. George Lipsitz, *Time Passages: Collective Memory and American Popular Culture* (Minneapolis: University of Minnesota Press, 1990), 16. Lipsitz is discussing the forms of popular culture here, but I am extending his notion of form and memory to scientific culture and its forms (particularly, the form that practices take in their enactment, what Lefebvre [*Space*] might call rhythm analysis). For more on memory embedded in the forms of practice, see Connerton, *Societies*.

10. Greene, *Malthusian*, 17. Butler, *Bodies*, 96.

11. See Butler, *Bodies*; duBois, *Torture*; Irigaray, *Revolution*; Laqueur, *Making Sex*; Lloyd, *Science*.

Bibliography

Primary Sources

"Abortion." *Medico-Legal Journal* 7 (1890): 170-87.

"Abortion and Murder." *Boston Medical and Surgical Journal* 42, no. 13 (1850): 275.

"Alleged Manslaughter by Procuring Abortion." *Boston Medical and Surgical Journal* 44 (1851): 288.

Andrews, J. S. "Infanticide." *Massachusetts Eclectic Medical Journal* 4, no. 7 (1884): 289-97.

"Attempt to Produce Abortion with Oil of Tansy, Followed by Death." *Boston Medical and Surgical Journal* 44, no. 19 (1851): 306.

Baker, William H. and Francis H. Davenport. "Methods of Gynæcological Examination and General Outlines of Differential Diagnosis." Pp. 26-86 in *Clinical Gynæcology: Medical and Surgical for Students and Practitioners by Eminent American Teachers*, edited by John M. Keating and Henry C. Coe. Philadelphia: J. B. Lippincott, 1895.

Balbirnie, John. *The Speculum Applied to the Diagnosis and Treatment of the Organic Disease of the Womb*. London: Longman, Rees, Orme, Brown, Green, and Longman, 1836.

Bedford, Gunning. "Clinical Lectures on Diseases of Women and Children." *Nelson's American Lancet* 7, no. 3 (1853): 101-19; 8, no. 1 (1853-1854): 3-22; 9, nos. 1, 3 (1854): 3-12, 85-92; 10, nos. 3-5 (1854): 99-106, 147-64, 186-96.

Bichat, Xavier. *Physiological Researches on Life and Death*. Translated by F. Gold. Boston: Richardson and Lord, 1827.

Birge, W. S. "A Case of Abortion with Peculiar Features." *Boston Medical Surgical Journal* 138, no. 17 (1895): 412-14.

Blackwell, Elizabeth. *Counsel to Parents on the Moral Education of Their Children*. 4th ed. New York: Brentano Bros., 1883.

———. *The Human Element in Sex*. London, 1884.

———. *A Medical Address on the Benevolence of Malthus, Contrasted with the Corruptions of Neo-Malthusiasm*. London, 1888.

———. *Pioneer Work in Opening the Medical Profession to Women*. London: Longmans, Green, and Co., 1895.

Brown, W. F. "Report of Medical Societies." *Boston Medical and Surgical Journal* 79, no.13 (1868): 200.

Buckingham, Charles E. "Two Cases of Labor in the Same Patient." *Boston Medical and Surgical Journal* 63, no. 8 (1860): 207-13.

Burdett, Everett W. "The Medical Jurisprudence of Criminal Abortion." *New England Medical Gazette* July (1883): 200-14.

Bush, J. Foster. "Medical History of a Case of Abortion, With a Synopsis of the Criminal Trial." *Boston Medical Surgical Journal* 107, no. 9 (1882): 205-6.

Calderone, Mary Steichen, ed. *Abortion in the United States: A Conference Sponsored by the Planned Parenthood Federation of America, Inc. at the Arlen House and the New York Academy of Medicine.* New York: Harper and Brothers, 1958.

"Case of Procidentia Uteri." *Boston Medical and Surgical Journal* 50, no. 4 (1854): 80-82.

C. K. B. "Marriage in America." *Boston Medical and Surgical Journal* 77 (1867): 153-57.

Chadwick, James R. *The Study and Practice of Medicine by Women.* New York: A. S. Barnes & Co., 1879.

"'Change of Life' in Women; With Remarks on the Periods Usually Called 'Critical.'" *Boston Medical and Surgical Journal* 50, nos. 3, 18 (1854): 54-57, 349-52.

Christison, Robert. "On the Present State of Medical Evidence." *Boston Medical and Surgical Journal* 46, no. 9 (1852): 176-81.

Churchill, Fleetwood. *The Diseases of Females.* Philadelphia: Lea and Blanchard, 1850.

Clarke, Edward. *Sex in Education.* Boston: James R. Osgood & Co., 1873.

Cleaveland. "The Powers of Life." *College Journal of Rational Medicine* 1, no. 9 (1856): 335-37.

Cleveland, C. H. "Poisoning by Oil of Cedar." *Boston Medical and Surgical Journal* 44, no. 17 (1851): 336-38.

Coale, W. E. "A Treatise on the Causes, Constitutional Effects and Treatment of Uterine Displacements." *Boston Medical and Surgical Journal* 47 (1852): 69-75, 109-15, 159-65, 206-12, 247-53, 323-26, 370-73, 423-26.

———. "Woman's Disease a Cause of Uterine Displacements." *Boston Medical and Surgical Journal* 45 (1852): 14-17.

Cocles, H. "Homeopathic Interference with Regular Practitioners." *Boston Medical and Surgical Journal* 50, no. 7 (1854): 136-41.

"Code of Medical Ethics." *Peninsular Journal of Medicine* 1, no. 2 (1853): 91-96, 135-38.

Coggeshall, George D. "Connection of Druggists with Quack Medicines." *Boston Medical and Surgical Journal* 50 (1854): 340-42.

Collins, Clarkson. "Diseases of Females." *Boston Medical and Surgical Journal* 47, no. 23 (1853): 476-80.

Commonwealth v. Follansbee, 155 MA Rep 274 (MA Sup Ct 1891/92).

Commonwealth v. Parker, 63 Am Dec 396 (MA Sup Ct 1845).

"Conviction for Criminal Abortion." *Boston Medical and Surgical Journal* 106, no. 1 (1882): 18-19.

Cornell, William M. "The Medical Education of Women." *Boston Medical and Surgical Journal* 49, no. 21 (1854): 419-22.

"Criminal Abortion." *Boston Medical and Surgical Journal* 56 (1857): 282-84.

"Criminal Abortion." *Boston Medical and Surgical Journal* 57 (1857): 45-46.

"Criminal Abortion." *Boston Medical and Surgical Journal* 62 (1860): 65-67.

"Criminal Abortion." *Boston Medical and Surgical Journal* 63 (1860): 66.

"Criminal Abortion." *The Colorado Medical Journal and Western Medical and Surgical Gazette* 9, no. 3 (1903): 170-74.

"Criminal Abortion." *Nelson's American Lancet* 7, no. 5 (1853): 183-84.

Crowe, Stephen. "Report of a Case of Septic Peritonitis Following a Criminal Abortion." *Maryland Medical Journal* 227, no. 21 (1892): 1013-14.

Cummings, A. I. "Tannin, As a Medical Agent." *Boston Medical and Surgical Journal* 47 (1850): 36-40.

———. "Use of the Tampon in Abortion." *Boston Medical and Surgical Journal* 49, no. 5 (1853): 98-99.

Curtin, R. G. "Pelvic Cellulitis from Abortion." *American Journal of Obstetrics* 8, no. 2 (1875): 330.

"Demonstrative Midwifery." *Boston Medical and Surgical Journal* 42 (1850): 257-58.

Dixon, Edward H. *Woman and Her Diseases.* New York: Edward H. Dixon, 1846.

Doe, John. " A Case of Abortion." *Boston Medical and Surgical Journal* 42, no. 15 (1850): 313-14.

Draper, F. W. "Criminal Abortion, with a 'Dying Declaration,'" *Transactions of the Massachusetts Medico-Legal Society* 3, no. 2 (1900): 35-42.

Dunne, P. C. and A. F. Derbois. *The Young Married Lady's Private Medical Guide.* Translated by F. Harrison Dunne. 1854.

Durell, Thomas M. "The Leach Case." *Boston Medical and Surgical Journal* 130, no. 16 (1894): 382-83.

"Editorial Notes," *Journal of the Gynæcological Society of Boston* 3 (1870): 269.

Editors. *Boston Medical and Surgical Journal* 76, no. 7 (1867): 145-46.

"Effects of Quinine on the Uterus." *Boston Medical and Surgical Journal* 54, no. 26 (1856): 528.

"Ergot and Galvanism as Ecbolics." *New Hampshire Journal of Medicine* 4 (1854): 225-27.

"Ergot vs. the Tampon in Puerperal Hemorrhage." *New Orleans Journal of Medicine* 23 (1870): 843-44.

"Female Abortionist." *National Police Gazette* 2, no. 27 (1847): 1.

"Female Doctors." *Medical Examiner* 8 (1854): 702-4.

"Female Education." *Boston Medical and Surgical Journal* 49, no. 9 (1853): 187-88.

"Female Medical Colleges." *Boston Medical Surgical Journal* 45, no. 5 (1852): 106-7.

Female medical student. In "Female Physicians." *Boston Medical and Surgical Journal* 76, no. 1 (1867): 43-44.

"Female Physicians." *Boston Medical and Surgical Journal* 48 (1854): 66.

"Female Physicians." *Boston Medical and Surgical Journal* 54, no. 9 (1856): 169-74.

"Female Practitioners of Medicine." *Boston Medical and Surgical Journal* 76, no. 13 (1867): 272-74.

"Female Practitioners of Medicine." *New Orleans Medical and Surgical Journal* 23 (1870): 394-96.

"Females as Physicians." *Boston Medical and Surgical Journal* 53, no. 14 (1855): 292-94.

Fernald, W. J. "A Sociological View of Criminal Abortion." *Illinois Medical Journal* 5, no. 2 (1903): 57-65.

Field. "Accidentally Produced Abortion." *American Journal of Obstetrics* 13 (1880): 405-8.

Finnell, T. C. "Chorea a Cause of Abortion." *Nelson's Northern Lancet* 2.4 (1852): 170.

Fish, E. F. "Criminal Abortion," *Milwaukee Medical Journal* 17, no. 4 (1909): 106-9.

Galbraith, Anna M. "Are the Dangers of the Menopause Natural or Acquired? A Physiological Study." Pp. 39-64 in *Transactions of the Twenty-Fourth Annual Meeting of
the Alumnæ Association of the Women's Medical College of Pennsylvania.* Philadel-
phia: Alumnæ Association of the Women's Medical College of Pennsylvania, 1899.
"Galvinism as a Substitute for Ergot." *Peninsular Journal of Medicine* 2, no. 2 (1854):
134.
Gannett, W. W. "A Case of Criminal Abortion Resulting in Death from Air-Embolism."
Boston Medical and Surgical Journal 106, no. 2 (1882): 28-31.
Gardner, Augustus. *The Causes and Curative Treatment of Sterility with a Preliminary
Statement of the Physiology of Generation.* New York: De Witt & Davenport, 1854.
———. "The Speculum and Its Modifications." *The Peninsular Journal of Medicine* 2
(1854): 39-42, 67-69.
Gerby, H. A. "Maternal Influence on the Fœtus." *Boston Medical and Surgical Journal*
44, no. 7 (1851): 137-38.
Ghent, H. C. "Criminal Abortion, or Foeticide, and the Prevention of Conception." *The
Texas Courier-Record of Medicine* 23, no. 5 (1906): 1-16.
Gleason, C. W. *Seven Lectures on the Philosophy of Life and the Art of Preserving
Health.* Columbus: Scott & Bascom, 1852.
Gleason, J. C. "A Medico-Legal Case of Abortion, Followed by Conviction of the Ac-
cused Abortionist." *Boston Medical and Surgical Journal* 101 (1879): 185-92.
Gleason, Rachel B. *Talks to My Patients: Hints on Getting Well and Keeping Well.* New
York: M. L. Holbrook Co., 1895.
Godfray, M. "Unusual Case of Abortion." *Nelson's American Lancet* 7, no. 1 (1854): 44.
Grant, John M. "Criminal Abortion." *Interstate Medical Journal* 13 (1906): 513-18.
Hale, Edwin. *The Great Crime of the Nineteenth Century: Why Is It Committed? Who Are
the Criminals? How Shall They Be Detected?* Chicago: 1867.
———. *A Systematic Treatise on Abortion and Sterility.* Rev. ed. Chicago: C. S. Halsey,
1868.
Hall, Marshall. "Assumed Frequency of the Ulceration of the Os Uteri." *New Orleans
Medical and Surgical Journal* 7 (1850): 229-31.
Hall, William Asbury. "Criminal Abortion and Its Treatment." *Northwestern Lancet* 8
(1888): 113-16.
Harris, F. A. "A Case of Abortion with Acquittal." *Boston Medical and Surgical Journal*
104, no. 15 (1881): 346-50.
Harris, S. N. "Case of Stricture of the Cervix Uteri." *Boston Medical and Surgical Journal*
42 (1850): 504-7.
Hartwell, James M. "Maternal Influence on the Fetus as Exhibited in a Cat." *Nelson's
American Lancet* 8, no. 8 (1853): 126.
Hastings, N. "Inflammation of the Uterus." *College Journal of Medical Science* 4, no. 6
(1859): 268-70.
Hatchard v. State, 79 WI Rep 35 (WI Sup Ct 1891).
Helmick, A. G. "A Case of Threatened Abortion." *Nelson's Northern Lancet* 10, no.1
(1854): 11-13.
Hendee, H. S. "Attempted Abortion by the Use of Veratrum Veride." *Boston Medical and
Surgical Journal* 57 (1857): 299.
Hender, H. S. "Chronic Prolapsus Uteri." *Boston Medical and Surgical Journal* 52
(1855): 197.
Herrick, G. E. "Abortion and Its Lessons." *Michigan Medical News* 4/5 (1881-1882): 7-

10.
——. "Specialties." *Michigan Medical News* 4/5 (1881-1882): 40-1.
Hoar, Sherman. "On the Duties of a Medical Examiner as a Witness." *Transactions of the Massachusetts Medico-Legal Society* 2 (1898): 328-30.
Hodge, Hugh."Marriage." Lecture. MS C98. National Library of Medicine, Bethesda, Md., 1857.
——. *On Criminal Abortion.* Philadelphia: T. K. and P. G. Collins, 1854.
——. "On the Rights of Women." Lecture. MS C98. National Library of Medicine, Bethesda, Md., 1851.
Hoitt, E. G. "Criminal Abortion." *Boston Medical and Surgical Journal* 135, no. 22 (1896): 541-43.
Holbrook, M. L. *Stirpiculture; or, the Improvement of Offspring Through Wider Generation.* New York: M. L. Holbrook, 1897.
Hollick, Frederick. *The Matron's Manual of Midwifery and the Diseases of Women During Pregnancy and in Child Bed.* New York: T. W. Strong, 1848.
Honestus. "Quackery in the Regular Profession." *Boston Medical and Surgical Journal* 43, no. 15 (1850): 280-81.
Howard, Henry. "The Somatic Etiology of Crime." *American Journal of Neurology and Psychiatry* 2, no. 2 (1883): 234-48.
Hunt, Lydia M. "Thesis," M.D. thesis, Women's Medical College of Pennsylvania, Special Collection on Women and Medicine at Allegheny University (hereafter SCWM), 1880.
Hunt, S. B. "The Cranial Characteristics and Powers of Human Races." *Boston Medical and Surgical Journal* 51, no. 4 (1954): 69-74.
Hurley, T. W. "The Prevention of Conception—Abortions, Justifiable and Criminal." *Transactions of the Arkansas Medical Society, Twenty-Eighth Session.* Little Rock: Thompson Litho. and Printing (1904): 262-74.
"Influence of a Mother's Mind on the Fetus." *Boston Medical and Surgical Journal* 55 (1856): 85-86.
Jacobi. "Case of Abortion in the Third Month." *American Journal of Obstetrics* 6 (1874): 632.
Jacobi, Mary Putnam. *The Question of Rest for Women During Menstruation.* New York: G. P. Putnam's Sons, 1877.
Jackson. "Gravid Uterus." *Boston Medical and Surgical Journal* 61 (1859): 239.
Jex-Blake, Sophia. *Medical Women: A Thesis and History.* Edinburgh: Oliphant, Anderson, & Ferrier, 1886.
Johnson, Joseph Taber "Abortion and Its Effects." *American Journal of Obstetrics* 33 (1896): 86-97.
Johnson, W. E. "The Actual Cautery of Diseases of the Uterus." *New Orleans Medical and Surgical Journal* 10 (1854): 397-99.
Johnston, Mackenzie. "Case of Retained Ovum after Death of the Fœtus." *American Journal of Obstetrics* 7, no. 4 (1875): 679-89.
Jones, William. *Practical Observations on Diseases of Women.* London: H. Bailliere, 1839.
Kellog, J. H. *Ladies' Guide in Health and Disease.* Battle Creek, Mich.: Modern Medicine Publishing, 1895.
Kelly, James E. "The Ethics of Abortion as a Method of Treatment in Legitimate Practice." *Transactions of the Gynecological Society of Boston* 1 (1889): 25-45.

Kessler, Adolph. "A Contribution to the Hypodermic Ergot Treatment of Uterine Myomata." *American Journal of Obstetrics* 13, no. 3 (1880): 548-62.

King, A. F. A. "A New Basis for Uterine Pathology." *American Journal of Obstetrics* 8, no. 2 (1874): 237-56.

King, Dan. "Quackery—Its Causes and Effects, with Reflections and Suggestions." *Boston Medical and Surgical Journal* 48, no. 11 (1853): 209-40.

Knowlton, Charles. *The Fruits of Philosophy.* In S. Chandrasekhar, *"A Dirty Filthy Book": The Writings of Charles Knowlton and Annie Besant on Reproductive Physiology and Birth Control and an Account of the Bradlaugh-Besant Trial: With the Definitive Texts of Fruits Philosophy, by Charles Knowlton, The Law of Population, by Besant, Theosophy and the Law of Population, by Annie Besant.* Berkeley: University of California Press, 1981.

Kratz, Annetta. "An Essay on Criminal Abortion." M.D. thesis, Women's Medical College of Pennsylvania, SCWM, 1870-71.

Lawrie. "New Views on Abortion." *Boston Medical and Surgical Journal* 79 (1868): 156-58.

Leonard, J. P. "Quackery and Abortion." *Boston Medical and Surgical Journal* 43 (1851): 477-81.

Lever, John C. W. *A Practical Treatise on Organic Diseases of the Uterus.* Newburgh, N.Y.: David L. Proudfit, 1846.

Litchfield, Thomas. "On the Use and Abuse of the Speculum." *New Orleans Medical and Surgical Journal* 7 (1850): 377-78.

Longshore-Potts, A. M. *Discourses to Women on Medical Subjects.* 12th ed. National City, Calif.: Longshore-Potts, 1897.

Martin, E. and J. P. Maygrier. *Atlas of Gynaecology and Obstetrics.* Translated and edited by Wm. A. Rothacker. Cincinnati: A. E. Wilde, 1881.

Massey, Thomas E. "Observations Upon Disease of the Uterus." *New Orleans Medical and Surgical Journal* 11, no. 1 (1855): 470-79.

"Maternal Impressions and the Fetus." *Boston Medical and Surgical Journal* 44, no. 7 (1851): 148.

Mauriceau, A. M. *The Married Woman's Private Medical Companion.* New York, 1848.

Maxwell-Christine, G. "The Medical Profession vs. Criminal Abortion." *Transactions of the Twenty-Fifth Session of the Homeopathic Medical Society of the State of Pennsylvania.* Philadelphia: Sherman Co., 1890.

McClintock. "Mechanical Tendency of Uterine Therapeutics." *Boston Medical and Surgical Journal* 77, no. 4 (1867): 87.

M'Cormack, M. J. "Influence of Maternal Impressions on the Fetus." *Boston Medical and Surgical Journal* 44, no. 4 (1851): 79-80.

Meadows, Alfred. "Remarks on Ovarian Physiology and Pathology." *American Journal of Obstetrics* 6, nos. 2-3 (1873): 215-47, 371-404.

Meigs, Charles D. *Females and Their Diseases.* Philadelphia: Lea and Blanchard, 1848.

———. *Woman: Her Diseases and Remedies.* Philadelphia: Blanchard and Lea, 1854.

Midland Surgeon. "The Genesis of Life." *Journal of the Gynecological Society of Boston* 7, nos. 5-6 (1872): 377-78, 392-93, 400.

Miller, Helen M. "Foeticide." M.D. thesis, Women's Medical College of Pennsylvania, SCWM, 1884.

Minnis, Maria. "Disquisition on Medical Jurisprudence." M.D. thesis, Women's Medical College of Pennsylvania, SCWM, 1853.

Minot, Francis. "Morbid Adhesion of the Placenta After Abortion." *Boston Medical and Surgical Journal* 53, no. 2 (1855): 35-38.

Mitchell, Mary. "Infanticide: Its Moral and Legal Aspects." M.D. thesis, Women's Medical College of Pennsylvania, SCWM, 1884.

Mitchell v. Commonwealth 39 Am. Rep. 227. KY Sup. Ct. 1879.

"Multiplication of Medical Schools." *Boston Medical and Surgical Journal* 76 (1867): 203-4.

Nebinger, Andrew. *Criminal Abortion: Its Extent and Prevention.* Philadelphia: Collins, 1870.

"New Vaginal Speculum." *American Journal of Obstetrics* 2 (1869): 544-46.

"New Views on Abortion." *Boston Medical and Surgical Journal* 79 (1868): 156-58.

Nightingale, Florence. *Introductory Notes on Lying-In Institutions.* London: Longmans, Green, and Co., 1871.

Nivison, Samantha S. "Priest of Nature and Her Interpreter." M.D. thesis, Women's Medical College of Pennsylvania, SCWM, 1855.

Nott, J. C. "On a New Duck-Bill Speculum, for Private Practice." *New Orleans Journal of Medicine* 22 (1870): 146-52.

Nourse, Amos. "Menstruation and Its Connection with Utero-Gestation." *Boston Medical and Surgical Journal* 71, no. 25 (1864): 492.

Nowlin, J. B. W. "Criminal Abortion." *The Southern Practitioner* 9, no. 5 (1887): 177-82.

Ohio General Assembly. *General and Local Laws and Joint Resolutions, Passed by the Fifty-Seventh General Assembly 1867.* Columbus, Ohio: L. D. Myers & Bro, 1867.

———. *Journal of the House of Representatives of Ohio of the Fifty-Seventh General Assembly, 1867.* Columbus, Ohio: L. D. Myers & Bro, 1867.

———. *Journal of the Senate of the State of Ohio for the Adjourned Session of the Fifty-Seventh General Assembly Commencing on January, 2 1867.* Columbus, Ohio: L. D, 1867.

"On the Reciprocal Agencies of Mind and Matter." *Boston Medical and Surgical Journal* 45, no. 9 (1851): 169-201.

"Opening Address." *Peninsular Journal of Medicine* 1 (1853): 139-40.

Oreman, Jennie G. "The Medical Woman's Temptation and How to Meet It." *The Woman's Medical Journal* 11, no. 3 (1901): 87-88.

"Our Editorial of Last Week." *Boston Medical and Surgical Journal* 73, no. 26 (1866): 504.

Palmer, Charles. "Attempted Abortion by American Hellebore." *Boston Medical and Surgical Journal* 57 (1857): 436.

Parsons, Mary. "The Written Law in Reference to the Unborn Child." *Washington Medical Annals* 9 (1910/11): 153-60.

Pendleton, E. M. "The Comparative Fecundity of the Black and White Races." *Boston Medical and Surgical Journal* 44, no. 19 (1851): 365-66.

People v. McGonegal, 17 NY Sup 147 (NY Sup Ct 1891).

People v. Sessions, 58 MI Rep 594 (MI Sup Ct 1886).

Pettingill, Eliza F. "A Thesis on the Ovaries." M.D. thesis, Women's Medical College of Pennsylvania, SCWM, 1864.

Pomeroy, H. *The Ethics of Marriage.* New York: Funk & Wagnalls, 1888.

Porter, William W. "A Discussion of the Medico-Legal Aspect of Criminal Abortion." *Medical and Surgical Reporter* 48 (1893): 655-60.

"Procuring Abortions." *Boston Medical and Surgical Journal* 51, no. 10 (1855): 204-5.

"Profits of Quackery." *Boston Medical and Surgical Journal* 46, no. 20 (1852): 406.

"Quackery." *New Hampshire Journal of Medicine* 1 (1850): 128-13.

"Quackery, Versus the Regular Medical Practice." *Boston Medical and Surgical Journal* 44, no. 12 (1851): 239-40.

"Quarterly Report on Obstetrics." *American Journal of Obstetrics* 7, no. 2 (1874): 286-89.

"Question Which Should be Settled." *Boston Medical and Surgical Journal* 73, no. 25 (1866): 481-83.

Ramsay, H. A. "Abortion in the Earlier Months, and in Fever." *Nelson's American Lancet* 7 (1853): 76-80.

Randall, O. W. "Suits for Mal-Practice." *Boston Medical and Surgical Journal* 45, no. 7 (1851): 137-41.

Reamy. "Reply to Dr. Underhill." *American Journal of Obstetrics* 3, no. 2 (1879): 392-93.

"Report of the Committee Upon Criminal Abortion." *Boston Medical and Surgical Journal* 56 (1857): 386-87.

"Report upon Criminal Abortion." *Boston Medical and Surgical Journal* 57 (1857): 67.

Reynolds, John P. "The President's Annual Address." *Transactions of the American Gynecological Society* 15 (1880): 3-24.

Rogers, Edmund J. A."The Attitude of the Profession Toward Abortion." *The Colorado Medical Journal and Western Medical and Surgical Gazette* 9, no. 3 (1903): 149-51.

Satterthwaite, Laura H. "Thesis: Menstruation." M.D. thesis, Women's Medical College of Pennsylvania, SCWM, 1888.

Saur, Prudence B. *Maternity: A Book for Every Wife and Mother*. Rev. ed. Chicago: L. P. Miller & Company, 1888.

Scott, James Foster. "Criminal Abortion." *American Journal of Obstetrics* 33 (1896): 77-86.

Scott v. People, 30 NE Rep 329 (IL Sup Ct 1892).

Scruggs, R. L. "On the Use of Ext. Belladonna in the Treatment of Obstinate Vomitings in Pregnant Women." *Peninsular Journal of Medicine* 1, no. 4 (1853): 165-69.

Simpson, James Y. *Obstetric Memoirs and Contributions of James Y. Simpson, M.D., F.R.S.E.* Vol. 1. Edited by W. Priestley & H. Storer. Philadelphia: J. B. Lippincott, 1855.

Sims, J. Marion. *Clinical Notes on Uterine Surgery*. New York: William Wood & Co., 1866.

Slusser, L. "Influence of the Imagination of the Mother upon the Fœtus." *Medical Examiner* 8 (1852): 344-46.

Small, A. E. "Jurisprudence of Abortion." Pp. 313-37 in *A Systematic Treatise on Abortion and Sterility*, rev. ed., by Edwin Hale. Chicago: C. S. Halsey, 1868.

Souchon, Edmond. "Speculum Holder or Retainer, an Apparatus for Keeping in Place Sims' Duck-Bill Speculum, Without an Assistant." *New Orleans Journal of Medicine* 23 (1870): 81-84.

"Standards for Drug Inspectors." *Boston Medical and Surgical Journal* 45, no. 12 (1851): 246-47.

State v. Cooper, 51 Am Dec 248 (NJ Sup Ct 1849).

State v. Leeper, 22 IA Rep 748 (IA Sup Ct 1887).

State v. McIntyre, 19 MN Rep 65 (MN Dup Ct 1882).

State v. Smith, 53 Am Dec 578 (ME Sup Ct 1851).

Stevenson, Sarah Hackett. *Physiology for Women*. Chicago: Fairbanks, Palmer, 1882.

Stockham, Alice. *Tokology*. 2nd ed. Chicago: 1883.

Stone, Warren. "Observations Upon Disease of the Uterus." *New Hampshire Journal of Medicine* 5 (1855): 74-82.

Storer, D. H. "An Address on Medical Jurisprudence." *Medical Examiner* 7 (1851): 572-73.

———. "Two Frequent Causes of Uterine Disease." *Journal of the Gynecological Society of Boston* 6 (1872): 194-203.

Storer, Horatio Robinson. "Contributions to Obstetric Jurisprudence." *New York Medical Journal* 3, no. 18 (1866): 422-33.

———. *Criminal Abortion: Its Nature, Its Evidence, and Its Law.* Boston: Little, Brown, 1868.

———. "The Gynæcological Society of Boston and Women Physicians; A Reply to Mr. Wm. Lloyd Garrison." *Journal of the Gynæcological Society of Boston* 2 (1870): 95-99.

———. *Is It I? A Book for Every Man.* Boston: Lee and Shepard, 1868.

———. "Studies of Abortion." *Boston Medical and Surgical Journal* 68, no. 1 (1863): 15-20.

———. *Why Not? A Book for Every Woman.* Boston: Lee and Shepard, 1868.

Storer, H. R. et al. "Report on Criminal Abortion." *Transactions of the American Medical Association* 13 (1859): 75-79.

Studley, W. H. "Is Menstruation a Disease?" *American Journal of Obstetrics* 8, no. 3 (1876): 487-512.

Taylor, George H. *Health for Women.* New York: American Book Exchange, 1880.

Thomas. "Attempted Criminal Abortion with a Long Wire—Penetration of Right Lung—Death." *American Journal of Obstetrics* 6, no. 1 (1863): 103-5.

Thomas, T. Gaillard. *Practical Treatise on the Diseases of Women.* Philadelphia: Henry C. Lea, 1868.

———. *Practical Treatise on the Diseases of Women.* 3rd ed. Philadelphia: Henry C. Lea, 1872.

Thomson, Anthony Todd. "Lectures on Medical Jurisprudence." Lecture XIII, XIV, XV, XVI, XVII. *Nelson's Northern Lancet* 1, no. 1, nos. 3-4 (1851): 95-107, 156-63, 208-15; 1, nos. 5-6 (1852): 246-53, 289-97; 2, nos. 1-2 (1852): 49-52, 88-97.

Tilt, Edward John. *Handbook of Uterine Therapeutics and of Diseases of Women.* 4th ed. New York: William Wood & Co., 1881.

———. *On the Diseases of Menstruation and Ovarian Inflammation.* London: John Churchill, 1857.

Tower. "Pelvic Viscera from a Patient Dead of a Criminal Abortion." *Journal of the Gynæcological Society of Boston* 1 (1869): 202-3.

Treadwell, J. B. "Case of Criminal Abortion with Retained Placenta, Followed by Metritis, Pelvic Cellulitis, and Pyæmia. Recovery." *Boston Medical and Surgical Journal* 78/79 (1, no. 7 New Series) (1868): 97-99.

"Ulceration of the Cervix Uteri." *Boston Medical and Surgical Journal* 43 (1851): 285-86.

Underhill, J. W. "The Female Generative Organs in Their Medico-Legal Relations." *American Journal of Obstetrics* 12, no. 1 (1879): 91-111.

"Use of Ergot in Abortion." *American Journal of Obstetrics* 11, no. 3 (1878): 772-73.

"Uterine Displacements." *New Orleans Journal of Medicine* 12 (1856): 98.

Valleix, M. "Displacements of the Uterus." Parts 1-7, 9-16, translated by L. Parks, Jr. *Boston Medical and Surgical Journal* 48 (1853): 169-72, 229-34, 269-74, 318-22,

351-56, 392-96, 456-61; 49 (1853): 89-93; 50 (1854): 269-77; 334-39, 412-18; 51 (1855): 15-20, 129-35, 236-41, 335-42.

"Vaginal Speculum." *Massachusetts Eclectic Medical Journal* 3, no. 6 (1883): 268-69.

Van de Werker, Ely. "Detection of Criminal Abortion." Parts 2 and 3. *Journal of the Gynæcological Society of Boston* 5 (1871): 229-45, 350-70.

Ward, Samuel B. "Criminal Abortion by Inflation of the Uterus With Air." *Albany Medical Annals* 10, no. 1 (1889): 1-8.

"What Female Medical Students Are Capable Of." *Boston Medical and Surgical Journal* 76, no. 26 (1867): 503.

Whitefield, R. H. "The Practice of Midwifery." *New Orleans Medical and Surgical Journal* 7, no. 2 (1855): 196-99.

Whitehead, James. *On the Causes and Treatments of Abortion and Sterility*. Philadelphia: Blanchard and Lea, 1854.

Whitehead Ross, Charlotte. "Abortion." M.D. thesis, Women's Medical College of Pennsylvania, SCWM, 1875.

"Why Not? A Book for Every Woman. The Prize Essay to Which the American Medical Association Awarded the Gold Medal for 1865." *Boston Medical and Surgical Journal* 75 (1865): 104.

Wife of a Christian physician. "'Why Not? A Book For Every Woman.' A Woman's View." *Boston Medical and Surgical Journal* 75, no. 14 (1866): 273-76.

Williams, N. "A Dissertation on 'Female Physicians.'" *Boston Medical and Surgical Journal* 43, no. 4 (1850): 69-75.

Williamson, T. J. "Influence of the Mother's Mind on the Embryo in Utero." *New Orleans Journal of Medicine* 23 (1870): 94-96.

Wilson, Ellwood. "Death of a Fetus Caused by Fright of the Mother." *American Journal of Obstetrics* 10 (1877): 340.

Wright, C. O. "Maternal Impressions Affecting the Fetus in Utero." *American Journal of Obstetrics* 11, no. 3 (1878): 634-40.

Wright, Henry C. *Marriage and Parentage*. Boston: Bela Marsh, 1854.

W. S. C. "Preparation and Sale of Domestic Medicines." *Boston Medical and Surgical Journal* 45, no. 22 (1852): 447-49.

Secondary Sources

Acevedo, Zoila. "Abortion in Early America," *Women & Health* 4 (1979): 159-67.

Adams, Alice. *Reproducing the Womb: Images of Childbirth in Science, Feminist Theory, and Literature*. Ithaca: Cornell University Press, 1994.

Allen, Amy. "Power Trouble: Performativity as Critical Theory." *Constellations* 5 (1998): 456-71.

Ardener, Shirley. "Ground Rules and Social Maps for Women: An Introduction." Pp. 1-30 in *Women and Space: Ground Rules and Social Maps*, edited by Shirley Ardener. Oxford: Berg, 1993.

Barker, Francis. *The Tremulous Private Body: Essays on Subjection*. London: Methuen, 1984.

Benjamin, Walter. *Illuminations: Essays and Reflections*. Translated by Harry Zohn. Edited and introduced by Hannah Arendt. New York: Schocken Books, 1968.

Ben-Ze'ev, Aaron. "The Alternative to the Storehouse Metaphor." *Behavioral and Brain*

Sciences 19 (1996): 192-93.

Blewett, Mary H. *Men, Women, and Work: Class, Gender, and Protest in the New England Shoe Industry, 1780-1910*. Urbana: University of Illinois Press, 1990.

Bodnar, John. *Remaking America: Public Memory, Commemoration, and Patriotism in the Twentieth Century*. Princeton, N.J.: Princeton University Press, 1992.

Bordo, Susan. *Unbearable Weight: Feminism, Western Culture, and the Body*. Berkeley: University of California Press, 1993.

Braidotti, Rosi. *Nomadic Subjects: Embodiment and Sexual Difference in Contemporary Feminist Theory*. New York: Columbia University Press, 1994.

Brodie, Janet Farrell. *Contraception and Abortion in 19th-Century America*. Ithaca: Cornell University Press, 1994.

Browder, Clifford. *Madame Restell the Abortionist*. Hamden, Conn.: Archon Press, 1988.

Browne, Stephen H. "Counter Science: African American Historians and the Critique of Ethnology in Nineteenth-Century America." *Western Journal of Communication* 64 (2000): 268-84.

Burbick, Joan. *Healing the Republic: The Language of Health and the Culture of Nationalism in Nineteenth-Century America*. Cambridge: Cambridge University Press, 1994.

Burke, Kenneth. *A Grammar of Motives*. Berkeley: University of California Press, 1969.

———. *Language as Symbolic Action: Essays on Life, Literature, and Method*. Berkeley: University of California Press, 1966.

Butchart, Alexander. *The Anatomy of Power: European Constructions of the African Body*. London: Zed Books, 1998.

Butler, Judith. *Bodies that Matter: On the Discursive Limits of "Sex"*. New York: Routledge, 1993.

———. *Gender Trouble: Feminism and the Subversion of Identity*. New York: Routledge, 1990.

———. "Performative Acts and Gender Constitution: An Essay in Phenomenology and Feminist Theory." Pp. 401-17 in *Writing the Body: Female Embodiment and Feminist Theory*, edited by Katie Conboy, Nadia Medina, and Sarah Stanbury. New York: Columbia University Press, 1997.

Cabot, A. "Survey of Abortion Law: History of Abortion Law." *Arizona State Law Journal* (1980): 73-127.

Campbell, Karlyn Kohrs. *"Man Cannot Speak for Her"*. Vol. 1, *A Critical Study of Early Feminist Rhetoric*. New York: Greenwood Press, 1989.

Canguilhem, Georges. *Ideology and Rationality in the History of the Life Sciences*. Translated by Arthur Goldhammer. Cambridge, Mass.: MIT Press, 1988.

Casper, Monica. "Operation to the Rescue: Feminist Encounters with Fetal Surgery." Pp. 101-12 in *Fetal Subjects, Feminist Positions*, edited by Lynn Marie Morgan and Meredith W. Michaels. Philadelphia: University of Pennsylvania Press, 1999.

Cassedy, James H. *Medicine in America: A Short History*. Baltimore: Johns Hopkins University Press, 1991.

Cayleff, Susan E. "Gender, Ideology, and the Water-Cure Movement." Pp. 82-98 in *Other Healers: Unorthodox Medicine in America*, edited by Norman Gevitz. Baltimore: Johns Hopkins University Press, 1988.

Certeau, Michel de. *The Capture of Speech & Other Political Writings*. Translated by Tom Conley and edited by Luce Giard. Minneapolis: University of Minnesota Press, 1997.

————. *The Practice of Everyday Life*. Translated by Steven Randall. Berkeley: University of California Press, 1984.

————. *The Writing of History*. Translated by Thomas Conley. New York: Columbia University Press, 1988.

Condit, Celeste. *Decoding Abortion Rhetoric: Communicating Social Change*. Urbana: University of Illinois Press, 1990.

Connerton, Paul. *How Societies Remember*. Cambridge: Cambridge University Press, 1989.

Corea, Gena. *The Mother Machine: Reproductive Technologies from Artificial Insemination to Artificial Wombs*. New York: Harper & Row, 1986.

Cott, Nancy F. *The Bonds of Womanhood: "Woman's Sphere" in New England, 1780-1835*. 2nd ed. New Haven, Conn.: 1997.

Coulter, H. "Political and Social Aspects of Nineteenth Century Medicine In the United States: The Formation of the American Medical Association and Its Struggle with Homeopathic and Eclectic Physicians." Ph.D. diss., Columbia University, 1967.

Crary, Jonathan. *Techniques of the Observer: On Vision and Modernity in the Nineteenth Century*. Cambridge: MIT Press, 1990.

Curran, William J. "An Historical Perspective on the Law of Personality and Status with Special Regard to the Human Fetus and the Rights of Woman." *Health and Society* 61 (1983): 58-73.

Daston, Lorraine and Peter Galison. "The Image of Objectivity." *Representations* 40 (1992): 81-128.

Degler, Carl N. *At Odds: Women and the Family in America from the Revolution to the Present*. New York: Oxford University Press, 1980.

Deleuze, Gilles. *Foucault*. Translated by Seán Hand. Minneapolis: University of Minnesota Press, 1988.

Deleuze, Gilles, and Fèlix Guattari. *Anti-Oedipus: Capitalism and Schizophrenia*. Translated by R. Hurley, et al. Minneapolis: University of Minnesota Press, 1983.

Derbyshire, Lynne. "Paulina Kellog Wright Davis." Pp. 309-320 in *Women Public Speakers in the United States, 1800-1925: A Bio-Critical Sourcebook*, vol. 1, edited by Karlyn Kohrs Campbell. Westport, Conn.: Greenwood Press, 1993.

Derrida, Jacques. *Archive Fever: A Freudian Impression*. Translated by Eric Prenowitz. Chicago: University of Chicago Press, 1995.

————. *Dissemination*. Translated by Barbara Johnson. Chicago: University of Chicago Press, 1981.

Descartes, René. *Discours de la méthode/Discourse on the Method*. Translated, edited, and introduced by George Hefferman. Notre Dame: University of Notre Dame Press, 1994.

————. *Meditations on First Philosophy*. 3rd ed. Translated by Donald A. Cross. Indianapolis: Hackett, 1993.

————. *Treatise of Man*. Translated by Thomas Steele Hall. Cambridge: Harvard University Press, 1972.

Deutsch, Sarah. *Women and the City: Gender, Space, and Power in Boston, 1870-1940*. New York: Oxford University Press, 2000.

Donegan, Jane B. *Women & Men Midwives: Medicine, Morality, and Misogyny in Early America*. Westport, Conn.: Greenwood Press, 1978.

Douglas, Mary. *Natural Symbols: Explorations in Cosmology*. London: Routledge (1970) 1996.

Drachman, Virginia G. "Women Doctors and the Women's Medical Movement: Feminism and Medicine, 1850-1895." Ph.D. diss., University of New York at Buffalo, 1976.

Dreyfus, Hubert L. and Paul Rabinow. *Michel Foucault: Beyond Structuralism and Hermeneutics*. 2nd ed. Chicago: University of Chicago Press, 1983.

duBois, Page. *Torture and Truth*. New York: Routledge, 1991.

Duden, Barbara. *Disembodying Women: Perspectives on Pregnancy and the Unborn*. Cambridge: Harvard University Press, 1994.

———. "The Fetus and the 'Farther Shore': Toward a History of the Unborn." Pp. 13-25 in *Fetal Subjects, Feminist Positions*, edited by Lynn Marie Morgan and Meredith W. Michaels. Philadelphia: University of Pennsylvania Press, 1999.

———. *The Woman Beneath the Skin: A Doctor's Patients in Eighteenth-Century Germany*. Cambridge: Harvard University Press, 1991.

Duncan, Nancy. "Renegotiating Gender and Sexuality in Public and Private Spaces." Pp. 127-45 in *Bodyspace: Destabilizing Geographies of Gender and Sexuality*, edited Nancy Duncan. London: Routledge, 1996.

Durkheim, Emile. *Suicide: A Study in Sociology*. Translated by John A. Spalding and George Simpson, edited and introduced by George Simpson. Glencoe, Ill.: Free Press, 1951.

Dyer, Frederick N. *Champion of Women and the Unborn: Horatio Robinson Storer, M.D.* Canton, Mass.: Science History Publications, 1999.

Ehrenreich, Barbara and Deidre English. *Complaints and Disorders: The Sexual Politics of Sickness*. New York: Feminist Press, 1973.

———. *For Her Own Good: 150 Years of Experts' Advice to Women*. Garden City, N.Y.: Anchor Books, 1978.

Etienne, Robert. "Ancient Medical Conscience and the Life of Children." *Journal of Psychohistory* 4 (1976): 131-61.

Evans, Sara M. *Born for Liberty: A History of Women in America*. New York: Free Press, 1989.

Farquhar, Dion. *The Other Machine: Discourse and Reproductive Technologies.* New York: Routledge, 1996.

Fausto-Sterling, Anne. *Sexing the Body: Gender Politics and the Construction of Sexuality*. New York: Basic Books, 2000.

Fentress, James, and Chris Wickham. *Social memory*. Oxford: Blackwell, 1992.

Figlio, Karl M. "The Metaphor of Organization: An Historiographical Perspective on the Bio-Medical Sciences of the Early Nineteenth Century." *History of Science* 14 (1976): 17-53.

Foucault, Michel. *Archeaology of Knowledge*. Translated by A. Sheridan. New York: Pantheon Books, 1972.

———. *The Birth of the Clinic: An Archaeology of Medical Perception*. Translated by A. M. Sheridan Smith. New York: Vintage, 1973.

———. "Body/Power." Pp. 55-62 in *Power/Knowledge: Selected Interviews & Other Writings, 1972-1977*, translated by Colin Gordon et al. and edited by Colin Gordon. New York: Pantheon Books, 1980.

———. "Different Spaces." Pp. 175-85 in *Michel Foucault: Aesthetics, Method, and Epistemology*, edited by James B. Faubion; *Essential Works of Foucault, 1954-1984*, vol. 2, series edited by Paul Rabinow. New York: New Press, 1998.

———. *Discipline and Punish: The Birth of the Prison*. Translated Alan Sheridan. New

York: Vintage, 1979.

———. *The History of Sexuality: An Introduction*. Vol. 1. Translated by Robert Hurley. New York: Vintage, 1990.

———. "Nietzsche, Genealogy, History." Pp. 139-164 in *Language, Counter-Memory, Practice: Selected Essays and Interviews*, translated by Donald F. Bouchard and Sherry Simon, edited by Donald F. Bouchard. Ithaca: Cornell University Press, 1977.

———. *The Order of Things: An Archeaology of the Human Sciences*. New York: Vintage Books, 1994.

———. "Security, Territory, and Population." Pp. 67-71 in *Ethics: Subjectivity and Truth; Essential Works of Foucault, 1954-1984*, vol. 1, edited by Paul Rabinow. New York: New Press, 1997.

———. "Society Must Be Defended." Pp. 59-65 in *Ethics: Subjectivity and Truth; Essential Works of Foucault, 1954-1984*, vol. 1, edited by Paul Rabinow. New York: New Press, 1997.

———. "Two Lectures." Pp. 78-108 in *Power/Knowledge: Selected Interview & Other Writings, 1972-1977*, translated by Colin Gordon et al. and edited by Colin Gordon. New York: Pantheon Books, 1980.

Franklin, Sarah. "Fetal Fascinations: New Dimensions to the Medical-Scientific Construction of Fetal Personhood." Pp. 190-205 in *Off-Centre: Feminism and Cultural Studies*, edited by Sarah Franklin, Celia Lury, and Jackie Stacey. London: HarperCollins Academic, 1991.

Gaonkar, Dilip Parameshwar. "Rhetoric and Its Double: Reflections on the Rhetorical Turn in the Human Sciences." Pp. 341-66 in *The Rhetorical Turn*, edited by Herbert Simons. Chicago: University of Chicago Press, 1990.

Gilman, Charlotte Perkins. "Why I Wrote 'The Yellow Wallpaper.'" Pp. 51-53 in *The Captive Imagination: A Casebook on "The Yellow Wallpaper"*, edited by Catherine Golden. New York: Feminist Press, 1992.

Gilman, Sander L. *Difference and Pathology: Stereotypes of Sexuality, Race, and Madness*. Ithaca, N. Y.: Cornell University Press, 1985.

Glass, Ruth. *Clichés of Urban Doom and Other Essays*. Oxford: Basil Blackwell, 1989.

Glausser, Wayne. "Locke and Blake as Physicians: Delivering the Eighteenth Century Body." Pp. 218-43 in *Reading the Social Body*, edited by Catherine Burroughs and Jeffrey David Ehrenreich. Iowa City, Iowa.: University of Iowa Press, 1993.

Golberg, David. "The Social Formation of Racist Discourse." Pp. 295-318 in *Anatomy of Racism*, edited by David Goldberg. Minneapolis: University of Minnesota Press, 1990.

González, Jennifer A. "Autotopographies." Pp. 133-50 in *Prosthetic Territories: Politics and Hypertechnologies*, edited by Garbriel Brahm, Jr. and Mark Driscoll. Boulder, Colo.: Westview, 1995.

Gordon, Linda. *Woman's Body, Woman's Right: Birth Control in America*. Rev. ed. New York: Penguin Books, 1990.

Gould, Stephen Jay. "American Polygeny and Craniometry before Darwin." Pp. 84-115 in *The Racial Economy of Science: Toward a Democratic Future*, edited by Sandra Harding, Bloomington: Indiana University Press, 1993.

———. *The Mismeasure of Man*. New York: W. W. Norton & Co., 1981.

Greene, Ronald Walter. "The Aesthetic Turn and the Rhetorical Perspective on Argumentation." *Argumentation & Advocacy* 35 (1998): 19-30.

———. *Malthusian Worlds: U.S. Leadership and the Governing of Population Crisis*.

Boulder, Colo.: Westview Press, 1999.

Grosz, Elizabeth. *Space, Time, and Perversion: Essays on the Politics of Bodies.* New York: Routledge, 1995.

———. *Volatile Bodies: Toward a Corporeal Feminism.* Bloomington: Indiana University Press, 1994.

Halbwachs, Maurice. *On Collective Memory.* Edited and translated by Lewis A. Coser. Chicago: University of Chicago Press, 1992.

Haraway, Donna J. *How Like a Leaf: An Interview with Thyrza Nichols Goodeve.* New York: Routledge, 2000.

———. *Modest_Witness@Second_Millenium.FemaleMan©_Meets_Onco-Mouse™: Feminism and Technoscience.* New York: Routledge, 1997.

———. "The Promises of Monsters: A Regenerative Politics for Inappropriate/d Others." Pp. 295-337 in *Cultural Studies*, edited by Lawrence Grossberg et al. New York: Routledge, 1992.

———. *Simians, Cyborgs, and Women: The Reinvention of Nature.* New York: Routledge, 1991.

Harrison, Michael R. "Unborn: Historical Perspective of the Fetus as a Patient." *The Pharos* Winter (1982): 19-24.

Hartouni, Valerie. "Fetal Exposures: Abortion Politics and the Optics of Allusion." *Camera Obscura* 29 (1992): 131-49.

Haskins, Ekaterina V. "Rhetoric between Orality and Literacy: Cultural Memory and Performance in Isocrates and Aristotle." *Quarterly Journal of Speech* 87 (2001): 158-78.

Hayles, Katherine. *How We Became Posthuman: Virtual Bodies in Cybernetics, Literature, and Informatics.* Chicago: University of Chicago Press, 1999.

Herndl, Diane Pierce. *Invalid Women: Figuring Feminine Illness in American Fiction and Culture.* Chapel Hill: University of North Carolina Press, 1993.

Hodgson, Dennis. "The Ideological Origins of the Population Association of America." *Population and Development Review* 17 (1991): 1-34.

Horkheimer, Max and Theodor Adorno. *Dialectic of Enlightenment.* Translated by J. Cumming. New York: Continuum Press, 1993.

Irigiray, Luce. *Speculum of the Other Woman.* Transl ted by Gillian C. Gill. Ithaca, N.Y.: Cornell University Press, 1985.

Jacobson, Matthew Frye. *Whiteness of a Different Color: European Immigrants and the Alchemy of Race.* Cambridge, Mass.: Harvard University Press, 1998.

Jamieson, Kathleen Hall. *Beyond the Double Bind: Women and Leadership.* New York: Oxford University Press, 1995.

Jay, Martin. *Downcast Eyes: The Denigration of Vision in Twentieth-Century French Thought.* Berkeley: University of California Press, 1993.

———. *Marxism & Totality: The Adventures of a Concept from Lukács to Habermas* Berkeley: University of California Press, 1982.

Joffe, Carole. *Doctors of Conscience: The Struggle to Provide Abortion before and after* Roe v.Wade. Boston: Beacon Press, 1995.

Jordanova, Ludmilla. *Sexual Visions: Images of Gender in Science and Medicine between the Eighteenth and Twentieth Centuries.* Madison, Wisc.: University of Wisconsin Press, 1989.

Kaufman, Martin. "Homeopathy in America: The Rise and Fall and Persistence of a Medical Heresy." Pp. 99-123 in *Other Healers: Unorthodox Medicine in America*, edited by Norman Gevitz. Baltimore: Johns Hopkins University Press, 1988.

Keller, Alan. *Scandalous Lady: The Life and Times of Madame Restell.* New York: Antheneum, 1981.

Keller, Evelyn Fox. *Secrets of Life, Secrets of Death.* New York: Routledge, 1990.

Keller, Evelyn Fox and Christine R. Grontkowski. "The Mind's Eye." Pp. 187-202 in *Feminism & Science,* edited by Evelyn Fox Keller and Helen E. Longino. Oxford: Oxford University Press, 1996.

Kerber, Linda K. *Women of the Republic: Intellect and Ideology in Revolutionary America.* Chapel Hill, N. C.: University of North Carolina Press, 1980.

King, Charles R. "Abortion in Nineteenth Century America: A Conflict Between Women and Their Physicians." *Women's Health Issues* 2 (1992): 32-39.

Kristeva, Julia. *Pouvoirs de l'horreur.* Paris: Seuil, 1980.

———. *Revolution in Poetic Language.* Translated by Margaret Waller. New York: Columbia University Press, 1984.

Kroker, Arthur, and Marilouise Kroker. "Theses on the Disappearing Body in the Hyper-Modern Condition." Pp. 20-34 in *Body Invaders: Panic Sex in America,* edited by Arthur Kroker and Marilouise Kroker. NewYork: St. Martin's Press, 1987.

Kushner, Howard I. "Suicide, Gender, and the Fear of Modernity in Nineteenth-Century Medical and Social Thought." *Journal of Social History* 26 (1993): 461-90.

Kuypers, Mary Shaw. *Studies in the Eighteenth Century Background of Hume's Empiricism.* New York: Garland Publishing, Inc., 1983.

Laqueur, Thomas. *Making Sex: Body and Gender from the Greeks to Freud.* Cambridge: Harvard University Press, 1990.

———. "Orgasm, Generation, and the Politics of Reproductive Biology." Pp. 1-41 in *The Making of the Modern Body: Sexuality and Society in the Nineteenth Century,* edited by Catherine Gallagher and Thomas Laqueur. Berkeley: University of California Press, 1987.

La Sorte, Michael A. "Nineteenth Century Family Planning Practices." *Journal of Psychohistory* 4 (1976): 163-83.

Latour, Bruno. *Pandora's Hope: Essays on the Reality of Science Studies.* Cambridge, Mass.: Harvard University Press, 1999.

Lees, Andrew. *Cities Perceived: Urban Society in European and American Thought, 1820-1940.* Great Britain: Columbia University Press, 1985.

Lefebvre, Henri. *The Production of Space.* Translated by Donald Nicholson-Smith. Oxford: Blackwell, 1995.

Leonardo, Richard A. *History of Gynecology.* New York: Froben Press, 1944.

Leppert, Richard. *Art and the Committed Eye: The Cultural Functions of Imagery.* Boulder, Colo.: Westview, 1996.

Linke, Uli. *Blood and Nation: The European Aesthetics of Race.* Philadelphia: University of Pennsylvania Press, 1999.

Lipsitz, George. *Time Passages: Collective Memory and American Popular Culture.* Minneapolis: University of Minnesota Press, 1990.

Litoff, Judy Barrett. *American Midwives: 1860 to the Present.* Westport, Conn.: Greenwood Press, 1978.

Livingstone, Frank. "On the Nonexistence of Race." Pp. 133-41 in *The Racial Economy of Science: Toward a Democratic Future,* edited by Sandra Harding, Bloomington: Indiana University Press, 1993.

Lloyd, G. E. R. *Science, Folklore and Ideology: Studies in the Life Sciences in Ancient*

Greece. Cambridge: Cambridge University Press, 1983.

Lowe, Donald M. *History of Bourgeois Perception*. Chicago: University of Chicago Press, 1982.

Ludmerer, Kenneth M. *Learning to Heal: The Development of American Medical Education*. New York: Basic Books, 1985.

MacDowell, Linda. "Spatializing Feminism: Geographic Perspectives." Pp. 28-44 in *Bodyspace: Destabilizing Geographies of Gender and Sexuality*, edited by Nancy Duncan. London: Routledge, 1996.

Mahon, Michael. *Foucault's Nietzschean Genealogy: Truth, Power, and the Subject*. Albany, N.Y. : State University of New York Press, 1992.

Manion, Elizabeth. "A Ms.-Managed Womb." Pp. 183-200 in *Body Invaders: Panic Sex in America*, edited by Arthur Kroker and Marilouise Kroker. New York: St. Martin's Press, 1987.

Marcuse, Herbert. *The Aesthetic Dimension: Toward a Critique of Marxist Aesthetics*. Boston: Beacon Press, 1978.

———. *Counter-Revolution and Revolt*. Boston: Beacon Press, 1972.

———. *Eros and Civilization: A Philosophical Inquiry into Freud*. Boston: Beacon Press, 1966.

———. *One Dimensional Man: Studies in the Ideology of Advanced Industrial Society*. Boston: Beacon Press, 1964.

Marshall, Gloria A. "Racial Classifications: Popular and Scientific." Pp. 116-27 in *The Racial Economy of Science: Toward a Democratic Future*, edited by Sandra Harding. Bloomington: Indiana University Press, 1993.

Martin, Emily. *The Woman in the Body: A Cultural Analysis of Reproduction*. Boston: Beacon Press, 1992.

Massey, Doreen. *Space, Place, and Gender*. Minneapolis: University of Minnesota Press, 1994.

McClintock, Ann. *Imperial Leather: Race, Gender and Sexuality in the Colonial Contest*. New York: Routledge, 1995.

McLaren, Angus. "The Pleasures of Procreation: Traditional and Biomedical Theories of Conception." Pp. 323-41 in *William Hunter and the Eighteenth-Century Medical World*, edited by W. F.Bynum and Roy Porter. Cambridge: Cambridge University Press, 1985.

Merchant, Carolyn. *The Death of Nature: Women, Ecology and the Scientific Revolution*. New York: HarperCollins, 1983.

Michaels, Meredith W. "'Fetal Galaxies': Some Questions About What We See." Pp. 113-32 in *Fetal Subjects, Feminist Positions*, edited by Lynn Marie Morgan and Meredith W. Michaels. Philadelphia: University of Pennsylvania Press, 1999.

Mohanram, Radhika. *Black Body: Women, Colonialism, and Space*. Minneapolis: University of Minnesota Press, 1999.

Mohl, Raymond, ed. *The Making of Urban America*. Wilmington, Del.: SR Books, 1988.

Mohl, Raymond A. and Neil Betten, eds. *Urban America in Historical Perspective*. New York: Weybright and Talley, 1970.

Mohr, James. *Abortion in America: The Origins and Evolution of National Policy, 1800-1900*. New York: Oxford University Press, 1978.

———. *Doctors and the Law: Medical Jurisprudence in Nineteenth-Century America*. New York: Oxford University Press, 1993.

Monkkonen, Eric. H. *America Becomes Urban: The Development of U. S. Cities and*

Towns 1780-1980. Berkeley: University of California Press, 1988.

Morantz, Regina Markell, Cynthia Stodola Pomerleau, and Carol Hansen Fenichel, eds. *In Her Own Words: Oral Histories of Women Physicians*. New Haven: Yale University Press, 1982.

Morantz-Sanchez, Regina. "The Making of a Woman Surgeon: How Mary Dixon Jones Made a Name for Herself in Nineteenth-Century Gynecology." Pp. 178-220 in *Women Healers and Physicians: Climbing a Long Hill*, edited by Lilian R. Furst. Lexington, Ky.: University Press of Kentucky, 1997.

———. *Sympathy and Science: Women Physicians in American Medicine*. New York: Oxford University Press, 1985.

Mosse, George L. *Nationalism and Sexuality: Respectability and Abnormal Sexuality in Modern Europe*. New York: Howard Fertig, 1985.

Nast, Heidi J. and Audrey Kobayashi. "Re-corporealizing Vision." Pp. 75-93 in *Bodyspace*, edited by Nancy Duncan. New York: Routledge, 1996.

Neisser, Ulric. "Remembering as Doing." *Behavioral and Brain Sciences* 19 (1996): 203-4.

Newman, Karen. *Fetal Positions: Individualism, Science, Visuality*. Stanford: Stanford University Press, 1996.

Omi, Michael, and Howard Winant. *Racial Formation in the United States: From the 1960s to the1990s*, 2nd ed. New York: Routledge, 1994.

Packard, Francis R. *History of Medicine in the United States*. Vol. 2. New York: Hafner Publishing, 1963.

Pateman, Carole. *The Disorder of Women: Democracy, Feminism and Political Theory*. Cambridge: Polity Press, 1989.

———. *The Problem of Political Obligation*. Berkeley, Calif.: University of California Press, 1986.

———. *The Sexual Contract*. Stanford, Calif.: Stanford University Press, 1988.

Petchesky, Rosalind. "Foetal Images: The Power of Visual Culture in the Politics of Reproduction." Pp. 57-80 in *Reproductive Technologies: Gender, Motherhood and Medicine*, edited by Michelle Stanworth. Minneapolis: University of Minnesota Press, 1987.

Plato. *Phaedrus*. Translated by Alexander Nehemas and Paul Woodruff. Indianapolis, Ind.: Hackett Publishing, 1995.

Poirer, Susan. "The Weir Mitchell Rest Cure: Doctors and Patients." *Women's Studies* 10 (1983): 13-40.

Pollack, Griselda. "The Dangers of Proximity: The Spaces of Sexuality and Surveillance in Word and Image." *Discourse* 16 (1993-94): 3-50.

Poovey, Mary. "The Abortion Question and the Death of Man." Pp. 239-256 in *Feminists Theorize the Political*, edited by Judith Butler and Joan W. Scott. New York: Routledge, 1992.

———. *Uneven Developments: The Ideological Work of Gender in Mid-Victorian England*. Chicago: University of Chicago Press, 1988.

Porter, Roy. "The Rise of Physical Examination." Pp. 179-97 in *Medicine and the Five Senses*, edited by W. F. Bynum and Roy Porter. Cambridge: Cambridge University Press, 1993.

Radley, A. "Artefacts, Memory and a Sense of the Past." Pp. 46-59 in *Collective Remembering*, edited by David Middleton and Derek Edwards. London: Sage, 1990.

Rajchman, Jonathan. "Foucault's Art of Seeing." *October* 44 (1988): 89-117.

Reagan, Leslie. *When Abortion Was Crime: Women, Medicine, and the Law in the United States, 1867-1973*. Berkeley: University of California Press, 1997.

Reiser, Stanley Joel. *Medicine and the Reign of Technology*. Cambridge: Cambridge University Press, 1978.

Ricci, James V. *The Development of Gynaecological Surgery and Instruments*. Philadelphia: Blakiston Company, 1949.

————. *One Hundred Years of Gynaecology, 1800-1900*. Philadelphia: Blakiston Company, 1945.

Rimé, Bernard and V. Christophe. "How Individual Emotional Episodes Feed Collective Memory." Pp. 131-46 in *Collective Memory of Political Events: Social Psychological Perspectives*, edited by James W. Pennebaker, Darí Páez, and Bernard Rimé. Mahwah, N.J.: Lawrence Erlbaum Associates, 1997.

Roediger, David. *The Wages of Whiteness: Race and the Making of the American Working Class*. London: Verso, 1991.

Rolfe, W. D. Ian. "William and John Hunter: Breaking the Great Chain of Being." Pp. 297-319 in *William Hunter and the Eighteenth-Century Medical World*, edited by W. F. Bynum and Roy Porter. Cambridge: Cambridge University Press, 1985.

Rose, Gillian. *Feminism & Geography: The Limits of Geographical Knowledge*. Minneapolis: University of Minnesota, 1993.

Rosenberg, Charles. *The Care of Strangers: The Rise of America's Hospital System*. Baltimore: Johns Hopkins University Press, 1987.

Rothman, Barbara Katz. *Recreating Motherhood: Ideology and Technology in a Patriarchal Society*. New York: Norton, 1989.

Rothstein, William G. *American Physicians in the Nineteenth Century: From Sects to Science*. Baltimore: Johns Hopkins University Press, 1972.

————. "The Botanical Movements and Orthodox Medicine." Pp. 29-51 in *Other Healers: Unorthodox Medicine in America*, edited by Norman Gevitz. Baltimore: Johns Hopkins University Press, 1988.

Rubin, Gayle. "The Traffic in Women: Notes on the 'Political Economy' of Sex." Pp.157-210 in *Toward and Anthology of Women*, edited by Rayna Rapp Reiter. New York: Monthly Review Press, 1976.

Russett, Cynthia Eagle. *Sexual Science: The Victorian Construction of Womanhood*. Cambridge, Mass.: Harvard University Press, 1989.

Said, Edward. *Orientalism*. New York: Pantheon Books, 1978.

Sawday, Jonathan. "The Fate of Marsyas: Dissecting the Renaissance Body." Pp. 111-35 in *Renaissance Bodies: The Human Figure in English Culture, c. 1540-1660*, edited by Lucy Gent and Nigel Llewellyn. London: Reaction Books, 1990.

Schiebinger, Londa. *The Mind Has No Sex?: Women in the Origins of Modern Science*. Cambridge: Harvard, 1989.

————. *Nature's Body: Gender in the Making of Modern Science*. Boston: Beacon Press, 1993.

Schouls, Peter A. *Descartes and the Possibility of Science*. Ithaca: Cornell University Press, 2000.

Schultz, Stanley K. *Constructing Urban Culture: American Cities and City Planning, 1800-1920*. Philadelphia: Temple University Press, 1989.

Scully, Diana. *Men Who Control Women's Health: The Miseducation of Obstetrician-Gynecologists*. Rev. ed. New York: Teacher's College Press, 1994.

Seigel, Rudolph E. *Galen's System of Physiology and Medicine*. Basel, Switz.: S. Karger,

1968.

Sepper, Dennis L. *"Ingenium*, Memory Art, and the Unity of Imaginative Knowing in the Early Descartes." Pp. 142-61 in *Essays on the Philosophy and Science of René Descartes*, edited by Stephen Voss. New York: Oxford University Press, 1993.

Shands, Kerstin W. *Embracing Space: Spatial Metaphors in Feminist Discourse*. Westport, Conn.: Greenwood Press, 1999.

Shapin, Steven. *A Social History of Truth: Civility and Science in Seventeenth-Century England*. Chicago: University of Chicago Press, 1994.

Shapin, Steven and Simon Schaffer. *Leviathan and the Air-Pump: Hobbes, Boyle, and the Experimental Life*. Princeton: Princeton University Press, 1985.

Showalter, Elaine. *The Female Malady: Women, Madness, and English Culture*. New York: Pantheon Books, 1985.

Smith-Rosenberg, Carroll. *Disorderly Conduct: Visions of Gender in Victorian America*. New York: Oxford University Press, 1985.

Soja, Edward W. *Thirdspace: Journeys to Los Angeles and Other Real-and-Imagined Places*. Cambridge, Mass.: Blackwell, 1996.

Solinger, Rickie. *Wake Up Little Susie: Pregnancy and Race Before* Roe v. Wade. New York: Routledge, 1992.

Sontag, Susan. *Illness as Metaphor and Aids and its Metaphors*. New York: Anchor Books, 1990.

Spain, Daphne. *Gendered Spaces*. Chapel Hill: University of North Carolina Press, 1992.

Spivak, Gayatri Chakrevorty. "French Feminism Revisited." Pp. 54-85 in *Feminists Theorize the Political*, edited by Judith Butler and Joan W. Scott. New York: Routledge, 1992.

Srebnick, Amy Gilman. *The Mysterious Death of Mary Rogers: Sex and Culture in Nineteenth-Century New York*. New York: Oxford University Press, 1995.

Stabile, Carole. "Shooting the Mother: Fetal Photography and the Politics of Disappearance." *Camera Obscura* 28 (1992): 179-205.

Stafford, Barbara Maria. *Body Criticism: Imaging the Unseen in Enlightenment Art and Medicine*. Cambridge: MIT Press, 1993.

Stansell, Christine. *City of Women: Sex and Class in New York, 1789-1860*. New York: Alfred A. Knopf, 1986.

Starr, Paul. *The Social Transformation of American Medicine: The Rise of a Sovereign Profession and the Making of Vast Industry*. New York: Basic Books, 1982.

Stepan, Nancy. *The Idea of Race in Science: Great Britain, 1800-1960*. London: Macmillan, 1982.

Stepan, Nancy, and Sander Gilman. "Appropriating the Idioms of Science: The Rejection of Scientific Racism." Pp. 170-93 in *The "Racial" Economy of Science: Toward a Democratic Future*, edited by Sandra Harding. Bloomington, Ind.: Indiana University Press, 1993.

Stoler, Ann Laura. *Race and the Education of Desire: Foucault's* History of Sexuality *and the Colonial Order of Things*. Durham, N. C.: Duke University Press, 1995.

Stormer, Nathan. "Embodying Normal Miracles." *Quarterly Journal of Speech* 83, no. 2 (1997): 172-91.

———. "In Living Memory." *Quarterly Journal of Speech* 88, no. 3 (2002): 265-83.

———. "Prenatal Space." *Signs: Journal of Women in Culture and Society* 26, no. 1 (2000): 109-44.

———. *"Why Not?* Memory and Counter-Memory in 19th-Century Abortion Rhetoric."

Women's Studies in Communication 24, no.1 (2001): 1-29.

Taussig, Frederick J. *Abortion, Spontaneous and Induced: Medical and Social Aspects.* St. Louis: C. V. Mosby, 1936.

Temkin, Owsei. *Galenism: Rise and Decline of a Medical Philosophy.* Ithaca: Cornell University Press, 1973.

Theriot, Nancy M. *Mothers & Daughters in Nineteenth-Century America: The Biosocial Construction of Femininity.* Lexington, Ky.: University Press of Kentucky, 1996.

Thornton, John L. "William Hunter (1718-1783) and His Contributions to Obstetrics." *British Journal of Obstetrics and Gynecology* 90 (1983): 787-94.

Tolnay, Stewart E. "Black Fertility in Decline: Urban Differentials in 1900." *Social Biology* 27 (1980): 249-60.

Trachtenberg, Alan. *The Incorporation of America: Culture & Society in the Gilded Age.* New York: Hill and Wang, 1982.

Twigg, Reginald. "The Performative Dimension of Surveillance: Jacob Riis' *How the Other Half Lives.*" *Text and Performance Quarterly* 12 (1992): 305-28.

Ulrich, Laurel Thatcher. *A Midwife's Tale: The Life of Martha Ballard, Based on Her Diary, 1785-1812.* New York: Vintage Books, 1991.

Walker, Lynne. "Home and Away: The Feminist Remapping of Public and Private Space in Victorian London." Pp. 65-75 in *New Frontiers of Space, Bodies and Gender*, edited by Rosa Ainley. London: Routledge, 1998.

Walsh, Mary Roth. *"Doctors Wanted: No Women Need Apply": Sexual Barriers and the Medical Profession.* New Haven, Conn.: Yale University Press, 1977.

Waxman, Wayne. *Hume's Theory of Consciousness.* Cambridge: Cambridge University Press, 1994.

Wells, Susan. *Out of the Dead House.* Madison, Wisc.: University of Wisconsin Press, 2001.

Welter, Barbara. *Dimity Convictions: The American Woman in the Nineteenth Century.* Athens, Ohio: Ohio University Press, 1976.

Wertz, Richard W. & Dorothy C. Wertz. *Lying-In: A History of Childbirth in America.* Exp. ed. New Haven: Yale University Press, 1989.

Wilson, Kirt H. "Toward a Discursive Theory of Racial Identity: *The Souls of Black Folk* as a Response to Nineteenth-Century Biological Determinism." *Western Journal of Communication* 63 (1999): 193-215.

Wood, Ann Douglas. "'The Fashionable Diseases': Women's Complaints and Their Treatment in Nineteenth-Century America." *Journal of Interdisciplinary History* 4 (1973): 25-52.

Wright, John P. *The Sceptical Realism of David Hume.* Manchester: Manchester University Press, 1983.

Yates, Wilson. "Birth Control Literature and the Medical Profession in Nineteenth Century America." *Journal of the History of Medicine and Allied Sciences* 31 (1976): 42-54.

Yolton, John W. *Thinking Matter: Materialism in Eighteenth-Century Britain.* Minneapolis: University of Minnesota Press, 1983.

Young, Robert J. C. *Colonial Desire: Hybridity in Theory, Culture, and Race.* London: Routledge, 1995.

Yuval-Davis, Nira and Floya Anthias. Introduction to *Woman-Nation-State*, edited by Nira Yuval-Davis and Floya Anthias. New York: St. Martin's Press, 1989.

Zelizer, Barbie. "Reading the Past Against the Grain." *Critical Studies in Mass Communi-*

cation 12, no. 2 (1995): 214-39.

———. *Remembering to Forget: Holocaust Memory Through the Camera's Eye*. Chicago: University of Chicago Press, 1998.

Zerubavel, Yael. *Recovered Roots: Collective Memory and the Making of Israeli National Tradition*. Chicago: University of Chicago Press, 1995.

Zinn, Howard. *A People's History of the United States 1492-Present*. Rev. ed. New York: HarperPerennial, 1995.

Index

abortifacients, 27, 97
abortion(s); botched, 32, 109, 136; criminal, 7, 22, 28, 35, 71, 76, 97-100, 115, 117, 123, 135-38, 143; induced, 21, 28, 83, 97, 136; instrumental, 97; rates, xii-xiv, 17, 27, 33, 87, 107, 144; septic, 32; services/practice, 4-6, 51, 97, 128-29, 144-45; spontaneous, 28, 75, 97. *See also* rhetoric, abortion
abortionists, 27, 34-35, 38-39, 73, 81, 99, 115, 128
Acton, William, 69
Adams, Alice, 48
Adorno, Theodor, 34, 46
African Americans, 27-29, 55
Africans, 28-29, 83
Albany Medical College, 37
Allen, Amy, 75
allopathy, 9, 22, 35-38, 110
aloe, 97
American Medical Association (AMA), xiii, 7, 9-10, 21-22, 27, 34-35, 37-38, 71, 73, 99-100, 105, 107, 111, 123, 128-29
amnesia, cultural, xiii, 3-4, 6, 18, 88 144-46, 150
anamnesis, 12-13, 42-46, 51, 84, 86-87, 117, 121
anatomy, 9-10, 16-17, 37, 41, 51, 59, 63-66, 72, 76, 78, 80, 84-85, 87, 101, 108, 134
Andrews, J. S., 29
Anglo-Americans, 28-29, 74, 82-83,

127
Anthias, Floya, 32, 122
antiabortion, xi, xiii, 3-4, 6, 8, 14, 16, 19, 22, 29-30, 33, 35, 38, 42, 81, 90, 126, 129, 144, 146; campaign, 6-7, 15-16, 18, 22, 32, 83, 124-25, 144, 150; climate, 50; legislation, 7, 22, 100, 129. *See also* rhetoric, antiabortion
antiabortionists, xii, 4, 6, 12-13, 15-16, 18-19, 23, 27, 29, 32, 41, 46-47, 53, 55-56, 63, 75, 80, 82, 84, 87, 99, 102, 134, 136, 146-48
archive, 17, 41-42, 52, 55, 58, 63-64, 67, 74, 84, 89, 91, 103, 107, 119, 123, 127, 145-47, 149-50
Aristotle, 36, 47-48, 73, 77
articulation, xii-xv, 4, 6-8, 20, 23, 31, 33, 36, 42-43, 47, 51-53, 63-64, 77, 83-85, 87-89, 91, 98, 107, 117, 119-20, 122, 130-32, 134-35, 138-41, 145, 147-49
Ashton, James, 37
Asians, 29
assemblies. *See* legislatures
auscultation, 92
autopsy, 127-28

Bacon, Francis, 44, 46
Balbirnie, John, 95-96, 105-7
Ballard, Martha, 36
Becklard, Eugene, 37
Bedford, Gunning, 14, 45, 67-68, 136
Beecher, Catherine, 37

223

About the Author

Nathan Stormer is assistant professor of Communication and Journalism at the University of Maine. His work on the intersections of articulation, embodiment, memory, and abortion is part of an ongoing line of research that traces the rhetorical dynamics of biomedical knowledge production about abortion. He has published in several venues, most notably the *Quarterly Journal of Speech* and *Signs: Journal of Women in Culture and Society*. He holds a bachelor's in Speech, as well as a master's and a doctorate in Rhetoric from the University of Minnesota, with doctoral minors in Feminist Studies and Cultural Studies.